Music, Postcolonialism, and Gender

Music, Postcolonialism, and Gender

THE CONSTRUCTION OF IRISH NATIONAL IDENTITY, 1724–1874

LEITH DAVIS

University of Notre Dame Press

Notre Dame, Indiana

Published in the United States of America

Library of Congress Cataloging-in-Publication Data

Davis, Leith, 1960–
Music, postcolonialism, and gender : the construction of Irish
national identity, 1724–1874 / Leith Davis.
p. cm.
Includes bibliographical references and index.
ISBN 0-268-02577-0 (cloth : alk. paper)
ISBN 0-268-02578-9 (pbk. : alk. paper)
1. Music—Ireland—18th century—History and criticism.
2. Music—Ireland—19th century—History and criticism.
3. Popular culture—Ireland—History.
4. Gender identity—Ireland.   I. Title.
ML287.D38   2006
306.4'8420941509033—dc22
2005029467

For Rob, Ciaran, Devin, and Nia,

and

in memory of my parents, Nancy and Eric Davis

Justly has Ireland been called "The Land of Song," the very atmosphere is poetical—the breezes that play around us seem the very breathings of melody. The spirits of our ancient bards are looking down, inviting the youth of the soil to participate in their glory.

—Thomas Furlong,
quoted in James Hardiman's *Irish Minstrelsy*

[M]uch indeed do we stand indebted to the most charming of all the sciences for the eminence it has obtained us; for in *music only*, do *you* English allow us poor Irish any superiority.

—Sydney Owenson,
The Wild Irish Girl

Contents

Illustrations

Acknowledgments

This book is the product of a number of years of thinking, writing, and presenting conference papers and has benefited greatly from the help of a number of people along the way. In particular, I would like to thank Miranda Burgess, Helen Burke, Andrew Carpenter, Ian Duncan, David Johnson, Paul Keen, and Janet Sorensen for important comments and conversations. In addition, I spent a very productive semester as a Visiting Scholar at the Institute for the Advanced Study of Humanities at Edinburgh University, enjoying the benefits of conversations ranging from eighteenth-century Scottish philosophy to contemporary Nigerian literature. My colleagues in the Print Culture Group at Simon Fraser University (SFU) provided a forum at a crucial early point in the work's development and support along the way. Thanks especially to Margaret Linley for observations on art, exchange, and commodification and to Betty Schellenberg for thoughts on the nature of *concordia discors,* eighteenth-century public culture, and the roles of women writers in the eighteenth century. The two anonymous readers of the manuscript offered extremely valuable suggestions that gave me direction in shaping the manuscript as a whole. I have also been very lucky to have had the help of a number of excellent research assistants at SFU over the last number of years, and I would like to acknowledge the contributions of: Sharon Alker, Chris Lendrum, Laila Ferreira, Jason King, Ryan Miller, Jackie Rea, Leanne Romane, and Karina Vernon. Also thank-you to my graduate classes of Spring 1997 and Spring 2001 who were so enthusiastic about eighteenth-century Irish music and literature. Sara Maurer at the University of Indiana at Bloomington helped me obtain a vast number of Irish American song sheets.

The germ of the idea for this book was planted a number of years ago when I discovered the Captain O'Neill Collection in the University of Notre Dame's Special Collections. Thanks to Laura Fuderer for her enthusiasm about the collection. I am also grateful to Barbara Hanrahan and Rebecca DeBoer at the University of Notre Dame Press for helping bring the seed to fruition and to Elisabeth Magnus for help in the editing process. The Social

Sciences and Humanities Research Council of Canada provided generous funding for the research involved in this book. The Department of English and the Dean of Arts Office at SFU also helped provide the research time for the project.

My sons, Ciaran and Devin, and my daughter, Nia, were all born during the course of writing this book. Their lives are interwoven with every chapter. Most recently, Nia's early arrival meant that I learned to type with one hand while holding her in the other. I'm very grateful to all three of my children for helping me keep my work in perspective. The book is also dedicated to my parents, Nancy and Eric Davis, both of whom passed away before they could see it in published form. I will always be grateful for their love and encouragement. Finally, none of this would have been possible without the support—in innumerable ways both tangible and intangible—of my husband, Rob McGregor.

Earlier versions of chapters 3 and 4 appeared as "Birth of the Nation: Gender and Writing in the Work of Henry and Charlotte Brooke" (*Eighteenth-Century Life* 18:1 [1994]: 27–47) and "Sequels of Resistance: Edward Bunting's *Ancient Irish Melodies* and the Irish Nation" (*Nineteenth-Century Contexts* 23 [2001]: 29–57). Chapter 6 has been extensively reworked from its initial form as "Irish Bards and English Consumers: Thomas Moore's *Irish Melodies* and the Colonized Nation," in *ARIEL: A Review of International English Literature* 24:2 (1993): 7–25.

Music, Postcolonialism, and Gender

Introduction

GIRALDUS CAMBRENSIS AND THE "DISCORDANT CONCORD" OF IRISH MUSIC

This book examines how texts concerning Irish music and the social contexts within which those texts emerged contributed to the imagining of the Irish nation from the eighteenth to the mid–nineteenth century. In particular, it focuses on the processes by which Ireland became identified to its own inhabitants and to those of the British archipelago and North America as having a particular affinity for music. It considers how this identification of Ireland as a musical nation was produced within the colonial dynamic between Ireland and Britain, and it explores the effects of the growth of print culture and consumer capitalism on the perception of Irish music at home and abroad. Moreover, it is concerned with how the discourse on music became increasingly gendered in the eighteenth and nineteenth centuries as gender was utilized variously in the representation of both national and colonialist formations.

The centrality of concerns regarding postcolonialism and gender to a study of Irish music is evident as far back as the twelfth century in a text that, because of its various republications and translations, became the most widely cited authority on Irish music in the eighteenth century: Giraldus Cambrensis's *Topography of Ireland* (1188). A grandson of the erstwhile king of South Wales, Rhys Ap Tewdwr, and a culturally "hybrid" character himself, Giraldus participated in the conquest and colonization of his own nation of Wales.[1] In 1183, he made a visit to Ireland, where a number of his relatives had acquired lands. The *Topography*, a compilation of his observations during his next few years in Ireland, constitutes a survey over a conquered nation by one who adopts an outsider's perspective but professes an insider's knowledge. The second preface, dedicated to Henry II and written after Giraldus's second visit to Ireland in conjunction with Prince John's mission of conquest, frames the *Topography* as part of a larger project of promoting the Angevin colonization of Ireland. More practically, the preface serves to advance the cause of Giraldus's own family, as Giraldus asserts his own importance in memorializing "by the aid of letters" the royal family whose "virtues and victorious honour" have conferred such "great glory . . . on our age."[2] The *Topography* is presented as a permanent monument to Henry's dynasty and as a work that will inspire future generations: "[T]he perusal of these pages may have the same effect [on minds of future readers] as the statues and portraits of their ancestors had on men of old, rousing a laudable spirit of emulation, not only in ardent minds, but in those which are feeble and sluggish; fanning the sparks of impetuous valour in the one, and lighting up the fire of innate courage in the other."[3]

The observations that Giraldus offers throughout the body of the *Topography* establish a power/knowledge conjunction that places the Irish at the bottom of a political and cultural hierarchy. While he acknowledges that the Irish are handsome and tall in person and "richly endowed with the gifts of nature," for example, Giraldus concludes that their want of civilization, "shown both in their dress and mental culture, makes them a barbarous people."[4] Their rustic lifestyle makes them by definition "rude" and backward: "In the common course of things, mankind progresses from the forest to the field, from the field to the town, and to the social condition of citizens; but this nation, holding agricultural labour in contempt, and little coveting the wealth of towns, as well as being exceedingly averse to civil institutions— lead the same life their fathers did in the woods and open pastures, neither willing to abandon their old habits or learn anything new."[5] Giraldus emphasizes that the lack of cultivation in Ireland is due not to any natural phenomenon, but to the people's "want of industry."[6] As David Cairns and Shaun Richards point out, however, Giraldus does not see the Irish as "irremediably . . . inferior";[7] rather, he implies that their culture can be improved by coming into contact with that of more "civilized" nations:

> [H]abits are formed by mutual intercourse; and as this people inhabit a country so remote from the rest of the world, and lying at its furthest extremity, forming, as it were, another world, and are thus excluded from civilized nations, they learn nothing and practise nothing but the barbarism in which they are born and bred, and which sticks to them like a second nature. Whatever natural gifts they possess are excellent, in whatever requires industry they are worthless.[8]

The "worthlessness" of Irish efforts and the necessity of intervention are nowhere more apparent than in Giraldus's use of Irish chronicles in the third part of the *Topography*. Giraldus comments that he has had to revise the work of "native writers" because the information contained in their chronicles was "heaped together . . . in a loose and disorderly manner, with much that is superfluous or absurd." Furthermore, because the chronicles were "composed in a rude and barbarous style," he notes, "I have digested them, with much labour, as clearly and compendiously as I could, like one seeking and picking up precious stones among the sands on the sea-shore, and have inserted whatever was of most value in the present volume."[9] Not only does Giraldus make his subject the political incorporation of Ireland, but he also embodies this incorporation in the text of the *Topography* as he "digests" and reformulates material from the Irish chronicles.

As disparaging as Giraldus is in general about the Irish "want of industry," there is one exception to his account of Irish barbarism. He acknowledges that the Irish are superior musicians, commenting, "The only thing to which I find that this people apply a commendable industry is playing upon musical instruments; in which they are incomparably more skilful than any other nation I have ever seen."[10] Not pausing with this brief mention, he continues to praise Irish harpers in a lengthy digression:

> For their modulation on these instruments, unlike that of the Britons to which I am accustomed, is not slow and harsh, but lively and rapid, while the harmony is both sweet and gay. It is astonishing that in so complex and rapid a movement of the fingers, the musical proportions can be preserved, and that throughout the difficult modulations on their various instruments, the harmony is completed with such a sweet velocity, so unequal an equality, so discordant a concord, as if the chords sounded together fourths or fifths. . . . They enter into a movement, and conclude it in so delicate a manner, and play the little notes so sportively under the blunter sounds of the base strings, enlivening with wanton levity, or communicating a deeper internal sensation of pleasure, so that the perfection of their art appears in the concealment of it.[11]

Native music serves to trouble Giraldus's description of Ireland as a barbarian land crying out for the civilizing power of England.[12] Instead, it suggests Irish supremacy in a field that Giraldus values highly. Giraldus's elevation of music is evident in the subsequent section of the *Topography*, "On the Beneficial Aspects of Music,"[13] in which he digresses on the general power of music. Music can provide the highest form of inspiration, he suggests: "[O]f all the most pleasant things in the world, nothing more delights and enlivens the human heart."[14] But its power to inspire can also prove dangerous: "[I]ts influence may be used to heighten the pleasures of the vicious as well as to animate the virtuous and brave."[15] Giraldus illustrates the Janus-faced nature of music in his story about Alexander of Macedon, who, when he hears the tones of the harp at table with friends, orders the strings to be broken. When asked the reason for such a command, he replies, "It is better that chords should be broken than hearts."[16] Giraldus concludes, "For our passions are by no means in our own power."[17] The power of music is ambiguous for Giraldus: it heightens the passions, but it diminishes self-control.

The *Topography* establishes music as a positive aspect of Irish identity, the only positive aspect, in fact, during the early years of the colonization of Ireland, and it situates that musical identity within the framework of the relationship with England. In addition, Giraldus's ambiguous formulation of Irish music suggests the existence of postcolonial possibilities at the moment of articulation of colonial power. It is notable that the exact nature of Irish music, according to Giraldus, is paradoxical, as he describes it as "unequal in its equality, discordant in its concord, most noticeably perfect when its perfection is concealed."[18] Giraldus's comments laid the foundation for a number of competing uses—both complicit and resistant—for Irish music. Finally, the *Topography* foreshadows what would become a central issue in eighteenth- and nineteenth-century texts concerning Irish music: the gendering of the discourse on Irish music and the intersections between that gendering and the construction of national identity. The harpers whom Giraldus describes are all male, yet they are described in terms that suggest their sensibility. The connection between sensibility and gender was the subject of heated debate in eighteenth-century discourse, a subject that in turn reflected back on the imagining of the national community. Music itself is accorded a questionable effect on masculinity in the *Topography*, as Giraldus writes that Alexander saves his warriors from "heartbreaking" situations by breaking the strings of the musicians' harps.

MUSIC AND IRISH STUDIES

In *Musical Elaborations*, Edward Said suggests that musicologists have traditionally practiced a form of disciplinary isolationism, identifying their subject as a phenomenon removed from ideological concerns or criticisms: "[M]usic's autonomy from the social world has been taken for granted for at least a century."[19] Only recently, he suggests, has the "new musicology" subjected music to the kinds of cultural criticism employed in the literary and fine arts fields. As Said himself argues, "Music, like literature, is practised in a social and cultural setting."[20] Richard Leppert, too, emphasizes the cultural contexts that shape any understanding of music, asserting that "music . . . is not an act of self-expression but of externally imposed identity,"[21] while in *Musica Practica* Michael Chanan regards music, like language, as a process of social competition: "[L]ike every art form, music is a site where as well as the dialogue of individual voices, competing ideologies engage in battle to express themselves, often through a kind of artistic guerilla warfare."[22] However, Chanan, like Said, notes that this understanding of music "is largely obscured by the dominant modes of public discussion of music, which fail to see the links between music and society."[23]

Within the field of music in Ireland, however, the problem seems to be a little different. Irish musicologists traditionally have been only too aware of "the links between music and society," links that were explicitly forged by figures such as Joseph Cooper Walker, Thomas Davis, George Petrie, and others considered throughout this book.[24] Historically, however, Irish musicologists have too often accepted the particular form those links have taken rather than examined the complexities involved in their formation. In other words, their investigations have been shaped by what David Lloyd describes as "the organizing concerns of official history," which coalesce around the promotion of national formations.[25] In chapter 1, for example, I discuss the impact that an acceptance of the "organizing concern" of a fundamental gap between Gaelic and Anglo-Irish music has had on our understanding of Irish music. A more general implication of the acceptance of "official history" in the study of Irish music is the relative weight given to imaginative literature over music in the recently burgeoning canon of Irish studies.[26] While several important interventions in the field of Irish studies have attempted to right this imbalance by focusing on the ideological uses of music, for the most part literature has been seen as the stage on which the ambivalences of Irish national identity have been richly expressed and debated.[27] Music and the discourse on music have most often been seen, where considered at all, as constituting a prefabricated background to these struggles. It is the overall contention of this book, however, that the examination of Irish music and of the discourse that links that music to Irish society is as crucial to our understanding of the complexities involved in the construction of Irish identity—both at home and abroad—as the examination of Irish literature is already acknowledged to be.

In the chapters that follow, I probe the "externally imposed identities" and "competing ideologies" that Leppert and Chanan identify as bound up with the practice of music by employing perspectives derived from postcolonial and gender studies. Attempting to contextualize the music, I focus in particular on the historical discourse that has framed the social contexts in which the music was created, performed, and consumed. As Pierre Bourdieu asserts, "[D]iscourse about a work is not a mere accompaniment, intended to assist its perception and appreciation, but a stage in the production of the work, of its meaning and value."[28] Throughout this book, I consider how music was written down and what was written about the music. I examine introductions, prefaces, and contents of musical collections, lyrics, histories, fictional texts, and reviews, all of which, I argue, contributed to the imagining of Ireland as the "Land of Song." I have made a consideration of the genre through which each representation of music is conveyed—whether song collections, antiquarian history, novels, or poetry—part of my analysis, taking into consideration what Bourdieu describes as the "field of cultural production" in which each genre occupies a particular position in relation to other genres and the entire cultural field is related to a network of power relations.

In analyzing the social contexts of music in Ireland, I draw particular attention to Said's assertion that "[n]o social system, no historical vision, no theoretical totalization, no matter how powerful, can exhaust all the alternatives or practices that exist within [music's] domain."[29] As Said intimates, music has a tendency to transgress any boundaries inside which it is placed. In this book, I argue that it is precisely music's ambivalence that has historically been responsible for its playing so vital a role in the articulation of Irish national identity. We have already seen Giraldus's representation of Irish music's paradoxical power and unruliness in the *Topography*. At the same time that it articulates the terms of colonial hegemony, the *Topography* acknowledges the conditions for Irish music's potential threat to that hegemony. In chapter 1, I investigate the ambivalence accorded to music more fully as I examine the position of music in the eighteenth-century hierarchy of the fine arts. Music, in the words of the Irish Protestant turned Catholic philosopher James Usher, is "too confused and fluid to be collected into a distinct idea."[30] In subsequent chapters, I trace how this "fluidity" and ambivalence attributed to music made it a peculiarly compelling means through which to address the terms of the colonial relationship between Ireland and Britain.[31] Music's hybrid ability to cross the borders that attempt to contain it unsettles the binaries on which colonial power—and its mirror opposite, nationalism—is so dependent.

Postcolonialism and Irish Music

To apply the term *postcolonial* to an Irish context is to invite controversy.[32] I employ the term cautiously here, hoping not to close down debate by defining it either too narrowly or too broadly but rather to subject our understanding of the relationship between Irish studies and postcolonialism to more scrutiny. Like many others, I reject the chronological relationship between the terms *colonialism* and *postcolonialism,* the belief that postcolonialism follows logically on from the destruction of the vestiges of colonialism. Instead, I see an intimate relationship between the two terms. The combination of *post-* and *colonial* for me suggests that the agency for contesting colonial power is always already present in the instantiation of colonialism and, conversely, that colonialism features as a historic presence in any postcolonial formulation.[33] This is not to say that we can never get beyond colonialism, but only that to do so involves a continuing critical awareness of the historical conditions of colonialism, conditions that are specific to each particular geographical and temporal context but that can be usefully considered together. I believe that it is crucial to acknowledge the circumstances specific to Irish history—or any other local site—but that important critical gains can be made by considering the Irish situation in relation to other postcolonial positions.[34] Like many other critics working from a postcolonial perspective, however, I hope to avoid imposing rigid definitions on the Irish situation. Rather, I advocate what Colin Graham and Willy Maley refer to as a "postcolonial theory which at once questions and revises itself."[35]

With that caveat, I suggest that a postcolonial approach can help us read the meanings of Irish music outside the bounds of what Lloyd calls "official history" and to bring into question the way music in Ireland has been evaluated. Rather than reading musical texts like the Neals' *Colection [sic] of the most Celebrated Irish Tunes* (c. 1724) as simply a reflection of Anglo-Irish co-optation of the Gaelic musical tradition, for example, I examine the ways in which the work also serves as a site of potential resistance and challenge to Anglo-Irish hegemony. Conversely, I suggest that an examination of Irish music can prove useful in critiquing our understanding of postcolonial criticism. In her study of the use of English in India, Sara Suleri points to what she sees as one of the flaws in postcolonial criticism: "Even as the other is privileged in all its pluralities, in all its alternative histories, its concept-function remains too embedded in a theoretical duality of margin to centre ultimately to allow the cultural decentering that such critical attention surely deserves."[36] A close examination of the role of music in the construction of Irish identity suggests the untenability of the binaries of self and other, colonizer and colonized, as it reveals the ambivalences involved in both terms. In Graham and Maley's terms: "Ironically, Ireland, so susceptible to binaries, undoes the double bind of the West and the rest."[37]

In *After Colonialism*, Gyan Prakash discusses the manner in which colonial authority is subject in practice to "dislocation and transformation," due to "the functioning of colonial power as a form of transaction and translation between incommensurable cultures and positions."[38] This is evident in Giraldus's concern with the impact of the "translation" of Irishness on the identity of the colonizers, as he fashions the appreciation of Irish music as an occult practice not available to everyone. He notes that "those very strains which afford deep and unspeakable mental delight to those who have skillfully penetrated into the mysteries of the art, fatigue rather than gratify the ears of others, who seeing do not perceive, and hearing do not understand."[39] The colonial authority, far from being an omnipotent presence, is divided from within through its interaction with the Irish, split into those who can appreciate Irish music and those who cannot. The position of the colonial surveyor who "translates" the colonized is also troubled here. Giraldus's ability to appreciate Irish music indicates his power in "penetrat[ing] the mysteries" of the foreign practice. But this ability also hints at a fundamental similarity between colonized and colonizer that enables the one to understand the culture of the other. In chapter 1, I read the popularity of printed Irish tunes on the London market similarly as a form of "translation" that implicates the colonial power in the culture of the colonized, while in chapter 8, I discuss how the representation of Irish music at the Great Exhibition in London in the form of a "Temple of Music" constructed of bogwood serves to remind the colonial authority of its dependence on its outlying colonies for its cultural and economic identity.

An examination of Irish music also reveals the internal fractures within the position of the colonized. In chapter 1, for example, I consider the difficulties involved in applying the terms *native* and *Anglo-Irish* to music when the musical traditions of each group were marked by internal divisions. I suggest that Gaelic Irish music represents an amalgam of the music of different traditions, and I trace how that music becomes further hybridized through interaction with an Anglo-Irish musical culture that is itself reflective of both local and metropolitan concerns. Chapters 4 and 7 explore how later commentators on Irish music as diverse as Edward Bunting and Thomas Davis attempt to identify characteristics of "pure" Irish music. Not only do their efforts prove impossible, but their texts reveal how the ideal of cultural purity that they promote actually mirrors the paradigms of colonial ideology.

This book, then, considers music as a location of "double inscription" in Ireland, a site that reflects the various ways in which colonizing and colonized identities were shaped, changed, and articulated through encounter.[40] It argues that the discourse on Irish music reflects a continuous negotiation between the original cultures of the native Irish and the dominant cultures, both Anglo-Irish and English. In their anthology on colonial discourse and postcolonial theory, Patrick Williams and Laura Chrisman suggest that the examination of such negotiations will prove important in the future of postcolonial theory:

> What has been less explored is the extent to which the subaltern may have played a constitutive rather than a reflective role in colonial and domestic imperial discourse and subjectivity. Rather than being that other onto which the coloniser projects a previously constituted subjectivity and knowledge, native presences, locations and political resistance need to be further theorised as having a determining or primary role in colonial discourses, and in the attendant domestic versions of these discourses. In other words, the movement may have been as much from "periphery" to "centre" as from "centre" to "periphery."[41]

Stuart Hall, too, refers to the necessity of "re-read[ing] the binaries [of the colonial encounter] as forms of transculturation, of cultural translation, destined to trouble the here/there cultural binaries for ever."[42] The readings I offer—of eighteenth-century printed collections of Irish tunes, of historiographies that promote Irish bardic culture, of translations of Irish songs and of novels that highlight Irish musical culture, to name only a few—are all characterized by the hybridity derived from encounter and translation, despite the creators' frequent claims for the purity of the musical tradition on which they draw.

At the same time, I use the interactionist model through which I examine Irish music to argue for the necessity of situating hybridity. David Lloyd identifies the peculiar kind of hybridization evident in Ireland:

> It should be recalled that the experience of colonized cultures such as Ireland's, with differing but increasing degrees of intensity, is to be subjected to an uneven process of assimilation. What is produced, accordingly, is not a self-sustaining and autonomous organism capable of appropriating other cultures to itself, as imperial and post-modern cultures

alike conceive themselves to be, but rather, at the individual and national-cultural level, a hybridization radically different from Bakhtin's in which antagonism mixes with dependence and autonomy is constantly undermined by the perceived influence of alien powers.[43]

Lloyd's description of ambivalence proves a salutary warning against a tendency that is too prevalent in postcolonial studies: the alignment of hybridity with resistance. In the case studies that I examine, I eschew making the connection between hybridity and liberation or resistance suggested by Homi K. Bhabha.[44] The hybridity that I consider here, for example, does not necessarily register either resistance or co-optation; rather, it illustrates the multiple ways these positions intersect with each other across a variety of fields. Srinivas Aravamudan writes of these kinds of intersections:

> Rather than reifying a voice of resistance or dissent, the act of reading makes available the differing mechanisms of agency that traverse texts, contexts, and agents themselves. . . . Though some critics would have us choose between hybridity and authenticity, or collaboration and opposition, the messy legacies of empire do not always afford such clear-cut choices. One manifestation of agency may look like assimilation, incremental change, or liberal reformism.[45]

What is important in Aravamudan's intervention is the shift he makes from the site of writing to the site of reading, from the ambivalence of the text to ways in which a reader constructs the meaning of that ambivalence. In keeping with Aravamudan's articulation, I argue for the necessity of situating textual ambivalence in the experiences of a text's readers or consumers. A text like Moore's *Irish Melodies*, for example, which was seen by some as promoting political resistance, was also constrained by its position in the marketplace as a commodity for eager bourgeois consumers of Irish culture. Conversely, a text that appears ideologically complicit with the colonizing power, such as Bunting's last version of the *Ancient Music of Ireland*, can also be seen as figuring resistance in the marketplace by representing a continual revising and refashioning of Irish identity. Hybridization, then, will be seen in this study as a crucial formulation, although one that does not serve unconditionally as either a complicit or a liberatory strategy, and one that must be considered in relation to the particular material circumstances of its articulation and the interests of its perceivers.[46]

One way of situating the political valence of the hybridity that I identify in particular texts is to consider those texts from a print culture perspective.[47] The print culture approach I take allows for an examination not just of texts but of the circumstances surrounding their creation, dissemination, and consumption. While all of the texts I consider demonstrate a form of hybridity, the political resonance of that hybridity depends to a great extent on the text's physical manifestation and its reception: how and where it was published, who its consumers were, and what expectations they possessed for making meaning of the text. Again, the *Topography* serves as a point of reference. It was first written in manuscript form and presented to Archbishop Baldwin while Giraldus was in Wales in 1188 to promote a crusade. It was subsequently copied, translated, and abridged in manuscript form and was eventually printed in the sixteenth and early seventeenth centuries.[48] However, Giraldus's comments, originally presented in a text whose purpose was to promote the conquest of the Irish, were taken up by later writers in Ireland who employed them for their own purposes of promoting a positive Irish national image. In "The Progress of Music in *Ireland*. To Mira" (1725), for example, the Anglo-Irish poet Matthew Pilkington echoes Giraldus's ambiguous assessment of Irish music in describing the harp-playing of Carolan:

> Sweetly irregular, now swift, now slow,
> With soft Variety, his Numbers flow,
> The shrill, the deep, the gentle, and the strong,
> With pleasing Dissonance adorn his Song.[49]

Strikingly, however, it was a Catholic writer, Charles O'Conor, a spokesperson for the Catholic Committee in its campaign to end the penal laws, whose reference to Giraldus ensured the *Topography*'s continued influence during the eighteenth and nineteenth centuries. In his *Dissertations on the History of Ireland* (1755), O'Conor observes that "Cambrensis, who lived when the art was in greater perfection, seemed enraptured with our music" and suggests that the evidence of Irish musical skill calls into question the contemporary image of the Irish as barbaric.[50] Joseph Cooper Walker followed in O'Conor's footsteps, providing his readers with an English translation and the original Latin of Giraldus's remarks. In the nineteenth century, Thomas Moore and Sydney Owenson register a more complex sense of how Giraldus's comments framed a positive Irish identity only within the confines of the colonial relationship. In the advertisement to the *Irish Melodies* (1808), Moore writes that music is "the only Talent for which our English Neighbours ever deigned to allow us any Credit."[51] Owenson's character Glorvina in *The Wild Irish Girl* reiterates this idea: "[M]uch indeed do we stand indebted to the most charming of all the sciences for the eminence it has obtained us; for in *music only*, do *you* English allow us poor Irish any superiority."[52] By the mid–nineteenth century, the connection between music and the Irish nation that Giraldus articulated had become so naturalized in the writing of Irish nationalists that in 1845, Thomas Davis, one of the leaders of Young Ireland, could write assuredly that "[m]usic is the first faculty of the Irish. . . . [T]he use of this faculty and this power, publicly and constantly, to keep up their spirits, refine their tastes, warm their courage, increase their union and renew their zeal is the first duty of every patriot."[53] The image of Ireland as the "Land of Song" was employed as a reflection of both colonial hegemony and its discontents, depending on how that image was packaged and on the political allegiances of those who read or consumed it.[54]

Gender and the Irish Nation

The editors of *Gender and Sexuality in Modern Ireland* comment on the lack of attention to gender issues as a systemic problem in Irish studies: "The study of gender in Ireland has been suppressed, with some notable exceptions, in the dominant male-centered discourses of historiography and literary criticism, which have until very recently assumed an understanding of culture that marginalizes gender in revising nationalism or in analyzing Ireland's postcolonial status."[55] Éibhear Walshe concurs, suggesting that "the primacy of a particular form of masculinist nationalism in Irish writing led, inevitably, to the suppression of a number of counterdiscourses (i.e. feminism, radical socialism, lesbianism, the homoerotic)."[56] Often where concerns regarding gender have arisen, they have tended to reinforce certain stereotypes of femininity. The pervading symbolization of Ireland as a woman, for example, has been investigated by Adele Dalsimer and Vera Kreilkamp and Belinda Loftus, among others.[57] Dalsimer and Kreilkamp make an exceptionalist argument for the connection between gender and national identity in Ireland, asserting that "[i]n Ireland—more insistently than in other countries—national identity is gendered, rooted in an ancient native iconography."[58] But such observations tend to reinforce rather than interrogate the use made of woman as symbol in nationalist projects.

Luke Gibbons and Joseph Valente provide more nuanced examinations of the identification of Ireland with the feminine by relating it to the processes of colonialism. Gibbons argues that representations of the Irish nation as female actually constitute a way of contesting colonial power. He acknowledges the limitations that the typical allegorical gendering of national identity imposes on actual women, asserting that "female figures are endowed with allegorical status at the expense of the interests of living women in the real world."[59] But at the same time he asserts the efficacy of such allegory in a colonial context, suggesting that the appeal to such "enigmatic, allegorical figures" as "Queen Sieve," "Dark Rosaleen," or "Cathleen Ní Houlihan" by Whiteboys or other insurgents does two things. First, the reliance on allegory in which "it may not be at all clear where the figural ends, and the literal begins"[60] constitutes a "blurring of the boundaries between the personal and the political, inscribing the physicality of the body in public space," a situation that he suggests is sympathetic with the feminist project of transforming the public sphere. Second, the use of allegorical figures facilitates an "unmask[ing]" of "power relations."[61] Gibbons seems to reinforce the very limitations he acknowledges, however, when he argues, regarding this second point, that

> [t]he figuration of Ireland as a woman intensified under a system of cultural apartheid in which the entire native population, both male and female, shared the condition of women in the metropolitan centre. In these circumstances, the recourse to female imagery in poetry and popular protest turns the colonial stereotype against itself, positing an alternative "feminized" public sphere (imagined as the nation) against the official patriarchal order of the state.[62]

Such a statement dismisses the lack of actual participation of Irish women in such a project, for it is clear that this is not a "feminized" public sphere; rather, it is a public sphere still constructed through the use of female symbols.[63] At the same time Gibbons homogenizes the "condition of women in the metropolitan centre," disregarding the reminder that Yuval-Davis and Anthias give us: "[I]t is important to remember that there is no unitary category of women which can be unproblematically conceived as the focus of ethnic, national or state policies and discourses."[64]

Joseph Valente also addresses the relationship between gender and colonialism in Ireland, picking up on what Dalsimer and Kreilkamp describe as the "rooted" notion of gender identity: "[M]any properties attaching to the feminized idea of the Celt had come to be cherished by the Irish people as the *differentiae* of their ethnic and cultural definition."[65] Where Gibbons argues for the radical use of female images from this ethnic and cultural repertoire, however, Valente suggests that these images were used to justify English liberal policy regarding ruling Ireland. He asserts that in order to oppose English stereotyping of Ireland as feminine, Irish writers fell back on a "colonial hypermasculinity," to use the term of Ashis Nandy, that "tended to underwrite vigorously the normative code of gender hierarchy but to contest its customary translation into the register of ethno-cultural difference"[66] between Ireland and England. Valente reads this "colonial hypermasculinity" as an "oedipalized identification with the aggressor," as it "concedes . . . that the colonial subjacency of the Irish people would in fact be justified if they did in truth harbor the 'feminine characteristics' attributed to them."[67] But in his very description of this relationship as "oedipal," Valente uses a model that limits the literal and figurative place of women in the nation and that reinscribes the colonial relationship as familial. Even an actual woman, Maud Gonne, is seen as rehearsing the oedipal struggle of the son, Ireland, against the parent, England. Both Gibbons and Valente, then, use models that essentialize gender relations while placing women on the sidelines.

In this book, I analyze the connections between music, gender, and postcolonialism with attention to the ambiguities that complicate any simple rhetorical model. I read music as one of those "nationalist projects" that, as Nira Yuval-Davis suggests, "affect and are affected by" actual "relations between women and men" and that in turn construct notions of "femininity and masculinity."[68] But I also read the discourse on music within the larger framework of Ireland's colonial relationship. Within the colonial dynamic, I suggest, the gendering of the Irish nation and its music possesses a peculiar resonance; it is overdetermined, expressed at different times as a representation of continuing colonial domination and as an attempt to resist that domination. Accordingly, the symbolic positions of dominant and resisting, male and female, become inherently unstable, subject to a multiplicity of readings that, in turn, are capable of destabilizing the systems that they ostensibly represent.[69] What I present in the chapters that follow is not a linear development of how the discourses of gender and music map onto the discourse of nation in the eighteenth and nineteenth centuries; rather, I focus on the many ways each field both constitutes and unsettles the others. Moreover, these chapters demonstrate how, in Ireland, as elsewhere, the categories of gender and nation inflect and are inflected by issues of class and, particularly in the nineteenth century, racialization. As Anne McClintock argues, "[R]ace, gender and class are not distinct realms of experience, existing in splendid isolation from each other; nor can they be simply yoked together retrospectively. . . . Rather, they come into existence *in and through* relation to each other—if in contradictory and conflictual ways."[70] In my chapter on Thomas Moore, for example, I examine how Moore's feminization was bound up with his position as a performer in middle-class drawing rooms, while in chapter 7, I examine how Thomas Davis's racialization of Ireland—making its culture "racy with the soil"—corresponds with his masculinization of the nation in response to Moore.

A number of recent critics have addressed the connection between "relations between men and women" and "nationalist projects." G. J. Barker-Benfield, for example, suggests that the post–Civil War shift to a consumer-based society in Britain underlies changes in "relations between the sexes" in the eighteenth century. Specifically, he argues that "the prospect of creating and furthering commerce led men to change themselves as males, changes nourished by and nourishing the elaboration of a public, popular, male culture in a process dating back to the English Reformation."[71] Women's roles also changed: "[T]he home became the primary site for consumption on a broad social scale and women gained significant authority over the relations of new objects to human activities therein, creating what we think of as domesticity."[72] Barker-Benfield identifies how these changes were accommodated by what he calls a "culture of sensibility": "Women's entering public space for pleasure (making it heterosocial) and men's being attracted into more comfortable homes (promising pleasurable heterosociality there, too) began to transform previous alignments of gender. This permeability contributed to the attempted clarification and hardening of new definitions of being female and male, and the spheres with which women and men were most usually identified."[73] In drawing attention to the "hardening of new definitions," Barker-Benfield quotes Mary Wollstonecraft's critical characterization of the discourse on gender roles: "[T]he sexes ought not to be compared; man was made to reason, woman to feel."[74] For Barker-Benfield, the "new definitions" of male and female activity were intimately connected with economic changes in the nation.

In "Women, Literature and National Brotherhood," Mary Louise Pratt examines the ideological uses of "relations between men and women" in the development of national identity. Situating her argument in the work of feminist historians like Joan Landes and in opposition to what she calls Benedict Anderson's "androcentrism" in describing the nation as a fraternal link, Pratt argues that the modern nation of the "bourgeois republican era" developed not only simultaneously with, but in direct relation to, the evolution of separate, gendered spheres.[75] As the national community developed, she argues, women came to be imagined as "dependent rather than sovereign . . . practically forbidden to be limited and finite, being obsessively defined by their reproductive capacity."[76] In Pratt's formulation, women are important not because they participate in the activities of the nation but because they reproduce new citizens. The nation requires them, but they are "precariously other to the nation."[77]

Both Barker-Benfield's and Pratt's analyses are dependent on and, to a certain extent, reproduce a binary that divides a male public from a female private domestic sphere. This binary, equated with the development of modernity, has, however, been subject to dispute by a number of other scholars. Lawrence Klein, for example, argues that "although the distinction between 'public' and 'private' *is* common in the eighteenth century, each term in the opposition has several meanings. Thus, there is no one 'public/private' distinction to which interpretation can confidently secure itself. As in the case of the diversity of distinctions, recognizing this mobility of meanings increases the complexity of mapping discourse."[78] Klein advocates a closer examination of issues of "both space and language" in order to determine more accurately the relation of gender to publicity and privacy.[79] In *Small Change: Women, Learning, Patriotism, 1750–1810,* Harriet Guest intervenes in the debate by investigating the "small changes in the network of meanings that constitute publicity" that allow and even make it "necessary for some women to define their gendered identities through the nature and degree of their approximation to the public identities of political citizens."[80]

In this book, I read the division between a male public and a female private sphere as a general scheme that was prevalent in textual discourse and that allows us to make useful observations at times. As Klein suggests, "Most historians agree that over the course of the eighteenth century, and more insistently in the nineteenth, a private and a public sphere were constructed ideologically and endowed with gender and class meaning."[81] However, I acknowledge the interventions of Klein, Guest, and others who have drawn our attention both to the slipperiness of the concepts themselves and to the fact that in practice, in Guest's words, "the relation between public and private may be permeable, may be fluid."[82] Moreover, I am very conscious that historians' and literary critics' assessments of these categories are derived primarily from English sources. There has to date been no book-length attempt to consider how issues of public and private map onto gender relations in eighteenth-century Ireland, nor how that mapping is connected to the development of modernity. For the nineteenth century, however, Margaret Kelleher and James Murphy have drawn together a series of useful essays regarding the gendered nature of the public/private binary in *Gender Perspectives in Nineteenth-Century Ireland: Public and Private Spheres,* in which they suggest that "[i]nterconnectedness, rather than separateness, is frequently evident: the domestic realm influenced by and itself shaping the public domain; male and female roles [are] . . . 'intermeshed and interdependent.'"[83] I believe it fair to say that eighteenth- and nineteenth-century middle- and upper-class Irish people were extremely influenced by the gendered constructions operative at least provisionally across the Irish Sea. After all, as I discuss in chapter 1, Irish men and women, especially in urban areas, practiced patterns of consumption similar to those of inhabitants of London and would have had access to the same forms of print culture in which gendered constructions were articulated. However, the social and political realities in Ireland were significantly different from those in England. Klein suggests a number of ways of understanding the definition of "public": as "the State" or the "civic public sphere" or the "economic public sphere" or "an associative public sphere, a sphere of social, discursive and cultural production."[84] While each of these definitions was exclusive in England, serving to draw a line between people who could claim participation in "public" activity and those who could not, the exclusions were even greater in Ireland, where penal laws were operative. Not only women, for example, but also Roman Catholic men were not officially allowed to participate in any form of state or civic political activity, including land ownership. For a majority of the population in Ireland who didn't have access to political positions, "public" didn't correspond with the official definition of "political" at all, although, as the work of Kevin Whelan on Catholics' manipulation of the penal laws to their own advantage suggests, the political realm was different in practice than in theory.[85] If the boundary between the public and the private was permeable in England, then it was even more porous in Ireland. Moreover, rather than equating the divide between public and private with the development of modernity in Ireland, we should observe that Ireland was subject to a process of uneven modernization. The division between public and private in Ireland's case signified variously both the development of modernity and an obstacle to it.

If Ireland both mirrors and interrogates the divisions between private and public that Barker-Benfield describes, it both emulates and confounds the gendered model of national imagining that Pratt discusses. Pratt suggests that Anderson's "three key features" of modern nations—their finiteness, their sovereignty, and their fraternal connection—are "metonymically embodied in the finite, sovereign, and fraternal figure of the citizen-soldier." Women, on the other hand, are imagined as "dependent, rather than sovereign; they are practically forbidden to be limited and finite. . . . [T]heir bodies are sites for many forms of intervention, penetration, and appropriation."[86] But Ireland's national imagining does not fit neatly into this formulation. While it was finite geographically as an island, it was severely divided from within and disturbingly connected to the interests of a larger nation-state. Though a number of people in Ireland attempted in various ways to exercise their sovereignty through promoting an Irish parliament and through staging a rebellion, for example, Ireland was ultimately absorbed into the political framework of Britain. Ireland's colonial position was productive of more complex "metonymical" embodiments of the Irish nation. While Joseph Cooper Walker, for example, promotes a masculine image of the nation in the figure of the bard, attempting to represent a self-assured finite national identity, he also turns what he refers to as the "unbounded" nature of women into a powerful aspect of national identity, noting the role that women played in "guiding in secret the helm of the state, and proving the primary cause of great revolutions."[87]

As well as encouraging complex rhetorical constructions involving women, the unique political situation in Ireland sanctioned women's participation in the literary realm and other varieties of "public" activity. Pratt acknowledges the ambiguities in her gendered model of the nation resulting from women's participation in the realm of print culture: "As writers, readers, critics, salon-keepers, and members of literary circles, [women of privilege] were legitimate, though far from equal, participants in the sphere of letters."[88] In the case of Charlotte Brooke and Sydney Owenson, this participation was directly linked to the promotion of the nation. In *Reliques of Irish Poetry*, Charlotte Brooke justifies her venture into the "associative public sphere" of publishing by claiming that she is advancing Ireland's cause by "strew[ing] flowers in the paths of these laureled champions of my country."[89] Sydney Owenson, too, describes her project of collecting songs in the *Twelve Original Hibernian Melodies* as a contribution to the development of "national taste."[90] Owenson would later embrace the cause of Catholic emancipation. The work of Nancy Curtin, John Gray, and Kevin O'Neill on the involvement of Matilda Tone, Mary Ann McCracken, and Mary Shackleton Leadbeater in the 1798 Rebellion further suggests the ways eighteenth- and nineteenth-century Irish women participated not only as writers but as activists and political thinkers.[91]

MUSIC, POSTCOLONIALISM, GENDER

The considerations I have discussed above—music, postcolonialism, and gender—interweave in the chapters that follow. I examine their particular articulations in each moment, but rather than build a linear narrative, I endeavor to trace the complications in each articulation that refuse any master narrative. Chapter 1, "Nation and Notation: Irish Music and Print Culture in the Eighteenth Century," examines the changing concept of native Irish music from its emergence in print as a commodity in the early eighteenth century to its deployment in later eighteenth-century national projects in Ireland. I discuss three intersections of native Irish music and print culture. First, I consider early-eighteenth-century attempts to render native music in printed forms, exploring how issues of gender and class came to play a part in the process of publication as Irish music was consumed by a middle-class male and female population in search of novelty and "accomplishments" respectively. Second, I examine later eighteenth-century comments on native Irish music intended to promote Irish national identity, focusing on how the association between Irish music and sensibility was articulated in gendered terms. Chapter 1 ends with a discussion of the figure who came to embody native Irish music at the end of the eighteenth century, Turlough Carolan, whose different representations epitomize the complex gendered identities—virile and effeminate—that Gaelic Irish, Anglo-Irish, and English observers sought to project onto Irish music and the Irish nation.

Chapter 2, "Harping on the Past: Joseph Cooper Walker's *Historical Memoirs of the Irish Bards* and the 'Horizontal Brotherhood' of the Irish Nation," explores how Walker creates an association between Irish music and a masculine community of bards. Walker's work is a response to the "general histories" of music by Charles Burney and John Hawkins, which concern themselves with asserting an English presence on the musical scene but ignore the contribution of Ireland. Walker's construction of the Irish nation in the *Memoirs* (1786) is extremely contradictory. He represents Ireland as both foreign and similar to England, and he negotiates an ambiguous history of the English invasion of Ireland. However, ambiguities in the text also call into question Walker's representation of the gendered political and socioeconomic relationship between Ireland and England. These ambiguities reveal how dependent English hegemony is on establishing Ireland as a negative mirror image for itself.

Chapter 3 examines how, in publishing the first translations of Irish poetry in *Reliques of Irish Poetry* (1789), Charlotte Brooke inserted herself into the discourse of those attempting to imagine the Irish nation. Brooke consciously situated herself in relation to the male mentors in her life—her father, Henry Brooke, Joseph Cooper Walker, and Thomas Percy—only to refute many of their positions and claims. In particular, in her original poem "Mäon: An Irish Tale" she revises her father's use of women as symbols of sacrifice for the national imaginary community, presenting instead a woman poet, Moriat, who saves the nation through her writing. I consider how later publications of Brooke's work recontextualized her and her work. The posthumous inclusion of some of her translations in *Bolg an tSolair* (1796), by Patrick Lynch, a member of the United Irishmen, served to call attention to and politicize Brooke's poems. But twenty years later, Aaron Crossley Seymour's republication of the *Reliques* reinscribed Brooke as a nonpolitical model of female domesticity.

In chapter 4, "Sequels of Colonialism: Edward Bunting, the *Ancient Irish Music*, and the Cultural Politics of Performance," I examine the publication of the three editions of the *Ancient Irish Music* in 1796, 1809, and 1840 in light of the changing political circumstances in Ireland. I argue that the three volumes of Bunting's collection offer multiple, sometimes contradictory, interpretations of the Irish nation, interpretations that, although presented as projects of cultural nationalism, often reflect nationalist practices shared by, and even derived from, characteristic forms of British imperial ideology. Despite this fact, however, and regardless of Bunting's possible intentions, I suggest that the sequelization of the *Ancient Irish Music* offers an important intervention into the politics of colonial domination in Ireland. Bunting, like Walker, imagines the work of creating national identity as a peculiarly male activity that takes place in the public realm, while his work, designed for the pianoforte, a typically female instrument, serves both to facilitate the participation of women as performers of Irish national identity and to feminize the representation of the Irish nation.

In chapter 5, I suggest that in the *Hibernian Melodies* (1805) and *The Wild Irish Girl* (1806), Owenson attempts to assert an Irish cultural identity connected to music in the wake of the loss of its parliament, but she also complicates that national identity by reconfiguring its gendered terms. The songs in the *Hibernian Melodies* portray essentially disembodied women as images of the nation. But the songs also leave readers questioning the basis of the use of women as symbols of the nation, as the women seem ultimately to be projections of the speakers' own desires. Although the nation produces women in "permanent instability with respect to the imagined community,"[92] in the words of Pratt, the deployment of the image of woman to represent the nation also suggests the instability of the national imagining. This is a stance that Owenson takes up again in *The Wild Irish Girl*, commenting this time on English colonial imagining of Ireland. In the last section of that novel, Glorvina recalls the insubstantial women in the *Hibernian Melodies* in that she is seen as either totally silent or shrieking. Owenson implies that Ireland under the Union is a product of the colonizing power's gaze, but she constructs a site of resistance to that gaze by concentrating on the oral realm; the voice rather than the eye becomes the source of ultimate power. I also consider Owenson's ambiguous representation of Ireland as she assumes the guise of her wild Irish heroine, Glorvina, in her own harp and voice performances, simultaneously making Irishness into cultural performance and herself into an object of cultural consumption for upper-class English audiences.

The last three chapters attend to the gendering of taste and the development of cultural imperialism in the nineteenth century. In chapter 6, "A 'Truly National' Project: Thomas Moore's *Irish Melodies* and the Gendering of the British Cultural Marketplace," I examine the *Melodies* (1808–34) as a logical extension of the ambiguities surrounding Irish music, gender, and national identity that I have been tracing so far, taking into account the various factors influencing the work's conception, dissemination, and reception. I consider not just the way Moore portrays women in the nation but the way he represents the "slippages" of gender that occur in the imagining of the colonized nation. Critical opinion on Moore ran the gamut of gendered stereotypes of the Other: in the beginning he was presented as licentious and dangerous to the "fair sex," but he later became feminized, his body the object of close critical scrutiny. And as Moore's own body became feminized and made representative of an Irish nation incapable of self-government, so the body of his work also underwent important changes: the lyrics were published separately from the music, resulting in the erasure of the effect of the hybridization of Gaelic and Anglo-Irish cultures. Elaborate illustrations further served to call attention to the *Melodies* as material commodities. These changes, I argue, functioned to relocate Moore's work from the realm of Irish politics to that of the British cultural marketplace.

Chapter 7, "In Moore's Wake: Native Music in Ireland after *The Irish Melodies*," examines the discourse on Irish music in Ireland in the years after Moore, concentrating on the work of James Hardiman, Thomas Davis, and George Petrie. In his *Irish Minstrelsy* (1831), Hardiman was anxious to reassert a Gaelic presence in Irish music that he felt Moore's ambivalent representations had erased. On the other hand, in his essays and in *Spirit of the Nation* (1843), Davis was concerned to represent an essential Irish "raciness" in Irish music that would include Catholic and non-Catholic people from the lower and middle classes. Davis's work in particular also emphasized the masculine nature of Irish culture in response to what he saw as Moore's feminization of the nation. Finally, I turn to George Petrie's *Ancient Music of Ireland* (1855). Written in the aftermath of the Famine, Petrie's *Ancient Music* is a collection of Irish tunes with all the local variants, designed to fill what he called "this awful, unwonted silence" that had affected the "imaginations" of the Irish people as a result of the devastation of the Famine.[93] Petrie turns to the pre-Famine Irish past in order to imagine a national identity for contemporary Ireland. His project becomes confusing, however, as he attempts to appeal to both oral and print culture for authority. He suggests that only through the voice can an authentic line of Irish music be drawn. However, his ultimate sources of authority are previously printed versions of the tunes. The *Ancient Music* asserts a direct connection between music and the body but also attempts to modify that connection through the intervention of the mechanism of print. In Petrie's work, this is also a gendered disjunction that regulates the organic body (gendered female) through the technology of print. Petrie's work connects Irish music with the feminine and with physical loss.

Chapter 8, "Irish Music, British Culture, and the Transatlantic Experience," examines the way that representations of Irish music contributed to but also contested the establishment of British imperial interests and American national identity. I begin by discussing British perceptions of Irish national music during and after the Famine, when cultural representations of Ireland as an exotic "Land of Song" contrasted with representations of Irish incivility. At the same time that Ireland was suffering through economic crisis and Famine, and was the subject of much scrutiny by the English press, Irish music was presented in evenings of entertainment in London venues, and Irish goods were on display for the Great Exhibition in London. These entertainments and displays both asserted an independent Irish identity and defined Ireland as a consumer commodity. I next consider how Irish music functioned within the context of Irish emigration to North America.[94] Emigrant song sheets reinforce a female image of Ireland in order to create an emotional bond between the country left behind and the new nation, but at the same time this image of a feminized, traditional Ireland contributes to an image of a masculine, modern American nation. Finally, I examine how the Irish plays of Dion Boucicault challenge this binary gendered opposition, presenting a hybrid image of the Irish nation as rooted and fluid, female and male.

In "Questioning the Frame: Hybridity, Ireland and the Institution," Richard Kirkland reflects on the "usage of the concept of hybridity and the heterogeneous in a number of recent and important studies of Irish culture," suggesting that such readings are "deeply implicated in the process of the institution and yet are marked by a concomitant desire to make such implication appear as discreet as possible."[95] He adds, however, that it is possible to see such readings as indications of "a moment of (as yet unrealized) potential within the discursive practices of Irish studies."[96] I trust that the investigations of hybridity that emerge in the following chapters, although obviously marked by the institutional experiences and prejudices of its author as an academic working outside Ireland, will encourage other scholars of Irish studies to look anew at the vast range of material that constitutes the discourse on Irish music. If this book contributes in any way to a continued and nuanced understanding of the relationship between music, postcolonialism, gender, and Irish studies, it will have achieved its purpose.

I

Nation and Notation

Irish Music and Print Culture in the Eighteenth Century

Critics have tended to encourage the division of the music of Ireland before the eighteenth century into two entirely separate traditions, setting up rigid boundaries between the "hidden Ireland" of the Gaelic world and the Anglo-Irish world. As Marie McCarthy suggests, "The tendency has been to approach music in Irish culture as a dualism and to equate classical music with colonial, Anglo-Irish society and traditional music with Gaelic, Irish-Ireland."[1] Certain scholars, like Ann Buckley and Ríonach Uí Ógáin, have concentrated on reconstructing an idea of the Gaelic musical tradition using references to music found in visual arts or literature.[2] Their accounts, necessarily limited to the privileged classes of Irish society, indicate the importance of the figure of the bard, whose accolades and genealogies, probably accompanied by improvised harp, helped to heighten the prestige of noble Irish families. Other scholars, like I. M. Hogan and Brian Boydell, have concentrated more on the Anglo-Irish tradition, which they see beginning with the sacred music promoted by St. Patrick's Cathedral in Dublin and other churches in the provinces and which they interpret as following, in general, the pattern of musical evolution in England. Both Hogan's and Boydell's work reflects a separation of the two traditions. Hogan refers to "the chasm, political, social and religious, which existed between the Anglo-Irish and the native Irish."[3] Similarly, Boydell emphasizes "the sharp division between the native Gaelic community and the colonial ruling society, each with its separate culture insulated from the other by strong political and religious barriers."[4] More recently, Harry White discusses the "cultural polarisation" between the colonial and the ethnic ideologies of culture: "Within the folds of Ascendancy thought, the formation of two cultures in Ireland did not rest with the unprecedented revival of interest in Irish antiquities; rather it extended to an acute appraisal of their incompatibility."[5]

The distinction between the Irish and Anglo-Irish musical worlds has an undeniable basis in history. But there are also consequences to setting up this division.[6] First, such an oppositional model tends to homogenize each of the two traditions and to produce false binaries. In actuality, even in its most ancient form, Irish Gaelic music was itself a mixed tradition of pre-Celtic, Celtic, and Scandinavian influences.[7] Similarly, the Anglo-Irish culture consisted of diverse elements. Along with the so-called Old Irish contingent and Church of Ireland Anglicans, there were Presbyterians and Dissenters, each of whom had differing attitudes to music. Anglo-Irish music, like music in England, was also greatly influenced by other European music. Attempting to identify "pure" Gaelic or Anglo-Irish parts of the traditions is as misleading as it is impossible.[8] In addition, the unquestioning assumption of the divide between native and Anglo-Irish music obscures the interaction that did occur between them. That interaction did take place is clear from the occasional comments of scholars examining one or the other tradition.[9] But while such interaction is frequently acknowledged, it is not foregrounded.

While it is not my intention in this book to provide such a survey of musical interactions between the Gaelic and Anglo-Irish cultures in Ireland, I want to set the stage for my argument in this chapter concerning Irish music and print culture by suggesting that the narrative of the two musical traditions before the advent of eighteenth-century printed collections can be productively reformulated as a history of both interaction and contestation. In fact, music can provide one example of the "transverse, transnational, transcultural movements" that Stuart Hall suggests have been "carefully overwritten by more binary forms of narrativisation,"[10] overwritten in Ireland's case by both colonial and national formations based on assumptions of "authenticity" or "purity." Furthermore, such a reformulation can offer a new way of reading Irish music after it began to be printed. The destruction of the Gaelic order obviously had devastating effects on bardic music and poetry. Gaelic music changed significantly over time as a result of its encounter with Anglo-Irish culture. But it was not a one-way interaction. Gaelic Irish music also had an impact on the evolution of Anglo-Irish music. In fact, the first written evidence of interest by Anglo-Irish individuals in Gaelic music appears during the era when the two cultures were supposed to be furthest apart. "Callion Casturame" or "Cailin o chois tSiuire mé" (I Am a Girl from the Banks of the Suir River) appears in *William Ballet's Lute Book* and in the *Fitzwilliam Virginal Book*, both dating from the seventeenth century.[11] Although he concentrates on linguistic activity, Andrew Carpenter suggests a model of the interaction between the Gaelic and Anglo-Irish cultures that can be usefully applied to the musical field as well: "Ireland was made up of many distinct but interdependent and interwoven social and cultural communities in which two main languages, English and Irish—or versions of them—were living side by side, and influencing each other at a local level. There were many forms of English and many forms of Irish, and many places (hedge schools for instance) where, in their local forms, these languages rubbed against and influenced each other."[12] The two musical traditions were involved in a dynamic relationship that began well before the eighteenth century. This relationship was transformed, however, by two interrelated phenomena that occurred during the eighteenth century: an increasing interest in the consumption of leisure and the growth of the printed music industry.

In *The Birth of a Consumer Society: The Commercialization of Eighteenth-Century England*, Neil McKendrick, John Brewer, and J. H. Plumb map out what they call a "consumer revolution," an eighteenth-century precursor to the nineteenth-century Industrial Revolution, a precursor that created a "convulsion on the demand side of production to match the [later] convulsion of the supply side."[13] According to McKendrick, "[T]he closely stratified nature of English society, the striving for vertical social mobility, the emulative spending bred by social emulation, the compulsive power of fashion begotten by social competition—combined with the widespread ability to spend (offered by novel levels of prosperity) to produce an unprecedented propensity to consume: unprecedented in the depth to which it penetrated the lower reaches of society and unprecedented in its impact on the economy."[14] In his contribution to the volume, J. H. Plumb notes in particular the growth in the areas of "books, music, entertainment and holidays."[15] Ann Bermingham and John Brewer take up this exploration of consumerism in their collection *The Consumption of Culture, 1600–1800: Image, Object, Text*, suggesting that "in addition to revealing a great deal about the texture of everyday life, the production and consumption of consumer items reveals a changing attitude towards labor, fashion, built-in obsolescence, economy and national identity."[16] More specifically, they focus on the ways in which "the activity of consuming culture enables individuals to construct social identities."[17] While these authors' observations are concentrated on England, a similar expansion of consumption and leisure is evident in urban centers in Ireland, although not, as I suggested in the Introduction, as a result of identical economic and social experiences. This new expansion included the performing and printing of native Irish music.

In the eighteenth century, Dublin became a center for music, attracting a great number of foreign musicians and composers.[18] In his poem "The Progress of Music in Ireland. To Mira," Matthew Pilkington places Ireland in a superior position to England musically, as he depicts the Muses migrating from England to Ireland: "The *Muses* now from *Albion's Isle* retreat, / And here with kind Indulgence fix their Seat."[19] Music was included in theatrical evenings, where singing, dancing, and other entertainments were presented between acts in the plays.[20] Beginning in the 1720s, ballad operas enjoyed a vogue in Ireland, as they did in England, as a response to Italian opera. In addition, numerous charity concerts were held in venues around Dublin.[21] Not less significant were the increase in the number of concerts held in great rooms, halls, and taverns and the encouragement of amateur playing. Amid this musical expansion, native Irish tunes began to appear in nontraditional contexts. Charles Coffey of Dublin picked up on the vogue for ballad operas, including Irish tunes in his *Beggar's Wedding* (1729) and *The Devil to Pay* (1732).[22] Certain Irish songs such as "Eileen Aroon," included in Coffey's *Beggar's Wedding,* became popular items in Dublin concerts as well.[23] Matthew Dubourg, an English violinist who served as Master and Composer of State Music in Dublin from 1728 to 1752, produced a series of variations on "Eileen Aroon." Writing in 1855, George Petrie takes this process of cultural encounter for granted, noting that the air of "Cormac Spaineach, or The Drummer" "will be familiar to many of my readers as one of the Irish tunes first, as far as I am aware, introduced to the English public by O'Keeffe, the dramatist, in his once highly popular musical farce of 'The Poor Soldier' in which it is sung to the silly words, 'Good Morrow to your Nightcap.'"[24] Native Irish tunes were part of the cultural context of the eighteenth-century Anglo-Irish music scene in Dublin. They were recognizable and appealing.[25]

But this use of native tunes by members of the Anglo-Irish population needs to be read in the context of Ireland's colonial situation. On the one hand, it can be seen as an attempt to construct a national identity distinct from that of England. David Johnson suggests that the substantial crossover between native and elite cultures in eighteenth-century Scotland was a direct consequence of the Act of Union, which badly damaged Scottish upper-class self-esteem: "Edinburgh tried to compensate culturally for its lost political power by starting a new artistic movement which was both aggressively nationalistic and aggressively fashionable."[26] The work of J. C. Beckett and J. G. Simms suggests that in a similar fashion the Anglo-Irish, too, were concerned with asserting their independence from England. According to Beckett, "The 1690s saw a revival of the claim, inherited from the past, that Ireland was a distinct and self-governing kingdom, united to England only by the link of the crown; and that, consequently, only the Irish parliament could pass legislation for Ireland."[27] Simms refers to this new national conception as "colonial nationalism."[28] The Anglo-Irish promotion of the music of the native Irish can be seen, like the promotion of Irish goods, as part of the creation of an identity distinct from England.[29]

But viewing the use of Irish tunes solely as a form of "colonial nationalism" is made complicated by the hegemonic cultural relationship between Ireland and Britain. As late as 1770, Ferdinando Warner noted that, "though to be born themselves in Ireland, and to enjoy estates and emoluments from father to son through several generations will make it their own country, or one does not know what will, yet the inhabitants of the English race at this day have their eye and inclination rather fixed on England as their country."[30] Thomas McLoughlin, quoting Chris Tiffin and Alan Lawson in *De-scribing Empire*, describes the situation of the Anglo-Irish settlers: "Caught between the authority of the metropole and the 'otherness' of the colonised, the settler tries to find an identity in this 'half-empowered limbo' where 'he fetishizes yet disparages' the metropole."[31] Regardless of whether they fetishized or despised it, however, the Anglo-Irish elite still considered London a center of cultural power. Musical fashion was established in London, then disseminated to provincial centers such as Dublin. In addition, music, libretti, and scores were for the most part published in London, which had a thriving music publishing industry. In fact, it was an English production, *The Beggar's Opera* (1728), that first encouraged the use of Irish tunes in ballad opera, an innovation that people like Charles Coffey then followed. As Nicholas Carolan notes, *The Beggar's Opera* contains the "Irish howl" and the "Irish Trot" amidst English, Scottish, and French tunes.[32]

Rather than see the eighteenth-century Anglo-Irish interest in Irish tunes as a result solely of either colonial nationalism or the hegemony of a London-based market, I read it as an indication of the ambiguities inherent in the colonial situation. From the beginning, the popularity of Irish songs among the Anglo-Irish was connected to their popularity across the Irish Sea. The songs assert an Irish identity, but they link that identity both to the culture of consumption and to the consumption of culture in England. The market, both at home and abroad, became a site of negotiation (or what Stuart Hall calls "double inscription") between the Gaelic and certain Anglo-Irish elements of the Irish nation. And the most significant change in the interaction between Gaelic and Anglo-Irish musical traditions, the one that would have the most profound effect on both traditions, was the printing of collections of Irish tunes.[33] In *Strange Country*, Seamus Deane comments on the process of translating oral sources into print:

The sounds that issue from the mouths of the Irish—as speech, song, or wail—pose a challenge for those who wish to represent them in print. . . . What is taken in by and emitted from the mouth cannot easily be represented in print. The movement from an oral to a print culture is not simply a matter of translating folk tales or customs from the mouths of the people to the page. It involves an attempt to control a strange bodily economy in which food, drink, speech and song are intimately related.[34]

The printing of native music undeniably both altered that music's form and cultural significance and changed the terms on which native Irish music confronted Anglo-Irish culture. I argue, however, that it is possible to look at the process of translation as one of encounter and even contestation. Controlling the "strange bodily economy" of Irish music was never easy and never final. Traces of past meanings that challenged hegemonic control existed within the pages of certain collections. The ambiguous nature that was accorded music in the eighteenth century also affected the music's meaning. Moreover, in printed form, music became "embodied" in a different way, subject, as we shall see, to a process of gendering that rendered it ambivalently masculine and feminine. At the same time, the position of music in the market for leisure limited the possible ways its hybridity could be interpreted.

Native Irish tunes were traditionally passed on through oral tradition. Printing, however, enforced more uniformity on the Irish tunes.[35] The printed texts of Irish music were still open to local variation, as contemporary purchasers of the music in Ireland would have learned the tunes from native players in their midst and would certainly have added their own embellishments. Then, as with folk music now, printing would have served to give an outline to the tune, not to constitute absolute instructions. But notation of any kind, published or longhand, imposes a different system of order on music. Anne Willis discusses the alterations made to Irish tunes by printing, especially in the case of later editors, who would often sharpen the seventh.[36] As Chanan observes, "[T]he development of notation has the effect of shaping musical materials to satisfy its own demands, thereby marginalizing and excluding from its syntax whatever it is unable to capture."[37] While many amateur musicians in Ireland would have had the example of native players to imitate, this would not have been so common in locations like London. Moreover, when the Irish tunes were printed they were designated for a variety of instruments foreign to the Irish tradition: the German flute, the violin, and, later, the pianoforte, for example.

Printing also changed the relationship between music, musician, and audience implicit in the performance of Irish tunes. Shepherd comments on the important difference between oral and written music: "The orality of face-to-face communication cannot help . . . but emphasize the social relatedness of individual and cultural existence."[38] The social contexts in which Irish tunes traditionally appeared were now replaced by the context of marketplace transactions. Chanan observes generally that the development of music printing in history "marked the entry of music into commodity relations. Thereafter the evolution of European music and the improvement of its notation is powerfully affected by what is printed, for whom, who prints it, and how it is paid for."[39] What is at stake in the Irish context is a change from one variety of economy to another. Both the native Gaelic and the Anglo-Irish cultures attributed both symbolic and economic value to the native music, but the nature of those values was different. In the native Irish political economy, music was often exchanged for food, drink, and lodging (in the case of patronage of harpers) or for hospitality and status in the community (in the case of musicians playing for popular entertainment). In printed form and circulating among Anglo-Irish consumers, native Irish music exchanged its original context of "face-to-face communication" for new contexts. Now people unconnected with the social contexts of native Irish music would buy and play the tunes. For these new audiences, Irish music had the symbolic appeal of novelty and exoticism. But, in turn, their interests affected what was selected to be printed and, in consequence, the body of Irish music that was passed on in print form. Irish music continued to appear within oral cultural contexts. Nicholas Carolan notes, for example, that funeral laments and work songs continued to be practiced by the Irish population. But only the more accessible tunes were of interest to the Anglo-Irish individuals who disseminated them and interpreted them as "instrumental melodies and song airs."[40] Lawrence Whyte, a mathematics teacher, poet, and friend to the foremost music publishers in early eighteenth-century Dublin, the Neals, comments on this situation in his poem "A Dissertation on *Italian* and *Irish* Music, With Some Panegyrick on *Carralan* Our Late *Irish Orpheus*" (1740). Whyte notes that while certain Irish tunes have been rejected even in the remotest parts of Ireland, "Drimin duh" and "Eveleen a Rune," tunes that appeared often in printed form, are "by the *Muses* kept in Tune" and "doom'd by fate to be long liv'd."[41]

While the advent of printed music for the urban, leisured class without doubt altered, even partially effaced, native Irish music, it also pointed out—even in this highly mediated form—the presence of native music and served, if not exactly to assert the culture from whence it came, then at least to call attention to the uneven nature of the Irish nation, its anomalous state. Printing helped create what Mary Hamer refers to as "sites for the contestation of meaning."[42] Luke Gibbons observes that the "remnant of oral culture" is "characteristic of the most resilient strains in Irish nationalism—or any subaltern culture . . . which attempts to speak in the aphasic condition of colonialism."[43] While the "remnant of oral culture" perceptible in the rendering of native music into print culture cannot be confused with a nationalist ideology in the later sense of the word, it does nevertheless indicate the translated presence of the Gaelic culture. As Chanan suggests: "Even if music seems unable to express anything definite—because it has no vocabulary—the fluid mixture of different levels in the way music communicates produces great semiological complexity, for each level leaves traces of different kinds to produce a confusion of signs extremely complex to unravel."[44]

"A Confusion of Signs": The Neals's *Colection [sic]* of the most *Celebrated Irish Tunes*

The "confusion of signs" to which Chanan refers is evident in the earliest printed collection to call attention to itself as Irish music, *A Colection [sic] of the most Celebrated Irish Tunes,* printed in Dublin by the father-and-son team of John and William Neal (c. 1724) (figure 1.1).[45] The pervading influence over this important collection is neither Irish nor Anglo-Irish, but Italian. The tunes have all been set as performed at the "Subscription Consort" by an Italian musician, Lorenzo Bocchi.[46] A subtitle to "Plea Rarkeh na Rourkough or ye Irish weding" (*sic*) notes that it is "improved with diferent divitions [*sic*] after ye Italian manner with A bass and Chorus by Sigr. Lorenzo Bocchi."[47] Even the name of one of the Irish composers, Turlough Carolan, appears in Italianized form in the tune "The Fairy Queen" as "Sigr. Carrollini" (figure 1.2).[48] The impact of the European classical tradition is further seen in the fact that while the tunes are designated "Irish" they have been arranged for "Violin, German Flute or Hautboy," none of which is a particularly Irish instrument.[49] Moreover, on the cover of the *Celebrated Irish Tunes,* the publishers note that they have lately "Printed a Quarto Book of the Best Scotch Tunes and another of the Finest English Ayres & Newest Minuets." The "Scotch" tunes in that publication, *A Colection [sic] of the Most Celebrated Scotch Tunes For the Violin,* are in fact presented in a virtually identical fashion; the only difference is in the nationality ascribed to them. The "English" tunes are "arias from Italian

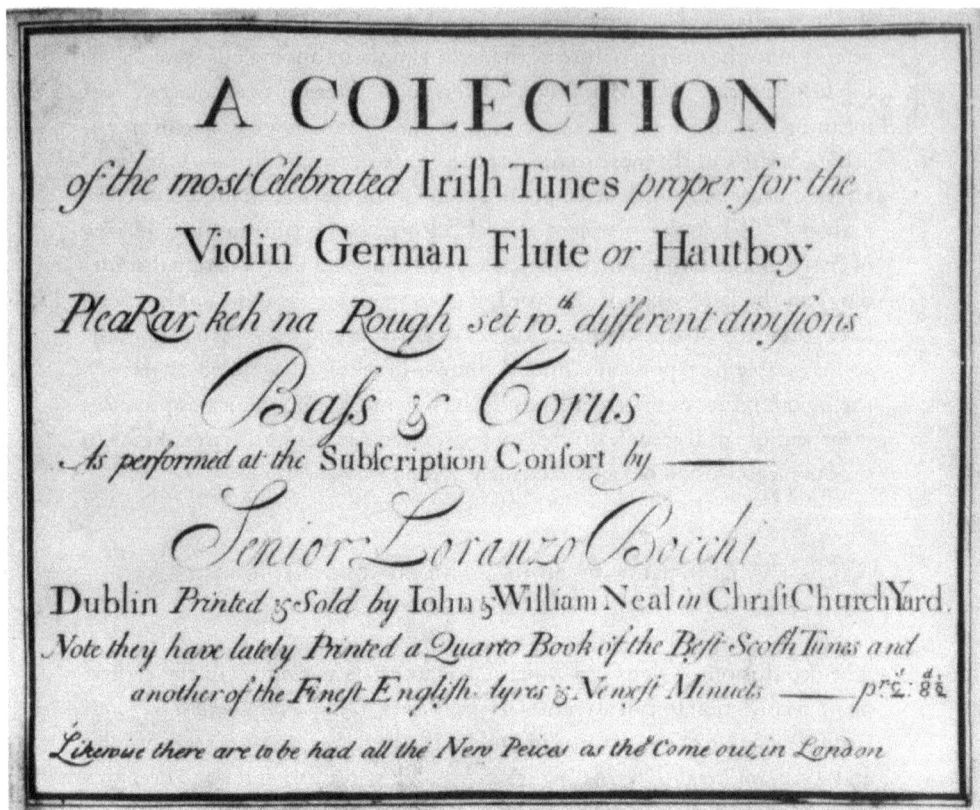

Figure 1.1. Title page of John Neal and William Neal, *A Colection[sic] of the most Celebrated Irish Tunes* (Dublin, c. 1724). Courtesy of the National Library of Ireland.

operas produced in London by Handel, Scarlatti, Bononcini and Ariosti."[50] The Neals's commercial interest is also indicated by the fact that they published *Favourite Songs from Comus* by Thomas Arne in 1740[51] and a collection of the tunes from *The Beggar's Opera*. There would seem to be little Irish influence on the way these tunes are presented.

However, while the *Celebrated Irish Tunes* alters the substance and the social context of the native music, it also provides traces of the native Irish culture from which the tunes derive. Almost one-third of the forty-nine tunes in the collection have titles in Irish. The Neals attempt to convey the original Gaelic

Figure 1.2. Music of "The Fairy Queen," from John Neal and William Neal, *A Colection[sic] of the most Celebrated Irish Tunes* (Dublin, c. 1724), p. 13. Courtesy of the National Library of Ireland.

words as accurately as possible in Roman type in tunes like "Eiry n Greany" (The Rising of the Sun) and "Ta me ma Chullas na doushe me" (I Am Asleep and Don't Waken Me). The title page even draws attention to the collection's inclusion of one of the Irish tunes, "PleaRar keh na Rough," composed by Carolan for words written in Gaelic by Hugh McGauran.[52] Moreover, the Irish tunes in this collection were probably written down directly from native sources, suggesting their origin in a process of cultural transmission. Willis notes that "it is unlikely that the tunes in Neal's *Celebrated Irish Tunes* were obtained from previously printed sources,"[53] unlike many of the other tunes that the Neals published; the Scottish tunes, for example, were "Carefully

Corrected by the Best Masters," and the tunes from the *Beggar's Opera* were "carefully engraved on plates from the London copy."[54] While many of the tunes in the Irish collection are anonymous (although they were no doubt in the repertoire of contemporary players), over half of them were composed by harpers, possibly with accompanying words. The tunes would have been notated by Bocchi, or by other individuals, as the title of "Ye Ragg set by A gentleman" suggests, and then sent on to the printers. The collection's claim that the tunes are the "most celebrated" also suggests the existence of a wide variety of popular native Irish tunes from which the editors were able to choose and implies an active interest by Anglo-Irish musicians in Irish tunes. The fact that the Neals thought to include the name of the composer Carolan ("Carrollan") in three tunes in the collection ("The Fairy Queen," "Luke Dillon," and "Grace NUGENT") also suggests that his name was well-known enough to deserve such attention.[55]

Mary Helen Thuente asserts that "there was clearly no concern for preserving ancient musical traditions or for the music as revealing a significant cultural achievement" in the Neals's collection.[56] However, I would argue that what we see in the *Celebrated Irish Tunes* is an example of the kind of hybridization discussed in the Introduction, a hybridization that does in fact reveal significant cultural achievement, albeit ambiguously. Tunes with Irish and English titles (and Latin, in one case) and tunes named after both Irish and Anglo-Irish individuals are interspersed. Tunes with important political connotations for both cultures appear together in the pages of the Neals's collection, although if anything there are more tunes that promote the Gaelic cause. "PleaRar keh na Rough" refers to a feast given by a "powerful and turbulent Chieftain . . . in the reign of Elizabeth," according to Walker in his *Historical Memoirs of the Irish Bards*.[57] "Coun[sello]r Mac Donagh's Lamentation" elegizes "the only Roman Catholic lawyer allowed to plead at the bar in his day."[58] Many of the tunes in the *Celebrated Irish Tunes* are Jacobite in sympathy. "Gye Fiane," for example, or "The Wild Geese," was, according to Edward Bunting, "sung as a farewell to the exiles after the capitulation of Limerick in 1691."[59] On the other hand, "Sqr. Woode's Lamentation on ye Refusall of his HALF PENCE" would have had more symbolic appeal for an Anglo-Irish audience. It celebrates the boycott proclaimed by the Dublin merchants in 1724 in protest against the British government's disregard of the Irish parliament in authorizing Wood, a Dublin mine owner and iron merchant, to strike 100,800 pounds' worth of halfpennies underweight at his Bristol mint, while profiting from the difference.[60] The *Celebrated Irish Tunes* embodies the hybrid history of Ireland. While the collection may have been consumed in the parlors of the best houses of Dublin, and while it contains pieces like "Sqr. Woode's Lamentation" that might be considered evidence of "colonial nationalism," the violence of a history not long past—and certainly not forgotten—can also be glimpsed in its pages.

However, the perception of this hybridity was dependent upon the location in which the text was consumed. The Neals's collection was published in Ireland, in Dublin, where the Siege of Limerick would have been familiar to the population. But there were also collections of Irish music published outside Ireland in the early part of the century that capitalized on Irish tunes as commercial novelties and as exotic reliques of a nation that was now controlled from the metropolitan center. Consumers outside Ireland would not have been quite so conversant with the particulars of Irish history. Several collections printed shortly after the *Celebrated Irish Tunes* package Scottish and Welsh with Irish tunes. Daniel Wright's *Aria di Camera*, printed in London (c. 1730), for example, advertises itself as *"A Choice Collection of Scotch, Irish & Welsh Air's" (sic)*, compiled by representatives of the three nations: "Mr. Alex: Urquahart, of Edinburgh," "Mr. Dermt. O'Connar [*sic*], of Limrick" (*sic*), and "Mr. Hugh Edwards, of Carmarthan." Eighteen of the Irish tunes included in *Aria di Camera* appear to have been copied unaltered from the *Celebrated Irish Tunes*,[61] but to quite different effect.[62] The tunes are interspersed with no distinguishing comments regarding their national origin. Wright's collection appeals to a cultivated audience by labeling itself chamber music—"aria di camera," or airs for the chamber—and the editor does not seem as concerned with establishing an accurate transliteration of each language into English as the Neals were. Burke Thumoth's collection of songs from the Celtic periphery was also published in London: *Twelve Scotch and Twelve Irish Airs with Variations* for the German flute, violin, or harpsichord (c. 1750).[63] Its title page also advertises "Two Collections of all the most favorite old and new Scotch Tunes several of them with Variations entirely in the Scotch Taste," by James Oswald. Such collections that combine the music of the three Celtic nations ostensibly assert the identity of those nations. However, by presenting the tunes in an identical manner, they actually obscure the particular history of each nation and promote the centrality of England as the place in relation to which marginality is defined. While collections like the Neals's suggest trace elements of the cultures from which they derive, these elements become more and more faint for audiences in collections that are published and disseminated further from the geographical point of origin of the tunes.

EIGHTEENTH-CENTURY DISCOURSE ON IRISH MUSIC: REFORMING MANNERS OR DEFYING COMPREHENSION?

A shift to much more self-conscious claims for the uniqueness of Irish music occurred in the later eighteenth century as Ireland came to be seen by its own citizens and by those of other nations as intimately connected with music.[64] The proponents of these claims share a reliance on Giraldus's account in order to substantiate their own claims. In his *Dissertations on the History of Ireland* (1755), for example, Charles O'Conor enlists Giraldus for a discussion of "the excellence and civil uses" of Irish music: "Cambrensis, who lived when the art was in greater perfection, seemed enraptured with our music. 'Of all the nations within our knowledge, this (said he) is, beyond comparison, the chief, in musical compositions.' He little reflected, that a nation, so instructed, could not possibly be the barbarians he represented them."[65] O'Conor asserts that "a knowledge of the arts of music and poetry was absolutely necessary" to the nation's early legislators.[66] Thomas Campbell, a Protestant clergyman, expands on this in his *Philosophical Survey of the South of Ireland* (1778) to include all Irish, not just the legislators: "[T]he Irish were, in a very early period, addicted to music."[67] Campbell praises the Irish for their veneration of learning, including musical learning: "We have already seen that the Druids, Bards, *Musicians,* &c. of Ireland had portions of land assigned them for their maintenance. It may well be supposed that the musicians had this legal establishment, not only as they were officers of the court, but as they were ministers in the public worship of the Gods. The high honour and emoluments, attendant on this art must naturally have produced eminence in many of its numerous professors."[68] Joseph Cooper Walker, whose work will be examined in greater detail in chapter 2, pronounces in *The Historical Memoirs of the Irish Bards* that "[a] musical taste . . . seems to have been innate in the original inhabitants of this island. . . . [E]very hero, every virgin could touch the Harp, long ere the useful arts got foot in this country."[69] In his *Vindication of the Ancient History of Ireland* (1786), Charles Vallancey, an Englishman of Huguenot descent who devoted himself, somewhat eccentrically, to Irish antiquarianism, went so far as to claim that the Irish had notation before the Greeks: "The Ogham served also for Musical Notes. . . . [B]y casting the eye on the Ogham figure will be readily discovered the origin of the Greek musical notes, consisting of letters standing in all directions."[70] Even Scottish publishers like Samuel, Ann, and Peter Thompson acknowledge the preeminence of Irish music in their brief history of Irish music affixed to their collection, *The Hibernian Muse: A Collection of Irish Airs* (1787): "[T]he Scots probably derived a great part of their Music from the Irish; and there is reason to think the Welsh were indebted to the same masters."[71] By the end of the century, the identification of music with the Irish nation was complete. As Campbell asserts in 1778: "The *Cognoscenti*, I think, allow that Ireland is a school of music."[72]

The relationship of each one of these writers to the Irish past is different, but they unite in focusing on music as a defining characteristic of Irish society.[73] The claim of Ireland's affinity for music, however, had complex implications, a result of the ambiguous status accorded music at the time. On the one hand, music was perceived as a necessary component of civilized society. Beginning with Charles Avison, author of *An Essay on Musical Expression* (1752), discussions of music had moved from concern with music as imitation to concern with music as expression.[74] Increasingly, music came to be explained as a reflection of the moral inclinations necessary for the progress of civilization. In his "Essay on the Origin of Languages which treats of Melody and Musical Imitation," Rousseau used the capacity to respond to music as an indication of civility: "Unless the influence of sensations upon us is due mainly to moral causes, why are we so sensitive to impressions that mean nothing to the uncivilized? Why is our most touching music only a pointless noise to the ear of a West Indian? Are his nerves of a different nature from ours? Why are they not excited in the same way?"[75] Music was understood to promote the sympathy and moral feelings so integral to eighteenth-century ideas of civil society. The association between Ireland and music was therefore useful as a corrective to representations of the Irish as barbaric.

By representing the Gaels as a civilized nation before the time of the conquest, for example, Charles O'Conor sought to alter negative stereotypes about Catholics and to encourage political change. In his *Dissertations*, he concerns himself with proving that the Irish enjoyed the use of law and letters well before the Roman conquest and the advent of Christianity. He emphasizes the integral relationship between good government and music and poetry in ancient Gaelic society. The history of the nation, the legislative acts, and "all their systems, philosophical, metaphysical, and theological," were "conveyed in the harmonious measures of sound and verse,"[76] sung by princes and bards, he suggests. O'Conor notes the morally uplifting powers of music: "This charm in the combination of music and poetry, smothered the seeds of mean, little, and opprobrious sentiments, in their cradle, elevated the passions to their best ends, and became the source of intrepidity, exalted sentiments, and virtuous emulation."[77] And it is this kind of positive association that Matthew Pilkington conveys in his poem "The Progress of Music in *Ireland*":

"Musick and Love the savage World refin'd, / Reformed the Manners, while they rais'd the Mind."[78]

But the appeal to the civility of music is only half the story. In attempting to show how music could "humanize the manners of a secluded martial nation," O'Conor omits to mention a characteristic of music that Giraldus Cambrensis was only too quick to perceive: its uncontrollability. When we are influenced by music, Giraldus had written, "our passions are by no means in our own power."[79] Eighteenth-century discussions of music are almost all in accord about music's inscrutability. In one of the earliest eighteenth-century treatises on the effects of music, *The Musical Grammarian* (1728), Roger North suggests: "[N]o art is more enveloped in dark diallect, and jargon, than Musick is."[80] In "A Discourse on Music, Painting and Poetry" (1744), James Harris alludes to the cause of this by suggesting that music has the weakest power of imitation of the three fine arts. Working from the assumption that "the *Definite* and *Certain* is ever preferable to the *Indefinite* and *Uncertain*,"[81] Harris concludes that music is inferior to poetry (which is itself inferior to painting in terms of imitative ability) because "MUSICAL IMITATIONS, tho' *Natural*, aspire not to raise the *same* Ideas, but only Ideas *similar* and analogous."[82] John Brown echoes Harris's view, observing in his *Dissertation on the Rise, Union, and Power, the Progressions, Separations, and Corruptions, of Poetry and Music* (1763) that the "Expressions" of music are *"general* and *vague"* in comparison with those found in poetry, which he considers *"particular,* and unalterably *appropriated* to their subject."[83] In his *Essay on Musical Expression*, Avison goes so far as to ascribe the characteristic of secrecy to music: "[I]f it works at all, it must work in a secret and unsuspected Manner."[84]

Significantly, it was an Irishman, James Usher, who, in the second edition of *Clio: Or, A Discourse on Taste* (1769), a work that "was revised, enlarged and annotated through eight editions between 1767 and 1809,"[85] presented the most telling theorization of music's ambiguous force. Usher locates music's power in its sublime intangibility:

> The most elevated sensation of music arises from a confused perception of ideal or visionary beauty and rapture, which is sufficiently perceivable to fire the imagination, but not clear enough to become an object of knowledge. This shadowy beauty the mind attempts, with a languishing curiosity, to collect into a distinct object of view and comprehension; but it sinks and escapes, like the dissolving ideas of a delightful dream, that are neither within reach of the memory, nor yet totally fled. The noblest charm of music then, though real and affecting, seems too confused and fluid to be collected into a distinct idea.[86]

For Usher, music is appealing because it "fires" the imagination and avoids being harnessed to pure reason. It acts as a metaphor for desire, insatiable and constant. Given that Usher was a Protestant educated at Trinity College who converted to Catholicism, his biography suggests his own powerful investment in such concepts as fluidity. Filtered differently through the lenses of Rousseau or Usher, then, the Irish capacity for music could be interpreted as either a corrective to barbarism or a dangerous practice, a threat to established order.

In his "Dissertation on *Italian* and *Irish* Music," Laurence Whyte comments on the ambivalence that characterizes music:

> Sounds elevate the Soul to Prayers,
> They mitigate our Toils, and Cares,
> Rouse and excite us all to Arms,
> Allay our Fury by their Charms,
> Compose the Mind, lull us to sleep,
> And mollify or make us weep.[87]

Whyte also registers an awareness of music's essential "strangeness" and power as he suggests that notes have "Energy and Meaning / Which all the Passions strangely move, / To Joy, or Grief, to Mirth, or Love."[88] Eighteenth-century Scottish writers like David Hume, William Robertson, Adam Smith, and Adam Ferguson turned to history and philosophy as a way of writing their culture into the hegemony of Britain. Eighteenth-century Irish writers—of varying backgrounds—turned to music. The association of Ireland with music ensured that nation a unique place in British culture as a site of historical interest and importance, but it also served as a means through which Ireland and its citizens could defy complete "comprehension," in Usher's words. If Irish music collections like the Neals's embodied the hybridity of Irish culture in their pages, the general association of Ireland with music heightened that sense of hybridity, as it positioned that hybrid society within both highly civilized and highly threatening contexts.

Eighteenth-Century Irish Music and Gender

The hybridity and ambivalence associated with Irish music in the eighteenth century were also mapped onto a discourse of gender, whereby gendered representations of Irish music served variously to promote and detract from Irish national identity. In two early-eighteenth-century Anglo-Irish poems, Irish music is represented as part of a masculine ethos. The first, by Jonathan Swift, is a translation of Hugh MacGauran's "Pléaráca na Ruarcach," for which Carolan composed his tune of the same name.[89] It describes the feast given by a late-sixteenth-century chieftain, Brian O'Rourke, in Leitrim. Swift's title for the poem, "Description of an *Irish-Feast* Translated Almost Literally Out of the Original *Irish*," suggests an attempt to describe Irish customs to those unfamiliar with them. In fact, the poem is not an anthropological description by an outsider but a rollicking reflection by a narrator who is intimately involved in the feast that will be remembered "By those who were there / And those who were not." In the "Description," harp music is presented as an integral part of the celebration, accompanied by copious amounts of drinking:

> Come, Harper, strike up,
>> But first by your Favour,
> Boy, give us a Cup;
>> Ay, this has some Savour:
> O *Rourk*'s jolly Boys
>> Ne'er dream't of the Matter,
> Till rowz'd by the Noise,
>> And musical Clatter,
> They bounce from their Nest,
>> No longer will tarry,
> They rise ready drest,
>> Without one *Ave Mary*.[90]

This is a world of "jolly Boys," where females only provide partners for the dancing that occurs in between the fights. The "musical Clatter" serves as martial inspiration for the men. Although the event to which the poem refers is situated in the past, in a pre-1690s environment, nothing in the poem indicates that this way of life has ceased to exist. Instead, the masculinized image of Irish music that Swift translates into English promotes an image of Irishmen—and an Irish nation—who are potentially dangerous if "rowz'd."

The "Parson's Revels," by Swift's friend William Dunkin, also describes a harper at a drinking party held by an Irish county squire. This time, the harper is given a name, Murphy. Murphy plays his music "without rule," in other words, without music. To him, "[Matthew] Dubourgh [*sic*]" (who presumably played with written music) is "but a fool." Murphy's rejection of Dubourg signals a rejection of the politics and also the refinement of the

Anglo-Irish. In contrast, Murphy considers it his role to recount the glories of the Gaelic past, a past that is masculine and martial:

> He sounds in more majestic strains,
> How brave Milesians with their skanes [knives or daggers]
> Had butcher'd all the bloody Danes
>   Like weathers [wethers, or castrated rams].
>
> While Brian Borough with a yell
> Flat on the bed of honour fell,
> When he might sleep at home as well
>   On feathers:
>
> He celebrates with lofty tone
> Tyrconnel, Desmond, and Tyrone,
> Renown'd O Neal, who shook the throne
>   Of Britain.[91]

The tunes Murphy plays are associated with military prowess and, in particular, resistance to Britain. Murphy himself boasts of being a "foster-brother" to one of the O'Neills of Ulster. However, Dunkin's poem also represents a corrective to this glorious Gaelic tradition in the form of asides by a Presbyterian character, Oaf, who comments:

> His harp is hollow; so is he;
> Both make one popish jubilee:
> What can he play but Garran-buoy,
>   Or Planksty?[92]

Oaf lists a specific dance tune, "Gearrán Buí" (Yellow Pony) and a general dance form, the *plancstaí*. His remark detracts from the heroic nature of the songs that Murphy is singing by suggesting that he plays only frivolous music. Nevertheless, the comment also reveals Oaf's intimate knowledge of Irish tunes. He uses an insider's understanding of Irish music to insult Murphy. Oaf's comment signals an attempt to contain the threat of Irish music, but it also indicates the pervasiveness of Irish music beyond Gaelic-speaking circles.

Swift represents Irish music within the context of a Gaelic chieftain supporting bardic culture. Dunkin presents a post-1690s world, where the bard has become an itinerant entertainer, dependent on pleasing patrons of different cultures. In Dunkin's poem, the "throne-shaking" power of Tyrconnel, Desmond, Tyrone, and O'Neill has been contained. But Dunkin also depicts a different kind of menace that Irish music represents: the ability to deceive. Murphy, perceiving the political inclinations of his listeners, ends his recital with a song ridiculing King James and celebrating King William's victory at the Boyne. His listeners are delighted, but it is clear that this is a deliberate strategy on his part, for he is described as combining his "Orphean art" with "cunning." In both Swift's and Dunkin's poems, Irish music is presented as a form of homosocial bonding, along with drinking and fighting. Such representations tended to reinforce the perception that the native Irish were less civilized than their English-speaking contemporaries, but the poems also depict the Irish as potentially threatening.

We see a different kind of representation in the prose work of Charles O'Conor. For O'Conor, music is not just riotous entertainment with or without an implied threat but entertainment with a purpose of conveying information that binds the Irish nation together:

> [A]ll their systems, philosophical, metaphysical, and theological, were conveyed in the harmonious measures of sound and verse. Such subjects formed the chief diversion of their entertainments and festivities. They were sung by their princes, bards, and crotaries, in vocal and instrumental accompaniments: and, by such means, (means, indeed, pointed out by nature, and improved by art,) they roused the soul to manly, noble, and heroic actions.[93]

Irish music for O'Conor is also a masculine, public practice, but O'Conor's work situates that practice within the discourse of sensibility. Music "rouses the soul" to "manly, noble and heroic actions" rather than merely "rowz[ing]" the body to fight. O'Conor divides Irish music into three types: "Golltraidheacht, Geantraidheacht, Suantraidheacht; that is the Martial, the Sorrowful, and the Reposing."[94] The first, the Martial, worked "to instil courage, displayed the glory of true valour, and excited the feelings of heroic love, whilst it celebrated the virtuous deeds of the hero and the legislator." In the "Sorrowful" mode, "heroes were bewailed; and the human soul was cast into that deep distress, which administers a kind of comfort in the midst of our tears; rage and revenge were not excited, or were exchanged for tender feelings."[95] The "Reposing" was designed to encourage relaxation between actions. In each of these categories, the primary concern is with music as affect.

But the concern with feelings that connects O'Conor's description of Irish music to the discourse on sensibility also implicates that music in the debate about the gendering of sensibility. While sensibility could be seen as an indication of refinement and heightened social responsibility in men, it could also suggest a kind of effeminacy. G. J. Barker-Benfield and John Brewer discuss the fine line that existed between masculine sensibility and effeminacy in the eighteenth century. Barker-Benfield comments, "It was in the interests of commerce that men cultivated politeness and sensibility, this tendency coinciding with the goals of 'the reformation of manners.'"[96] At the same time, however, "they marked their apprehensions over relinquishing the older male ideals associated with classical warriors and farmers at a boundary they named 'effeminacy.'"[97] Brewer notes that eighteenth-century notions of sensibility accorded women a prominent role in the refinement of manners and the reformation of male behavior. The "company and conversation" of women "were widely held to make men less rude and brutal, more refined and polite."[98] There were increasing opportunities for women and men to mingle during public concerts, theatrical performances, and other entertainments. But, Brewer notes, "such an arrangement brought its dangers: men would be led away from their civic responsibilities, seduced by women into a life of pleasure rather than duty; they would behave effeminately, wallowing in the luxury that modern life afforded."[99] Brewer notes the implications of a potential demasculinization for national identity in England. The Jacobite Rebellion, the loss of American colonies, the French Revolution, and the constant wars with France raised questions about England's martial abilities, he suggests: "[C]ritics agonized over the state of the nation. Was a bold, masculine, martial nation becoming effete and effeminate?"[100]

In Ireland, the charge of effeminacy had profound implications for Ireland's colonial relationship with England. An image of an effeminate Irish nation could potentially promote a colonial relationship in which Ireland was seen to be the weaker partner.[101] Commentators on Irish music, then, were faced with a dilemma. To depict Irish music as the cultural production of a virile masculine nation meant encouraging a view of Gaelic Ireland as a primitive society. To situate that music within a discourse of sensibility, however, was to threaten its masculine identity and hence compromise the image of Ireland as capable of political self-representation. O'Conor wants to ensure that the demonstration of sensibility does not call into question the masculine nature of the Irish "classical warriors." He notes that the "Geantraid-heacht," or "Sorrowful" mode of Irish song helped exercise the warriors' "tender feelings," but he portrays these feelings as being lavished on a fellow warrior, a bewailed hero. In O'Conor's account, sensibility reinforces a collective martial identity.

Matthew Pilkington's "Progress of Music in *Ireland*" also draws on a discourse of sensibility to encourage a positive attitude toward Ireland and its music, but with more ambiguous results. In the beginning of the poem, Pilkington writes that Hibernia was long distressed at seeing "Her Poets and her Sons in Arts unskill'd: / Sons! dead to Fame, nor comely to the sight, / Their Customs wild, their Manners unpolite."[102] "The Progress of Music in *Ireland*" suggests that Irish music has its origins in the efforts of a shepherd "Swain" to counteract his "Despair" over unrequited love. Although he is unable to sing his grief, he makes a pipe out of a reed and plays upon that. Pilkington's shepherd, like O'Conor's warriors, is positively represented as a "man of feeling," but in his case, sensibility also compromises his masculinity: the "Despair" that the shepherd feels "quite unmans his Soul."[103] Irish music still partakes in some of this effeminacy, suggests Pilkington, as it is a reflection of the shepherd's "unmanned Soul": "And still the Tenor of *Hibernian* Strains / . . . From his a melancolly [*sic*] Turn receive, / The Airs are moving, and the Numbers grieve."[104] Pilkington depicts Irish music "improving" over time as it becomes more urban and as it becomes a subject of interest to foreign musicians like William Viner, Nicolo Grimaldi, Matthew Dubourg, and Lorenzo Bocchi. But this improvement also means that the original Irish music is no longer valued:

> The first rude Lays are now but meanly priz'd,
> As rude, neglected, as untun'd, despis'd:
> Dead—(in Esteem too dead) the *Bards* that sung,
> The *Fife* neglected, and the *Harp* unstrung.[105]

The "Progress of Music" concludes with an elegiac account of Irish music that has now fallen into disrepute, displaced by more "excellent" sounds, but it also suggests that there may be some way of reversing this process by appealing to individual female taste. The end of the poem presents the Muse tuning her "artless Voice and Reed" in order to please Mira. The term *artless* suggests the Muse's association with the original "rude" strains, as opposed to the music that has been subject to the improvement of art. And Mira's approval is more important than that of the rest of the "World": "Approv'd by thee she scorns the World beside." In "The Progress of Music," the association of Irish music with the feminine compromises the masculine identity of the nation but proves salutary in suggesting changes to a standard of taste that disparages Irish music.

Laurence Whyte's "Dissertation on *Italian* and *Irish* Music" avoids a feminization of Irish music by displacing that feminization onto foreign music, particularly Italian music. "Corinna," the generic female spectator, is sent into "Extasies" by listening to foreign artists, and "the *Beaus*" who watch her applaud the music because she likes it. In contrast, Irish music is presented as favored by the Anglo-Irish male, the "Country *Squire* dress'd like a *Hero*, / Who'd rather hear *Lil'bolero*." He asks the musicians to play "Black Joke," "Jack Lattin," and "Larry Grogan," then "rushes out with seeming Haste, / And leaves that sample of his taste."[106] Like "The Progress of Music," "A Dissertation" depicts Irish music waning in popularity, but for Whyte the native tunes are not altered and "improved" by foreigners but completely eradicated by foreign tunes. An Italian song, "Ariadne," for example, "cross[es] the Shannon" and "expels" songs "of *Irish* Race."[107] "A Dissertation" also ends with an elegy on Irish music, situating it in the person of Turlough Carolan,

> The greatest *Genius* in his way,
> An *Orpheus*, who could sing and play,
> So great a *Bard* where can we find,
> Like him illiterate and blind.[108]

Whereas the poem's earlier association of Irish music with the masculine in the person of the Squire detracted from the image of Irish music, the reference to Carolan suggests a more positive masculine identity for Irish music. Despite his poor education and his disability, Carolan shines forth as a "Genius," an Irish "Orpheus." He is a contemporary manifestation of the ancient order of bards that O'Conor endowed with both sensibility and heroism.[109]

Turlough Carolan

Whyte was not the only eighteenth-century writer who used Carolan as an embodiment of Irish music. In "The Progress of Music in *Ireland*," Pilkington makes a similar reference to Carolan, acknowledging him as "The Vagrant Bard" who "charms the Villages with venal Lays."[110] In including references to Carolan in their poetry, Whyte and Pilkington could be sure that their readers would be familiar with the harper and composer because Carolan was one of the few Irish composers who was identified by name in early collections.[111] In addition to featuring Carolan in their *Celebrated Irish Tunes*, for example, the Neals apparently published a collection of tunes specifically by Carolan around 1721.[112] Another collection, *A Selection of Tunes by Carolan*, published in conjunction with Turlough's son, Terence, came out in 1748.[113]

In "What Is an Author?" Michel Foucault discusses his notion of the "author function." According to Foucault, the "aspects of an individual, which we designate as an author (or which comprise an individual as an author), are projections, in terms more or less psychological, of our way of handling texts: in the comparisons we make, the traits we extract as pertinent, the continuities we assign, or the exclusions we practice."[114] Michael Chanan's discussion of the roles that composers are made to serve parallels Foucault's concerns regarding authors: "The composer as a historical person with a biography is a site where different forces meet, cultural and economic, historical, aesthetic and political, large-scale and small-scale, social and psychological, conscious and unconscious."[115] We might designate what Chanan describes, then, as the "composer function." Part of Carolan's "composer function" involved his representation of a precapitalist ethos of hospitality in contrast to the current marketing concerns of music. Thomas Campbell notes, for example, the practice of naming tunes after a patron, associating it in particular with Carolan: "I have heard divers [*sic*] others of his tunes called *Planxties*, which are in the convivial strains, and evidently calculated to inspire good humour, and heighten the jollity of the festive hour. They go by the names of those gentlemen, for whose entertainments they were composed, as Planxty-Connor, Planxty-Johnston, Planxty-Jones, &c."[116] Ironically, it was in part Carolan's representation of noncommodification that made him such a popular commodity.

Another important aspect of Carolan's "composer function" is the fact that he was made to represent an ancient Gaelic culture that could also be appreciated by the Anglo-Irish. In his essay "The History of Carolan, the Last Irish Bard," published in the *British Magazine* in 1760, Oliver Goldsmith refers to native Irish music as exemplifying "rude Celtic simplicity" as opposed to "modern refinement."[117] "The Irish," he suggests, "preferably to all other nations I have seen," are "still untinctured with foreign refinement, language, or breeding."[118] Moreover, he depicts native Irish music as a potentially subversive threat to the dominant English hegemony. In Irish society, he writes, bards would "rehearse the actions of the ancestors of the deceased, *bewail the bondage of their country under the English government*, and generally conclude with advising the young men and maidens to make the best use of their time."[119] But

Goldsmith uses Carolan to serve as a link between "Celtic simplicity" and "modern refinement," as he suggests that "even some of the English themselves, who have been transplanted" to Ireland find his music extremely pleasing."[120] And Carolan is able not only to re-create a concerto of Vivaldi upon hearing it once but to compose his own "in the same taste."[121] Goldsmith uses the harping of Carolan as an example of a native tradition that just happens to reinforce European standards.

In his *Philosophical Survey,* Thomas Campbell also refers to Carolan as a representative of the Gaelic population: "They talk of a wonderful master they had of late, called *Carolan,* who, like Homer, was blind, and like him, went about singing and playing his rhapsodies. His poetry was in Irish, and not much praised, but his music is celebrated."[122] But Campbell, like Goldsmith, praises Carolan's native art by relating it to the European classical and neoclassical traditions. Carolan is "like Homer," and his ear is "so exquisite, and his memory so tenacious, that he has been known to play off, at first hearing, some of the most difficult pieces of Italian music, to the astonishment of Geminiani."[123] Campbell implies that both populations can appreciate Carolan's music, although he does note the "improvements" on lyrics of Carolan's made by an Anglo-Irish gentleman: "Planxty Jones" "has been dignified by better words than those of the Bard, by Mr. Dawson, late Baron of the Exchequer, and is now called *Bumper Squire Jones.*"[124] In these comments, Campbell suggests that the lyrics were inferior in their original form.

It is worth examining Goldsmith's and Campbell's use of Carolan as a representative of an acceptable form of native music more closely, however. Carolan lived and wrote during the final collapse of the Gaelic patronage system, a system that promoted itinerant musicians, but his music was highly influenced by Italian music of fashionable centers like Dublin.[125] He enjoyed the patronage of both Gaelic Catholic and Anglo-Irish Protestants. As Harry White suggests, he "intermittently stood between the two traditions of displaced native and ruling Ascendancy."[126] Carolan may have been used by writers like Goldsmith to represent "rude Celtic simplicity," but he was in fact a culturally hybrid figure to begin with.

The vogue for Macpherson's Ossian provided the basis for still another "composer function" that Carolan served, as, toward the end of the eighteenth century, he was repackaged as a Celtic bard. In later eighteenth-century collections, Carolan is specifically given the designation of "bard." For example, John Lee's *Favourite Collection of the So Much Admired Old Irish Tunes* (Dublin, 1780) featured "The Original and Genuine Compositions of Carolan, The Celebrated Irish Bard" set for the harpsichord, violin, and German flute. Similarly, the Thompsons' *Hibernian Muse* also included "the most Favorite Compositions of Carolan, the Celebrated Irish Bard," along with "An Essay on Irish Music" and "Memoirs of Carolan." In *Bardic Nationalism*, Katie Trumpener argues that eighteenth-century "Irish and Scottish antiquaries reconceive national history and literary history under the sign of the bard."[127] In their accounts, she contends, "bardic performance binds the nation together across time and across social divides; it reanimates a national landscape made desolate first by conquest and then by modernization, infusing it with historical memory."[128] But as we see in the case of Carolan and Ireland, that "binding" of the nation is not unequivocal.

In a number of accounts, Carolan's own body serves as a site of resistance. Even as his work was being embodied in printed collections, his bodily excess was being deployed by commentators as a sign of the continuing presence of native Irishness. Cheryl Herr suggests that "in traditional as well as in colonial and postcolonial Ireland, the body has frequently been associated representationally with danger and has been scrutinized with an intensity that *stills* (photographically),"[129] and this is indeed the image we see in Goldsmith's representation of Carolan. Goldsmith ends his account with an anecdote regarding Carolan's "intemperance," which he relates to the ultimate "stilling" process, death:

> Homer was never more fond of a glass than he; he would drink whole pints of Usquebaugh, and, as he used to think, without any ill consequence. His intemperance, however in this respect, at length brought on an incurable disorder, and when just at the point of death, he called for a cup of his beloved liquor. Those who were standing round him, surprised at the demand, endeavored to persuade him to the contrary; but he persisted, and when the bowl was brought before him, attempted to drink but could not; wherefore, giving away the bowl, he observed with a smile, that it would be hard if two such friends as he and the cup should part at least without kissing; and then expired.[130]

Goldsmith comments vaguely on the medical "disorder" that Carolan's appetite brought on, but his drinking is also associated with a disruption in the social and linguistic order, as Goldsmith uses the Irish word *Usquebaugh* to denote the whisky that the larger-than-life Carolan is imbibing in "whole pints." Goldsmith's essay is otherwise written in standard English.

Thomas Campbell also notes Carolan's fondness for whisky, associating his bodily appetite for liquor with his musical skill: "They tell me, that in his latter days he never composed without the inspiration of whiskey, of which at that critical hour, he always took care to have a bottle beside him."[131] Joseph Cooper Walker, however, concerned to make Irish music acceptable to a wider British public, attempts to downplay the unruly nature of Carolan. He links the harper's intemperance to "an error in his education,"[132] suggests that "he seldom drank to excess,"[133] and, as a last resort, argues that Carolan was not "the only Bard who drew inspiration from the bottle."[134] But he picks up on Campbell's association, commenting that "Carolan, at an early period of life, contracted a fondness for spirituous liquors, which he retained even to the last stage of it"[135] and that "he seemed to think, nay, was convinced from experience, that the spirit of whiskey was grateful to his Muse, and for that reason generally offered it when he intended to invoke her."[136] A lengthy anecdote in Walker's account recounts how Carolan, on the advice of his physicians, attempted to give up drinking, resulting in the extinguishing of his musical powers. When he resumed imbibing, "every latent spark within him was rekindled."[137] Such accounts represent Carolan's body as a link between the material and cultural products of Ireland. He literally imbibes the "spirit of nation" and then produces its national music. But these accounts also suggest a desire to control, or to "still," as Herr suggests, that bodily energy.

In Reverend Charles O'Conor's account of his grandfather Charles O'Conor's life, *Memoirs of the Life and Writings of the Late Charles O'Conor of Belanagare ESQ, M.R.I.A* (1796), Carolan's unruliness is made more explicitly anti-English as his fondness for whisky is linked with anti-English sentiment in a list of his characteristics: "[I]t appears that a religious enthusiasm, a peculiar fondness for the old Irish families, an irreconcilable hatred to the English nation, an habitual attachment to intoxicating liquors, and a constitutional devotion, were the leading features of Carolan's character."[138] Moreover, the harper himself becomes associated with a "patriotism" that is "imbibed" by others: "It was thus that Mr. O'Conor imbibed from his infancy, that enthusiastic patriotism which is so conspicuous in all his writings, as well as that partiality for the harp, which in memory of old Carolan, he retained to the day of his death."[139] Patriotism and music are linked together with drink in O'Conor's account.[140]

The figure of Carolan took on particular significance at the end of the eighteenth century in the context of growing Irish unrest and, eventually, the Union of Great Britain and Ireland. Luke Gibbons argues that the Irish substituted the figure of Carolan as an image of a vital national identity in place of the image of cultural loss that Macpherson embodied: "That Ossian should have been enlisted ultimately in the cause of Empire was, perhaps, the fate of Scottish patriotism: that the bard should become central to the quest for political independence was the fate of its Irish counterpart, a process that was brought about by the radical transformation of Ossian into the more politically charged figure of Carolan."[141] Gibbons credits Robert Owenson in particular with "converting Carolan from being an elegiac figure, 'the last of the bards,' to being an icon of a resurgent Irish nation"[142] and notes the "ritualistic use of Carolan's music to mediate important occasions in the political culture of the United Irishmen (and women)."[143] He observes that Carolan's "Plansky [sic] Connor" was "suggested in *Paddy's Resource* as the air for the rousing sentiments of 'The Trumpet of Fame.'"[144]

But at the same time that this "rousing" song was circulating, other images of Carolan appeared that complicate the image of "a resurgent Irish nation." An article on the "Life of Carolin" in the October 1809 issue of the *Irish Magazine*, for example, illustrates a more hybrid image of Carolan: partly threatening and partly contained. Repeating Charles O'Conor's list of Carolan's characteristics verbatim, this piece uses Carolan to indicate the injustices done to the Gaelic population. Carolan is said to have sought "the hospitable society of the decendants [sic] of the Milesian race, whose little properties and narrow means left them by the English invader, were always devoted to administer relief and refuge to their persecuted countrymen, who were unhappy enough to survive the loss of their patrimonies, or fortunate enough to escape the vigilance of religious intolerance."[145] Carolan's drinking and "undisciplined" nature are noted.[146] However, these aspects are also countered by the disciplining of the harper's body effected by the engraving that accompanies the essay (figure 1.3). Far from depicting a dangerous figure of Irish unrest, the sketch represents Carolan as an old man who is dwarfed in comparison to his harp. In the only actual portrait of Carolan that we know, commissioned by Dean Massey of Limerick in 1720, Carolan is shown as a young man dressed in the costume of the day holding a hefty-looking harp (figure 1.4). His blindness is indicated by his slightly rolled eyes. In the image in the *Irish Magazine*, however, Carolan's harp is placed in an impossible position for playing, although one that serves to emphasize the delicacy of his hands. The harper himself is dressed in flowing robes. His eyes are open, but he is gazing off into the distance with a gentle expression. *A Favorite Collection of Irish Melodies, The Original and Genuine Compositions of Carolan, The Celebrated Bard,* published around the same time and dedicated to "The Irish Harp Society of Belfast," features a similar engraving to that found in the illustration accompanying the *Irish Magazine,* but without the suggestion of the threat that the article itself represents.[147]

Carolan

The Celebrated Irish Bard

Figure 1.3. Image of Carolan accompanying article "Life of Carolin" in the *Irish Magazine* (October 1809). Reproduced from the original held by the Department of Special Collections of the University Libraries of Notre Dame.

Figure 1.4. Portrait of Carolan, frontispiece of James Hardiman, ed., *Irish Minstrelsy, or Bardic Remains of Ireland* (London, 1831). Reproduced from the original held by the Department of Special Collections of the University Libraries of Notre Dame.

The case of Carolan suggests how Irish music and the figures that represent it were constantly under negotiation. Carolan himself provides a point of intersection for the concerns of national identity, print, and gender that lie at the heart of this book. In Goldsmith's, Campbell's, and Walker's accounts, Carolan is a contemporary descendant of O'Rourke's harper and Dunkin's Murphy, caught up in a masculine world of drinking and music. Their Carolan is clearly also threatening in his uncontrollability, needing to be disciplined into an image of Irish identity that could be used by Anglo-Irish culture as well. It is this virility and uncontrollability that Charles O'Conor and Robert Owenson cultivate in their image of Carolan as an assertion of powerful Irish national identity that resists Anglo-Irish domination. At the same time, the image of Carolan in the *Irish Magazine* article and on the cover of the *Favorite Collection of Irish Melodies* represents him as a model of sensibility, a figure capable of nurturing the "tender feelings" that O'Conor discussed in his *Dissertations*. In this guise, Carolan veers dangerously close to the effeminate: refined, full of feeling, definitely acceptable to the Anglo-Irish population, but incapable of representing a strong Irish national identity. The figure of Carolan, then, embodies what I have been referring to as the ambivalence of Irish music, its double valence, figured in gendered terms, as threat and containment. It was a doubleness that would play itself out in many different contexts throughout the next century.

Harping on the Past

Joseph Cooper Walker's *Historical Memoirs of the Irish Bards* and the
"Horizontal Brotherhood" of the Irish Nation

In 1776, two histories of music were published in England: the first of four volumes of Dr. Charles Burney's *General History of Music, From the Earliest Ages to the Present Period,* followed closely by Sir John Hawkins's five-volume *General History of the Science and Practice of Music.* As their titles suggest, both works purport to offer a "general" history of music. But in fact, their writers are also concerned with promoting the specific national interests of England.[1] Hawkins's "Dedication and Preface," addressed to George III, depicts England as a country of vast musical resources. The author notes that in his search for his materials, "recourse has been had to the Bodleian library and the college libraries in both universities; to that in the music-school at Oxford; to the British Museum, and to the public libraries and repositories of records and public papers in London and Westminster."[2] And he defends these research choices with a patriotic comment: "[T]o him that shall object that these sources are inadequate to the end of such an undertaking as this, it may be answered, that he knows not the riches of this country."[3] Burney did not limit himself to English materials; he drew upon his many travels abroad as a basis for his *History.* But he, too, was well aware of the national importance of his project. In his "Dedication" to the Queen, Burney suggests that his book will "fill a chasm in English literature,"[4] as he is the first English writer to chart the "progressive improvements and revolutions" of the history of music: "[A]lmost every country in Europe that has cultivated the polite arts, has, since the revival of learning, produced a history of Music, except our own."[5] Burney implies a link between his enterprise and an imperial overview as he equates writing the history of music with being "the historian of a great and powerful empire."[6]

Significantly absent from Hawkins's and Burney's accounts, however, is any meaningful discussion of Irish music. In a section dealing with secular music before 1300, Hawkins mentions that Vincenti Galilei ascribes the invention of the triangular harp to the Irish, but he corrects this by suggesting that "there is some ground to suppose that it was first constructed by those who were confessedly the most expert in the use of it, the ancient British bards,"[7] and moves quickly on to discuss a related instrument, the cruth. He devotes several pages to Scottish airs, which he describes as "borrowing very little from art, and yet abounding in . . . sweetness of melody,"[8] and compares Irish music to Scottish music but finds the former "far inferior . . . in sweetness of modulation."[9] He notes that Giraldus and John Fordun mention Irish music in their works, but he skips quickly over the quotation from Giraldus asserting that Irish music demonstrates *"tam discordi concordia"* (so discordant a concord)[10] and goes on to discuss the origin of harmony in Italy and Germany. Where mention of Irish music does arise in Hawkins's work, then, the author is quick to change the subject.

Burney devotes a large portion of his four-volume history to the ancient musical practices of the Egyptians, Greeks, and Romans, but Ireland is virtually absent from his account, too. The one Celtic nation Burney treats favorably is Wales. Burney notes that "[w]hoever reads the history of the most ancient inhabitants of this island, the CAMBRO-BRITONS, will find innumerable instances of the reverence that they paid to their Poet-Musicians, the Bards, both of Pagan and Christian times; and songs of very high antiquity have been preserved in the Welsh language, though not all the tunes to which they were sung."[11] In contrast to the positive reference to Wales, however, Ireland appears in Burney's *History* only as a footnote in which Burney uses a quotation from an unlikely Irish source, Geoffrey Keating, to discredit Giraldus Cambrensis's assertion that the Welsh sang in harmony. Burney cites Keating's comment that Giraldus's chronicle was "the most partial representation of the Irish history that ever was imposed on any nation in the world."[12] (In fact, Keating had noted that Giraldus was compelled to lay aside his partiality when discussing Irish music and had commented favorably on Giraldus.)[13] Burney clearly reshapes Keating's account of Giraldus Cambrensis to serve his own purposes. Moreover, as this passage suggests, even while Wales is held up for the most part throughout Burney's text as what Christopher Highly calls a "counterexample or model colony for a recalcitrant Ireland,"[14] Burney is careful to quash any musical pretensions by the Celtic nations. Burney's neglect of Ireland in his text was so notable as to deserve mention by James Hardiman, who, writing half a century later in the *Irish Minstrelsy*, quotes "an anonymous author" on Burney's lack of Irish material: "'Doctor Burney,' says our author, 'has been [so] extensive in his research, and elaborate in his detail of the anecdotes of music, as to dilate his history of them into several thousand quarto pages! Is it from the want of candour, or can it be from the want of information, that he has taken little or no notice of Irish music?'"[15]

Walker's *Historical Memoirs of the Ancient Irish Bards* (1786), published by the Dublin bookseller Luke White a decade after the first appearance of Burney's and Hawkins's works, corrects their omissions as it attempts to put Ireland and its music firmly on the historical map. Janet Harbison notes the alteration in national consciousness occurring at the end of the eighteenth century: "The atmosphere in Ireland approaching the year 1792 was one of national euphoria."[16] She attributes this euphoria to the fact that Ireland was experiencing developments in transportation, trade, and manufacture. Of equal, if not more importance, was the fact that it enjoyed its own parliament under the leadership of Henry Grattan.[17] This newfound independence, however illusory, was accompanied by a renewed interest in national history and culture. In the later eighteenth century, more Anglo-Irish writers in particular turned their attention to antiquarian research into traditional Gaelic culture as a means of connecting further with the native tradition.[18] According to Niall Ó Ciosáin, "Antiquarian and literary interests among landowners were . . . a way of establishing links with the old order and achieving a status based on antiquity of title."[19] Joep Leerssen, too, suggests that "[t]he adoption and central canonization of a Gaelic cultural affiliation and a Gaelic-oriented historical self-awareness . . . was to remain central to the Anglo-Irish sense of national identity."[20] The problem was, however, that the Anglo-Irish of the so-called "Grattan's Parliament" were an elite group ruling over a majority of a population who had a distinctly different history and language from them. The Anglo-Irish had limited experience on Irish soil, experience that was certainly not conducive to the fabrication of a history that would "loom out of an immemorial past."[21] Leerssen summarizes the confusion facing an Anglo-Irish population intent on imagining a nation for themselves: "[W]hat was the past, the 'national' past, to which [they] were to look? Alfred the Great or Brian Boru?"[22] Both Walker's narrative and his nation in *Historical Memoirs* reflect the presence of such questions. Walker's text exhibits a similar kind of hybridization to that found in the texts of Irish music examined in chapter 1, as it both promotes Anglo-Irish and British perspectives and undermines those perspectives. This chapter examines two manifestations of ambiguity that appear in the *Historical Memoirs*: Walker's representation of Ireland as both self and other and his ambivalent representation of the English invasion. Moreover, although Walker's text illustrates a common eighteenth-century investment in representing the nation as the product of male imagining, the

Historical Memoirs also contains slippages involving gender and the nation that further complicate the ambiguous construction of the Irish nation and that work to reconfigure its colonial relationship with England.

The *Historical Memoirs* presents a history of Irish music from the time of the Milesian invasion to the present with sections detailing such subjects as the musical instruments of the ancient Irish and the peculiarities of Irish music and nine appendices, including Appendix 9, "Select Irish Melodies," which features musical notation for fifteen tunes.[23] In the sections of the text that he authored, Walker positions Ireland alternately as other and not-other to an English self. Walker suggests Ireland's unique identity by presenting its music as a manifestation of the Rousseauvian "voice of nature" and a challenge to standard ideas of harmony. In his *Essay on the Origin of Language*, Rousseau contends that music in primitive societies was "natural": "[T]he first discourses were the first songs."[24] The section of the *Historical Memoirs* entitled "The Characteristic Features and Genera of the Irish Music" reiterates the Rousseauvian model of development, suggesting that "music, like language, the nearer we remount to its rise amongst men, the more it will be found to partake of a natural expression."[25] Walker admits that Irish music shares the characteristics of other ancient music: "The wildness of the ancient Irish music, carrying it beyond the reach of art, precludes the possibility of distinguishing it from the early music of other nations."[26] But Walker also suggests that the music of Ireland is distinct from that of any other nation: "[A]n ear formed in Ireland, would instantly recognize the native music of the country."[27] Walker presents music as a means of establishing a subconscious bond between the members of a nation. His claim for the "wildness" of Irish music relates to the fact that he wants to present Irish music as pure, untainted by influences that occur in a more "refined" state of society. As we shall see, it was a claim taken up by later commentators like Sydney Owenson. In each case, however, the claim for "wildness" is more a reflection of the desires of those creating the discourse on Irish music than of any specific characteristics that the music possesses.

Furthermore, it is clear that Walker associates Irish music with the Rousseauvian ideal of a pure communication of feeling: "The Irish music is, in some degree, distinguished from the music of every other nation, by an insinuating sweetness, which forces its way, irresistibly, to the heart, and there diffuses an extatic [*sic*] delight, that thrills through every fibre of the frame, awakens sensibility, and agitates or tranquillizes the soul."[28] Walker's words even echo Rousseau's own as he declares that Irish music "is the voice of

Nature, and will be heard."[29] Irish music is the natural expression that does not just contrast with the artifice of other music but surpasses it: Irish music is "beyond the reach" of art. Walker's identification of Irish music with sensibility also allows him to characterize English music in contrast as too artificial. The English are incapable of appreciating Irish music, he asserts: "Nothing can argue a great insensibility to pure melody in the English, than their disrelish for Irish music: amongst that people our best airs, so admired by foreigners, are hardly known."[30] Such comments appear as tacit criticisms of the efforts of Burney and Hawkins.

Like O'Conor, Walker is concerned to assert the masculine nature of the sensibility associated with Irish music. The "voice of Nature" in the *Historical Memoirs* is articulated exclusively by a male community of bards. But Walker is also concerned to avoid an association of a male community with barbarism or primitivity. His bards are not connected, as are Swift's and Dunkin's, with the rollicking world of drinking and fighting. For all the wildness of ancient Irish music, Walker's Irish bards are an extremely orderly group. "At an immemorial period," Walker writes, "Seminaries or Colleges were instituted in different parts of the kingdom for the education of the Bards." Although these institutions were "sunk in the bottom of deep woods of oak," they were designed like monasteries: "[T]he 'garish eye of day' was excluded from them, and their members studied by the light of tapers and lamps."[31] Walker's vision of the hermitlike bards appears as a deliberate contestation of Spenser's representation in *A View of the Present State of Ireland* of Irish bards as disorderly and morally corrupt. Walker quotes Spenser's assertion that bards were

> for the most part so far from instructing young men in moral discipline, that they themselves do more deserve to be sharply disciplined: for they seldom use to choose unto themselves the doings of good men for the arguments of their poems; but whomsoever they find to be most licentious of life, most bold and lawless in his doings, most dangerous and desperate in all parts of disobedience and rebellious disposition; him they set up and glorifie in their Rithmes, him they praise to the people, and to young men make an example to follow.[32]

In contrast, Walker's bardic schools serve to foster both aesthetic skill and moral values in their apprentices: "[T]he diet and dress of the students were regulated by the most rigid rules of prudence: the lures of pleasure were proscribed by the institution."[33] According to Walker, a young bard received a degree upon completing the seminary and was assigned a position as either "a Filea [poet], a Breitheamh, or a Seanacha," according to the rank of his family.[34] There was also an inferior order of musician. Walker's account constructs the ancient Irish bards as a kind of Royal Academy.[35] Although the Irish bardic seminaries were hidden in "deep woods of oak," the bards conformed to eighteenth-century models of civility and virtue. What Walker writes about in the *Historical Memoirs* is an ideal Irish nation: civilized, yet strong, and, most important, independent. Such a nation could be imagined only as masculine, for eighteenth-century constructions of the feminine precluded women's active participation in the affairs of government. As Linda Colley notes, "[A] woman would not by definition be a citizen and could never possess political rights."[36] If Ireland and the Irish were to be taken seriously by the English, they had to possess an impeccable masculine pedigree. In Walker's bardic community, knowledge and history are passed down by men through men. Walker's bards epitomize what Mary Louise Pratt refers to as the "androcentrism of . . . modern national imaginings": "Women inhabitants of nations were neither imagined as nor invited to imagine themselves as part of the horizontal brotherhood."[37]

As well as depicting the bards as a "horizontal brotherhood," Walker indicates that they are literate. In *Writing and Orality: Nationality, Culture and Nineteenth-Century Scottish Fiction,* Penny Fielding examines the way Scottish writers modified Rousseau's elevation of preliterate culture for their own purposes of promoting a positive image of Scottish culture.[38] In his discussion of the oral tradition of Irish music, Walker engages in a similar project for Irish culture, particularly by reworking the association of writing with authority.[39] Walker's promotion of orality is made explicit in the section entitled "The Characteristic Features and Genera of the Irish Music." He refutes the idea that the ancient "Aborigines of this island" possessed any means of musical notation, but he suggests that "[r]emains of their music have been handed down to us by tradition, in its original simplicity."[40] These remains, he contends, are considered "as classics" and have "obtained for Ireland the honourable title of A SCHOOL FOR MUSIC."[41] Faced with the dearth of written proof of Irish musical skill, Walker promotes oral culture as an alternative source of viable evidence and pedagogical value. This is also suggested in the first part of the *Historical Memoirs,* in which Walker discusses early Irish society. Walker quotes Keating's *General History of Ireland,* elaborating on the oral nature of Irish society: "Their laws, their systems of physic and other sciences . . . were poetical compositions, and set to music, which was always esteemed the most polite part of learning amongst them."[42] As Walker goes on to explain in his history, it was in fact the later separation of music from forms of authoritative knowledge that signaled the deterioration of Irish culture.

Yet despite his promotion of the unique, oral quality of Irish music, Walker wants to secure for the Irish the use of letters as a measure of civility in eighteenth-century terms. He refutes claims about the barbarity of early Irish culture, pointing out the civility of the golden age of Ireland, which he refers to as the "true aera of the orders of Druids and BARDS":[43] "Can that nation be deemed barbarous in which learning shared the next honors to royalty? Warlike as the Irish were in those days, even arms were less respected amongst them, than letters.—Read this, ye polished nations of the earth, and blush!"[44] The word *letters* is puzzling here. Walker emphasizes that the bardic system was based primarily on oral knowledge, yet he also wants to assert Irish civility in the terms of the cultural hegemony. He claims both that the Druids taught their knowledge *"verbum verbo"* and that they taught the use of letters, the Ogham script. In other words, he wants the best of both worlds. In Walker's representation of Irish history, the *Breithamh* (legislator) confirms the virtues of Irish orality, singing the laws "in a monotonous chant," accompanied on the harp by "a kind of *basse continue*" or harmony.[45] The *Seana-cha* (antiquarian or genealogist), on the other hand, confirms ancient Irish participation in the republic of letters, as Walker writes: "[W]e will venture to conjecture, that in each province there was a repository for the collections of the different Seanachaidh belonging to it."[46] Irish music may be the "voice of Nature" in the *Historical Memoirs,* but it is also a voice whose potential chaotic power is carefully tempered by an eighteenth-century promotion of print culture.

Further, despite Walker's attempt to frame Irish music as a connection between the nation's own members that is "beyond" both art and description, the *Historical Memoirs* suggests that Irish music *is* intelligible to an English audience. While eager to oppose the naturalness of Irish music to the "great insensibility" of the English, Walker anxiously draws analogies that situate Irish music within a context recognizable to a more classically oriented audience. One of the key sources for Walker's analogies is Greek civilization. He draws a number of parallels between Irish and classical Greek culture, noting, for example, that "[t]he respect for the person of the Bard we discover in Grecian story."[47] Similarly, in describing the Irish dance, he suggests, "Perhaps the classical reader will find . . . a similarity between our Riceadh-fada and the festal Dance of the Greeks."[48] Indeed, the Irish field dance "seems to have been of the nature of THE ARMED DANCE which is so ancient, and with which the Grecian youth amused themselves during the Siege of Troy."[49] Another source that Walker draws on is biblical Hebrew society. He comments that women of the lower classes in Ireland were instructed in the elegiac measure for the funeral song, and that "[t]his custom prevailed amongst the Hebrews, from whom it is not improbable that we had it mediately."[50] Both the Greek and the Hebrew traditions are used to legitimize the Irish keen: "David's lamentation for Jonathan, and the *conclamatio* over the Phoenician Dido, as described by Virgil, coincide with the Caoine, or Irish Cry."[51]

The poems of Ossian also provide Walker with a number of analogies to the Irish bardic tradition. Clare O'Halloran remarks that for "evidence of the manners and customs of the early bards" Walker was "forced" to look at "Macpherson's *Poems of Ossian,* Hugh Blair's *Critical Dissertations on the Poems of Ossian* (1763) and the works of John Smith, a successful imitator of Macpherson in Scotland."[52] According to O'Halloran, Walker drew on the Ossianic material when faced with a dearth of information about the early Irish bardic tradition. But it was not simply that Walker needed to draw on Ossianic material. Such material also provided a known context through which his readers could interpret his own text and Irish culture. Ossian had become a recognizable, albeit controversial part of British culture, as familiar as the Greek classics or the Bible.

As O'Halloran notes, Walker demonstrates his ambivalence about the poems of Ossian in his text: his "method was to quote from the poems in *Fingal* and *Temora* in the text, while in his footnotes hinting at the unreliability of Macpherson. In effect he used the footnotes as subtext to undermine the credibility of Macpherson's historical apparatus with the aim of salvaging the poems as evidence for his own argument."[53] Walker also "corrects" Macpherson's chronology: "Though Cucullin flourished about 200 years before the reign of Cormac, Mr. Macpherson has made him contemporary with Fin, whom he calls Fingal."[54] And he adjusts Macpherson's genealogy. Whereas the *Poems of Ossian* claimed the dominion of the Scots over the Irish, Walker indicates that the Scots were a colony of the Irish: "Cormac, at the head of the Fian, and attended by our hero, sailed into that part of North Britain which lies opposite to Ireland, where he planted a colony of Scots, (the name which the Irish then bore) as an establishment for Carbry Riada, his cousin-german."[55] Macpherson minimized Ireland's contribution to British culture by appropriating its heroic tales; Walker secures an eminent place for his nation by both drawing on Macpherson to justify his claims for Irish bardic culture and rewriting Macpherson's historical record. A footnote quoting O'Conor allows Walker to turn the tables even further, as he implies a direct link between the Irish and the present monarchy of Britain: "In process of time this colony gave Monarchs to the kingdom of Scotland, and their posterity reign at this day over the British empire."[56] Through such comments and analogies, Walker knits Ireland into the historical fabric of Britain.

A similar knitting together of the British cultures can be seen in Walker's triple association of the Irish bardic tradition, Ossianic poems, and English minstrelsy. Walker's proof for his assertion that the Ossianic poems were meant to be sung to the harp rests on his ability to show their similarity to English poems:

> [T]hey are, in general, in that short measure which was formerly sung to that instrument by the English Minstrels. Vide *Tale of Sir Topas, Sir Bevis of Southampton, Guy of Warwick,* and several other old English Ballads. . . . Many of these . . . begin with an introductory address to an auditory: Another proof that they were intended to be sung or recited in public.— Perhaps the Irish poems in question were of the nature of the Romance of Roncesvalles, which the peasant was singing as he passed Don Quixote and his 'Squire, in the streets of Toboso.[57]

This comparison of the three cultures, represented by Macpherson's *Ossian,* Percy's *Reliques of English Poetry,* and Irish poetry, suggests their essential similarity.

As well as juxtaposing the ancient English minstrel tradition and the Irish harp tradition, Walker provides a more immediate parallel between Irish and English culture by using quotations from more recent English poets to illustrate or fill in his historical narrative. To describe the "keirnine," an Irish musical instrument, Walker quotes from both Sylvester O'Halloran's *Collecteana de rebus Hibernicus* and Shakespeare's *Love's Labour's Lost.*[58] A line from Dryden's "Ode for St. Cecilia's Day" is used to describe the Irish bards raising "the martial fury of the soldiery" before battle.[59] The effect of Walker's constant contextualizing of Irish music is to destabilize the image of Irish music and of Ireland in his book. Irish music as depicted in the *Historical Memoirs* is at once "distinguished from the music of every other nation" and indistinguishable; it is recognizable only by the Irish and recognizable to anyone with a knowledge of the classics, the Bible, and English literature. Walker's *Historical Memoirs* makes Ireland as a nation simultaneously both unknowable and familiar to a British audience.

Walker's policy of translation is similarly ambiguous. The *Historical Memoirs* is remarkable for offering a number of untranslated poems. At times, the

Irish poems are merely assumed to comment on themselves. In Appendix 5, for example, Walker writes: "[H]ere I will gratify the Irish Reader with an Elegy of our Bard on the death of John Burke Carrentryle, Esq." The elegy on Carolan by MacCabe is also presented exclusively in Irish. Irish poetry, then, appears in Walker's text, albeit in standard Roman type, as an indication of an Ireland unknowable except to "the Irish reader." But Walker also makes an effort to reveal this hidden Ireland to the English readers. A number of poems are presented in translation in the *Historical Memoirs*, such as Charlotte Brooke's translation of Carolan's Monody on the death of his wife. Walker notes of this poem: "For the benefit of the English reader, I shall here give, with the original, an elegant paraphrase of this Monody by a young Lady."[60] At other times, Walker provides a synopsis for the English reader. He transcribes a specimen of the Ossianic poems "not only for the gratification of the Irish reader, but also to serve as a specimen of the metre, diction, and prevailing poetical fictions of these ages."[61] The textual ambiguity is augmented by Walker's own position with regard to the Irish language; he admits that he doesn't know Irish. If the Ireland of *Historical Memoirs* is at once both unknowable and familiar to a British audience, it is also both unknowable and familiar to the author. It is simultaneously both self and other.

Further evidence of narrative and ideological ambiguity is found in Walker's negotiation of the history of the English invasion. Walker's chronology of Irish history generates a conflicted representation of the confrontation between the native Irish and the English. While it presents the plight of the native Irish sympathetically, it complicates the impact of the English invasion by depicting a number of previous disruptions caused both by groups within the Irish nation itself and by invading peoples. Walker is explicit about the mistreatment of the native Irish during the Middle Ages, when the English "kept the natives in a state of absolute anarchy, refused them the privileges of subjects, and only left them the lands they could not subdue."[62] This mistreatment had a direct impact on Irish music, he suggests, although he notes that even under "the iron hand of tyranny," "yet did our music and poetry still flourish."[63] The Tudor period proved even more oppressive to Irish music. Walker comments that bards were forbidden to work within the Pale during Henry VIII's time, and he condemns the proclamation issued in the time of Elizabeth I forbidding anyone to pay "certen Idle men of lewde demeanor, called, *Rymors, Bards,* and dyce players."[64] Walker quotes Spenser's contemptuous account of Irish bards, indicating the important role of the bards in Spenser's time in trying to "preserve their country from the chains which were [being forged] for it."[65]

Included in the section on Tudor Ireland is an example of bardic protest by Fearflatha O Gnive, bard to the O'Neills of Clanna-boy, which Walker quotes from Charles O'Conor. The passage appears important to Walker because he quotes it at such length:

Oh the condition of our dear Countrymen! how languid their joys! how pressing their sorrows! . . . Are we not prisoners of the *Saxon* nation? the captives of remorseless tyranny? Is not our sentence therefore pronounced, and our destruction inevitable? Frightful, grinding thought! Power exchanged for servitude; beauty for deformity; the exaltations of liberty for the pangs of slavery—a great and brave people, for a servile desponding race. How came this transformation? . . . In truth, our miseries were predicted a long time, in the change these strangers wrought in the face of our country. They have hemmed in our sporting lawns, the former theatres of glory and virtue. They have wounded the earth, and they have disfigured with towers and ramparts those fair fields which Nature bestowed for the support of God's animal creation—that Nature which we see defrauded, and whose laws are so wantonly counteracted, that this late free Ireland is metamorphosed into a second Saxony. The slaves of Ireland no longer recognise their common Mother—she equally disowns us for her children—we both have lost our forms—and what do we see, but insulting *Saxon* natives, and native Irish aliens?[66]

The speech ends with a comparison between the Irish and "Ye Israelites of Egypt": "[Y]e wretched inhabitants of this foreign land! is there no relief for you? Is there no Hector left for the defence, or rather for the recovery, of Troy? . . . [U]nless the children of the Scythian Eber Scot, return to thee, old Ireland is not doomed to arise out of the ashes of modern Saxony."[67] Up to this point in the text, Walker's sympathies appear to be entirely on the side of the native Irish.

But Walker's description of the effect of English dominance moves into lurching contradictions when he details the effects of the destruction of the bardic order as "English Customs and Manners were universally adopted."[68] He comments that

[i]n [the] halls [of the exiled Chieftains] which formerly resounded with the voice of Minstrelsy and Song, and glittered with barbarous magnificence, there reigned

A death-like silence and a dread repose:
naught, save the slapping of the drowsy Bat, or shrieking of the moping
Owl, could now be heard within them.[69]

This gloomy imagery is immediately followed, however, by a comment on the
positive effects of English domination: "Agriculture was introduced, and
the face of the Country began to smile."[70] In a similarly contradictory vein,
the Hanoverian succession is described as having a detrimental effect on Irish
music and Irish society but also bringing peace to the nation and encouraging a return of swords to their scabbards.

Walker also registers ambivalence about the influx of foreign musical influences in Ireland resulting from English domination. Ireland is described as
subject to the European hegemony that is holding London in thrall: "Both
vocal and instrumental Musicians were brought, at an enormous expence [*sic*],
from Italy to London; and the Italian music began to reign with despotic
sway in that great City."[71] With the appearance of Handel, he notes, art music
became "the rage" in Ireland. But Walker seems to genuinely praise the effect
that this has: "In the education of the Youth of both Sexes, a knowledge of
some musical instrument was deemed an accomplishment indispensably necessary. Concerts were the favourite amusements in the houses of the Nobility
and Gentry; and musical Societies were formed in all the great towns in the
kingdom. In a word, every knee was bowed to St. Cecilia."[72] Ironically, this
"despotic sway" promotes a refinement that signals the death of Irish music:
"Our musical taste became refined, and our sweet melodies and native Musicians fell into disrepute."[73] Irish music, the "Voice of Nature," was lost to
"idle amusement, devoid of dignity, devoid of meaning, absolutely devoid of
any one ingredient that can inspire delightful ideas, or engage unaffected ap-
plause."[74] This loss of Irish music is directly associated with the dissolution
of Irish society: "Politics, Gaming, and every species of Dissipation have so
blunted the finer feelings of [onetime music lovers'] souls, that their warm
Devotion has at length degenerated into cold Neglect."[75] Walker notes that at
the time at which he writes, music—whether native or foreign—is "no longer
a favourite topic, nor a favourite study."[76] The last footnote of Walker's historical narrative serves as an illustration of the deterioration of music in Ireland that Walker seeks to portray, but it also suggests Walker's ambivalent
narrative stance. Walker ends his chronology not with a discussion of the fate
of Irish bards, or even with a discussion of O'Carolan; that appears as an appendix. Instead, he concludes by detailing the death of an Italian musician,
Castrucci, in Dublin.

The narrative of events in the *Historical Memoirs,* despite its ambiguous slant, suggests in general the gradual waning of a golden age of Irish musical life, occasioned chiefly by the invading presence of the English. But there are more complications in this scenario. Following the dubious researches of Colonel Vallancey, Walker begins his history of Irish music with the invasion of the Milesians, who, he says conquered the Danonians and who are the ancestors of the current inhabitants of Ireland. Notably, the Irish nation is founded in the *Historical Memoirs* at the moment of the conquest of native groups. The origin of the preconquest nation is accordingly displaced into fabulous time. Walker clarifies that "the arts of poetry and music obtained amongst the Milesians, both before and after their arrival" in Ireland.[77] From the beginning, then, the practice of music is associated not with actual native inhabitants of Ireland but with the conquering peoples.

Furthermore, in the early part of Walker's narrative, we see that the lapse into barbarism actually took place before the English invasion. Walker writes: "From the death of that great Monarch Brien Boiromh *to the invasion of the English,* the page of Irish history is defiled with domestic blood. . . . Chieftains rebelled against their Princes, or quarrelled amongst themselves . . . and the people once more relapsed into barbarism."[78] It becomes clear that there were considerable disruptions that affected the course of Irish music before the English came. The history of the bards themselves is a checkered one, characterized by internal disorder. Bards were respected and wise until the reign of Hugh, when they became "intolerably insolent and corrupted, and their order a national grievance."[79] Hugh called an Assembly at Drom-Chille in 580 to expel the bards but was prevented from doing so by St. Columba and subsequently merely reduced their numbers. The now registered bard was limited to singing about "the glory of the deity,—the honor of his country—of its heroes—of its females—and of his own patron."[80] The coming of the church also took its toll, causing Irish music to "lose its influence over the passions; for church music has nothing to do with them."[81] Then with the invasion of the Danes, "'the light of song' was eclipsed, and learning, and all the liberal arts, languished."[82]

Walker's description of the effect of English oppression on Irish music also registers a certain hybridity. Like O'Conor, Walker identifies three species of music that the ancient Irish cultivated: the festive, the dolorous, and that which was useful at "composing the soul to rest, and suspending the mental labours which might succeed the corporal toils of the day."[83] Walker says that it was the second, the dolorous, that prevailed as a result of English oppression: "After the invasion of the English, the Irish were very much confined to this species of music, for reasons which will appear elsewhere."[84] The "reasons," however, when they do appear some sixty pages later, complicate the earlier observation. Walker begins by restating his comments, again extending a sympathetic eye to the native Irish:

> Thus we see that music maintained its ground in this country, even after the invasion of the English. But its style suffered a change: For the sprightly Phrygian (to which, says Selden, the Irish were wholly inclined) gave place to the Doric, or soft Lydian measure. Such was the nice sensibility of the Bards, such was their tender affection for their country, that the subjection to which their kingdom was reduced, affected them with the heaviest sadness. Sinking beneath this weight of sympathetic sorrow, they became a prey to melancholy. Hence the plaintiveness of their music: For the ideas that arise in the mind are always congenial to, and receive a tincture from the influencing passion.[85]

He also suggests a more specific and scientific reason for the general melancholy that came to characterize Irish music at this time: "The Bards, often driven, together with their patrons, by the sword of Oppression from the busy haunts of men, were obliged to lie concealed in marshes, in gloomy forests, amongst rugged mountains, and in glyns and vallies [sic] resounding with the noise of falling waters, or filled with portentous echoes."[86] These scenes served to throw "a gloom over the fancy."[87] Accordingly, when the Bards attempted to sing, "it was not to be wondered, that their voices, thus weakened by struggling against an heavy mental depression, should rise rather by Minor thirds, which consist but of four semitones, than by Major thirds, which consist of five."[88] The physiological effect of the damp climate may also have been responsible for the fact that "almost all the airs of this period are found to be set in the Minor third, and to be of the sage and solemn nature of the music."[89]

But Walker's subsequent comments release the English invaders from responsibility for the change in Irish music. He conjectures that "the melancholy spirit which breathes through the poetry and music of the Irish, may be attributed to another cause; a cause which operated anterior to and subsequent to, the invasion of the English."[90] This "anterior cause" turns out to be "the remarkable susceptibility of the Irish of [sic] the passion of love; a passion, which the munificent establishments of the Bards left them at liberty freely to indulge."[91] To prove this point, Walker includes two Irish love "sonnets."[92] The description of previous invasion and disruption and the suggestion that Irish music's association with melancholy occurred "anterior to and subsequent to, the invasion of the English" problematize Walker's presentation of the relationship between Ireland and England.[93]

An elaborate anecdote that Walker includes by Chevalier O'Gorman involving the alleged harp of Brian Boru further suggests what a fluid position music occupies in the relationship between Ireland and England. After an internecine struggle on the death of Brian, his grandson, Turrlogh (*sic*), went on a pilgrimage to Rome, carrying "the Crown, Harp, and other regalia of Brien Boiromh" to the pope. The pope, however, "took these presents as a demonstration of a full submission of the kingdom of Ireland, and one of his successors Adrian IV (by name Brakspeare and an Englishman) alledged [*sic*] this circumstance as one of the principal titles he claimed to this kingdom, in his Bull of transferment to King Henry II."[94] The regalia were deposited in the Vatican until the reign of Henry VIII, when the pope "sent the Harp to that Monarch, with the title of *Defender of the Faith*, but kept the Crown."[95] The convoluted history of the harp suggests the hybrid nature of Irish national identity. The harp, presented, perhaps ambiguously, by the Irish themselves, is interpreted as a token of subordination and transferred to the English monarch to symbolize his lordship over Ireland. The story becomes more complex when seen in the context of elaborations in the first appendix to the *Historical Memoirs*, "Inquiries Concerning the Ancient Irish Harp in a letter to the Author," by the Reverend Edward Ledwich. Ledwich asserts: "It was Henry VIII. who, on being proclaimed King of Ireland, first gave us the Harp" as an armorial bearing.[96] Ledwich praises the monarch for choosing a bearing that "neither reminded us of our present dependence, nor upbraided us with our former rebellions," commenting, "[M]ay it long continue the ornament and support of the British Crown!"[97] In Ledwich's continuation, the symbol of music is given to the Irish by the English, who "allowed us eminence in nothing but music."[98] The identity of the colonized is limited to that which is recognized by the colonizing nation and, further, becomes involved in "the ornament and support" of that colonizing nation.[99]

The final appendix in the *Historical Memoirs* consists of notated music for fifteen tunes, designed, suggests Walker, as "specimens . . . for the purpose of illustrating" earlier points made about Irish music.[100] Like the rest of the *Memoirs*, this section raises the suggestion of Irish mistreatment by the English only to lay the subject aside. Walker begins his illustrations of Irish music chronologically with tunes that he suggests are drawn from "remote antiquity," the "Provincial Cries," but he prefaces them with a "wild air" which he claims that contemporary musicians have united with the Cries: the "Cath

Eachroma" or "Battle of Aughrim." After these tunes, which allude to the assertion and, in the case of the "Battle of Aughrim," the defeat of Irish martial power, Walker introduces a "melancholy tune," "Gol na mna'san ar," which, as he suggests, was "said to have been sung by the Irish women, while searching for their slaughtered husbands, after a bloody engagement between the Irish and Cromwel's [sic] troops."[101] Soon after this appears "Coulin," which, as Walker has explained earlier, refers to another act of oppression of the Irish by the English: an act made during the reign of Henry VIII "respecting the habits and dress in general of the Irish, whereby all persons were restrained from being shorn or shaven above the ears, and from wearing Glibbes or Coulins (long locks) on their heads, or hair on the upper lip called a Crommeal."[102] Walker's comments on the tunes up to and including the "Coulin" register the military and political tensions characterizing the historical relations between Ireland and England. However, these tensions are glossed over in the concluding comments on the tunes as Walker's interests shift to the actual collecting of the tunes. Several of the tunes included, he notes, were "pricked from the voice by the Rev. Dr. Young, while on a visit last winter in the county of Roscommon."[103] Apart from "Plough Tune" and "Carolan's Devotion," the titles of the tunes are all in Gaelic with Roman type, suggesting Walker's concern with representing them as artifacts of the Gaelic culture. But the notation, supplied by Gore Ousley, represents the tunes, even the "wild air" of "Cath Eachroma," as conventional, albeit elaborate, European music. The "Irish Melodies" included in the *Historical Memoirs,* like the narrative itself, assert an ambiguous relationship between Ireland and England.

The ambiguous representation of Irish national identity and of the relationship between Ireland and England in the *Historical Memoirs* is even further complicated by the relationship between gender and the Irish nation suggested in the *Historical Memoirs.* Walker's bardic community, along with the political realm, is exclusively male. Walker notes, "We cannot find that the Irish had female Bards, or BARDESSES, properly so called."[104] Like O'Conor, Walker is keen to suggest the sensibility of the Irish bards and warriors, a sensibility he depicts as promoting rather than detracting from their masculine activities. Rather than being completely excluded, however, women perform a supplementary role in the musical life of the nation. Quoting James Beattie's *Essay on Poetry and Music,* Walker points out how women serve to inspire feeling: "A fine female voice, modulated by sensibility, is beyond comparison the sweetest and most melting sound in art or nature."[105] Accordingly, women, or, at least lower-class women, are trained as singers at funerals, to heighten "the melancholy which that solemn ceremony was calculated to in-spire."[106] Where the training of the male bard prepared him for public duty as a religious leader, advisor to the monarch, prophet, or historian, a woman's role was to enhance the "manners" of the Irish people: "[T]hough women, during the heroic ages, held no rank in the order of Bards, yet it appears that they cultivated music and poetry, whose divine powers they often employed in softening the manners of a people rendered ferocious by domestic hostili-ties."[107] Walker's representation of the gender divisions in the Irish nation replicates an ideology of a gendered split between the public and private do-mains. He is intent on imagining the nation of Ireland as a construction of the male public sphere.

But Walker also depicts a different configuration of female and male do-mains, a configuration that works to destabilize and question the colonial re-lationship between Ireland and England. The positioning of women as sup-plementary, "[un]limited and [in]finite" also grants them a liquidity that threatens the established order. Walker notes what he calls the "unbounded influence" that women of the past must have commanded. This "unbounded-ness," while it prevents them from taking direct action in the public sphere, nevertheless proves uncontainable within the private sphere. Walker com-ments: "[W]e often find [women] guiding in secret the helm of the state, and proving the primary cause of great revolutions—While embattled ranks waited the arrival of expected invaders, women often walked through the lines, animating the soldiery with suitable war-songs, accompanying their voices, at the same time with Cruits or portable Harps, such as the Hebrews bore when they danced before the ark."[108] Women travel "through the lines" that are calculated to exclude them.[109] Women may be associated with elegiz-ing the nation, but, at least at a certain historical period, they also have an ac-tive effect on the future of the nation. Such a disruption of roles also puts into question the "vicious symbolic circle" of "imperialist discourse," in which, according to Joseph Valente, "sexual and socio-economic dominance reflect and authorize one another,"[110] as the patterns of dominance are no lon-ger stable.

Walker suggests a direct reversal of the "sexual and socio-economic" re-lationship between Ireland and England in the anecdote concerning O'Rourke and Elizabeth that he includes in the appended "Life of Carolan." O'Rourke, "a very powerful and turbulent Chieftain" of Ireland, was invited to London by Queen Elizabeth, who lured him with promises of honors, whereas in fact she "only intended by this invitation to lead him into a kind of exile, in order to secure his obedience."[111] Once he arrives, however, she is struck by "the elegant symmetry of his person, and his noble aspect" and resolves "to rank him with her *choicest* favourites."[112] He is given a "sumptuous apartment" and visited each night by an anonymous female, whom he eventually identifies as the queen by a ring that she wears. When he insinuates to the queen that he has "discovered his fair Visitor," however, she orders an assassin to "punish him for his idle curiosity."[113] The anecdote has the mythic quality of the story of Cupid and Psyche but also a political dimension: the lovers are antagonists occupying opposite positions in a colonial relationship of sexual and socioeconomic dimensions. Most importantly, however, the story reverses the "stereotyped feminization of the colonial."[114] In this case, the colonizer is female, the colonized, male. Walker's citation of the O'Rourke story both recalls and reformulates the allegory of Hibernia at the mercy of a male invader. In discussing the ambivalence of colonial discourse, Homi Bhabha notes that it "turns on the simultaneous recognition and disavowal of racial/cultural/historical differences."[115] O'Rourke, although a member of the uncivilized Irish, strikes the queen as "elegant" and desirable. But the colonial dynamic depends on the constant articulation of his "otherness." By revealing to Elizabeth that he knows her identity, O'Rourke asserts a form of power that threatens to upset the colonial dynamic. Even after his assassination, however, this threat remains. Its haunting presence is perpetuated both in the "wild story" that "wanders about the county of Leitrim"[116] and in the song "PLERACA NA RUARCACH," commemorating the feast O'Rourke gave before he left for England (see figure 2.1).[117]

Walker's depiction of Ireland and England in his text as two female nations further reconfigures the gendered relation of imperialist discourse. He notes: "This attention to the cultivation of the musical art, evinces a degree of refinement of manners and of soul amongst the Irish, that foreign writers, and *even those of a sister country*, are unwilling to allow them."[118] In this passage, rather than just reversing the gendered stereotypes of colonialism, as in the tale of O'Rourke, Walker portrays the two nations as both female. He thus replaces a relationship of sexual heterogeneity with one of homogeneity. In this model, dominance also gives way to a vision of equality.

It was the suggestion of the equality between England and Ireland with which Charles Burney took issue in his review of the *Historical Memoirs* for the *Monthly Review* of December 1787, published anonymously. In this review, Burney condemns as "wild and conjectural" Walker's depiction of the bardic schools.[119] He is outraged that Walker presumes to give Ireland such an impressive musical pedigree that he suggests is based on nothing but fiction: "Whatever poetry, romance, legends, or tradition can furnish to excite the

Figure 2.1. Music of "O'Rourke's Feast," from Joseph Cooper Walker, *Historical Memoirs of the Irish Bards* (Dublin: J. Christie, 1818), p. 16. Reproduced from the original held by the Department of Special Collections of the University Libraries of Notre Dame.

reader's wonder, has been carefully accumulated in Mr. Walker's book."[120] Burney's denunciation of Walker is constructed around an opposition of Englishness and Irishness, an opposition that depends crucially on the English people's ability to recognize fact and logic and on their mastery of the English language. Burney presents not just Walker but the Irish in general as incapable of rational thinking and incompetent in their use of the English language. He accuses the entire Irish population of promoting a false sense of Irish history: "Mr. W. says, 'it is in the fashion of the day to question the antiquity of Irish MSS.'; and we see plainly, in England, that it is the fashion of the day to give them an antiquity and a credence, in Ireland, that we are unable to allow."[121] The Irish are credulous where the English "see plainly." Walker himself is presented as mistaken and ignorant in numerous instances. Burney notes, for example, Walker's comment that Irish historians date the era of "Druids and BARDS in Ireland" to "*anno mundi* 2815," adding, "This, our Readers will doubtless recollect, was during the middle of the siege of Troy."[122] He suggests that Walker is so foolish as not to be able to distinguish between two entirely different instruments: "Now, how it is possible for the harp and sackbut [*sic*], a stringed and a wind instrument, to be synonymous, surpasses our comprehension."[123] He concludes with a general comment on Irish credulity:

> On the whole, it seems as if the Irish should abate in some of their Milesian claims to the extreme high antiquity of their civilization, refinement, literature, sciences, and arts, with which Colonel Vallancey and others are flattering them: as our late circum-navigators [*sic*] to the South Seas were obliged to lower their demands on our credulity, of nine feet for the size of the Patagonians; for after these giants had been visited and measured by other voyagers, they would have been very thankful to any one who would have allowed them six feet and a half.[124]

Katie Trumpener notes that "[t]hroughout the seventeenth and eighteenth centuries, ethnic joke books such as *Bogg-Witticisms* (1700) relentlessly evoked 'Irish bulls' and 'Macronian blunders,' the grammatical illogicalities or inadvertent puns purportedly uttered by Milesians in speaking and writing English, as a means of denigrating Irish intelligence."[125] Burney's review capitalizes on this common representation of the Irish, as he comments in a footnote: "It is left to the learned in *Bulls*, not of the name of JOHN, to determine, whether the Author of Memoirs of Irish Bards, and Irish Music of *remote antiquity*, as well as of the instruments of the *ancient Irish*, can without a solecism say, that his work 'has *novelty* to recommend it.'"[126] John Bull, a personification of English ability to "see plainly," is punningly contrasted here with the Irish bull, a representation of Irish confusion and equivocation.

Burney denounces not only Walker but the Irish music of which he speaks, promoting English music in its stead: "[C]an the Irish, with all their antiquity, colleges, bards, and harpers, produce specimens of such church music as the English could boast at least a 100 years earlier, by Tye and Tallis?"[127] He attempts to draw extreme differences between Irishness and Englishness. Quoting Spenser at length, he dismisses the character of the typical Irish bard of Spenser's time as "little better than that of piper to the *White Boys*, and other savage and lawless ruffians, who infested the country, to the great dismay of all those whose lives and property were at their mercy."[128] But Burney's comments also reveal an anxiety regarding the essential similarity between the Irish and the English, between "Mr. Walker's readers, and our own readers."[129]

Burney seeks to allay this anxiety by resorting to gender stereotypes. Although Walker only briefly mentions the participation of females in Irish musical tradition, Burney is quick to seize upon his remarks and turn them upside down: "Bardesses were not to be found in all these enquiries; but the Reader is made ample amends by an account of 'the melting sweetness of female voices' in the chorus of the funeral song. These females, we are told, 'were taken from the lower classes of life, and instructed in music.'"[130] By suggesting that women, too, help constitute the "school of music," Burney attacks the masculine identity of the bardic schools. Directly after this comment, Burney further undermines the masculinity of Irish musical identity by suggesting that in the ancient Ireland that Walker depicts, "music and poetry are still united, and form, as in high antiquity, a kind of Androgyne."[131] Irish music in Burney's terms is invalidated because of its uncertain gender, its unnaturalness. If certain incidences in Walker's text work to reconfigure the colonial relationship by means of gender, Burney works to reestablish a relationship of dominance by depicting Irish music as feminine or freakish in contrast to England's masculine normality.

In "Carolan and the Dislocation of Music in Ireland," Harry White juxtaposes Walker's and Burney's views on Ireland, suggesting that they represent two ways of viewing native music in Ireland. For Walker, Irish music serves as a symbol of "the mythic possibility of an ancient civilization in direct contrast to the degraded condition of Ireland under English rule," whereas for Burney, Irish music demonstrates "the notion of a wild and barbarous people hankering after an improbable past."[132] White compares the two authors in order to argue that "the development of an intelligible and enduring mode of Irish music was a virtual impossibility in the eighteenth century."[133] Specifically, he contends that in Ireland, music was "[d]eprived of shared social, aesthetic and political assumptions" and therefore "defined division and discord in the minds of commentators."[134] He implicitly contrasts Ireland with England, where a figure like Burney is seen as representing a healthy and concordant musical and social tradition. White's account of Walker and of native Irish music is valuable, but his assessment of native Irish music as failing in the attempt to assert an "intelligible and enduring mode of Irish music" bears further scrutiny. In particular, White's argument relies on a narrative of development that assumes a basis of "shared social, aesthetic and political assumptions" of the nation, or what Homi Bhabha calls its "sociological stability." According to Bhabha, "continuist national narratives," those that promote a homogeneous sense of national identity, "miss the 'zone of occult instability where the people dwell.'"[135] Any cultural site that claims to represent a homogeneous national identity can be destabilized by "the people's history,"[136] the history of displacement and discontinuity that exists within a nation—both the colonizing and the colonized. Given this revised understanding of nation-ness, I suggest that instead of regarding the *Historical Memoirs* as merely constituting a failure to represent a cohesive culture (and by so doing, confirming Burney's view of Ireland as freakish), one can fold Ireland back into the English colonial presence in order to reveal the fractured nature of that colonial power. Read in this context, the *Historical Memoirs* can help us revise our understanding of England as a model of "sociological stability." Walker's text, appearing a decade after Burney's own history, affronted Burney because it asserted the musical skill of an ancient culture that Burney dismissed as "rude and uncivilized" and because it threatened the universal model of history on which England's superiority rested. But, perhaps more importantly, Walker's *Historical Memoirs* also served as an indication that the "shared social, aesthetic and political assumptions" upon which the English sense of national identity was built were precariously dependent on a series of contradictions that allowed England hegemonic power over its Irish periphery, a periphery that would erupt in violent rebellion within the next decade.

A second edition of the *Historical Memoirs* was published in 1818 by James Christie in a two-volume set along with Walker's *Historical Essay on the Dress of the Ancient and Modern Irish* and *A Memoir on the Armour and Weapons of the Irish*. Between the 1786 and the 1818 editions of the *Historical Memoirs*, Ireland experienced a failed revolution, the dissolution of its parliament in Dublin and a union with Britain. In fact, Walker's original publisher, Luke White, after making a fortune in the lottery business, went on to become a member for the United Parliament after 1801.[137] The 1818 edition features significant changes. Christie, a printer and typefounder, substituted Gaelic type for the original Roman type used for the Gaelic words in the original text, suggesting his edition's concern to promote a Gaelic print culture (Christie himself was a member of the Gaelic Society of Dublin). What is also clear from the 1818 edition is the change in the status of Irish music that had occurred during the time between the two publications. Twenty-six more tunes were added to the fifteen that Walker included in the first edition, primarily Carolan tunes like "O'Rourke's Feast" and "Carolan's Concerto," but also other tunes that were in circulation in collections like those of Bunting, Owenson, and Moore: "Ellen A Roon," "Edmund of the Hill," and "The Pretty Maid Milking the Cow." The subject of Irish music had become not just an antiquarian pursuit but a cultural pastime for Irish and British readers.

3

"The United Powers of Female Poesy and Music"

Charlotte Brooke's *Reliques of Irish Poetry*

Seven years after the establishment of Grattan's Parliament in Ireland, and thirteen years after the appearance of Walker's *Historical Memoirs*, Charlotte Brooke, daughter of the Church of Ireland clergyman and author Henry Brooke, published the first translations of Irish Gaelic poetry and songs in English. In her *Reliques of Irish Poetry* (1789), Brooke inserts herself into the discourse of those attempting to imagine the Irish community through its music and literature. Joep Leerssen calls her "the first mediator of importance between the Irish-Gaelic and the Anglo-Irish literary traditions."[1] Seamus Deane praises her for achieving three "firsts": "the first extended translation of 'polite literature' from Irish into English; the first presentation of Irish and English enjoying 'parity of esteem' in a literary work; the first outspoken claim for literature to effect of conciliation that would prefigure and lead to political reconciliation."[2] This chapter argues that with her translations of Irish poetry and songs and, more particularly, with her "original Irish tale," a fictional poem based on authentic sources, Brooke attempts to fashion a role for women in the Irish nation of the past and the present. Her work is a direct reaction to Walker's alignment of Irish music with a male bardic community.

In her preface, Brooke presents herself as a handmaiden to both the male heroes and writers who have come before; her place, she suggests, is to "strew flowers in the paths of these laureled champions of my country."[3] She refers to her work with modesty, as she simultaneously introduces and excuses herself.[4] Her justification for writing, she suggests, is to help gain England's respect for Ireland, its history and its people. What is significant, however, is the way she characterizes the Irish nation and the relationship between Ireland and England in the preface:

As yet, we are too little known to our noble neighbour of Britain; were we better acquainted, we should be better friends. The British Muse is not yet informed that she has an elder sister in this isle; let us then introduce them to each other! together let them walk abroad from their bowers, sweet ambassadresses of cordial union between two countries that seem formed by nature to be joined by every bond of interest, and of amity. Let them entreat of Britain to cultivate a nearer acquaintance with her neighbouring isle. Let them conciliate for us her esteem, and her affection will follow of course.[5]

Like Walker, and in contrast to the sexualized dynamic of colonialism that Ashis Nandy discusses, Brooke presents both nations as female, as "sisters" rather than a male and female couple. What is striking, however, is the ambiguity surrounding the identity of the Irish muse. Brooke expresses her desire to let Britain know "[t]hat the portion of her blood which flows in our veins is rather ennobled than disgraced by the mingling tides that descended from our heroic ancestors."[6] Brooke's muse of Ireland is a vessel for the mingling of British and Gaelic blood. But while Brooke can use this muse to claim a stake in Gaelic Ireland's heroic ancestry, her key function in the preface is to mediate with a Britain with whom she is literally "joined by nature." The two muses are identical, except that the Irish muse is the elder. This is a meeting of sisters who share the same characteristics and expectations, not of half-sisters who are unlike. "Let them come," Brooke urges, invoking not one but two muses.[7] She then checks herself with a hyphenated pause: "—but will they answer to a voice like mine? Will they not rather depute some favoured pen, to chide me back to the shade whence I have been allured, and where, perhaps, I ought to have remained, in respect to the memory, and superior genius of a Father—it avails not to say how dear!"[8] This interjection expresses Brooke's sense of the inappropriateness of a woman participating in such overt political and public activity, particularly in this case, where she is confronting the legacy of the male bardic tradition. In the rest of the *Reliques,* however, Brooke's expressed confidence in her own powers is stronger. In particular, she becomes more "self-possessed" as she moves into the translations; neither of her immediate mentors, Henry Brooke, her father, and Joseph Cooper Walker, succeeded in learning Gaelic.[9] And as Brooke's powers of self-assertion change within the *Reliques,* the image she conveys of Ireland also changes. The Ireland she presents in the preface is a strange compound, mostly Anglo-Irish, but the Ireland that emerges from the rest of the text holds out against assimilation to English culture.

Brooke uses her male mentors, particularly Walker, to legitimize her enterprise, but she also asserts her right to participate in the imagining of the nation by disputing their ideas. It was Walker who first provided a forum for Brooke's works, as he published three of her translations in his *Historical Memoirs*, attributing them to a young lady who wished to remain anonymous and commenting that, "with the modesty ever attendant on true merit, and with the sweet timidity natural to her sex, she shrinks from the public eye."[10] Encouraged by Walker and by Thomas Percy, Brooke apparently overcame that timidity and published the *Reliques* under her own name. She acknowledges Walker's support in her preface, noting that he "afforded every assistance which zeal, judgment, and extensive knowledge, could give."[11] Brooke litters the *Reliques* with quotations from Walker—both his *Historical Memoirs* and his *Historical Essay on the Dress of the Ancient and Modern Irish* (1788)—inserting extensive passages from these works in her footnotes and in the "advertisements" to a number of her translations of the poems. Brooke stresses her own lack of expertise in comparison with the researches of Walker, Sylvester O'Halloran, and others.[12] She says, for example, that she is "unacquainted with the rules of translation"[13] and refers to her work as "my feeble efforts."[14] Nevertheless, although Brooke highlights her own lack of expertise, she gives the reader indirect proof to the contrary. She provides commentary that demonstrates her complete familiarity with the corpus of work that she translates, noting, for example, that "[h]air is a favourite object with all the Irish Poets."[15] She delivers authoritative criticism on the poetry and songs that she translates, directing the reader on how to read the pieces correctly. And she indicates that she is engaged in active correspondence with the experts she praises. Throughout the text she is careful to note from where she has procured her copies of the original Irish texts. When Walker cannot furnish her with a complete original of "The Chase," for example, she turns to Maurice Gorman. While this meticulousness is understandable, given the accusations being leveled at James Macpherson at the time, it also generates an impression of her belonging to the circle of scholars whom she admires.[16]

Moreover, Brooke clearly indicates her differences with those belonging to this circle. In her footnotes, for example, she notes that in his *Historical Essay on the Dress and Armour of the Irish*, Walker claims that "the poets of the middle ages describe the heroes of Oisin, as shining in polished steel," but she politely corrects this: "The poet before us is, however, (as well as many others) an exception."[17] Similarly, she disagrees with Walker's assessment that Carolan, who was blind, "remembered no impression of colours."[18] Brooke states, "I cannot acquiesce in this opinion."[19] She also asserts the accuracy of her translation of Carolan's "Gracey Nugent" as compared to Walker's, noting that, "a friend to whom I shewed this Song, observed, that I had omitted a very lively thought in the conclusion, which they had seen in Mr. WALKER's Memoirs." To "vindicate my fidelity," Brooke includes a "*literal* translation of the Song."[20] Such an inclusion indirectly criticizes Walker. Brooke's version is very different from Walker's. Walker employs rollicking anapestic trimeters in his translation:

> With delight I will sing of the maid
> Who in beauty and wit doth excel;
> My Gracey, the fairest, shall lead,
> And from Beauties shall bear off the belle.[21]

Brooke's iambic pentameter lines, on the other hand, render her version of "Gracey Nugent" more of an art song. Brooke's language is also considerably loftier than Walker's:

> Of Gracey's charms enraptur'd will I sing!
> Fragrant and fair, as blossoms of the spring;
> To her sweet manners, and accomplish'd mind,
> Each rival Fair the palm of Love resign'd.[22]

As well as taking issue with Walker on these points, Brooke parts ways with her mentor on larger issues such as the interpretations of Irish bardic culture and its relation to the present. Walker is fundamentally ambivalent about the cause of the disintegration of Ireland's superior musical and poetic culture. As was seen in chapter 2, he attributes it variously to foreign invasion, English invasion, internal strife, and a taste for Italian music. In his chronological account of Irish musical life from the invasion of the Milesians to the advent of the Hanoverian dynasty, Walker narrates a fundamental rift between the past superiority and the present failure of Irish culture. In contrast, Brooke attempts to build a seamless web between a past heroic age and the present. As she moves from the sections on "Heroic Poems," "Odes," and "Elegies" to a section on "Songs," she leaps from the age of the Fenii and Oisin to the early eighteenth century without indicating any fundamental difference between them. In fact, she says that the "songs of modern date" demonstrate "of what the native genius and language of this country even now, are capable, labouring, as they do, under every disadvantage."[23] In contrast to Walker, Brooke does not suggest a waning of Irish culture.

Moreover, Brooke offers a very different picture of Irish bardic culture in general from that found in Walker. In the *Historical Memoirs,* Walker's bardic culture in its most ancient form approximates a kind of Royal Academy. According to Walker, young bards attended a bardic seminary and, upon completing their studies, were assigned positions according to the rank of their families.[24] In contrast, Brooke's bards are learned chivalric knights. Drawing upon the questionable claims of Sylvester O'Halloran's *Introduction to the Study of the Histories and Antiquities of Ireland* (1771), a work that she notes is *"fraught with learning, rich with the treasures of ages, and animated by the very soul of Patriotism, and genuine Honor,"* Brooke asserts that the custom of creating knights in Europe actually originated among the Celts. According to Brooke, Irish knights were instructed in "Philosophy, History, Poetry and Genealogy" along with morality and "a reverence and tender respect for the Fair."[25] Brooke is concerned with emphasizing the courtesy of Irish bardic culture, contending that "[w]ith us chivalry flourished from the remotest antiquity."[26]

This is in fact the key to her disagreement with Walker's explanation of the "strain of tender pensiveness"[27] discernible throughout Irish music. As we have seen, Walker attributes the minor key that much Irish music was written in both to the oppression that the Irish labored under and, strangely, to "the remarkable susceptibility of the Irish of the passion of love,"[28] giving as his evidence for that conclusion the commentary of an anonymous traveler. Brooke corrects this view, distinguishing the heroic poetry from the songs: "[T]he heroic poetry of our countrymen was designed for the noblest purposes;—love indeed was still its object,—but it was the sublime love of country that those compositions inspired."[29] She continues: "I am not sufficiently conversant in the state of the antient [*sic*] music of this country, to say what that might once have been, or what degree of change it might have suffered; but it does not appear to me that the antient [*sic*] poetry of Ireland was *ever* composed in a very lively strain."[30] Walker's ambivalence about the melancholy nature of Irish music allows him to prevaricate about the specific nature of the relationship between Ireland and England, leaving unanswered the question of whether Irish musical melancholy was an effect of colonial domination or whether it existed prior to colonization. Brooke sidesteps this question, but she contests Walker's association of the ancient poetry with mundane concerns. She is determined first and foremost to assert ancient Irish poetry as a patriotic, chivalric, and noble activity.

In her commentary "The Nature of Irish Music," Brooke takes issue with the published ideas of another male mentor, the antiquarian Thomas Percy.[31] By entitling her work *Reliques of Irish Poetry,* Brooke flatteringly alludes to Percy's *Reliques of Ancient English Poetry,* published in 1765. And she echoes his aesthetic concerns to present works of ancient poetry to the general public. Percy wanted to present his ballads "not as labours of art, but as effusions of nature, showing the first efforts of ancient genius, and exhibiting the customs and opinions of remote ages."[32] But Brooke's project also directly opposes the politics of Percy's poetics, for where Percy makes his claim for the supremacy of the Anglo-Saxon tradition, Brooke asserts the superiority of the Irish bards. In "An Essay on the Ancient Minstrels in England," Percy contends that the minstrels of Britain were the successors of the ancient bards, "who under different names were admired and revered, from the earliest ages, among the people of Gaul, Britain, Ireland and the North; and indeed by almost all the first inhabitants of Europe, whether of Celtic or Gothic race; but," he adds, revealing his own ethnic predispositions, *"by none more than by our own Teutonic ancestors, particularly by all the Danish tribes."*[33] He continues, enlarging on the connection between the English and the Danes, whom he describes as particularly admiring of bards: "The Jutes and Angles in particular, who composed two thirds of the conquerors of Britain, were a Danish people, and their country at this day belongs to the Crown of Denmark."[34] The *Reliques of Ancient English Poetry* works to promote English national identity. The *Reliques of Irish Poetry,* however, presents the Irish bardic tradition as more authentic than the English, both because it is more ancient and because it includes works that outdo others in their ability to "interest the heart." Brooke implies that the Irish poems in their original forms are by nature more sublime than their English counterparts because they are "already Musick":

> It is scarcely possible that any language can be more adapted to Lyric poetry than the Irish. The poetry of many of our Songs is indeed already Musick, without the aid of a tune; so great is the smoothness, and harmony of its cadences. . . . But it is not in sound alone that this language [of Lyric poetry] is so peculiarly adapted to the species of composition now under consideration; it is also possessed of a refined delicacy of descriptive power, and an exquisitely tender simplicity of expression.[35]

Brooke claims that Irish poetry is characterized by more "enthusiasm" than English poetry. Because in Ireland poetry was "more universally in practice, and still more enthusiastically admired," than elsewhere, the Irish bards were able to practice their skill with the utmost freedom and to lose themselves "in the fine frenzy of exalted thought."[36] Such was not the case in England, where the poets had too long a tradition of playing with wit. Brooke takes aim at contemporary English poetry as well as the ancient varieties, observing that at least one-half of those "who bear the title of English Poets, are merely men of wit and rhyme; and I believe it will be acknowledged that those amongst them who possessed the sublimest genius, descended but seldom to sport with it."[37] While appearing to pay a compliment to Percy by imitating his project, Brooke actually sets herself up in direct opposition to his ideas and affirms the connection between music, poetry, and patriotism in Ireland.

In her commentary on the heroic poems, Brooke also emphasizes the idea of chivalry. She calls attention to the generous nature of the characters: "How exquisitely is the character of Fergus supported! He greets the enemy with courtesy: he is answered with insolence; yet still retains the same equal temper, for which he is every where distinguished. We see his noble spirit rise, but it is with something more noble than resentment."[38] The *Critical Review* explained this chivalric predisposition by suggesting that several of the poems, although "founded on, or framed from, traditionary tales of great antiquity," were actually "of later date." After all, the author reasons, "we cannot well suppose that . . . [the Irish bards] knew that knights bound themselves by 'the vow of chivalry.'"[39] But it is a particular kind of chivalry that Brooke portrays in the *Reliques*, one that is interpreted according to eighteenth-century ideas of sensibility, as is evident in her comments on Cucullin's lamentation over his son: "Here is one of those delicate strokes of nature and sentiment, that pass so directly to the heart, and so powerfully awaken its feelings!—Sympathy bleeds at every line of this passage."[40] In the *Reliques,* Cucullin and the other ancient characters are converted into "men of feeling."

Brooke employs the figure of Carolan to suggest a continuity between the ancient chivalric heroes and the present-day Irish. Where Walker placed his biography of Carolan in an appendix, relegating him to a footnote on the general narrative of deterioration, Brooke works the harper into her argument about the endurance of Irish culture, using him to demonstrate "of what the native genius and language of this country even now, are capable."[41] She includes a short biography of Carolan and two of his songs in the general body of her text. Although he was primarily known for his musical skills, Carolan is featured in Brooke's *Reliques* as a poet; Brooke seems anxious to re-create him as a man of letters. Earlier collections containing Carolan's work merely recorded the tunes; Walker was the first to provide a number of translations of his songs. But whereas Walker included examples of the variety of themes Carolan addressed—from drinking songs to satires—Brooke selects only two sentimental pieces: "Song for Gracey Nugent" and "Song for Mable Kelly." She interprets these songs with the same eye for sensibility that she had used in the earlier heroic poetry: "Every Reader of taste or feeling must surely be struck with the beauty of this passage.—Can anything be more elegant, or more pathetic, than the manner in which Carolan alludes to his want of sight!"[42] Moreover, in her "Thoughts on Irish Song," Brooke takes pains to point out the serious nature of Irish love songs: they are not the mere products of fancy and wit but rather expressions of "the heart" and "the sublime conceptions of the soul."[43] Brooke comments that "Love and War were the two favourite objects of passion and pursuit, with our antient [*sic*] countrymen, and of course, became the constant inspirers of their muse."[44] In the *Reliques*, Carolan is fit into the role of this kind of chivalric bard, demonstrating a "tender respect for the Fair,"[45] and is as serious about love as his forebears were.

In "Virtue and Manners in Macpherson's *Poems of Ossian*," Adam Potkay comments on the language of sensibility found in Macpherson's work, suggesting that the *Poems of Ossian* helped "bridge the gap separating the emerging 'feminism' of polite society from the male 'chauvinism' of both the ancient polis and its modern apologists."[46] I would suggest that in the *Reliques*, in addition to bridging the gap between eighteenth-century polite society and the ancient Irish polis, Brooke is attempting to bridge the gap that separates women from participating in the public discourse of the nation. While the poems in the *Reliques* deal with war and conquest, the paratext interprets the actions in terms of a discourse of sentiment, a discourse that feminizes the action of the poetry and also makes it more accessible to the commentary of women. For Brooke, translation and textual commentary are patriotic activities in which women can participate as much as men. In the preface she describes her literary endeavors as performing a "service to my country."[47] Later in the text, she again identifies the preservation of the ancient poetry with patriotism, as she exhorts: "*Irishmen*—all of them at least who would be thought to pride themselves in the name, or to reflect back any part of the honor they derive from it;—*they* are *particularly* called upon, in favour of their country, to rescue these little sparks from the ashes of her former glory."[48] Although she addresses her remarks to Irish*men*, it would appear that she is also concerned with providing a means by which Irishwomen can participate in "the horizontal brotherhood" of the nation. By reinterpreting Irish culture through the lens of sensibility, Brooke carves out a place for women in the discussion of national identity.

In this endeavor, she sets herself in direct opposition to another of her male predecessors, her father. In "Milton's Daughters: The Education of Eighteenth-Century Women Writers," Beth Kowaleski-Wallace comments, "Literary daughters are special kinds of daughters, women who adapt themselves to both a familial and a literary hierarchy."[49] Charlotte Brooke was one of two children surviving out of twenty-two. She was educated by her father, and like other literary daughters, went on to edit her father's works and write his memoirs after his death. But, while she did accept a familial hierarchy with her father in the privileged position, she also adapted his literary ideas. In Henry Brooke's work, women serve as a focus for male sentiment, but the sentiment must then be directed toward the nation. It is only when the female sign is eliminated that true patriotism is expressed. In *Gustavus Vasa*, for example, the crisis of the play occurs when Gustavus must choose between saving his mother and sister and saving the nation. His female kin are killed for the sake of Swedish independence. The moment at which Gustavus's sister, Gustava (tellingly described as a "lamb-like sacrifice"), is torn away from him to face execution provides the most pathetic scene in the play. Gustava's mother consoles her:

> . . . for these chains that bind thy pretty
> arms,
> The golden cherubim shall lend thee wings,
> And thou shalt mount amid the smiling choir
> Of little heavenly songsters, like thyself,
> All robed in innocence.[50]

Notably, the sacrifice of the woman becomes the proof of loyalty to the state. Augusta's words suggest that patriotism is born out of female suffering, although it is ultimately embodied in men:

> Blest were the throes I felt for thee, Gustavus!
> For from the breast, from out your swathing bands,
> You stepp'd the child of honour.[51]

Concluding with Gustavus's address to "my brothers all," *Gustavus Vasa* promotes a view of patriotism as a male prerogative and possession: "whene'er our country calls, / Friends, sons, and sires, should yield their treasure up, / Nor own a sense beyond the public safety."[52] Charlotte Brooke's concern was to write a new view of the nation, one that included women as patriots and writers of the nation, not just as passive sufferers in the achievement of national glory.

Brooke's concern to present women as participating actively in the imagining of the Irish nation is most evident in her creation of her own poem, "Mäon: An Irish Tale," a poem independent of any Gaelic original. By including her own original among ancient Irish texts and by altering the plot to suit her purposes, Brooke directly links female authority and authorship with Irish identity. She begins the poem with conventional modesty about her talents. Addressing a Mr. and Mrs. Trant, she begs them to accept the dedication of her "simple lays." Her Muse, she notes, has "ne'er, on Pindus' mount, / Trod inspiration's ground" but remains, rather, connected to the scenes of earth, inspired by Nature.[53] She refers to a national Muse, one who would have inspired the kinds of poems Brooke included in the *Reliques*: epics, war songs, elegies, and love songs. But we find out that this Muse is not one of the traditional nine maidens—or the two national muses alluded to in the preface—but a male bard, Craftine, and he appears to the narrator in the author's dream, urging her to take up the challenge of relating a story of Ireland. Whereas Brooke begins the *Reliques* with a preface that detracts from her own capabilities, she ends by asserting her authority in a notable twist on an old theme. What Brooke describes is in effect an *aisling*, a traditional Gaelic dream-poem, but she reverses the gender roles so that the figure in the vision is a man and the dreamer is a woman: herself. Furthermore, the male Muse encourages the literary expression of patriotism by women:

> For oft the Muse, a gentle guest,
> Dwells in a female form,
> And patriot fire, a female breast,
> May sure unquestioned warm.[54]

Brooke appropriates the role of a male authority figure and speaks with his voice.

Brooke's decision to write an original tale offers a counterperspective to Walker's comments regarding women's roles in ancient bardic times. Although he accords women some power to "soften the manners" of the people, Walker denies the existence of female poets: "We cannot find that the Irish had female Bards or BARDESSES, properly so called."[55] Nevertheless, soon after his comments regarding women's roles in bardic society, Walker makes the following statement: "Anno Mundi 3649, a great revolution was occasioned in Ireland by the united powers of female poesy and music."[56] The event he goes on to describe is the tale of Mäon. Brooke seized upon this tale as an invitation to write, appropriating and altering Walker's story so that it is a woman who performs the ultimate national activity and who serves as the national bard.

Brooke's tale of Mäon begins with the usurpation of the throne of Laoghaire Lork by his brother, Cobthach. In the ensuing slaughter in the palace, Craftine, the bard, manages to rescue Laoghaire's son, Mäon, by throwing himself between the boy and a dagger aimed at Mäon. Because bards are accorded such esteem in Irish society, the palace residents are outraged at the fact that the dagger wounds Craftine, and bard and boy are able to make their escape in the resulting chaos. Craftine transports Mäon to the kingdom of Munster, where he is trained in princely ways and becomes entangled in the inevitable love situation with the king's daughter, the "fair Moriat." But even as their love (still undeclared) grows and prospers in the bower of Munster's bliss, the long arm of Cobthach threatens to destroy their happiness. Mäon is forced to forego his Moriat and flee to France, or Gallia, as Brooke calls it:

> He must; there are no other means
> Of life or safety nigh;
> Our only hope on Gallia leans,
> And thither must he fly.[57]

He swears to return, however, and he leaves Craftine behind, instructing him to remind Moriat of her exiled lover, if ever she should show need of reminding.

Moriat soon perceives that it is Mäon and not herself who needs reminding of the bonds of love, for along with bulletins informing her of his increasing military skill, she receives word that he is to marry the daughter of the King of France, Aide, thus cementing the alliance between Ireland and France. Upset by these tidings, Moriat swoons and bemoans the inconstancy of love. However, after sufficient lamentation she recovers herself—and here is where the deviation of Brooke's version of the tale from Walker's becomes most evident. In Walker's tale of Mäon, there is no mention of Mäon marrying the princess of France. In Brooke's tale, however, Moriat must wrestle with her private love for Mäon and her realization of the public importance of securing the help of France. The latter impulse wins out in her sensibilities and she relinquishes her love for Mäon for the greater good of the country:

Tell [Mäon], he freely may espouse
My happy rival's charms;
Tell him, I give him back his vows,
I yield him to her arms.

So may the strength of Gallia's throne
Attend a filial prayer,
And force our tyrant to atone
For all the wrongs we bear.[58]

Ascertaining that Mäon still may be in love with her, she orders him into a contractual obligation with the Princess of France:

Tell him his country claims him now.—
To her his heart he owes;
And shall a love-breath'd wish, or vow,
That glorious claim oppose?—

Tell him to act the patriot part
That Erin's woes demand;
Tell him, would he secure my heart,
He must resign my hand.—[59]

Brooke is anxious not to sign away Ireland's independence through a marriage contract with France, however. Happily, the French princess, realizing that Mäon's affections lie elsewhere, frees him from his marital obligation. When Mäon regains his kingship, Mäon and Moriat are duly married with Aide's blessing, and the Irish kingdom remains solely in Irish hands.

Although the tale resolves with Mäon as ruler of the kingdom, in Brooke's retelling, it is Moriat who plays the role of the true patriot. She becomes a martyr to the national cause by sacrificing her personal interests for her country:

For me,—on duty I rely,
My firm support to prove;
And Erin shall the room supply
Of Mäon and of love.[60]

Further, in Brooke's version of the story of Mäon, writing becomes a key factor in saving the nation. Confirmed in her decision, Moriat composes a poem that she gives to Craftine to deliver to Mäon. The poem reveals to Mäon the truth regarding his family history and the murder of his father, information that Craftine had previously kept from Mäon, fearing he might do something rash. Brooke links Moriat's transformation into a patriot with the activity of writing that, by presenting the history of the nation, guarantees its future. It is Moriat's poem that ultimately effects the regaining of the kingdom. We note how, in turning from speaking to writing the poem, Moriat seemingly transcends earth as she transcends the limits of her gender:

> While thus the sweet Enthusiast speaks,
> She seems o'er earth to rise;
> Sublime emotions flush her cheeks,
> And fill her radiant eyes!
>
> In her soft hand the style she takes,
> And the beech tablet holds;
> And there the soul of glory wakes,
> And all her heart unfolds.[61]

Brooke alters her father's iconography of the passive and suffering woman as her heroine actively writes the nation.

The end of the tale provides further material for thought about assumptions concerning gender and patriotism. Brooke presents herself as uncertain of how to finish the poem: "How shall the Muse the Tale pursue? . . . Or paint to sympathy's fond view / What language fails to tell?"[62] In response to this dilemma, she ends "Mäon: An Irish Tale" with an encomium on patriotism, exhorting the reader to

> Think all that Glory can bestow!
> That Virtue's soul imparts!
> Conceive the nameless joys that flow
> From Love's selected hearts.
>
> Conceive the Patriot's glowing breast
> Whom grateful nations crown!
> With virtue, love and empire blest,
> And honor's clear renown.[63]

Knowing what we do of the story as Brooke has painted it, these stanzas actually confront us with an uncomfortable irony. "What language fails to tell" can be very telling. We may assume that these stanzas are to remind us of the importance of Mäon's exploits, but "the Patriot" remains anonymous, and, more importantly, genderless, in Brooke's description. The stanzas might apply equally well to Moriat, leaving us to ponder who, in fact, was the greatest patriot: Mäon, who was, after all, just obeying a filial duty in avenging his father's murder; or Moriat, who was willing to renounce the traditional female domestic and romantic role for the good of her country. The end of the poem challenges us to see how "grateful nations" as a rule "crown" and "honor" male patriots. In the case of the tale of Mäon, however, the nation was "conceived" by a woman—and a writing woman at that. In writing the role of Moriat, Brooke is writing her own job description as a female poet of her nation, taking over the position of those like Carolan whose work she is anthologizing. She herself becomes the hero she asked for in the preface: "Why does not some *son of Anak* in genius step forward, and boldly throw his gauntlet to Prejudice, the avowed and approved champion of his country's lovely muse?"[64] As becomes apparent in the *Reliques of Irish Poetry*, the "son of Anak" is in fact the daughter of Henry Brooke, Charlotte Brooke herself. The nation in "Mäon: An Irish Tale" is created, not through action and death, as in the Gaelic poems and songs that she translates earlier in the book, but through the act of writing.

The Irish nation that Brooke represents is curious in its appeal to both purity and hybridity. Perhaps partly in response to the criticisms leveled at Macpherson, Brooke is at pains to establish the authenticity of the poems and songs that she presents in the *Reliques*; hence she includes transcriptions of the poems in Gaelic. The *Critical Review* for 1790 confirms the sense of authenticity that the originals provide, even though the reviewer probably did not read Irish and could not judge the translations' "faithfulness" to the originals: "Miss Brooke, whatever [Macpherson] might be, is, we doubt not, faithful to her original."[65] But the presence of the originals also suggests the essential hybridity that lies at the root of Brooke's Ireland. Merely by being present, the Gaelic originals point out the inevitable compromise of translation and the violence of the translating letter. Brooke herself directs our attention to the originals' recalcitrance, their refusal to be translated. She comments that "there are many complex words that could not be translated literally."[66] According to Brooke, Irish is a language of multiple possibilities, multiple synonyms that "no modern language is entirely prepared to express."[67] Translation weakens the "force and effect" of the thoughts, "just as that light which dazzles, when flashing swiftly on the eye, will be gazed at with indifference, if let in by degrees."[68] In his comments on the translating process in his *History of Verse Translation from the Irish*, Robert Welch comments that "the translator was performing a public service in contributing to the advance of understanding and mutual accord, by providing versions of Gaelic poetry. In acknowledging that there was such a thing as Gaelic verse he was signalling the existence of a separate Irish culture; by translating it he was demonstrating the capacity of the English language to receive into itself a very different quality of human awareness and perception." [69] I would argue that, far from using translation as a way of "overcoming differences that mark Ireland and England off one from the other,"[70] Brooke reinforces difference by including the original Gaelic poems. Moreover, in addition to confronting the reader with their linguistic difference, the Gaelic poems also represent a typographical disorientation. As E. W. Lynam points out, the *Reliques* was "the first purely literary work containing printing in the Irish character which was ever published in Dublin."[71] The printer George Bonham used the Parker typeface for the *Reliques*, creating a text for the Gaelic poems that has closer affiliations to Irish script than to Roman type. In its content and its form, then, Brooke's *Reliques* holds up barriers that resist anglophone power because it resists anglophone knowledge. The book opens with a list of over three hundred subscribers drawn from the ranks of the Anglo-Irish gentry. Andrew Carpenter notes that "such a phalanx of Anglo-Irish respectability had never before been assembled in support of Irish culture."[72] However, what this "phalanx" was subscribing to was a hybrid representation of their nation that both intrigued them with its heroic depiction of ancient heroes and resisted their knowledge in its very typography.

Charlotte Brooke died in 1793. Later republications of her work suggest the very different contexts that she and her *Reliques* came to serve. In 1795, three years after the Belfast Harp Festival, and a year before Bunting produced his first edition of the *Ancient Irish Music*, "The Chase" and "a collection of choice *IRISH SONGS*, translated by Miss Brooke" were published in the first Gaelic-language magazine, *Bolg an tSolair*. *Bolg an tSolair* ("Bag of Goods" or "Miscellany") was complied by Patrick Lynch, a scholar and teacher of Irish living in Belfast, and published by the *Northern Star*, the newspaper of the United Irishmen in that city. An advertisement in the *Northern Star* on August, 27, 1793, announces the upcoming publication of the magazine: "The attempt which has been made by Mr. *Lynch*, to revive and preserve a knowledge and taste of the beauties of the Irish language, by his publication of the Gaelic Magazine, deserves, and we must trust will meet with every encouragement from his countrymen."[73] Instead of "conciliating" or developing "affection" between England and Ireland, like the *Reliques*, however, *Bolg an tSolair* is designed to foster unity at home through the medium of Gaelic. As the *Northern Star* suggests, the learning of Gaelic "is particularly interesting, to all who wish for the Improvement and Union of this neglected and divided Kingdom. By our understanding and speaking it, we could more easily communicate our sentiments and instructions to all our Countrymen; and thus materially improve and conciliate each other's affections."[74] Speaking Irish would be useful to both "Merchant and Artist," as "[t]hey would be qualified for carrying on Trade and Manufactures in every part of their native country."[75] To fulfill this purpose, *Bolg an tSolaír* featured an abbreviated grammar, a vocabulary (including useful phrases and words), and two "Dialogues" along with Brooke's poetry and songs. The dialogues concern a transaction between a merchant, a farmer who is trying to sell him some sheep, and a priest who is helping with the transaction. When the farmer notes that the merchant "speaks Irish tolerably well," the priest assures him that "[t]hat is a sign he is a [*sic*] Irishman."[76]

Bolg an tSolaír revised Brooke's work to make it suitable for United Irishmen propaganda. It discouraged Brooke's representation of the hybrid relationship between English and Gaelic and her notion that translating weakens the "force and effect" of the Gaelic. Instead, the grammar and vocabulary published in the magazine claim to make Gaelic accessible and usable to English speakers. The magazine implies that knowledge of the Gaelic language can grant everyone cultural ownership of the poems and songs of their nation. The typography of the text also works to lessen the essential difference of the Gaelic language. As Pat Muldowney and Brendan Clifford point out, a "Gothic type" was used in the original to give an "impression of Gaelic lettering."[77] This was no doubt an economic decision, the Parker type being very expensive, but the resulting text appears less like an Irish manuscript than Brooke's original text. In addition, *Bolg an tSolaír* narrowed the definition of patriot that Brooke had attempted to widen. While the magazine publicized Brooke's name as the translator of the Gaelic material, it undid her efforts to refashion that material in such a way as to emphasize female agency. *Bolg an tSolaír* published nothing from Brooke's story of Mäon. Moreover, it included none of the notes in which Brooke asserts her own opinion of the material.

In 1816, the *Reliques* was republished by James Christie, who would go on to republish Walker's *Memoirs of the Irish Bards* two years later. For the Gaelic poems, Christie used a special font which he had cut and cast himself. While Christie's version maintains the hybridity of the original text more closely than the *Bolg an tSolaír* version, the "Memoir of Miss Brooke" of that is conjoined to the text works to contain that hybridity by representing Brooke as a model of female submission.[78] This "memoir," written by Aaron Crossley Seymour, a vicar's son and author of several works on evangelical Christianity, describes Brooke as intelligent but ultimately focused on "domestic life": "To the tenderness and elegance of genius, Miss Brooke joined the most amiable social virtues. Few enjoyed the softened pleasures of the society of 'Home,' or entered with greater feeling into its interests and concerns than she did. . . . Disinterested and self-denied, she had no worldly ambition to gratify, no sordid appetites to indulge."[79] Seymour's account remakes Brooke's life into a Christian story of temptation resisted. He notes that Brooke was interested in the theater as a young woman and that she asked her father to introduce her to some celebrated actors: "Under such dangerous influences, Miss Brooke courted the acquaintance of those mock monarchs of the stage, who had assumed the regal honours for an evening, and whose wonderful exploits reigned completely paramount in her vivid imaginations." But he represents her as being saved from these temptations by a careful father: "Her rage for the amusements of the theatre soon carried all before it, and would doubtless have proved her ruin, had not Mr. Brooke hurried her from a scene so destructive to the happiness, and so pernicious to the morals of the youthful mind."[80]

Seymour is lavish in his praise for the *Reliques,* but only as a reflection of the author's modesty and struggles with life. He effuses: "To investigate the obsolete remains of other times, delivered in a language of which few have been hardy or inquisitive enough to attempt the acquisition; to elucidate those writings, and clothe them in the ungenial, I trust not ungraceful, vesture of modern rhyme, are achievements that might have staggered many a literary knight-errant and enterprising antiquary—yet all this has been attempted and accomplished by Miss Brooke, in her first poetical attempt, who stands forward 'the avowed champion of her country's lovely muse.'"[81] But he also comments that she went ahead with the endeavor only after she had duly asked Joseph Cooper Walker and other colleagues to help her with the project. Seymour notes that the work "abounds with many beauties" but that the "circumstances under which it was written" make it "especially" appealing: "a young lady in a state of ill health, the death of a tender mother, and an only brother, in a distant clime, with a father whom she tenderly loved, bending under a weight of years; without a single hand to guide her through an untrodden path, for she could scarce meet with any person that could read a word of the originals."[82] In the "Memoir," the patriotic image of "strew[ing] flowers in the paths of these laureled champions of my country"[83] is converted to a morality tale of a woman's individual "patient submission to the will of God."[84] Seymour includes an excerpt from an elegy on Joseph Cooper Walker by Eyles Irwin that praises the "female genius" of "BROOKE" who "revived the memory of the slain, / Who sleep in honour's bed, proud victors of the Dane." But it is the lines with which he concludes his account, lines written by a friend on her portrait, that define Charlotte Brooke for Seymour and for his readers:

> Religious, fair, soft, innocent, and gay,
> As ev'ning mild, bright as the morning ray,
> Youthful and wise, in ev'ry grace mature,
> What vestal ever led a life so pure!

The "Memoir" turns Charlotte Brooke into a character directly opposed to her Fenian heroes, who exert themselves in the challenges of battle, or to Moriat, who takes her place as a heroine of the nation. Where *Bolg an tSolair* erased female agency from national concerns, Seymour's "Memoir" actively confines that female agency to the domestic sphere.

In 1832, the *Dublin Penny Journal* featured an article on Brooke, asserting: "There are few writers, male or female, to whom we think Ireland owes a greater debt of gratitude than to Miss Charlotte Brooke, a lady whose patriotism led her to translate some of our most beautiful poetical remains, and whose talents enabled her to do them ample justice."[85] Despite the *Journal*'s desire to "see her genius more fully appreciated," however, Charlotte Brooke was largely forgotten by the general Irish public. Republished in a politically radical and then a socially conservative context, the *Reliques* vanished from view. Despite her own personal disappearance, however, Brooke paved the way for another more visible female figure who was to champion the cause of Ireland, music, and female participation in the nation, Sydney Owenson. As we will see in chapter 5, Owenson's Glorvina of *The Wild Irish Girl* is in many ways a direct descendant of Brooke's female poet-patriot, Moriat.

4

Sequels of Colonialism

Edward Bunting, the *Ancient Irish Music,* and the Cultural Politics of Performance

Three years after the publication of the *Reliques,* Doctor James McDonnell advertised a competition designed to revive interest in the ancient harping tradition of Ireland.[1] His advertisement for the event, which was held between July 11 and 14, 1792 in Belfast, was published in almost all the Irish newspapers and posits a close relationship between music and national identity: "[W]hen it is considered how intimately the *spirit* and *character* of a *people* are connected with their *national poetry* and *music,* it is presumed that the Irish patriot and politician will not deam [*sic*] it an object unworthy of his patronage and protection."[2] The Harp Festival, organized by McDonnell, Robert Bradshaw, Henry Joy, and Robert Simms, attracted ten harpers and ran concurrently with a celebration organized by the United Irishmen honoring the third anniversary of the fall of the Bastille.[3] Charlotte Milligan Fox notes that the Bastille celebrations, consisting of a procession, a review, "a convention, and finally, a banquet" at which the assembly sought to "declare themselves in favour of Catholic emancipation and the Rights of Man," shared the scene with the Harp Festival.[4] This overlap is not surprising given that, as Mary Helen Thuente points out, some of the same people were involved in both events.[5] In addition, the instrument the Belfast Harp Festival was designed to highlight, the harp, was the icon of the recently formed United Irishmen and the subject of their motto: "It Is New Strung and Shall Be Heard."

This double celebration encouraged the publication of at least two musical texts. The work inspired by the United Irishmen's celebration, *Songs on the French Revolution that took place at Paris, 14, July 1789. Sung at the Celebration thereof at Belfast, on Saturday, 14 July 1792,* consisting of six anonymous songs, appeared shortly after the event, although as Thuente suggests, the songs continued to play a part in political life in later manifestations. They were "subsequently published in the *Northern Star* or in the first *Paddy's Resource* songbook,"[6] both publications of the United Irishmen. The text which resulted from the Harp Festival appeared four years after the conclusion of the festivities and also had a long history of republication. McDonnell had employed a young organist, nineteen-year-old Edward Bunting, son of an English father and Irish mother, to copy down the compositions of the harpers engaged in the competition.[7] Working from his manuscript notes, and from material gathered during his travels around Ireland in the four years following the festival, Bunting published his collection of Irish tunes arranged for pianoforte, entitled *A General Collection of the Ancient Irish Music*, in 1796.[8] He published subsequent volumes in 1809 and 1840.[9]

Brian Boydell comments that Bunting's three volumes are the culmination of "a new stimulus [that] produced a remarkable increase in the number of publications of traditional Irish music" after about 1780.[10] The incentive for Bunting, according to Boydell, was "the growing sense of national consciousness that marked the closing decades of the century."[11] In fact, Bunting's 1796 *Ancient Irish Music* offered a perspective on the Irish past suitable for all religious and social affiliations as it combined antiquarian interest with political assertion. The cover proclaims the novelty of the project, announcing that the collection contains "Admired Airs" which have been "never before published." It draws attention to the tunes as a direct line to antiquity: some of the tunes are compositions of "Conolan and Carolan" which have been "Collected from the Harpers in the different Provinces of IRELAND." On one level, the 1796 *Ancient Irish Music* provides the same kind of positive image of the native Irish people that O'Conor's *Dissertations on the History of Ireland* and Walker's *Historical Memoirs* did. Like these texts, Bunting's volume suggests Irish historical superiority in the musical sphere. The preface begins with the assertion, "It is an extraordinary fact, that although Ireland has, from a remote antiquity, been celebrated for its cultivation of Music, and admitted to be one of the parent countries of that delightful art, the present is the first *general* collection of its national airs."[12] Bunting distinguishes his project from that of his predecessors, however, as he attempts to compile a larger corpus of material. The preface provides historical examples of the praise of Irish music. Bunting notes with relish, for example, that even though Giraldus was "probably not free from the prejudices that were then entertained against the Irish," he pronounced the skill of the Irish in music as "beyond all comparison superior to that of any nation I have seen."[13] Most importantly, Bunting claims a connection between Ireland and the originary moment of notation in Britain, as he argues that the piece that Charles Burney identifies in his *General History* as the "first piece of Music ever set in score in Great Britain" is in fact identical with an Irish tune, "Ta an samradh teacht," or "Summer Is Coming."[14] Bunting goes a step beyond Walker in revising Burney, as he declares that Ireland is the "parent" of British music.

Bunting is eager to emphasize the purity of his project, its authenticity. For as Colin Graham points out, in Ireland, "Authenticity and claims to authenticity underlie the conceptual and cultural denial of dominance."[15] In Bunting's case, the desire to stress authenticity is a way of combating claims like those of Burney against Walker which struck at the heart of an Irish sense of historical and—by implication—contemporary legitimacy. To stress the tunes' authenticity as embodiments of native Irish culture, Bunting gives them titles in solid Gaelic typescript, with English translations following in a smaller font (see figure 4.1). Asserting that he was "particularly cautioned against adding a single note to the old melodies, which would seem, from inferences that will afterwards be drawn, to have been preserved pure, and handed down unalloyed, thro' a long succession of ages,"[16] Bunting presents himself acting in accordance with a tradition which has kept the music intact throughout the centuries. He notes that the old musicians "seem never to have ventured to make the slightest innovation in [a tune] during its descent."[17] His proof for this assertion is the uniformity of playing throughout the island: "[H]arpers collected from parts far distant from one another, & taught by different masters, always played the same tune on the same key, with the same kind of expression, and without a single variation in any essential passage, or even in any note."[18] It is of utmost importance to Bunting that the tunes be seen as uncorrupted reliques of an Irish past which can serve as a connection to the present. In the process of making that connection, however, Bunting renders native Irish culture essentially homogeneous and static. Characterized as "without variation" even across geographical distance and associated with a continuous oral tradition, native music is figured in opposition to modernity. Bunting's choice of the word *ancient* in his title for the collection (even though many of the songs were composed by Carolan, who had died only sixty years previously) further suggests the music's separation from the present era. By identifying what is "ancient," Bunting's collection also works to define modernity.

Ironically, Bunting seeks to capture the antimodernity of the native music within a thoroughly modern medium as he shifts the music from a context of oral transmission to the realm of print culture. Chapter 1 discussed Michael Chanan's notions of the radical difference between oral and printed music. In a similar vein, Janet Harbison suggests that Bunting changed what had been flexible rhythm patterns into standard time and that he presented definitive

Figure 4.1. Music of "Love in Secret," from Edward Bunting, *New Edition of A General Collection of the Ancient Irish Music* (Dublin, 1796), p. 8, no. 14. Reproduced from the original held by the Department of Special Collections of the University Libraries of Notre Dame.

arrangements of right- and left-hand melody and harmony lines.[19] She argues that whereas the original players of the harp music would have used a great deal of improvisation, this improvisation was eliminated by Bunting's adapting the music for the piano. But the case of the *Ancient Irish Music* is more complicated than the work of Harbison suggests. What Bunting accomplished was not so much an eradication of spontaneity as a translation of it into the terms of Anglo-Irish and English consumption. Such a translation from oral to print culture meant that native Irish music was now placed in a commercial context of market demand and consumption, a context which rendered it intrinsically modern and involved it inevitably in the wider British marketplace.

Further complicating Bunting's enterprise is his reliance on contemporary aesthetic judgments. In particular, Bunting appeals to his audience's sense of harmony, derived from European musical rules, particularly from the work of the Italians. Bunting praises Carolan's work for being both contemporary and modern and ancient and native: "In Carolan's Concerto and in his Madam Cole the practitioners will perceive evident imitations of Corelli, in which the exuberant fancy of that admired composer he happily copied. In the ancient air *Grach gan fios,* or Love in Secret, he will be charmed with one of the most pleasing strains that any country has produced; it is accordingly so old, that no trace could be discovered of the century [in] which it was produced."[20] The ancient craft of harping is commended for its anticipation of contemporary harmonics. Bunting notes that the ancient authors were "versed in the scientific part of their profession, that they had originally a view to the addition of *harmony* in the composition of their pieces."[21] The effect is odd. The traditional music is most valuable when it is seen to be a retrospective reflection of currently admired musical qualities. Bunting suggests that Irish music was the point of origin for current European music, but he can make this assertion only by projecting contemporary aesthetics back onto the Irish music. Carolan himself becomes a strange figure here, most valuable for prefiguring the present, but also for disappearing: Bunting says he "seems to have been born to render the termination of his order memorable and brilliant."[22] The present folds back onto the past, suggesting that the ancient music was always already anticipating its progress into modernity.

If the ancient music is used to define modernity, it is reciprocally true that the modern also plays a part in the invention of the ancient. In particular, Bunting's collection bears something of the imprint of the Society of United Irishmen. Bunting himself was acquainted with a number of members of the United Irishmen, including Henry Joy McCracken (whose family he lived with for forty years), Patrick Lynch, and Thomas Russell. The 1796 edition owed its existence in a large part to Russell, who was keeper of the library of the Belfast Society for Promoting Knowledge and who would later lose his life as a result of his participation in Emmet's 1803 Rebellion. Russell convinced the society to donate some money to Bunting's project, without which it would have been abandoned.[23]

Several of Bunting's digs at English policy in Ireland echo the concerns of the United Irishmen to educate the Irish population in the history of their oppression.[24] Bunting notes, for example, that Carolan labored under the difficulty of being an "inhabitant of a country recently desolated by a civil war, the flames of which had scarcely subsided."[25] Further, the *Ancient Irish Music* seems to have an agenda akin to that of the United Irishmen to unite various divergent factors under the single cause of promoting Ireland. Bunting interprets the importance of his work as the transformation of local activity into national enterprise. He emphasizes that he has traveled around the entire country collecting material. This is, he notes, a "General" collection of tunes, a word he reuses in the 1809 collection. Music is presented as a connecting national practice, one capable of surmounting internal differences in the nation. Instead of advocating direct revolutionary activity to further the nationalist cause, however, Bunting directs oppositional political energy into cultural practice.[26] Ending his preface by urging people throughout the country to take up the cause of music, he exhorts those "in the southern parts of Ireland to follow the example of the Belfast society, by promoting similar meetings of the harp in their respective provinces."[27] He comments that "[i]t is a debt every man owes to his country, to search for and perpetuate the records of other days, to oppose, as far as he can, the destructive ravages of time and to render permanent the fleeting productions of every species of genius."[28] The language of military patriotism—"a debt every man owes his country" and "to oppose . . . the destructive ravages"—is converted into a cultural context here but still implies opposition.

The reference to "every man" also suggests another characteristic that Bunting's *Ancient Music* shares with the United Irishmen: the alignment of masculinity and national assertion. Kevin Whelan argues that "[w]omen began to take a more active role in the United Irish movement."[29] But he also points out that the separate societies of United Irishwomen were "derisively called 'teapot societies' by loyalists,"[30] suggesting the pervasive gendering of politics that reads women's participation in a political movement as cause for ridicule. At the same time, Whelan calls attention to the frontispiece of the United Irish songbook, *Paddy's Resource*, noting that it "blends references to the French Marianne with the Irish Caitlín Ní hUlacháin."[31] Pratt comments on such symbolism, arguing that "[t]he uneasy coexistence of nationhood and womanhood is played out in that paradoxical republican habit of using female icons as national symbols."[32] Nancy Curtin explores the gendered politics within the United Irishmen's own ideology, arguing that "[w]omen were most visible in the United Irish movement, invited in a sense into the public space of politics, as symbols prodding men to perform their national and re-publican duty."[33] Similarly, in her discussion of the representation of women in United Irishmen's song collections such as *Songs on the French Revolution,* Thuente asserts that the use of women as symbols accords them only passive participation.[34]

Tacitly promoting this gendered politics, Bunting's bardic community is also clearly masculine and based on the same kind of rhetoric of heroism prevalent in the songs of the United Irishmen. In the preface to the 1796 volume, Bunting speaks of the Belfast Festival as "the assemblage of the rem-nant of the Irish Bards"[35] and proceeds to create a heroic genealogy for them: "The Bards . . . existed among the ruder branches of the Celtic tribes, before the time of Augustus. We find them under the same name in Ireland from the earliest period of our history down to the year 1738, when Carolan died."[36] Even though one woman, Rose Mooney, was a contestant at the festival, Bun-ting refers to the festival performers as "men advanced in life,"[37] noting that they have learned from different "masters."[38] Like Walker, Bunting attempts to legitimize the Irish nation by presenting it as masculine.

The sequel to the *Ancient Irish Music* appeared in 1809 with the following elaborate title: *A General Collection of the Ancient Music of Ireland Arranged for the Piano Forte; Some of the Most Admired Melodies Are Adapted for the Voice, To Poetry Chiefly Trans-lated From the Original Songs, by Thomas Campbell, Esq. And Other Eminent Poets: To Which Is Prefixed a Historical and Critical Dissertation on the Egyptian, British and Irish Harp.* It is, like its predecessor, concerned with promoting Irish culture through presenting a positive image of Irish music. By 1809, the political situ-ation in Ireland had changed drastically, a consequence of the failure of the United Irishmen's rebellion, the institution of the 1800 Act of Union, and the failure of the 1803 uprising. The Irish parliament, for all its faults, was no more. Instead, as R. F. Foster notes, Ireland became subject to more direct and centralized British administrative policy: "Ireland came to be seen as an appropriate area for administrative energy, and even experiment, but this was without reference to the small proportion of Irish MP's, or to any larger con-stituency of opinion in Ireland at large."[39] The appearance of the 1809 volume of the *Ancient Music of Ireland* suggests Bunting's concern to market the book on both sides of the Irish Channel. The 1809 volume is attractively fashioned to highlight Irish culture, with a dark green cover embellished with gold, a title page that features a stylized shamrock border (see figure 4.2), and a text sup-plemented by illustrations of a variety of harps and harp players.[40] In the 1809 volume Bunting was much more concerned than previously with presenting the music as commodity.[41] But the 1809 volume of the *Ancient Music of Ireland*

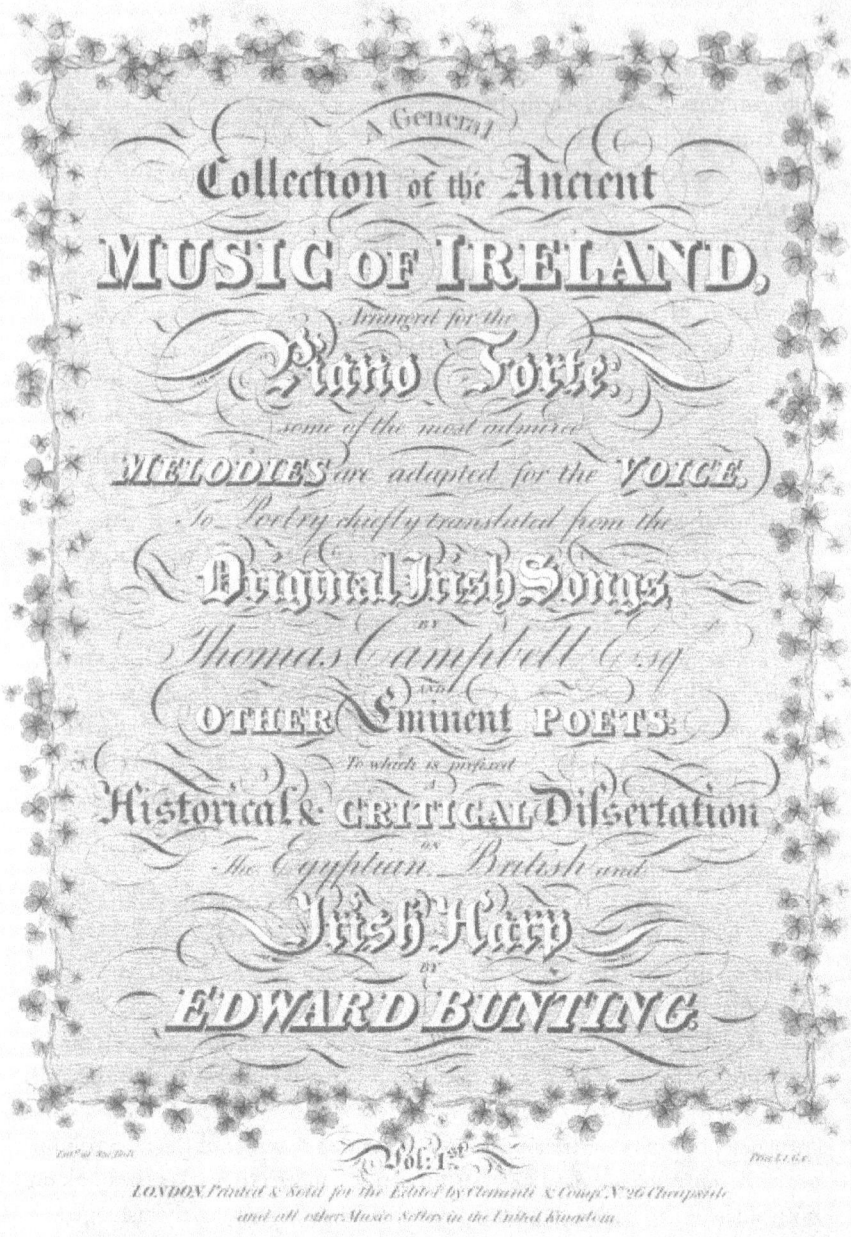

Figure 4.2. Title page of Edward Bunting, *A General Collection of the Ancient Music of Ireland* (London: Clementi, 1809). Reproduced from the original held by the Department of Special Collections of the University Libraries of Notre Dame.

offers an ambiguous picture of Irish national identity. Bunting's preface and the explanatory "Historical and Critical Dissertation on the Harp" that follows it assert an ancient and masculine pedigree for the Irish harp and for the Irish nation. The drinking songs like "O'Rourke's Noble Fare Will Ne'er Be Forgot" reinforce that image. But at the same time, the poems by Thomas Campbell, Mary Balfour, and "other Eminent Poets" in the collection work to feminize the music by aligning it with drawing-room performance.

The 1809 collection, like the 1796 volume, takes up the cause of "ancient" history. But the 1809 volume reverses the historical positions of the Irish and the English by showing the Scots and the Irish as pure nations and presenting the English as a colonized people. The "Historical and Critical Dissertation" included in the volume suggests that the Scots and the Irish are the most authentic nations: "One of the most certain criteria of the antiquity of a nation, is its being possessed of a native or original music."[42] It includes a quotation by John Brown, who, in his *A Dissertation on the Rise, Union, and Power, the Progressions, Separations, and Corruptions, of Poetry and Music*, says that countries peopled by colonies have no characteristic music of their own: "[T]he Irish, Welsh, and Scotch are strictly natives, and accordingly *have* a music of their own. . . . [T]he English, on the contrary, are a foreign mixture of lately established colonies, and in consequence of this, have no native music."[43] Carthage, for example, was a colony of Tyre, "and music which was of weight in the native city, was of no consideration in the descendent state."[44] The "Dissertation" concludes suggestively, "[T]he same principle applies to all times."[45] It even carries the superiority of the Celts into the realm of letters, observing that the Saxons did not have either *"the Harp or letters"* before their arrival in Britain at the 5th century."[46] The Irish, it is implied, had both.

The authenticity of the bards is connected in the 1809 volume of the *Ancient Irish Music*, as it is in the 1796 volume, with masculinity. The "Dissertation" notes that the bards "celebrated the brave actions of illustrious men in heroic times."[47] This discussion accords with Walker's account as it traces the evolution of the bards from their position as lawmakers to their role as minstrels retained by the nobility:

> Not only our kings, but almost all our nobility and men of fortune, had bands of secular musicians or minstrels in their service, who resided in their families, and even attended them in their journies [*sic*] for their amusement. These domestic minstrels . . . were permitted to perform in rich monasteries, and in the castles of the barons, for which they were handsomely rewarded.[48]

The drinking songs included in the 1809 volume further suggest the association between the minstrels and the Gaelic nobility, at the same time reinforcing the idea of the masculine community. Jonathan Swift's rollicking translation of "O'Rourke's Noble Fare Will Ne'er Be Forgot" is an extreme representation of feudal hospitality, as O'Rourke's guests are treated to "seven score sheep, fat bullocks, and swine" and "a hundred" pails of "usquebagh" by their host before they fight and fall into bed.[49] "Inspiring Fount of Cheering Wine" also conveys the valor and hospitality of the Gaelic order. It is described as "very ancient, and composed long before the time of Carolan" by David Murphy, a dependent of Lord Mayo who wrote it to regain the favor and protection of his patron. "Ye Good Fellows All" is listed as "imitated from the original Irish of Carolan" by Arthur Dawson, third Baron of the Exchequer of Ireland. Dawson's lyrics translate the hospitality of the Gaelic lords into an Anglo-Irish context, substituting claret for "usquebagh," but his song, too, promotes a masculine community in which women have no place. Poets are encouraged to "Forsake all the Muses, those senseless old crones,"[50] while lovers are advised to reject their objects of affection:

> Come hither I'll show you
> How Phillis and Cloe,
> No more shall occasion such sighs and such groans,
> For what mortal so stupid
> As not to quit Cupid,
> When called by good claret, and bumper 'Squire Jones.

The drinking songs suggest a seamless connection from the ancient bardic community to the more recent halls of the Gaelic chieftains and finally to the gentlemen's clubs that would have been frequented by Anglo-Irishmen like Swift and Baron Dawson.

But the authentic, ancient, masculine image of the nation that appears in the 1809 volume is problematic. While the 1809 volume offers scientific evidence of the mathematics and philosophy of the ancient harpers to assert the superiority of Irish music, it goes even further than the 1796 edition in presenting the ancient Irish music in terms of current European standards. In the preface to the new edition, Bunting justifies his qualifications to judge tunes by indicating that he is conversant "in the compositions of the Italian and German schools,"[51] suggesting that only such credentials can satisfy his public. The "Dissertation" in the 1809 edition wrenches Irish music from the earlier claims Bunting had made for its historical roots in the oral tradition as an "unlearned extemporaneous" art, instead claiming for it characteristics which make it more recognizably modern.[52] Drawing on the remarks of Dr. Ledwich and putting together the evidence that Welsh harp music appeared in written form with the assumption that the Irish gave the Welsh their harp music, the "Dissertation" concludes, "[T]hat we had music in score can hardly be disputed."[53] It also includes a more sweeping claim that Irish music anticipated European musical theory: "What is more extraordinary, most of the pieces for the Harp are in full harmony and counterpoint."[54]

Moreover, in the 1809 edition, Bunting aligns his ancient bardic culture with that of Macpherson's Ossian. A quotation from *Fingal* begins the new volume of the *Ancient Music of Ireland*: "Bards of other times! ye on whose souls the blue hosts of our fathers rise, strike the Harp in my hall, and let me hear the song. Pleasant is the joy of grief."[55] Bunting continues to refer to Ossian and Scotland, noting that he has found specimens of music "as sung in artless strains in the Highlands of Scotland, and also by the aborigines of different parts of Ireland, to OSSIANIC FRAGMENTS."[56] He does his part to relocate the focus to Ireland, however, by noting that the Scots derived both their language and their music from Ireland. Like Walker, Bunting seems to be both asserting the identity of the Irish in response to Macpherson's denigration of Irish culture and capitalizing on the success of Macpherson by presenting the ancient Irish as chivalric rivals of Macpherson's Highlanders.[57] Nevertheless, by drawing on Ossian's "joy of grief," Bunting enlists an enfeebled image to represent Ireland, an image that appears frequently throughout the 1809 volume in the poems of Thomas Campbell and Mary Balfour.

More generally, the poetry and lyrics included in the 1809 volume compromise the image of an ancient, masculine nation, as they are designed to appeal to a contemporary Irish and British audience, made up in particular of women, who are spending more and more time in the drawing room. In deciding to include texts to accompany the songs, Bunting was clearly influenced by the success of Thomas Moore. Moore's first volume of the *Irish Melodies*, which contained lyrics written by Moore with Irish tunes arranged by Sir John Stevenson for drawing-room performance, appeared in 1808 to high acclaim. Bunting's consciousness of competing with Moore is evident in his letter to Mary Ann McCracken dated March 8, 1809, in which he notes that "Power [Moore's publisher] endeavors to persuade every one that Moore's work and mine do not clash. Certainly they *do* clash, *unfortunately for me*."[58] A reflection of Moore's impact on Bunting can be seen in the latter's statement that his purpose has shifted somewhat since he came out with his original collection, which had been designed "to rescue [the tunes] from oblivion."[59] Now he registers more of a concern with marketing his work to English-speaking readers. He says he now aims "to collate the airs of different provinces with each other; to procure translations of some of the finest songs, and for several of the airs best adapted for the purpose to give English words with an instrumental accompaniment."[60]

The 1809 volume was also conceived under different terms which suggest its more radical nature. Unlike Moore, Bunting was concerned originally to include the Gaelic lyrics for the songs, and he employed Patrick Lynch, who, as we saw in the previous chapter, was editor of the *Bolg an tSolair* collection featuring Brooke's work, to collect songs, chiefly from sources in Connaught, and to provide translations. Bunting refers to Lynch in the preface as "a person versed in the Irish tongue," and he mentions his original plan, which was "to annex the original poetry in the Irish character."[61] Bunting's manuscripts for the 1809 edition contain the original Gaelic lyrics and translations of them with marks by Bunting indicating what he liked. In its originally planned form, the 1809 volume would have asserted more strongly the presence of the Gaelic society from which the music derived, representing the Gaelic lyrics in the "Irish character," as in Brooke's *Reliques*. But when Lynch, who was a member of the United Irishmen, turned King's evidence against fellow-member Thomas Russell, Bunting decided against including Lynch's contributions to the volume and against including the Gaelic lyrics.[62] These decisions had important implications for the gendered representation of Irish music in the volume.

Now, in his attempt to rival Moore's lyrics, Bunting capitalized on the popularity of Thomas Campbell, a Scottish poet who had risen to fame with his *Pleasures of Hope* (1799) and had been granted a government pension in 1805 for his patriotic verse. But Campbell apparently gave Bunting some difficulties. According to George Petrie, Bunting was "ultimately obliged to content himself with two indifferent songs and permission to use two of the poet's ballads written long previous to the agreement."[63] In the first song in the volume, "A Chieftain to the Highlands Bound," the Chief of Ulva elopes with the daughter of Lord Ullin. They attempt to cross over Lochgyle to escape Lord Ullin's wrath but are drowned in a storm. The poem is entirely set in Scotland, and even the name, Ullin, is derived from a Scottish source. Ullin was a bard of Fingal in Macpherson's Ossianic poems. "Twas the Hour When Rites Unholy," which Bunting notes was "written for this work," involves lovers from even further afield: a Crusader captured in Transylvania and a "paynim" lady. "To the Battle Men of Erin," which was also specifically "written for this work," moves from the theme of love to that of war. The song can be seen to have particular relevance to the British war against Napoleon, calling for the "Men of Erin" to each don a shamrock and prepare for battle against the French:

> What though France thine eagle standard
> Spreading terror far and nigh,
> Over Europe's skies hath wander'd
> On the wings of victory.[64]

The presentation of the "right true Irish band," with their plumes waving "To the trumpet's jubilee" would serve to alleviate any potential English fears about the kind of alliance between the Irish and the French which occurred during 1798. Campbell's final song for the 1809 volume, "There Came to the Beach a Poor Exile of Erin," although inspired by Campbell's meeting with a participant in the 1798 Rebellion, Anthony MacCann, in Hamburg, assuages anxiety about Irish militarism by displacing it into the personal sphere.[65] The exile in this song speaks in terms which could easily identify him as a participant in the failed rebellion. He dreams of Ireland but awakes to find himself in a "far foreign land,"[66] and he identifies the "brothers" who "died to defend me! or live to deplore!"[67] The description of his patriotism is similar to that found in United Irish ballads, even to the extent of utilizing Gaelic expressions:

> Yet, all its sad recollection suppressing,
> One dying wish my lone bosom can draw;
> Erin! an exile bequeaths thee his blessing!
> Land of my forefathers, Erin go bragh!

But the song introduces some confusion into the situation as the speaker suggests that he has been mistaken in his values. He laments the fact that he has doted "on a fast-fading treasure"[68] instead of his love for his "bosom friend": "Tears like the rain-drop may fall without measure, / But rapture and beauty they cannot recall."[69] If the song is read as a political allegory it is a confusing one that hints at the exile's conflict between his love of his country and his beloved and his love for "a fast-fading treasure." The political currency of the song is further devalued by the poem's conclusion, which reverts to an image of harpers who suggest an Ireland of the past rather than the present: "Thy harp-striking bards sing aloud with devotion, / Erin ma vournin! Erin go bragh!"[70] A footnote translates the Gaelic in this last line of the song as "Ireland my darling! Ireland for ever!"[71] but the burden of the song is to present Ireland as a focus of nostalgia, an embodiment of the same kind of "joy of grief" found in Macpherson's poetry. Petrie complains that "A Chieftain to the Highlands Bound" and "There Came to the Beach a Poor Exile of Erin," written earlier by Campbell, were "entirely out of place in a collection of Irish melodies."[72] In fact, all of Campbell's songs are in a sense out of place in this collection, as Bunting was more interested in songs that were done *"solely for this work* from literal translations of the original Irish."

Although Campbell is the only poet mentioned by name on the cover of the 1809 volume, the person who contributed the greatest number of songs— nearly half—was Mary Balfour, a schoolteacher from Limavady. All of Balfour's nine contributions are listed as "from a literal translation of the original Irish." As Seamus Deane notes, hers are "among the earliest translations from the Irish," but they are written as drawing-room pieces with "no serious attempt to come to terms with the original."[73] Balfour would go on to republish her contributions in *Hope: A Poetical Essay: With Various Other Poems* (1810). A number of Balfour's translations, like Campbell's, evoke an Ossianic nostalgia for a chivalrous past. "Full High in Kilbride in the Grass Seen to Wave" counters "Inspiring Fount of Cheering Wine" by lamenting the loss of the chief, Laughlin, and his hospitable hall: "The tones of the harp in that mansion have ceas'd, / No more it resounds with the mirth of the feast."[74] "Far Hence to Hail a Chief I Go" praises the manners of the chief but surrounds him with terms that evoke the past: "He loves the goblet's mantling flow, / The harp to festive music strung."[75] The majority of Balfour's songs concern a lover writing about his beloved, and Ireland becomes merely a poetic backdrop that is associated with quaint expressions and verdant natural scenery. Balfour's literal translation of "Ulican Dubh Oh" becomes the precious "Adieu! My Native Wilds, Adieu." The Gaelic phrase, "Ulican dubh, Oh!" is rendered into Roman characters and incorporated into English versification, with the Gaelic words being made to rhyme with the English words *go, know,* and *flow.*[76] Similarly, "The Moon Calmly Sleeps on the Ocean" uses the Gaelic phrase "cailin beog chruite na mbo" to rhyme with *draw, straw,* and *glow,*[77] even incorporating it grammatically into the English sentences, as in "my cailin beog chruite na mbo."[78] Like Campbell's "The Exile of Erin," both of these songs concern a young man forced into exile, not by politics, but by misplaced love. In "In Ringlets Curl'd Thy Tresses Flow," "Truigha's lonely green woods"[79] and "Uchais lovely plains" serve as an Edenic escape for the lovers:

There holly berries glowing red,
With nuts and apples sweet abound,
Green rushes there shall strew our bed,
And warblers chaunt their lov'd notes round.[80]

As Deane points out, "Truigha" and "Uchais" are possibly versions of the names of areas in County Sligo and County Mayo.[81] They serve to give an Irish flavor to a poem that could otherwise be set anywhere. Charlotte Milligan Fox observes that Balfour "sat down to modify the Gaelic songs of love and war and drinking into something more delicate."[82] And indeed, Balfour's poetry, along with Campbell's and the poems contributed by John Brown ("O Southern Breeze! Thy Nectar Breath"), Hector MacNeill ("O Lov'd Maid of Broka"), the Honorable W. R. Spencer ("Too Late I Staid: Forgive the Crime"), and even the erstwhile United Irishman William Drennan ("Branch of the Sweet and Early Rose") represents Irish music as suitable material for the drawing rooms of a now united Britain.[83]

Bunting projects the ambiguous sense of national identity suggested in the 1809 volume onto the music itself, implying that the Irish melodies represent the political and cultural conflicts inherent in the attempt to define the Irish nation. In a reference to John Leyden's *Preliminary Dissertation to the Complaint of Scotland*, Bunting suggests that the Irish tunes "take the very form and pressure of our history; and the conflict of spirits, naturally warm and vivacious, with the gloom which abasement and poverty would cast upon them, is no where more faithfully recorded than in these *bewildered* melodies."[84] The presentation of the music in written form in the 1809 edition presents a further example of this bewilderment, as the "conflict of spirits" (and of voices) is embodied in the textual apparatuses. In the index, the titles of tunes are given in English and in Irish using Roman typeface in two separate columns on the same page, but Bunting makes no attempt to correlate them. Each appears as a separate alphabetical listing. Bunting's methodology for providing titles for his tunes on the pages of the music itself has changed from the original edition, as he presents now an extra level of linguistic mediation. On the musical scores, the titles are written using large-print Gaelic typeface at the top of the page. On the next line in smaller print, the Irish name in Roman type and the English translation are stretched on either side of a long dash, almost poised like balancing scales. In addition, the language of European art music is applied to the musical score, which is filled with *crescendo, diminuendo,* and *forte* and *piano* signs, as well as Italian expressions to indicate time. (In the earlier volume, time had been indicated with English phrases.) The tunes are separated into melody and bass lines, as in the 1796 edition, but now, in the case of tunes accompanied by English translations, a melody line for the voice is added. Irish national identity, it would appear from the 1809 *Ancient Music of Ireland*, is indeed found within a "bewildered" combination of various voices.

The harp, the symbol of Irish identity, also embodies a "conflict of spirits" in the 1809 volume, as we see the opposing voices from which Irish identity is constructed embodied in the history of the harps. Brian Boru's harp, for example, in Bunting's volume, acts to confirm the subordination of the native Irish to their English colonizers. Picking up on a similar story in Walker, the "Dissertation" notes that after Brian Boru's defeat in 1014 at the battle of Clontarf, his harp was given to the pope.[85] It was eventually presented to Henry VIII with the title "Defender of the Faith." Henry gave it to an Irish earl, and it eventually ended up in the Protestant Trinity College in 1782. On the other hand, the frontispiece of this volume, a reconstructed image of the Dalway harp, marginalizes English influence. A seventeenth-century harp originally made by Donnchadh Fitzteige in 1621 for Sir John Fitzedmund Fitzgerald but existing only in fragments in Bunting's day, the Dalway harp is covered with inscriptions, not in English, but in Irish and Latin. The "Dissertation" notes that "[e]very part of the remaining fragments is covered with inscriptions in Latin and in the Irish character; the former containing mottos [*sic*], and the name of the maker . . . the latter the year it was made in, A.D. 1621, and the servants [*sic*] names of the household" (see figure 4.3).[86] If Brian Boru's harp, with its connection to battles, serves as a masculine musical representation of the nation, the Dalway harp suggests a feminine one, as it contains the inscription: "Ego sum Regina Citharum" (I am the Queen of Harps). Like the music, the illustrated harps represent the conflicted identity of Ireland suggested in the 1809 volume.

In his early-nineteenth-century commentary on Bunting, Captain Francis O'Neill implies that Bunting would have been content to have ended his publication of Irish music at two editions: "[I]t was hardly probable that he would venture to repeat his bitter experience, with a family now dependent on him for support had not the persuasion of friends and the goading of Dr. Petrie stirred his indolent spirit into renewed activity."[87] This "renewed activity" resulted in the 1840 edition of *The Ancient Music of Ireland*. Great changes had occurred between the 1809 and the 1840 editions. Catholic emancipation had been achieved finally in 1829. Daniel O'Connell's Repeal Movement was galvanizing the moneyed Catholic middle class. Such changes were accompanied by new ideas of how to represent the nation.[88] In the 1840 edition, Bunting rejects the romantic nationalism which can be seen in Moore

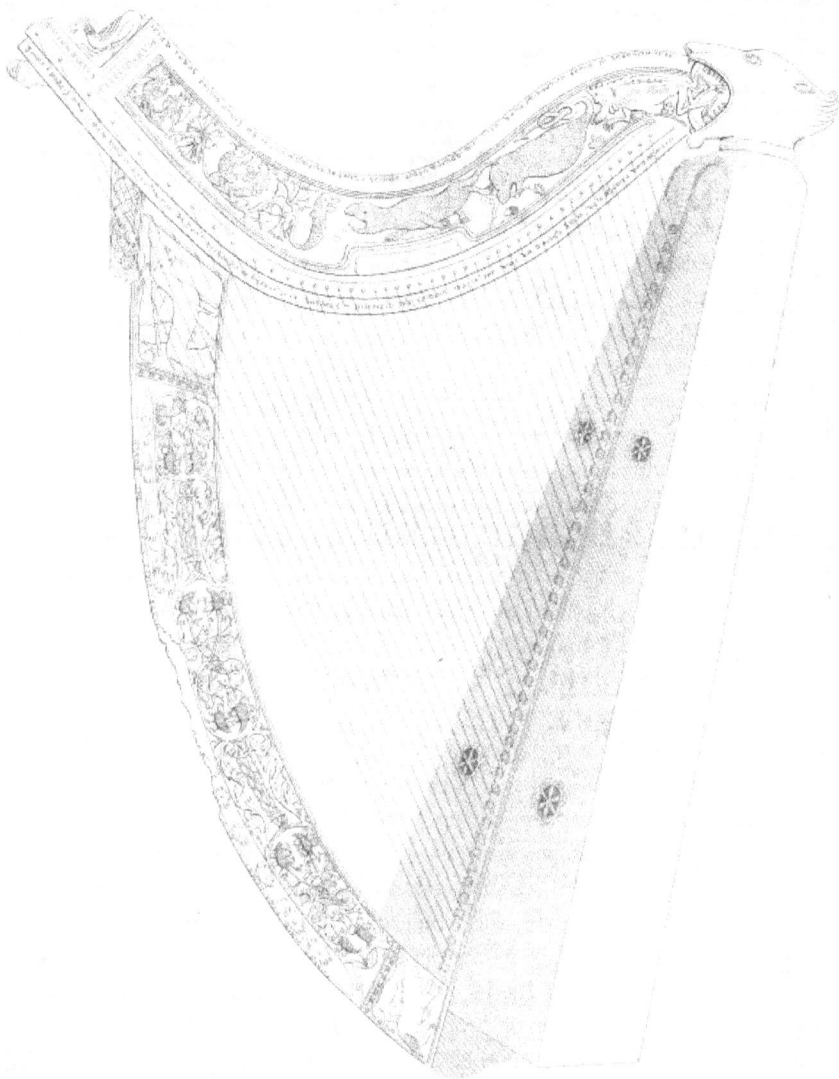

Figure 4.3. The Dalway Harp, frontispiece of Edward Bunting, *A General Collection of the Ancient Music of Ireland* (London: Clementi, 1809). Reproduced from the original held by the Department of Special Collections of the University Libraries of Notre Dame.

and which would prove so influential on the Young Ireland movement, situating his own enterprise firmly within an antiquarian quest for authenticity. This involved a renewed concern, albeit a problematic one, to recapture a sense of the purity of Irish music, a project similar to that of the first edition but now highly elaborated and expressed as opposition to Moore's modern corruptions of the music, an opposition also represented in gendered terms.

The success of Moore's *Melodies* was based on the popularity of the lyrics. Although he had tried to rival this aspect of Moore's work in the 1809 volume, Bunting sets out in the 1840 volume to promote music above lyrics. Instead of presenting music as just one of many sites of antiquarian activity, Bunting seeks to make music the preeminent source of information about the past. Whereas the exact nature of early Irish society has been disputed in many cases, Bunting suggests, the authority of Irish music is indisputable: "Whatever differences of opinion may exist as to the high degree of early civilization and national glory laid claim to by the Irish people, it has never been questioned that, in the most remote times, they had at least a national music peculiar to themselves, and that their bards and harpers were eminently skilful [*sic*] in its performance."[89] It is music, then, that offers the most perfect representation of the past. In "the uncertain, or at least debateable [*sic*] matter connected with the early condition of society among our ancestors," music is, of all historical subjects, "the one most capable of being handled with certainty and precision."[90] Music, not lyrics, conveys the purity of the past. A question mark hangs over Irish songs that are passed down by singing. But, suggests Bunting, "the case is totally different with music [passed down by instrumental playing]. A strain of music, once impressed on the popular ear, never varies. It may be made the vehicle of many different sets of words, but they are adapted to *it*, not it to *them*."[91] If the music collector confines his search to the native districts, he will find the "absolute and unimpeachable authenticity of every note he procures."[92] The object of Bunting's concern with authenticity soon becomes clear, as he suggests that the only time tunes are altered is when they are introduced "for the first time amongst those who had never heard them in their original state; as in the instance of Sir John Stevenson's supposed emendations of the Irish melodies."[93]

Now, instead of imitating Moore by providing English words to Irish tunes as he had done in the 1809 edition, Bunting sets his project of finding a pure Irish music in opposition to what he sees as Moore's musical frippery. He suggests that Moore, while popularizing Irish music, has also taken it away from its roots, the people from whom it came. In Moore's volumes, the tunes assumed a new dress—one indeed in point of poetic diction and classical ornament infinitely more elegant than they had ever worn before—under the hands of Mr. Moore; but the Editor saw with pain, and still deplores the fact, that in these new Irish melodies, the work of the poet was accounted of so paramount an interest, that the proper order of song writing was in many instances inverted, and, instead of the words being adapted to the tune, the tune was too often adapted to the words, a solecism which could never have happened had the reputation of the writer not been so great as at once to carry the tunes he deigned to make use of altogether out of their old sphere among the simple and tradition-loving people of the country—with whom, in truth, many of the new melodies, to this day, are hardly suspected to be themselves.[94]

Bunting relies on the association between fashion and the feminine to condemn Moore's work in gendered terms. Because of Moore, the ancient tunes have been put into new "dress"; they have become subject to the whims of fashion. Furthermore, according to Bunting, Moore has replaced the spirit of the people with the cult of the poet, a process he regards as unnatural and alien to the true sense of the music.

In the 1840 volume, Bunting sets out to remedy the situation. His aim, he states, is "to guard the primitive air with a religious veneration."[95] The 1840 volume is concerned with establishing the authenticity of the harpers from whom Bunting has gathered his music. Bunting devotes many pages in this volume to outlining their biographies and the specific peculiarities of each harper's playing style. In opposition to what he refers to as "Stevenson's supposed emendations of the Irish melodies," Bunting notes that he has learned about the "peculiar mode of playing and fingering" the harp from Denis Hempson and has attempted to arrange the newly collected tunes in the 1840 edition "in true harp style."[96] Bunting counters the feminizing influence that Moore's lyrics (and, for that matter, the lyrics in Bunting's own 1809 volume) have on the Irish tunes by relocating the tunes in the possession of male harpers. In this volume, however, unlike the 1796 volume, he concentrates not on the ancient bardic line but on the actual harpers who attended the Belfast festival. He provides information on the "lives and habits of the later harpers,"[97] concentrating almost exclusively on the men. Rose Mooney, the one female harper of the group of ten competing at the festival, is only briefly mentioned in a chapter entitled "Of the Various Efforts to Revive the Irish Harp," in which Bunting lists the contestants at the Belfast Festival. The note for Rose

Mooney reads merely: "(blind) from the county of Meath, aged 52, played 'Sir Charles Coote,' 'Mrs. Judge,' and 'Mrs. French,' or 'Fanny Power,' all by Carolan."[98] Even though Bunting notes that "formerly it was very usual for females to apply themselves to the harp,"[99] he devotes fifteen pages of chapter 5, "Anecdotes of the More Distinguished Harpers of the Last Two Centuries," to tracing a male genealogy for harping. The two women he does mention, Rose Mooney and Catherine Martin, are dealt with in five and a half lines.

Bunting's efforts were not lost on his reviewers. In the September 19, 1840, issue of *Chambers's Edinburgh Journal*, Robert Chambers elaborates on the distinction between Moore and Bunting in terms of gender:

> Were we to institute a literary comparison, we could say that Moore's *Irish Melodies* had about them all the fascination of poetry and romance, Bunting's collections all the sterner charms of truth and history. When we hear Sir John Stevenson's *Irish Melodies* played by a young lady on the pianoforte, or even on the pedal harp, we do not hear the same music, which O'Cahan, Carolan and Hempson played. It is as much altered as Homer in the translation of Pope. For the true presentment of this music to modern ears we require the old sets as preserved in the volumes of Bunting and the Irish harp played by an Irish harper.[100]

Chambers contrasts the "sterner" masculine material found in Bunting with the feminine material of Moore's *Melodies*, a gendered comparison which also implies an opposition between masculine age and "truth" and feminine newness and "romance."

In keeping with his desire to separate the authentic, ancient, and masculine body of music from that which is merely "disguised," Bunting divides the airs into three distinct epochs: "the very ancient, the ancient, and those composed from the time of Carolan to that of Jackson and Stirling."[101] He then proceeds to analyze the structure of the most ancient and observes that in these ancient tunes one can "trace a characteristic style which prevails more or less throughout all genuine Irish music, and constitutes the true test by which to distinguish our native melodies from those of all other countries."[102] These most ancient tunes bear witness to Ireland's strong past: "Tunes so unapproachably unique, so eminently graceful, so unlike any other music of the nations around us . . . can never with any shew of reason be attributed to composers living in times of civil discord and daily peril, in penury and comparative barbarism."[103] Instead, they "bear the impress of better days,"[104] and they are derived, not from the peasantry or harpers hiding in the countryside, but from the upper classes, at a time when "the native nobles of the country cultivated music as a part of education."[105] Bunting refers to but disagrees with Moore's historical narrative which asserts that Ireland's "finest airs are modern."[106] Claiming that, "perhaps, we may look no farther than the *last disgraceful century* for the origin of most of those wild and melancholy strains which were at once the offspring and solace of our grief,"[107] Moore situates the songs which are most Irish at the point of violent intersection between the colonizer and the colonized: "the *last disgraceful century*." In Moore's interpretation, the English play a part in creating what is most Irish. However, according to Bunting, it is the ancient songs, those written before the conquest and by the nobility, which are the most Irish.[108] Bunting seeks to remove the trace of English colonization from the most characteristically Irish music.

While Bunting attempts to situate the foundation of Irish identity in precolonial times, however, the colonizing presence is not so easily dismissed. In fact, it has leaked uncannily into the ideological foundation of Bunting's assumptions about an authentic nation. David Lloyd describes the process whereby resistant nationalism begins to take on the characteristics of the imperial ideology which it was intended to subvert:

> [W]hile nationalism is a progressive and even a necessary political movement at one stage in its history, it tends at a later stage to become entirely reactionary, both by virtue of its obsession with a deliberately exclusive concept of racial identity and, more importantly, by virtue of its *formal* identity with imperial ideology. Ultimately, both imperialism and nationalism seek to occlude troublesome and inassimilable manifestations of difference by positing a transcendent state of essential identity.[109]

While Bunting's musical project cannot be characterized as an exercise in self-consciously resistant nationalism, he is nevertheless concerned with the "essential identity" of Irish music and, correspondingly, of Ireland. His search for the pure products of the "native nobles" mirrors the "deliberately exclusive concept of racial identity" of the colonizing narrative which he has internalized. This internalized colonial identity is not only racial but gendered. It is a distinctly masculine identity from which the feminine influence has been purged by being transferred to an external site which is then considered inferior and inauthentic. While England's national identity is formed by projecting feminized "otherness" onto Ireland, the Ireland of Bunting's 1840 *Ancient Music* is created in contradistinction to Moore's feminized *Melodies*.

In his preface, Bunting indicates his hope that "the collection will be received with approbation by the lovers of music and the learned on both sides of the Channel."[110] In his private correspondence, Bunting expressed his concern regarding potential sales in Ireland: "[T]here are a few ardent lovers of their country whom I think will buy it, but, unfortunately, they are indeed few."[111] Bunting's London solicitor, James Sidebotham, was more encouraging regarding possible sales in London: "[T]he *dilettanti* if they will not play from it, would like to have it in their book case for occasional reference. If only one third of the musical people here take a copy the sale will be enormous."[112] By this time Bunting himself had more connections on the other side of the Channel, as he was working as an agent for Broadwoods of London, selling pianos. Appropriately, the title page of the 1840 edition of the *Ancient Music of Ireland* weaves images of Irish music into the symbols of British imperialism. In the illustrations of the historic harps flanking the title, Bunting suggests the evolution of the Irish harp from the classical lyre (see figure 4.4). These harps are linked to illustrations of Denis Hempson and Arthur O'Neill, two harpers who appeared at the Belfast Harp Festival. The focal image on the page, however, is the united British symbol of the lion and the unicorn, which appears at the top of the page under the British royal crown. A network of shamrocks connects all the images together. The 1840 title page encapsulates the ambiguous message of this edition, suggesting a pure lineage for Irish music but paradoxically placing it within the context of British imperial ideology. The musical score of the 1840 edition, too, reflects an internalization of the dominant ideology. Despite its claim to represent the "true harp style," Bunting's final edition, more than either of the earlier editions, presents standardized pianoforte music, although the directions for tempo have been mostly changed from Italian back to simple English. The titles of the tunes are now written in standard English, despite descriptions of them being "[v]ery ancient, Author and date unknown."

During the course of the three editions of his collections of music, written amidst three very different political situations, Bunting represents his nation in different ways. His work, then, maps the course of Ireland's colonial history, in which both political and cultural activity in Ireland is dominated by its relationship with England. Particularly in the 1840 edition, we see Bunting trying to write a redemptive identity for Ireland, but to represent that history he relies on the ideology of the colonizers of his nation; he is caught in the endless cycle of repeating the colonizing moment. Nevertheless, despite the personal and political factors which motivated Bunting's three editions,

Figure 4.4. Half-title, dedication page of Edward Bunting, *The Ancient Music of Ireland* (Dublin: Hodges and Smith, 1840). Reproduced from the original held by the Department of Special Collections of the University Libraries of Notre Dame.

his work as a whole serves to question the ideology on which colonialism depends, specifically the ideology of fixity. Although each version of the *Ancient Irish Music* attempts to fix Irish national identity in relation to the imperial self of England, each version in its way demonstrates the impossibility of doing so. The publication history of Bunting's three editions emphasizes the nation as process, not product. The editions of the *Ancient Irish Music* appear in sequel: one decade apart, then thirty years apart. All three present images of an Ireland which is constantly changing, never static, and therefore never completely co-optable. Bunting's presentation of such variant identities for Ireland suggests a nation which cannot be permanently defined, understood, and dominated. The "spirit of the nation" is constantly twisting and resisting its own previous definitions. There is no representable nation; there are only arrangements of influences which produce ambiguous cultural artifacts. The nation is revealed as what Homi Bhabha describes as a "transitional social reality."[113] The last volume of the *Ancient Music of Ireland* was dedicated by permission to Her Majesty, Queen Victoria; the title page announces this fact directly under the word *Ireland*.[114] The work ostensibly confirms the position of Ireland within the British Empire. But taken as the third in a sequence, the 1840 volume can be read as a disconcerting reminder of the trouble on the inside edge of the empire. Bunting's serial work both articulates the process of colonialism and represents the way Ireland continually challenges the administrative center.

What is crucial to bear in mind in examining Bunting's interventions in the process of colonialism, however, is the role for women and the subsequent feminization of the nation that the three editions of the *Ancient Music of Ireland* encouraged. Bunting's collections, unlike the songs of the United Irishmen, feature women not just as symbols of nation but rather as performers. Bunting suggests that he chose to adapt the tunes for pianoforte because music for the pianoforte, as a keyed instrument, most closely approximates the music played on the harp. He notes that all the other collections of Irish tunes published before his 1796 edition were "calculated for the flute or violin than for a keyed instrument, so that the tunes were to a great extent deprived of their peculiar character."[115] But rendering the music suitable for a "keyed instrument" had other consequences. Although Bunting represents a masculine bardic tradition in the commentary of all three volumes and refers to the "practitioners" of his tunes with the masculine pronoun *he*,[116] the majority of the performers of his music would have been female, as the pianoforte was very much considered a woman's instrument.

The association between women and keyboard instruments had begun in the eighteenth century, when, as Richard Leppert writes, "girls and women were restricted to two types of instruments, keyboards and plucked strings."[117] Jeffrey Kallberg points out that by the first half of the nineteenth century, "women were far and away the primary consumers of piano music"[118] and that "women played most of the keyboards found in middle-class homes throughout Europe and the United States in the eighteenth and nineteenth centuries."[119] But as Leppert notes, "The music females made, and were expected to make, was either tolerated or valued largely to the degree to which it kept within the bounds of the ideology of domesticity."[120] Women could perform the Irish nation through performing Bunting's tunes, but only in private and domestic environments, suggesting a circumscription of their national role. The correlative to this was that Bunting's "translation" of Irish music for piano also associated the Irish nation with the feminine and the domestic, reinforcing a gendered colonial dynamic that ran counter to his works' challenge to colonial preconceptions. By reworking the Irish harp tunes into music designed for the pianoforte, Bunting's three volumes of the *Ancient Irish Music* allowed for limited female participation in the musical imagining of the nation but also hinted at a feminization of Irish national identity, a feminization which was further encouraged by the reception of the work of Sidney Owenson and Thomas Moore in the nineteenth century.

5

Patriotism and "Woman's Sentiment" in Sydney Owenson's *Hibernian Melodies* and *The Wild Irish Girl*

In *The Culture of Sensibility*, G. J. Barker-Benfield comments on the renewed debate regarding the position of women in the British nation in the aftermath of the French Revolution: "Fluctuating struggles over the shaping of women's emergent, self-assertive consciousness were most explicitly politicized during the 1790s when they came to a head under the threat of revolution. Facing the bogey of a Wollstonecraft depicted as both an Amazon and a woman of sexually unbridled sensibility, literate women consolidated their claim to mind and domesticity at the expense of politics and the sexual promise in sensibility."[1] Linda Colley also asserts that "pre-existing anxieties about the position of women [became] still more intense in Britain after war with France broke out in 1793."[2] Colley qualifies the effect of this renewed debate, however, by indicating that "at the same time as they were being urged to look, feel and behave in ways that were unambiguously womanly, many female Britons were in practice becoming more involved in the public sphere than ever before, not least in terms of patriotic activism."[3] Harriet Guest also suggests that during the 1790s "women gain a clearly identifiable feminist political voice. Mary Wollstonecraft, and to some extent Mary Hays, Catherine Macaulay, and Anna Laetitia Barbauld, begin to articulate in the late century claims for women which are . . . recognizably claims to political identity."[4]

In the case of Ireland, the specter of revolution was even closer to home than in England, but it was also a revolution that was attempted and that failed twice. Despite, or perhaps because of, these circumstances, at least one woman responded to the political events going on around her by becoming more politically engaged. In the *Hibernian Melodies* and *The Wild Irish Girl*, Sydney Owenson promoted the cause of women participating in imagining the nation. But she did so in terms that were recognizably "womanly," as she made feeling patriotic. Owenson's use of the discourse of music was crucial to this project, as she disrupted the contemporary association between music, passivity, and feminine sensibility. Owenson made Ireland synonymous with a music that operated as the expression of both private sentiment and public patriotism. She was not the only writer whose work suggested a "dynamic model of the relation between the public and the private."[5] Colley, Guest, and other critics point out the many ways that men and women's actual lives contradict contemporary texts that assert such a division. What made Owenson's configuration of the relationship between the private and public and between female and male spheres unique, however, were its implications for the representation of Ireland's colonial relationship with England.[6]

On January 12, 1803, Owenson wrote a letter to her close friend Alicia Le-Fanu, concerned to counteract the latter's opinion that her writing was somehow "unwomanly." She begins by replicating the common assumptions that a woman's forte is sensibility and that it is her weakness that, paradoxically, grants her what power she has: "I entirely agree with you that *some women*, in attaining that intellectual acquisition which excites admiration and even reverence, forfeit their (oh! how much more valuable) claims on the affections of the *heart*, the *dearest, proudest* immunity nature has endowed her daughters with—the precious immunity which gives them *empire over empire*, and renders them sovereigns over the world's *lords*."[7] Owenson notes that she has curtailed certain of her intellectual interests because they were not conducive to this ambition: "Delighted with the pages of *La Voisine*, I dropped the study of chemistry, though urged to it by a favourite friend and preceptor, lest I should be thought less the *woman*. Seduced by taste, and a thousand arguments, to Greek and Latin, I resisted, lest I should not be a *very woman*."[8] She also assures her friend that those arts that she does pursue are acceptable: "And I have studied music rather as a sentiment than a science, and *drawing* as an amusement rather than an *art*, lest I should have become a musical *pedant* or a *masculine artist*."[9] Owenson's gendered distinction between music as female sentiment and as masculine science echoes her contemporaries' concerns regarding the gendering of music. Richard Leppert, for example, quotes Thomas Worgan's assessment of the difference between men's and women's relation to music: "I do not mean to say that music is not a proper accomplishment for a gentleman; tout au contraire; but I contend that, in men, it ought to be an elegant superstructure, founded on the basis of intellect."[10] But Owenson's letter to her friend also serves as an early indication of Owenson's desire to renegotiate gender roles, as she twists the paradox of women's achieving power through weakness a little more: "I must tell you, my dear madam, that I am *ambitious*, far, far beyond the line of laudable *emulations*, perhaps beyond the power of being happy. Yet the strongest point of my ambition is to be *every inch a woman.*"[11] Although ambition is not a womanly characteristic, she makes being a woman an ambition.

Well before she wrote this letter, Owenson had set herself up as an anomaly in terms of the current conventions regarding the proper feminine domain. In his discussion of gender and political economy in nineteenth-century Ireland, Timothy P. Foley comments that women of that era were seen as "by nature sensitive, altruistic, self-giving . . . virtually Christlike in their self-abnegation," and were considered "unfitted to the outdoor rigours of the public sphere" and thus in need of "the 'protection' afforded by the enclosing domestic circle."[12] Labour, which took women outside their own domestic circle, was considered distinctly unfeminine. The editor of Owenson's *Memoirs*, concerned for the most part to fit her into an ideal of feminine behavior, admits Owenson's shortcomings in this area: "Sydney's virtues were not of a patient, home-staying, household kind; she could go out into the world—she loved the adventure of it."[13] Disregarding her father's wishes, Owenson was interested in careers that disrupted conventional expectations of a woman of her class, working first as a governess, then as a professional writer. Her occupation as a governess foreshadows her later concerns with challenging gender roles, as she occupied what Anne McClintock identifies as a middle state between public and private life. Owenson was a working woman, but she worked inside a home, albeit someone else's.[14]

Her career as a writer also suggests her anomalous position, as she both assumes and eschews conventions of female authorship. Her description of the publication of her work in her *Memoirs* suggests the kind of modesty conventionally associated with female authors at the time. She claims that she deposited the manuscript of her first book of poems with Mr. Brown of Grafton Street, then forgot about it, only to pick up her own published novel in astonishment one day. However, as also becomes clear in her *Memoirs*, she was a very shrewd negotiator, playing one publisher off against the other in an attempt to extract the largest amount of money possible. When she was unhappy with Richard Phillips's offer for *The Wild Irish Girl*, she turned to Joseph Johnson. Johnson's letter to her suggests the negotiations in which she was engaging: "You have been offered a very liberal sum; not much more—say a hundred pounds per volume is the most, as far as my knowledge extends—than that which has been given to the most popular writers, after their characters were established, for works of this nature and size."[15] She eventually turned back to Phillips in order to publish *The Wild Irish Girl*.

Owenson found another means of disrupting social roles and social structures in her manipulation of musical discourse. Leppert discusses the place of women in reinforcing the "ideology of prestige."[16] He describes a historical change in the way music functioned. In the time of Castiglione and Pepys, he suggests, "music functioned integrally in the lives of the educated."[17] However, in the beginning of the nineteenth century, music's "role constituted the sonic replication of the divorce from larger reality that was possible for those of economic means. The alteration in function from a music that constituted action to one of inaction both mirrored and helped formulate the profoundest of socio-cultural changes at the advent of the modern world and the ascendancy of the bourgeoisie throughout western Europe."[18] In this process, he notes, women became "icons of privatization, success and respectability,"[19] with music's "insubstantiality mirroring perfectly the female social and gender roles."[20] In Owenson's hands, however, music is not just a symbol of passive bourgeois female sentiment, as Leppert suggests it was becoming. Rather, music is a vehicle for reforming and performing the nation. In Owenson's work, music is sentimental, but sentiment becomes the stuff of patriotism and the public sphere. As she writes in *Patriotic Sketches of Ireland* (1809): "Politics can never be a woman's science, but patriotism must naturally be a woman's sentiment."[21] Refiguring patriotism as sentiment, and showing how music conveys that sentiment, she not only justifies women's claim to patriotism but also disrupts the ideologically gendered divide between politics and the "patient, home-staying, household" of the private sphere. *Twelve Original Hibernian Melodies* and *The Wild Irish Girl* convey this disruption.

Published six years after the 1800 Act of Union, Owenson's *Twelve Original Hibernian Melodies, with English Words, Imitated and Translated from the Works of the Ancient Irish Bards* appears at first to reinforce the masculine gendering of the Irish nation that Walker and Bunting depict. Much of the preface to the work reiterates the observations of these predecessors. Owenson begins by describing the state of Irish music collecting in the present time, repeating the convention regarding the superiority of ancient Irish music promoted by Walker among others. Like Walker, Owenson portrays Irish music as "the voice of Nature,"[22] emphasizing its organicism and its origins in oral tradition. She writes: "Many of the airs and poems which compose this little selection, were orally collected in what may be deemed the classic wilds of Ireland."[23] The Irish songs must be understood, she suggests, quoting Milton's admiring comments on Shakespeare, as *"the native wood notes wild"* of those who were "unimproved by art, unrestrained by rule."[24] Owenson's comment that *"Emant*

Acnuick," or "Ned of the Hills," is the "epitome of the ancient Irish style of composition" because of its "characteristic wildness and melting pathos"[25] repeats Walker's observation that "[t]he Irish music is, in some degree, distinguished from the music of every other nation, by an insinuating sweetness, which forces its way, irresistibly, to the heart, and there diffuses an extatic [*sic*] delight, that thrills through every fibre of the frame, awakens sensibility, and agitates or tranquillizes [*sic*] the soul."[26]

For Owenson, however, the claim of wildness helps directly associate Irish music with female sensibility, as she compares her selection of the tunes in the *Hibernian Melodies* with the task of picking wild flowers. Owenson acknowledges Bunting and his endeavors in her preface, suggesting that despite the "celebrity" that the bards "obtained for their musical compositions from the remotest antiquity,"[27] there were no attempts to collect their works before Bunting applied himself to the task. But, according to Owenson, the goal was not completely achieved. Even at this point, when the "broad field of Irish music, even in its autumnal decline, afforded a rich harvest to the successful exertions of national taste, some few blossoms of poetry and song were still left."[28] Owenson emphasizes, however, that, as a woman, she belongs to a lesser group than previous collectors: "It was reserved for the minute and enquiring glance of the humble gleaner, to discover the neglected charms, and to behold them like the rose, fragrant even in decay."[29] Owenson echoes Brooke's description of herself in the *Reliques of Irish Poetry* as "strew[ing] flowers in the paths of these laureled champions of my country"[30] when she writes: "With a timid hand I have endeavored to snatch them from the chilling atmosphere of oblivion, and bound them in a wild and simple wreath, in the faint hope that public approbation would nourish and perpetuate their existence."[31]

Owenson also pays tribute to Brooke by confirming Brooke's sentimentalization of Carolan, as she connects his music with women and the "philosophy of love": "His first poetic and music effort was the effusion of an enamoured heart, elicited by the charms of *Bridget Cruise*; the high rank of his mistress proved an insurmountable barrier to his wishes, and like most other poetical enamoratos, his passion was as unsuccessful, as it was ardent. He, however, soon became an adept in the philosophy of love, and every song had for its theme a new mistress."[32] According to Owenson, Carolan's music comes out of frustrated desire and failure in love. At the same time that Moore was translating his *Odes of Anacreon*, Owenson represented Carolan as "the Anacreon of his country": "[O]f a roving and unsettled disposition, with his harp flung over his shoulder, he wandered like the bards of old, celebrating with Pindaric boldness the charms of love, the joys of social life, and the virtues of cordial hospitality."[33] Such comments suggest Owenson's complicity with her predecessors' gendered representations.

But Owenson also distinguishes her project from those of her predecessors. Where Walker and Bunting were eager to frame Irish music in terms that would render it acceptable to eighteenth-century standards, Owenson does not attempt to rationalize or explain Irish music's essential "wildness." Both Walker and Bunting, even though they emphasized the natural and spontaneous aspects of Irish music, ultimately concentrated on presenting it as reputable for scholarly study. The burden of Walker's *Historical Memoirs* is to show the Irish bards as suitable subjects of history. A similar desire motivates Bunting to undertake his antiquarian collecting and motivates his inclusion of essays like the "Historical and Critical Dissertation on the Harp" within his work. In the *Hibernian Melodies,* however, Owenson shifts the judgment of Irish music away from "professed votarists of science."[34] For Owenson, musical excellence is not a question of scientific calculation; rather, a piece "is to be estimated by the effect it produces on the human mind, by its power over the passions, or its influence over the heart."[35] Given such terms, she argues, "the Irish melodies, it must be allowed, graduate to a very high degree on the scale of musical excellence; always composed under the operation of the feelings, whether the warm inspirations of gratitude—whether the tender effusions of love, or the bold spirit of martial enthusiasm awakens the strain—it still breathes the truest intimation of the soul."[36] Owenson is concerned here with the female aspect of music: music "rather as a sentiment than a science," as she described it in her letter to LeFanu.[37] She associates Irish music with a certain feminization by grounding it in sentiment, but she shows that sentiment is also the vehicle of patriotism. And just as she distinguishes herself from her male predecessors, she voices a different perspective from that of her female predecessor. Whereas Brooke was concerned with including women in the public sphere, Owenson is intent on reconfiguring the gendered division between public and private spheres that produces and is produced by androcentric national imaginings in the first place.

In part, the complexity surrounding the process of translating the Gaelic songs allows Owenson to posit a new kind of relationship between the masculine and feminine in the *Hibernian Melodies.* Owenson associates the original songs with the productions of men. In the distant past, she suggests, it was the male bards who spread the "light of song" over "the gloom of unillumined ignorance."[38] Women were relegated to serving merely as inspiration, as in the case of "Ned of the Hill." Owenson notes that the original "Author, and the Hero" of this song was "an outlaw'd gentleman," "a warrior and poet," who took a woman, Eva, as his "*inspiration* and his *theme*."[39] In addition, Owenson's father, Robert Owenson, served as a contemporary male point of origin for the songs. In *Patriotic Sketches,* she discusses how she "caught from the paternal lip, the transmitted 'song of other times.'"[40] In the process of translating the songs, however, Owenson relocates them from these male points of origin to a female site as she makes them her own productions. In so doing, she also plays with the notion of originality contained in the title of the work. The "Original Hibernian Melodies" are "original" both in the sense that some of them are claimed as artifacts of an authentic bardic tradition that is male and in the sense that they are new creations written by a woman.

The songs, which are derived from men but translated by Owenson, all have male speakers, yet within them the voice of the woman character is extremely powerful. The collection begins immediately with a reference to a woman's voice: "Ah! who is that whose thrilling tones, / puts my tranquil sleep astray."[41] In "Oh tell me sweet Kate or Cathleen O'Tyrell," the voice becomes more ominous, as the speaker notes that "in thy voice in thy song lurks the dangerous spell."[42] In "As on the Wave, or The Mountain Sprite," the speaker is inspired to sing by the appearance of the fairy woman, but the sounds that she utters also cause his silence:

As near the charming phantom stole,
She paused to hear and hearing sighed;
Her sigh thrill'd o'er my very soul,
But oh! my song still murmuring died.[43]

Although he is moved to take up the harp and try singing again, the "breathing chords," mixed with the woman's "sweet accents," again render him mute:

Then bolder grown my strain I tried,
In harmony with her sweet lay;
But still my voice in murmurs died,
And every note would fade away.[44]

Similarly, in "My Love's the Fairest Creature or Shelah na Conolan," the speaker observes: "Her voice is like the soft strain, / Which steals its soul from passions [*sic*] dream."[45] The woman's voice is presented as overpowering the male speaker's ability to speak. In fact, Owenson presents a Chinese box of gendered voices which suggests an interrelation of the male and female spheres: the songs are written by Owenson, who assumes the perspective of a male speaker, who is ultimately controlled by a woman's voice. The songs, originally part of the public sphere of the male bardic circle, are translated by a woman into marketed sheet music designed primarily for domestic female consumption.

Owenson's depiction of the relation between male and female contexts also has implications for her representation of Irish identity. Commenting on Owenson's "complex" relationship with the "Anglicized Gaelic background of her father," Tom Dunne suggests that Owenson's attitude was "that of the sympathetic outsider," despite "being so close to the authentic Gaelic source":[46] "[W]hile her father's background gave her a romantic interest in the west of Ireland, her perspective on it was more that of Longford house, the residence of her [Anglo-Irish] Crofton relations, where she stayed while gathering materials for *The Wild Irish Girl*."[47] Leerssen, too, categorizes Owenson as a writer "whose perspective . . . is almost invariably non-Irish, tracing an approach *towards* Ireland from outside (rather than describing Ireland from within)."[48] Such readings of Owenson negate the subtle negotiations that Owenson does perform. She does more than gaze upon one tradition from the perspective of the other. She shows them to be interrelated in the process of imagining the nation.

Like Brooke before her, Owenson notes that the sound of Irish poetry bids "defiance to the adapting [*sic*] any other language to its melodies."[49] In Brooke's *Reliques,* this claim served to hybridize Irish identity. In Owenson's *Hibernian Melodies,* the woman's association with Erin and her mysterious voice suggest a female Gaelic Ireland that is constantly evading understanding. But Owenson associates the non-Gaelic world with the female too. The English translations are, as we have seen, associated with Owenson's own female voice and with drawing-room culture. Moreover, there is a middle ground on which Anglo-Irish and Gaelic interests can meet in Owenson's work. Brooke placed the Gaelic poetry and her English translations of them in direct opposition, including the Gaelic originals in a separate section in her book. Owenson excludes the Irish words, depicting instead a working conjunction of the "Hibernian Melodies" and the "English Words, imitated or translated from the Works of the Ancient Irish Bards." They are presented as inseparable from each other.

Moreover, Owenson is as concerned with using representations of Irish identity to revise gender roles as she is with using gender roles to revise conventional representations of Irish identity. Owenson foregrounds but also

questions the traditional association between woman and Ireland in the lyrics of the *Hibernian Melodies* themselves. Women serve as "inspiration and
theme," and all of the lyrics concern the relationship between a lover and a beloved. "When Floating O'er, or Cathleen Nolan" makes the relationship between woman and Ireland explicit, as the woman is described as having "Her
mantle of old Erins [*sic*] green" flung over her arm.[50] The speaker of the verses
concludes, "To me more splendidly she beams, / Then [*sic*] the proud Saxons
[*sic*] mighty king."[51] "Oh Farewell Dear Erin" (see figure 5.1) also connects the
woman, Eveline, with the nation, as the speaker notes his exile from both:

> Oh! farewell dear Erin my country adieu,
> And farewell my souls [*sic*] dearer Idol to you
> Tho' forc'd from my love and my country to part,
> yet Eveline and Erin still hold my sad heart.[52]

Similarly, in "Say Can'st Thou Oh Maid," Norah and Ireland are conflated,
as the speaker asks the woman to go into exile with him. "Open the Door
'Tis Your True Love" portrays a lover returning to both his beloved and his
nation: "Long was my absence and far have I strayed, / Still parted from Erin
and thee love."[53] His love for his beloved is associated with patriotic duty:

> When I fought for my Country its freedom and laws,
> My soul was still fired by thee love,
> I thought on my love and I conquered my foe,
> Then open the door to me love.[54]

Such depictions suggest an association between woman and the Irish nation
similar to that found in the *aisling* tradition in eighteenth-century Irish
poetry.

In all of the songs, however, the beloved is described as constantly vanishing. She is the "girl of the melting eye,"[55] who comes "floating o'er th' im-
pending steep . . . like the golden clouds"[56] or who appears "like a breeze."[57]
As a practitioner of "sorcery," a "fairy form,"[58] she is associated with ethereality, and the speaker's relationship with her is accordingly ephemeral. Either
the speaker is entranced by a woman he cannot call his own, or the woman is
dead, or, as in "Away with the Tear," the woman doubts the constancy of the
lover's affection. The final song concerns a woman who has betrayed her
lover. The relationship between lover and beloved is constantly in question
in the *Hibernian Melodies,* and this uncertainty suggests the limitation of the

Figure 5.1. Music and words for "Oh Farewell Dear Erin," from Sydney Owenson, *Twelve Original Hibernian Melodies* (London, 1805), p. 13. Courtesy of the National Library of Ireland.

conventional association between woman and the Irish nation. In essence, the lyrics of the *Hibernian Melodies* create a politics of the voice in direct opposition to a politics of the eye. Owenson presents a male speaker who attempts to control the object of his national gaze, the woman. In contrast, however, as we have seen, the voice of the woman in the songs overpowers the desires of the speaker, representing not just the resistance of the object of the gaze but a relocation of the basis on which the gaze's power is constructed. Where the politics of the gaze depends on a separation between the powerful observer and the powerless observed, Owenson's politics of the voice complicates such binary oppositions. Owenson confounds the association between woman and Ireland and so calls into question the basis of national representation.[59]

Owenson continues her challenges to the gendering of the nation in *The Wild Irish Girl*. Although she shifts from the medium of music to the medium of fiction, she continues to use music as a theme in her work. She describes her concerns about her right as a woman to write of national affairs in this novel in *Patriotic Sketches*, published three years after *The Wild Irish Girl*, noting that "I came to the self-devoted task, with a diffidence proportioned to the ardour which instigated me to the attempt; for, as a *woman*, a *young woman*, and an *Irish woman*; I felt all the delicacy of undertaking a work which had for the professed theme of its discussion, circumstances of national import, and national interest."[60] Despite this professed diffidence, she persevered and again succeeded in asserting a form of female "patriotism." Her particular variety of patriotism is discernable in the relationship between the novel's text and paratext, in its representation of Irish music, and in its portrayal of Ireland's colonial relationship with England.

In *Remembrance and Imagination*, Joep Leerssen indicates the importance of *The Wild Irish Girl*, suggesting that it "marks the introduction, the translation of the antiquarian iconography into Anglo-Irish literature."[61] Leerssen discusses the oppositional tension between the text and the footnotes, contending that "the narrative core text is the medium for the love story while the footnotes are the medium for discursive referential discourse."[62] His representation is not entirely accurate, however, as the narrative also contains a certain kind of "referential" discourse about Ireland that is mixed with sentimentalism. Likewise, the footnotes also provide a mixed discourse, as they combine antiquarian references with Owenson's own personal reminiscences. By depicting the interpenetration of sentimentalism and antiquarianism in both text and paratext, Owenson troubles the opposition between masculine and feminine constructions of the nation.

Far from constituting merely a "love story," the text of *The Wild Irish Girl* offers another way in which Owenson combines "sentiment" with "science." The narrative intermingles Horatio's sentimental and sublime descriptions of the Irish landscapes and the Princess of Inismore with references to actual antiquarian texts. Details of a specific antiquarian publication, for example, are included in the priest's diatribe about the Irish origin of the heroes of Macpherson's works: "Take then their history, as extracted from the book of Howth into the Transactions of the Royal Irish Academy in 1786."[63] Notably, it is a female character who best embodies the combination of the two discourses. Glorvina represents simultaneously both a sentimental and an antiquarian perspective on Ireland.

Glorvina is characterized by feeling, a consequence of what Horatio describes as her "naturalness." She is "tender-hearted for man or beast"[64] and described as "the most sensient of all created beings."[65] She also has the capacity to inspire others to feel deeply. Before Horatio comes into the presence of Glorvina, he describes himself as destitute of emotion: "[N]othing touches, nothing interests me."[66] This inability to feel is made literal as he actually becomes "bereft of sense"[67] when spying on the Inismore household. After meeting Glorvina, however, he begins to experience feelings "up to that vehement excess which forbade all expression, which left my tongue powerless, while my heart overflowed with emotion the most powerful."[68] Such emotions are "of a character, an energy, long unknown to my apathized feelings."[69] Glorvina awakens the sensibility that has lain dormant within Horatio.

Owenson most frequently conveys Glorvina's sensibility by associating her with music. Horatio observes: "She was created for a musician—there she is borne away by the magic of the art in which she excels, and the natural enthusiasm of her impassioned character. . . . The sensibility of her soul trembles in her song, and the expression of her rapt countenance harmonizes with her voice."[70] Avoiding the convention of woman as passive symbol, however, Owenson is careful to depict Glorvina as both active and passive, as in the scene in which Glorvina plays the tunes of Carolan: "Wrapt in her charming avocation, she seemed borne away by the magic of her own numbers, and thus inspired and inspiring as she appeared, faithful, as the picture it formed was interesting, I took her likeness. Conceive for a moment a form full of character, and full of grace, bending over an instrument singularly picturesque."[71] Glorvina here is both "inspired and inspiring."[72] She is a "picture" of sentimental virtue, but at the same time she is an accomplished musician herself. Owenson's descriptions of Glorvina are modeled on representations of a sentimental and feminized Carolan such as those discussed at the end of chapter 1: "The expression of the divinely touching countenance breathed all the fervour of genius under the influence of inspiration, and the contours of the face, from the peculiar uplifted position of the head, were precisely such, as lends to painting the happiest line of feature, and shade of colouring."[73]

But in addition to representing sentiment, Glorvina is the spokesperson of sober antiquarian discourse, delivering extensive speeches on Irish music, dress, and culture. She notes, for example, sounding herself a little like a footnote, that: "we learn from musical record, that the first piece of music ever seen in *score*, in Great Britain, is an air sung time immemorial in this county on the opening of summer—an air which, though animated in its measure, yet still, like all the Irish melodies, breathes the very soul of melancholy."[74] She indicates her own close relationship with an actual antiquarian artifact when she comments that her harp is "precisely the same form as that preserved in the Irish university, which belonged to one of the most celebrated of our heroes, Brian Boru."[75] Her representation of antiquarian discourse is further suggested by her association with Irish texts, specifically those found in the Earl of M—'s Lodge. His secret library, containing books "related to the language, history, and antiquities of Ireland,"[76] is also Glorvina's literal point of origin: she was born in "the rooms where my Lord keeps his books."[77]

A combination of sentiment and antiquarian discourse similar to that found in the narrative is also found in the footnotes. Leerssen traces three sources for the footnotes: antiquarian discourse, sentimental comedy, and travel writing.[78] But in fact much of the material for the footnotes comes from Owenson's own life, which is conveyed in conventional terms of sensibility. Whereas Glorvina represents the intermixture of sensibility and antiquarian discourse in the narrative, Owenson herself embodies this intermixture in the footnotes. The first footnote in the book, regarding the scene that Horatio describes upon his arrival at Dublin Bay, inserts the author's presence at once into the book as someone who is an afficionado of the sublime: "This little marine sketch is by no means a fancy picture; it was actually copied from the life, in the summer of 1805."[79] While a number of footnotes are taken from sources such as O'Halloran, Walker, Ledwich, and Young, they are mingled with scenes from Owenson's biography. We learn from the footnotes, for example, all about Owenson's experiences in an Irish hovel,[80] her encounter with a character like Murtoch,[81] her grandmother's life,[82] and her father's account of meeting the Fanny Power made famous by O'Carolan's tune.[83]

In one instance, she includes a footnote to a footnote. In this "meta-footnote" she includes material that personalizes the first footnote. Regarding the theory that the Irish obtained the harp from Scandinavia, Owenson says: "The supposition is advanced by Dr. Ledwich, but neither among the 'Sons of Song,' or [sic] by those of the interior part of the island, who are guided in their faith by 'tradition's volubly transmitting tongue,' could I ever find *one* to agree in the supposition."[84] She further quotes Percy's "Essay on Ancient Minstrels" from the *Reliques of Ancient English Poetry* and his etymological argument for the word *harp* being Gothic, but she says that "the national *Lyre of Erin*" claims a "title independent of a Gothic origin," being known as a *clarseach,* which is closer to the Greek cithera or Hebrew chinor "than the Anglo-Saxon harp."[85] The word *harp* in this footnote becomes an excuse for a further footnote, in which Owenson mentions playing Spanish guitar for the peasants: "A few months back the Author having played the Spanish guitar in the hearing of some Connaught peasants, they called it a *clarseach beg,* or little harp."[86] In contrast with the impersonal footnotes found in Walker and other antiquarians, Owenson inserts her personality—and her gender—into the paratext. She combines the antiquarian discourse conventionally associated with footnotes of scholarly texts (and with a male perspective) with her own personal experiences as a woman. Leerssen suggests that in Owenson's footnotes, eighteenth-century antiquarians like "Charles Vallancey, Joseph Cooper Walker, Sylvester O'Halloran or Thomas Campbell" make "their last discernible presence in the realm of literature, perhaps, before they disappear from sight under new sediments and in a new stratification of discursive practice."[87] For Leerssen, *The Wild Irish Girl* "marks the introduction, the translation of the antiquarian iconography into Anglo-Irish literature."[88] But Owenson is not just translating one medium into another. She is hybridizing the two.

Owenson's conflation of antiquarian discourse and sentiment in her fictional character and in her authorial voice allows her to treat the subject of music in a manner quite different from that found in Walker and other antiquarian writers. Owenson relies heavily on Walker, incorporating into her narrative some of the tunes he included in the final appendix of his *Historical Memoirs*. At times, she makes her debt to Walker explicit. When Horatio is traveling through the Irish countryside, he notes that "[n]othing could be more wildly sweet than the whistle or song of the ploughman or labourer as we passed along; it was of so singular a nature, that I frequently paused to catch it; it is a species of voluntary recitative, and so melancholy, that every plaintive note breathes on the heart of the auditor a tale of hopeless despondency or incurable woe."[89] In the footnote to this passage, Owenson comments, "Mr. Walker . . . has given a specimen of the Irish plough-tune, and adds, 'While the Irish ploughman drives his team, and the female peasant milks her cow, they warble a succession of wild notes which bid defiance to the rules of composition, yet are inexpressibly sweet.'"[90] At other times, she borrows from Walker without comment. The "wild and plaintive melody" that Murtoch sings is identified as "the lamentation of the poor Irish for the loss of their *glibbs*, or long tresses, of which they were deprived by the arbitrary will of Henry VIII."[91] Walker used the story behind this song as an example of Irish resistance to English law and included the tune in his appended collection.[92] Owenson writes of this tune merely that "[t]he Cualin is one of the most beautiful and popular Irish airs extant" without acknowledging her source.[93]

But, as we saw in chapter 2, Walker's narrative was subject to the comments of critics like Burney who objected to his praise of Irish culture and music. Owenson, on the other hand, is able to script disagreements into her text and rework the outcome in her narrative. In one scene, for example, Glorvina comments on her "national enthusiasm" for her "national music": "[M]uch indeed do we stand indebted to the most charming of all the sciences for the eminence it has obtained us; for in *music only*, do *you* English allow us poor Irish any superiority; and therefore your King, who made the *harp* the armorial bearing of Ireland, perpetuated our former musical celebrity beyond the power of time or prejudice to destroy it."[94] Horatio suppresses a verbal response to this comment but thinks to himself that "we [English] thought as little of the music of her country, as of every thing else which related to it; and that all we knew of the style of its melodies, reached us through the false medium of comic airs, sung by some popular actor, who, in coincidence with his author, caricatures those national traits he attempts to delineate."[95] His remarks in fact echo those of Walker: "Nothing can argue a great insensibility to pure melody in the English, than their disrelish for Irish music: amongst that people our best airs, so admired by foreigners, are hardly known."[96] But the fictional medium of *The Wild Irish Girl* allows Glorvina to win the debate as Owenson shows the power that Irish music actually has over Horatio. His arguments are rendered invalid by Glorvina's playing and singing. Glorvina's performance is shown as an embodiment of the kind of observations regarding the power of Irish music that writers from Giraldus to Bunting had made: "[H]er round and sighing voice modulated in unison with each expression it harmonized."[97] The reader sees the literal impression which the music has upon Horatio as he is moved beyond words: "Who dares to translate the language of the soul, which the eye only can express? . . . What a sublime assemblage of images!"

In Walker, music is a masculine and public tradition. In *The Wild Irish Girl*, the force of music is depicted as at once personal and political, private and public. The "plaintive notes" of the plowman's tune convey not just his own situation, but that of Ireland in general. Glorvina explains the way music affects the individual: "The susceptibility to the influence of my country's music, discovered itself in a period of existence, when no associating sentiment of the heart could have called it into being; for I have often wept in convulsive emotion at an air, before the sad story it accompanied was understood."[98] But this personal sentiment is later connected with a political understanding. The conflation of the two, the personal and the political, is evident in the scene in which Horatio sees the Prince listening to the harp music "which at once spoke to the heart of the father, the patriot, and the man—breathed from the chords of his country's emblem—breathed in the pathos of his country's music—breathed from the lips of his apparently inspired daughter."[99] Music, as presented in *The Wild Irish Girl*, is a form of patriotic sentiment that unites the "politics" of the male sphere with the "sentiment" of the female sphere. Glorvina notes that she learns her songs from a combination of female and male sources, her nurse and her father: "Long before I could read, I learned on the bosom of my nurse, and in my father's arms, to recite the songs of our national bards."[100]

Owenson also uses the confusion of gender divisions in the *Wild Irish Girl* to comment on the issue of Ireland's relationship to England. Glorvina, as the harp-playing "wild Irish girl," symbolizes Gaelic Ireland. Horatio calls her "thy country's muse, and the bright model of the genuine character of her daughters, when unvitiated by erroneous education, and by those fatal prejudices which lead them to seek in foreign refinement for those talents, those graces, those virtues, which are no where to be found more flourishing, more attractive, than in their native land."[101] Glorvina's marriage to Horatio rather than to his father suggests on one level the rejection of a paternalistic relationship with England in favor of a political union that includes more equality and respect.[102] This connection between the characters and the larger political situation is suggested in Horatio's comment: "I perceive my father emulates the policy of the British Legislature, and delegates English ministers to govern his Irish domains."[103] The father's blessing also suggests a union of equals:

[L]et the names of Inismore and M— be inseparably blended, and the distinctions of English and Irish, of Protestant and Catholic, for ever buried. And, while you look forward with hope to this family alliance being prophetically typical of a national unity of interests and affections

between those who may be factiously severed, but who are naturally allied, lend your *own individual efforts* towards the consummation of an event
so devoutly to be wished by every liberal mind, by every benevolent
heart.[104]

But Owenson also complicates this symbolic representation of a union
between Ireland and England. For one thing, with one exception, she never
gives the reader an impression of Glorvina that is not mediated by Horatio's
vision of her.[105] We see her almost exclusively through Horatio's or his father's
letters, and what becomes evident is the way Horatio frames her throughout
the narrative. Horatio describes his first glance of the Prince and Glorvina as
"some pictured story of romantic fiction."[106] He talks about it in pictorial
terms: the scene is completed as the figure of the nurse "finished the picture."[107] Glorvina at the harp also appears "framed": by the casement at first,
then by "the vista of a huge folding door, partly thrown back."[108] It is not co-
incidental that Horatio assumes the identity of "an itinerant artist,"[109] as he
is constantly representing what he perceives. Even at the point where Glorvina, having control of a canvas, is positioned in the role of artist, she is
turned into a represented subject. On a blank canvas, Glorvina inscribes
Horatio's false name and the time of his arrival at the castle. Subsequently, he
draws her on the paper, with an inscription: "'Twas thus Apelles bask'd in
beauty's blaze, / Nor felt the danger of the stedfast gaze."[110]
    Just as he frames Glorvina, Horatio also frames Ireland, choosing the
way he will perceive it. He describes Ireland in terms of works of art: "Every
feature that constitutes either the beauty or the sublime of landscape is here
finely combined."[111] Dublin is different from London, he notes, but still a
"miniature copy of our imperial original."[112] The situation is made even more
complex by the fact that Horatio's descriptions of Glorvina and of Ireland are
being presented to us by Owenson herself, who occupies an ambiguous position in terms of both national affiliation and gender. She is linked both to
Horatio by virtue of "possessing" and arranging his letters and to Glorvina
by the fact that she has made her heroine embody aspects of herself. Owenson writes, for example, that Glorvina inherited her name from her mother,
"who obtained the appellation of *Glorvina,* from the sweetness of her voice,"[113]
and she notes that her own "grandmother was known in the neighbourhood
where she resided . . . by the apellative [*sic*] of *Clarseach na Vallagh,* or, the *Village
Harp*; for the superiority of her musical abilities."[114] In contrast to Leerssen's
argument that the book's leading desire is "to represent a Real Ireland whose
identity is untainted by foreign presence,"[115] I would argue that Owenson is

making the point that it is impossible to gain an image of a "Real Ireland." Representations of Ireland are always mediated by the desirer's gaze.

To emphasize this point, Owenson deliberately foregrounds the self-conscious and mediated nature of Horatio's imaginings. Arriving at the Castle of Inismore just as the sun is setting to hear vespers, he comments, "And surely, Fancy, in her boldest flight, never gave to the fairy vision of poetic dreams, a combination of images more poetically fine, more strikingly picturesque, or more impressively touching."[116] He himself suggests that it is partly the situation that is affecting his perception of Glorvina: "[W]ith what indifference I should have met her in the drawing-room, or at the Opera!—there she would have been merely a woman!—here, she is the fairy vision of my heated fancy."[117] Owenson most clearly articulates the slipperiness of Horatio's image of Glorvina, and of Ireland, in the incident of the nightmare, where Horatio's subconscious figuring of Glorvina as Gorgon acts as the logical reversal of his romantic exoticization of her:[118] "[W]hile the sound of the Irish harp arose from the hall below, and the nurse muttered her prayers in Irish over her beads by my side, I fell into a gentle slumber, in which I dreamed that the Princess of Inismore approached my bed, drew aside the curtains, and raising her veil, discovered a face I had hitherto rather guessed at, than seen. Imagine my horror—it was the face, the head, of a *Gorgon!*"[119] When he wakes up, the "horrid spectre of my recent dream" becomes "the form of a cherub hovering near my pillow."[120] Gorgon or cherub, Glorvina is figured as other to the English self. The dangerous nature of this other is also suggested at other times in the text. Horatio claims that it is Glorvina's voice that drew him up to the castle to look: "the voice of a syren!"[121] He calls this incident the "decline, and fall, of my physical empire."[122]

It is Glorvina's voice, too, that Owenson ultimately draws on to complicate the allegory of union between Ireland and England that the novel represents. As in the *Hibernian Melodies,* in *The Wild Irish Girl,* Owenson provides an alternative to the politics of the gaze, in this case not the national gaze, but the colonial gaze. In the penultimate section of the novel, written from the perspective of a third-person narrator, Owenson reinforces the impossibility of the reader's ever gaining a true perception of Ireland. This is the only section of the novel in which the reader does not see events through Horatio's eyes. It is a telling segment, for in contrast to Horatio and his father, who are presented as seeking and obtaining verbal explanations that will enable them to understand the truth, and therefore gain power over the situation, Glorvina is presented as nonrational. She is described as "shriek[ing],"[123] overcome with grief,[124] "mad" and maniacal,[125] or, most frequently, "lifeless."[126]

Owenson suggests that it is primarily Horatio's representations, symbolic of the colonizing power in Ireland, that are responsible for the image of the Irish nation in *The Wild Irish Girl*. But for a fleeting moment we have an indication of a Glorvina who is not framed by the gaze of the colonizer—and this Glorvina is represented not visually but orally.[127] Like the voices of the women portrayed in *Hibernian Melodies*, Glorvina's voice is powerful. In her famous essay "Can the Subaltern Speak?" Gayatri Spivak postulates that "[i]f in the context of colonial production, the subaltern has no history and cannot speak, the subaltern as female is even more deeply in shadow."[128] In Owenson's text, Glorvina herself does not and cannot speak; she is described as "inarticulate."[129] Nevertheless, her inarticulate ravings—and her body—speak louder than words, serving to resist the desire of the colonizer for knowledge of the other. Owenson deliberately relocates the androcentric terms of national construction out of the all too familiar terrain of the gaze to a new site, or rather, a new sense: orality. The last section of *The Wild Irish Girl* also suggests this relocation of the basis of power from vision to bodily noise. As a result of Glorvina's shrieking and ravings, the reader becomes aware of the distinction between the voice of Glorvina and Horatio's vision of her. While *The Wild Irish Girl* ends by allegorizing a union between England and Ireland in the marriage of Glorvina and Horatio, the text itself questions this harmonious conclusion, as it questions both the colonizing and desiring gaze that has mediated the image of the Irish nation presented in the novel.

By breaking down distinctions between the masculine and feminine and by representing Irishness as a constantly mediated phenomenon, Owenson's work serves to reconfigure both the Irish national imaginary and the colonial relationship between Ireland and England. Music as both event and theme is crucial to this project. But Owenson's own use of Irish music to perform national identity complicated the effects of that reconfiguration. According to her *Memoirs*, with money from her first novel, *The Novice of St. Dominic*, she bought herself a costume: "The first purchases she made for herself out of her literary earnings were an Irish harp, from [John] Egan (a Dublin harp maker), and a black mode cloak."[130] Equipped with these national "signs" and eventually taking on the name of the heroine of *The Wild Irish Girl*, she set out to represent Irishness to the English by playing the harp at gatherings of friends and acquaintances. In a letter to a friend, she registers an awareness of herself as a national representative in a foreign land: "I must tell you that my Irish melodies are doing wonders in London, and that I have published a song at Holden's, Parliament Street, dedicated to Lady Charlotte Homan."[131] Owenson's reliance on Irishness as costume and as performance can on the one hand be read as a counterbalance to views of Irishness as a set of racial characteristics.[132] However, her representations of Irishness as performance also merged into representations of Irishness as commodity, as Owenson, her book, and her paraphernalia became consumer items on English markets. The *Wild Irish Girl* went through seven editions in two years. Ian Dennis notes that it "launched a craze" for Wild Irish Girl paraphernalia: "Gaelic accessories and a Wild Irish Look helped create the disposable identity of the moment, a commodified romantic femininity with a Celtic Twilight flavour."[133] Owenson promoted the consumption of Irish harps by gentry—both Irish and British—living in England. Charlotte Milligan Fox notes that Lady Abercorn wrote to Owenson upon receiving a harp that she had been sent: "Your harp is arrived, and for the honour of Ireland, I must tell you, is very much admired and quite beautiful. Lady Aberdeen [her married daughter] played on it for an hour last night, and thought it very good. . . . Pray tell poor Egan I shall show it off to the best advantage, and I sincerely hope he will have many orders in consequence."[134] As Barra Boydell points out, however, Egan's harps "had little in common with their forbears."[135] They were painted green with "golden, painted shamrocks"; rather than being authentic, they were "a reinvention" designed to represent Irishness.[136] Owenson encouraged a representation of the Irish harping tradition that was an invention of the market for Irish exoticism.

She also promoted the sales of other pieces of Irishness. The name by which Owenson performed, "Glorvina," came to designate a "golden bodkin for fastening up the hair, after the pattern of an antique Irish ornament," according to Owenson's *Memoirs*.[137] Mary Campbell discusses the "Glorvina" craze: "Ladies in the vice-regal court were now wearing their hair held in place by golden bodkins, as worn by Glorvina. Dublin jewellers were competing with each other in turning these out, and thus putting up the price of Irish gold. The drapers were advertising the 'Glorvina' mantle, a scarlet cloak, as a companion for the ornament."[138] Owenson helped promote the display of Ireland in upper-class English Regency homes. In addition, Owenson herself became something of a commodity, selling an image of Ireland as she performed on her harp. Despite her sincere efforts on behalf of Catholic Ireland, Owenson provided the means through which Irishness became a consumer product after the Union. It would be another figure, however, who was responsible for the mass consumption of Ireland. The popularity of Owenson, with her green and gold harps and her golden glorvinas, faded into the background as middle-class Irish and English consumers turned eagerly to the *Irish Melodies* of Thomas Moore.

6

A "Truly National" Project

Thomas Moore's *Irish Melodies* and the Gendering of the British Cultural Marketplace

In a letter to John Stevenson, printed in the first volume of the *Irish Melodies* (1808), Thomas Moore announced his excitement over the "truly National" project that he was undertaking: reclaiming Irish songs that had, "like too many of our countrymen, passed into the service of foreigners."[1] Daniel O'Connell's speech at a meeting of the Dublin Political Union indicates his confidence that the *Melodies* fulfilled this nationalist function: "I attribute much of the present state of feeling, and the desire for liberty in Ireland to the works of that immortal man [Moore]—he has brought patriotism into the private circles of domestic life."[2] Several British journals, including *Blackwood's* and the *New Monthly Magazine*, confirmed the politically subversive nature of Moore's work by labeling it "mischievous," "a vehicle of dangerous politics," and "jacobinical." But despite their protestations, Moore was extremely popular east of the Irish Channel. He eventually made more than twenty thousand pounds for his literary endeavors in England.[3] The publication of the ten volumes of the *Melodies* from 1808 to 1834 coincided with a period of intense debate about the Irish, particularly the Irish Catholic, question in the Westminster Parliament. English consumers of the *Melodies* had the issue of Ireland foregrounded for them in the daily papers during this time.[4] Moore's representation of Ireland in the *Melodies* was able to perform seemingly contradictory activities. It inspired O'Connell and the radical writers of the *Nation* in their quest for cultural nationalism and repeal of the Act of Union. At the same time it made Ireland consumable in English parlors where, although there may have been sympathy for the Irish, there was no question of accepting Irish Home Rule.[5] Moreover, as we will see, the political ambiguity that surrounds the *Melodies* was further complicated by their critical reception in relation to contemporary concerns about gender and the market.

Moore's earliest work indicates his sympathies for the 1798 Rebellion.[6] He began his writing career in Ireland while at Trinity College when he published several nationalistic articles in the *Press*, a journal operated by Arthur

O'Connor and Thomas Addis Emmet. His article of December 2, 1797, admonishes his fellow students to "show these ministerial minions [the university administration] . . . that Ireland has Sons untutored in the school of corruption, who love her Liberties, and, in the crisis, will die for them."[7] His next piece was a prose effusion in the style of Ossian: "O! children of Erin! you're robbed: why not rouse from your slumber of Death? Oh! Why not assert her lov'd cause, and strike off her chains and your own, and hail her to freedom and peace?"[8] He also published several translations in the periodical *Hibernica*. Harry White notes the close connection between politics and music that informed Moore's sensibility at this time, encouraged as he was by Emmet and by Edward Hudson, two United Irishmen: "It was Hudson who introduced Moore to Bunting's collection and to Irish music generally, in 1797. It was Emmet to whom Moore played from the collection, exciting the apocryphal response: 'Oh, that I were at the head of twenty thousand men marching to that air.'"[9]

The *Irish Melodies*, the first volume of which appeared in 1808, are, on one level, an extension of Moore's earlier concerns to encourage nationalist sympathies. But this objective is tempered by the facts surrounding the works' publication: the *Melodies* were conceived from the beginning by their publishers to appeal to an English market. Moore's case illustrates the complexities that occurred as Irish music became involved in the developing system of commodification of culture in Britain. It exemplifies how the English market system determined the fate of Irish music and, subsequently, the Irish national image that music helped to create. Moore's success as a writer did not occur until he moved to London. There he gained the favor of Lord Moira and received permission from the Prince of Wales to dedicate his translations of the *Odes of Anacreon* (1800) to him. This patronage assured Moore's popularity on the English market as a protege of the prince. In a letter to his mother dated June 6, 1801, Moore indicates the importance he places on the English market and English criticism in comparison to their Irish counterparts: "My little poems are very much admired here [in London]. . . . You cannot imagine how much my name is gone about here; even of those poems my bookseller sells at the rate of 20 copies a day; and the shabby demand of Ireland for 50 copies . . . will surely appear very contemptible to this."[10] Moore's concern with the marketing of his work is visible here, as he contrasts the "shabby demand" of Ireland for his books with his immense popularity in London.

The two Irishmen who published the *Melodies*, James and William Power, makers of military instruments, were originally inspired by the success of collections of Scottish melodies with English words such as James Johnson's *Scots Musical Museum* (1787–1803) and George Thomson's *Select Collection of Original Scotish [sic] Airs for Voice* (1793–1818). In an attempt to capitalize on the contemporary interest both in folksong and in pianoforte music, the Powers contracted John Stevenson to arrange a number of Irish melodies for the piano. Initially intending to feature several poets as lyricists, they approached Moore to write lyrics for the first edition. What is crucial to understand here is how the dictates of the English market determined Moore's selection as lyricist for the prospective *Irish Melodies*. The Powers did not choose Moore because of his dedication to or experience with authentic Irish material; although Moore had applied to help Edward Bunting with later volumes of his *General Collection of the Ancient Irish Music*, he had been turned down. Rather, the Powers selected Moore because his translations of classical material, the *Odes of Anacreon* and his *Epistles, Odes and Other Poems* (1806) had caught the interest of a British readership. Subsequently, the acclaim with which the public greeted the first volume of the *Melodies* with Moore's lyrics made the Powers settle on him as sole author for the remaining volumes. The *Melodies* were produced from the beginning to meet the desires of an English as well as an Irish reading public.

James Power purchased the copyright of the first number of the *Melodies* from Moore for fifty pounds. Veronica ní Chinnéide notes that with the volume's great success, James and William Power settled with Moore to pay him five hundred pounds a year to produce an annual volume for the next seven years.[11] Part of Moore's contract of five hundred pounds per year included his performance of the *Melodies* in English parlors. He came to represent Ireland for the English, and his popularity in England in turn affected his reputation in Ireland. In a gesture that suggests the importation of English values to the Irish cultural arena, Lord Moira proposed creating for Moore the position of Irish Poet Laureate. Even more suggestive of the power that England exercised over Irish artists is the fact that Moore rejected the offer because he preferred to wait for "advancement under the government [in Westminster]."[12] He believed that the position of Irish Poet Laureate would bring him less of an income and preclude him from accepting a more lucrative English political position. Moore's expectation was that Lord Moira's connections with the prince would prove useful. When the prince, upon assuming the role of regent, decided to retain the Tory ministry, Moore's hopes for preferment were dashed.[13] Nevertheless, after 1811, Moore lived in England, making only the occasional visit back to Ireland. The patronage possibilities had fallen through for him, but he was still dependent on the English market for his success.[14]

The poems in the *Melodies* that seem, paradoxically, to espouse an English perspective can be attributed to Moore's attempt to woo Moira. "The Prince's Day," for example, was written in celebration of the Prince of Wales' birthday. The poem advises that the Irish can be loyal followers if treated fairly: "Tho' fierce to your foes, to your friends you are true."[15] It suggests that, if summoned, the Irish will "cast every bitter remembrance away, / And show what the arm of old Erin has in it, / When roused by the foe, on her Prince's Day."[16] The poem's monarchical sympathies are understandable considering that at the time Moore wrote this piece he was still expecting preferment from the prince and aid for the Irish cause.

The fight between the Power brothers regarding the publication location of the *Melodies* is a further example of the considerable influence of the London market on Irish publishing. The Powers first agreed to publish two simultaneous editions of the *Melodies*: one in Dublin, where William resided, and one in London, where James lived. The Dublin edition appeared first. But, as Miriam De Ford notes, because London was the more important publishing center, "James Power (and Moore with him) came to think of the growing series as his property."[17] As early as 1813, the brothers were in dispute about the copyright of the *Melodies*.[18] Although William was granted a renewal of the copyright in 1815, James filed a bill in the Irish court of chancery "to compel William to give him the exclusive right to sell the *Melodies* in Great Britain."[19] An arbitration was attempted, but James did not accept the decision. In July 1817, William sued James in London for five thousand pounds. An eventual compromise was reached, but the situation still proved troublesome. James won the right to publish the rest of the volumes of the *Melodies* on the condition that he send copy to William. He did so for volume 7, but not for the rest, and William took to pirating the remaining editions. Moore's letters to James Power indicate his concern about public opinion on his role in the matter. He fears that "the world should suspect I stood quietly by, *taking advantage of the dissention of two brothers,* and *leaving* to the side that *it is* most for my *interest.*"[20] He indicates his own sense that the agreed settlement was unfair to William: "I certainly feel it due to candour to declare that I think he has every right to the sort of arrangement he demands, and that however we may be borne out by the *bond* in resisting him, we shall never stand clear in the code of honour & fairness for it."[21] Nevertheless, in the ensuing battle, Moore supported James, who had the best access to the English market, and continued to send James the words for subsequent editions of the *Melodies*. The settlement of the editorial seat of power in London also resulted in another displacement of Irish by English interests, as James Power contracted Henry

Rowley Bishop, an Englishman, to arrange the melodies instead of the Irish Stevenson, who had sided with William in the dispute.[22]

Though the publication history of the *Melodies* situates them so firmly within the English market for culture, the *Melodies* in their original form also served to resist the homogenizing effects of that culture. Moore's earlier college pieces asserted an Irish identity reliant on an ideology of nationalism that, in David Lloyd's terms was identical with an imperial ideology in its attempt to posit "a transcendent realm of essential identity."[23] But the *Melodies*, although clearly embedded within the structures of an English market, also represent an attempt to break out of the imitative pattern of colonial nationalism. Instead of appealing to an idea of the nation as a homogeneous group, they depict the Irish nation as a site of contestation and hybridization, much like the eighteenth-century publications of Irish music like the Neals'. Terry Eagleton suggests that Moore's poems work to "distil the pure essence of national feeling" by "loosening up the relations between signified and signifier."[24] According to Eagleton, the poems themselves approach the condition of music that is "a kind of discourse beyond signification."[25] I would argue, however, that, far from constituting a "discourse beyond signification," music does in fact signify much: it is overdetermined rather than indeterminate. Accordingly, I suggest that the tunes in Moore's *Melodies* as they were originally published played an extremely important part in constructing their political meaning.

In contrast to Bunting before him and Petrie after him, Moore is not concerned with identifying his immediate source for the tunes with which he works. Ní Chinnéide suggests that tunes from the *Melodies* derive from both printed and manuscript sources, with the majority coming from printed sources. In fact, most of the tunes Moore used came from Bunting's collection.[26] In addition, music in manuscript form was sent to him by James Kelly, Thomas Crofton Croker, George Petrie, William Crotch, and William Power. But the particulars of attribution have been discovered only through the efforts of recent scholarship.[27] Moore himself was not trying to construct a genealogy that would connect the *Melodies* to the work of his contemporaries. He mentions the efforts of Bunting and Owenson only briefly in the first volume of the *Melodies*—and then only as an afterthought.[28] Nor was he concerned with establishing the authenticity of the tunes. Rather, he was more intent on representing them as a generally known body of material, a body of material that was hybrid by nature.

The one genealogical connection that Moore did seek to make was to Carolan. Volume 1 begins with four pieces of music without words, two of

which, "Carolan's Concerto" and "Planxty Drury," are by Carolan. But Carolan for Moore is himself a figure of hybridity. In his "Prefatory Letter on
Music" addressed to the Marchioness Dowager of Donegal and prefixed to
the third volume of the *Melodies,* Moore depicts Carolan as a figure of an Ireland already invaded. Carolan, Moore suggests, recollects a time "when our
poor countrymen were driven to worship their God in caves, or to quit forever the land of their birth—like the bird that abandons the nest which
human touch has violated."[29] As I argued in chapter 4, Moore identified the
true essence of Irish music with the time of colonization, while Bunting
sought to locate Irish music in a time before colonization. Moore comments
on the relative youth of the material that he claims is "truly national," asserting that the tunes that best characterize the Irish nation did not come into
existence until after the mid–sixteenth century: "[I]t is certain that our finest airs are modern."[30] But it is precisely because these moments of conflict
also symbolize moments of hybridization that they become so valuable for
Moore. Irishness, for Moore, is a state of tension and translation rather than
a static state of authenticity. Moore's volumes, as they appear in the original
editions, highlight this idea of dynamic encounter, as they represent overlap-
ping layers of meaning. The cover illustrations, the music, and the lyrics of
the *Melodies* represent an Ireland characterized by tension and ambiguity.

Each volume of the *Melodies* appeared with a different cover. Volume 1
features a harp against the background of a landscape with a ruined fortress
(figure 6.1). The background itself can be interpreted variously. As Anne
Janowitz suggests:

> Though the spectacle of ruins in the landscape offers evidence of a na-
> tion possessed of a long history, the materials that ruinists draw on to
> make figures may produce different meanings within some other group's
> imagination. . . . Martello towers assert to the Irish the continuous and
> material presence of English domination. So, too, the evidence of ruined
> castles may remind those in opposition to central government that there
> has been a time when government was neither central nor uncontested.[31]

The blasted Irish oak in the middle ground is a similarly ambiguous image.
The top part of the tree appears to be dead, its main trunk cut off and without leaves, but there is a side branch that appears strong and vigorous. The
harp in the foreground emphasizes this vigor, as its bow curves in the direction of the living branch. This harp is positioned directly in the center of the
page and, because of the peculiar angle of the bottom corners, appears oddly

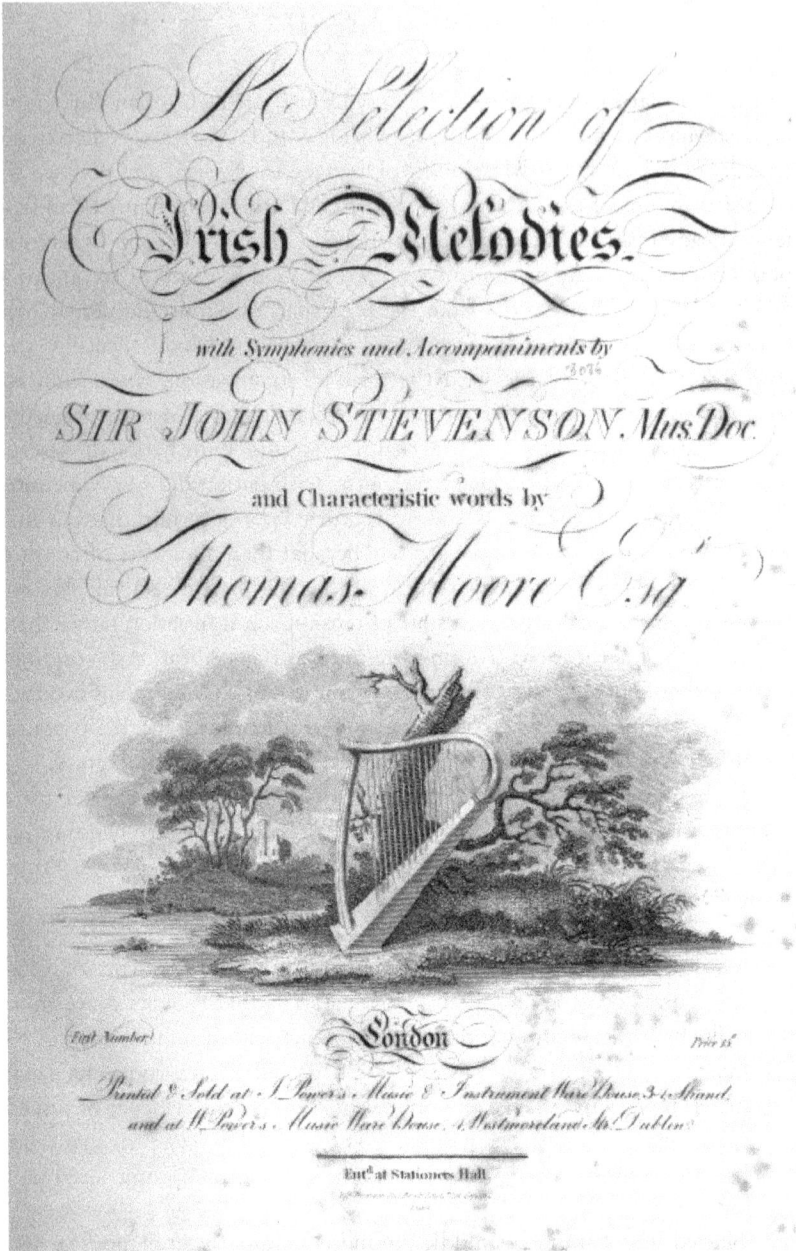

Figure 6.1. Title page of Thomas Moore, *A Selection of Irish Melodies, with Symphonies and Accompaniments by Sir John Stevenson* . . . (London: J. Power's [1808–1815]), vol. 1 ("First Number of First Volume"). Reproduced from the original held by the Department of Special Collections of the University Libraries of Notre Dame.

to be rising out of the ground. Whereas the harps that adorned Bunting's collection were designed to represent antiquarian objects, Moore's harp is a new model. Moore himself cannot have been unconscious of the connection between the harp and the United Irishmen, and volume 1 of the *Melodies* resonates with the unspoken slogan: "It Is New Strung and Shall Be Heard." Volume 1 depicts a defeated Ireland, a picturesque ruin, alongside an image of the nation's resurrection.

The images on the covers of subsequent volumes also suggest similar readings in tension. Like volume 1, volume 2 depicts a landscape with ruins, but the focal point on the cover of the second volume is not a harp but a bardic figure with a harp. While the bard's long white beard and his position against the ruins suggest he is an ancient Ossianic figure, this image is countered by the exposure of a powerful, well-muscled, and young leg from beneath the robes, directly under his harp. On the cover of volume 3 a female figure representing Ireland rests with a pen in hand against an upright harp. Her hand clenches a rolled-up parchment, and she appears either to have just set down or to be about to pick up her spear, shield, and helmet. The images on the fourth volume are even more assertive. A female Ireland is crowning the bard, who this time appears more youthful. She has now picked up her spear, on the end of which is hanging a Phrygian cap, symbol of revolutionary France (figure 6.2). The covers of the *Melodies,* then, produce a dynamic blend of different kinds of identities for Ireland. Nostalgic and contemporary, passive and active images of the Irish nation are represented together.

The multiple titles in the original volumes of the *Melodies* also suggest alternate identities for the Irish nation. Moore supplied new titles for the tunes to represent his new lyrics, but he also made sure that the titles of the original airs appeared directly below the new titles. That this multiple labeling was of great concern to him is evident from a letter he wrote to James Power in 1815, asking to be supplied with the title of "Has Sorrow Thy Young Days" because "I have just hunted through all my music for Kelly's book and cannot find it."[32] The original titles are presented as either English titles (many of which are translations from original Irish titles) or approximations of Gaelic. Ní Chinnéide writes: "Where titles are given they prove to have been copied fairly faithfully, including those that, being written in a rough phonetic script intended to represent the original Irish, may have presented some difficulty, e.g., 'Thamama hulla' or 'Cummilum.'"[33] The fact that Moore includes the original tune titles for his songs suggests his concern with including traces of the musical past in his present construction of Irish identity.

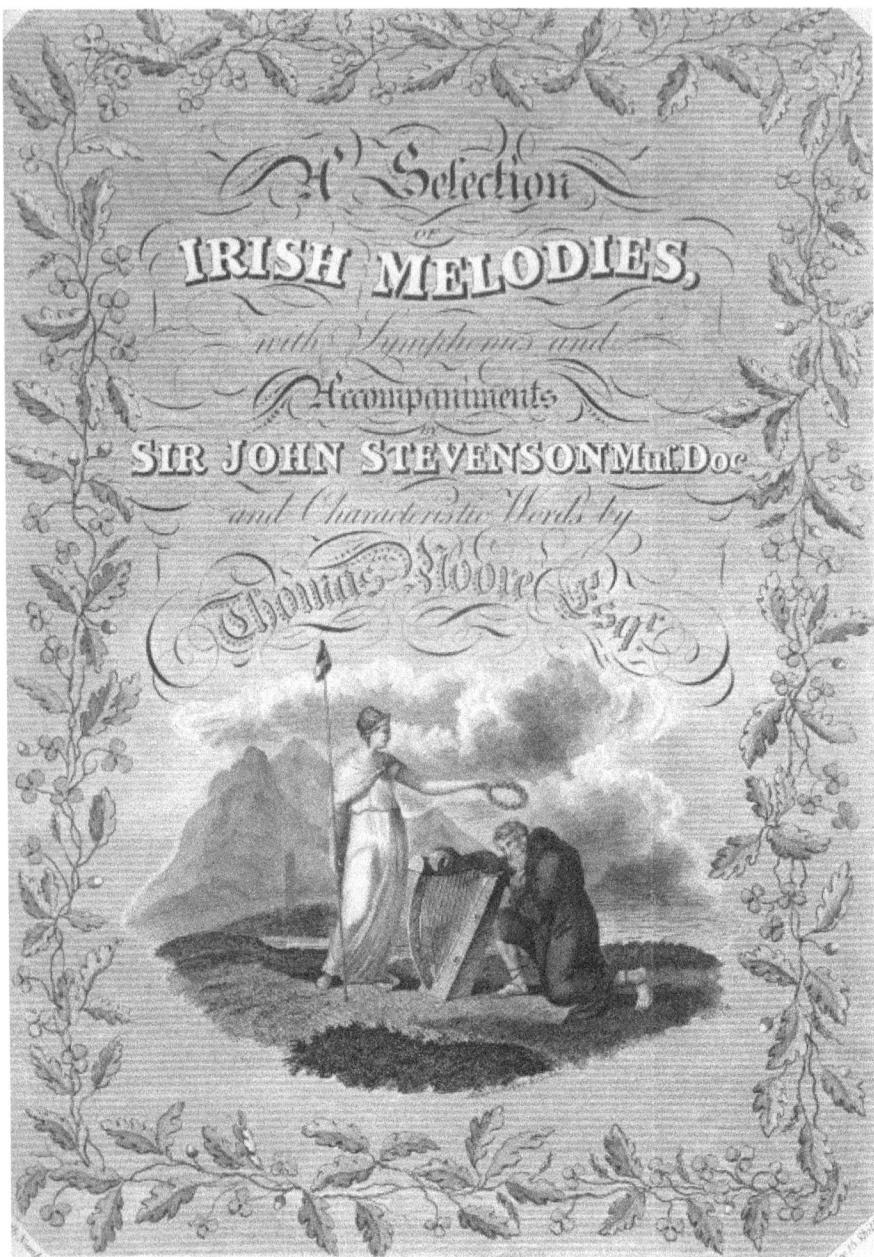

Figure 6.2. Title page of Thomas Moore, *A Selection of Irish Melodies, with Symphonies and Accompaniments by Sir John Stevenson* . . . (London: J. Power's [1808–1815]), vol. 4 ("Second Number of Second Volume"). Reproduced from the original held by the Department of Special Collections of the University Libraries of Notre Dame.

Moore is often accused of altering the meaning of the original songs, rendering them languid and romantic. But Moore could also go the other way. "Remember the Glories of Brien the Brave," for example, recalling the exploits of Brian Boru, is written to "Molly Macalpine," a tune that did not originally have anything to do with Ireland's military prowess. What is most notable is that Moore did not just write random lyrics. Many of his lyrics are inspired by original tunes, and these new lyrics often comment, albeit obliquely, on the original tunes. As ní Chinnéide suggests, "'The Song of Sorrow' inspired him to write his 'Weep on, weep on, your hour is past' . . . and 'The Lamentation of Aughrim' gave rise to 'Forget not the field where they perished.'"[34] "Tho' the Last Glimpse of Erin" was written to the tune "Coulin" (see figure 6.3), a tune which Walker identified as registering political defiance and Owenson described as an Irish "lamentation" concerning "the arbitrary will of Henry VIII." Moore remakes the song into a nostalgic reminiscence of the homeland from the perspective of an exile, but his song, like the original, also defies English attempts to control Irish culture, as the speaker notes that in the new land, she and her lover will not "dread that the cold-hearted Saxon will tear/One chord from that harp, or one lock from that hair."[35] By referencing the original songs, however indirectly, the *Melodies* create a sense of Irish identity as a dynamic interrelation of the old and the new.

The texts of the *Melodies* also promote multiple readings of the Irish nation. Tom Dunne contends that "[t]he audience for which the *Irish Melodies* were written was, above all, an English audience, and their main intention was the creation of a sentimental sympathy with Irish wrongs."[36] Similarly, Augustine Martin suggests that the *Melodies* "struck at an English sense of guilt which had been stirred by the crushing of two rebellions and the corrupt passage of the Act of Union."[37] But the truth is that the *Melodies* were designed for both Irish and English audiences. The lyrics illustrate Moore's awareness of this double audience as he cultivates a strategy of ambiguity in his texts. He elaborates on this strategy in his "Prefatory Letter on Irish Music," in which he feels it necessary to stave off criticism of the subversive nature of his work by explaining that the songs in the *Melodies* are not designed to "appeal to the passions of an ignorant and angry multitude" because they are not intended to circulate among the lower classes. They are rather aimed for the parlors of "the rich and educated," "those who can afford to have their national zeal a little stimulated, without exciting much dread of the excesses into which it may hurry them."[38] Still, he wants to claim some bite for his work, as he indicates that many of the parlored class have nerves that can be "now and then,

Figure 6.3. Music and words for "Tho' the last glimpse of Erin," from Thomas Moore, *A Selection of Irish Melodies, with Symphonies and Accompaniments by Sir John Stevenson* . . . (London: J. Power's [1808–1815]), vol. 1 ("First Number of First Volume"), p. 37. Reproduced from the original held by the Department of Special Collections of the University Libraries of Notre Dame.

alarmed with advantage" because "much more is to be gained by their fears, than could ever be expected from their justice."[39] Moore also notes with seeming satisfaction the rumor that the fourth edition was delayed because it was suppressed by the government. Although he dismisses the rumor, the fact that he points it out to his public suggests that he wants them to be aware of his work's potential for subversion. He plays back and forth, at times suggesting his *Melodies* as politically radical, then recovering himself by claiming that the "ballads have long lost their revolutionary powers, and we question if even a 'Lillibulero' would produce any serious consequences at present."[40] This last assertion can be read as either a statement of fact or, in the hands of a reader like O'Connell, a provocation to change.[41]

Certain of the *Melodies* promote the cause of Ireland, although the sentiment is tempered in comparison with Moore's earlier college pieces. In "Remember the Glories of Brien the Brave," for example, Moore writes:

> Forget not our wounded companions, who stood
> In the day of distress by our side;
> While the moss of the valley grew red with their blood,
> They stirr'd not, but conquer'd and died.[42]

The speaker urges the reader to take up the cause of "the star of the field": "enough of its glory remains on each sword, / To light us to victory yet." "Erin, Oh Erin" focuses similarly on achieving liberty. It envisages the spirit of Ireland appearing through "a long night of bondage" and conveys optimism about the future:

> The nations have fallen, and thou still art young,
> Thy sun is but rising, when others are set;
> And tho' slavery's cloud o'er thy morning hath hung
> The full noon of freedom shall beam round thee yet.[43]

"Avenging and Bright" registers an even stronger sense of righteous indignation and gives a historical example of the Irish spirit of vengeance, using the story of Deirdre and the sons of Usna: "Though sweet are our friendships, our hopes, our affections, / Revenge on a tyrant is sweetest of all!"[44] In poems like this, Moore seems to reiterate in poetic form his earlier assertion that "Ireland has Sons untutored in the school of corruption, who love her Liberties, and, in the crisis, will die for them."

Poems like "Sublime Was the Warning" and "Erin, Oh Erin" introduce a revolutionary note into the collection. "Sublime Was the Warning" draws a parallel between the Spanish resistance to the Napoleonic forces and the Irish cause: "If deceit be a wound, and suspicion a stain, / Then, ye men of Iberia, our cause is the same!"[45] It suggests that even England herself will sheepishly come to recognize the parallel and defend the rights of the Irish as she has the Spaniards'. At that time, lovers of liberty will "forgive even Albion while blushing she draws, / Like a truant, her sword, in the long-slighted cause / Of the Shamrock of Erin and the Olive of Spain!"[46] The phrase "God prosper the cause!—oh it cannot but thrive, / While the pulse of one patriot heart is alive"[47] is sufficiently ambiguous to be applicable to both national struggles.

But such political assertions are compromised for the most part by the fluid time frame within the *Melodies*. In the majority of Moore's poems, contemporary Ireland does not appear. Although the poems welcome the idea of an independent Ireland, they constantly defer the fulfillment of that nation. Either Ireland's independence is situated in the past and now only dimly remembered, or it is still to occur. The poems that address the plight of the Irish nation and accuse England of subjugating the Irish people avoid reference to present-day situations. "Let Erin Remember the Days of Old," for example, situates an independent Ireland only in the past. The poem recalls a time before Erin's "faithless sons betrayed her."[48] But that time is perceived only in a dream when "Memory" looks "through the waves of time / For the long-faded glories they cover."[49] The proud nation of Ireland is thus triply occluded by a combination of dream, memory, and lapping waves.[50] Conversely, in poems like "The Legacy," the freedom of Ireland is deferred to the future. The narrator requests that certain emblems of his affection—his heart, his harp, and his cup of wine—be preserved after his death. But only in the future when "some warm devoted lover" appears will the hovering "spirit" of the speaker (and of the nation) find its fulfillment.[51] In the end, even though the oppressors may weep at the laments of their captive, they nevertheless continue to "rivet [the] chains."[52]

Moore's depiction of gender relations in the *Melodies* is even more complex than his depiction of time. Belinda Loftus comments that "Tom Moore's *Irish Melodies*, so frequently sung in English drawing rooms . . . made Irish womanhood . . . sentimental, melancholy . . . and submissive."[53] However Moore's portrayal of women in the nation is more ambiguous than Loftus suggests. The songs do speak endlessly of the Irish nation as the female beloved. The first volume begins with "Go Where Glory Waits Thee," which presents a female speaker imploring her lover to remember her as he moves on to new fame and friendship. The phrase "Oh! still remember me" and the alternate "Oh! then remember me," appear nine times in a poem of thirty-nine lines, haunting the poem as the speaker haunts her lover.[54] "Erin, Oh Erin" also portrays the Irish nation as a woman besieged by trials: "Erin, oh Erin, thus bright thro' the tears / Of a long night of bondage, thy spirit appears."[55] "Eveleen's Bower," too, draws upon the allegorical representation of Ireland as a woman wronged by England:[56]

Oh! weep for the hour,
When to Eveleen's bower
The Lord of the Valley with false vows came;
The moon hid her light
From the heavens that night,
And wept behind her clouds o'er the maiden's shame.[57]

Moore, like Brooke and Owenson before him, is clearly drawing on the *aisling* tradition. But as Murray Pittock points out, the *aisling* tradition itself was utilized in the service of politics, where the young woman became representative of Ireland.[58] This allusion to a previous poetic form of political resistance situates Moore's work partly within that same politics. Indeed, in his *Ancient Music of Ireland*, George Petrie comments that *aisling* poems used the "guise of a love-song put on to conceal treason" and notes that this "has been so skillfully adopted by Moore in some of his finest lyrics."[59]

Moore complicates the politics of the *aisling* tradition further by situating it within a cult of domesticity closely bound up with a politics of colonialism. As Anne McClintock argues, the cult of domesticity in the nineteenth century was "an indispensable element both of the industrial market and the imperial enterprise."[60] Moore's *Melodies* appear at first glance to reinforce this domestic ideology. In "Lesbia Hath a Beaming Eye," the narrator rejects the charms of the beautiful but wayward Lesbia for the more solid loyalty of his "gentle, bashful Nora Creina."[61] Ireland in the *Melodies* is not just a woman wronged and waiting for rescue by her male lover. She is also the "dear woman" who represents hearth and home to the man who roams the world "like a child at a feast."[62] In the lines "When a cup to the smile of dear woman goes round, / Oh! remember the smile which adorns her at home,"[63] we hear echoes of "O, still remember me," but in this case, the remembrance is not a call for national consciousness but an indication of how closely Moore reiterates an ideology connected with England's dominance. This depiction of an "Erin" that fit into notions of domesticity also encouraged the image of Ireland as feminized, thus further reinforcing the gendered colonial relationship between Ireland and England.

At times, however, Moore rejects the ideals both of domestic ideology and of the gendered identity of Ireland. Poems like "One Bumper at Parting" and "Fill the Bumper Fair" espouse an ideology of pleasure antithetical both to the cult of domesticity and to the depiction of the Irish nation as feminine. "To Ladies' Eyes," for example, rejects domestic loyalties in favor of a multiplicity of possible attachments:

Fill up, fill up—where'er, boy,
Our choice may fall, our choice may fall,
We're sure to find Love there, boy,
So drink them all! so drink them all![64]

The desire for "Freedom, whose smile we shall never resign" expressed in "Remember the Glories of Brien the Brave"[65] is curiously echoed and parodied here in the celebration of man's liberty to chose a mate. Moreover, Moore reverses the gendered stereotypes of Ireland, most notably in two of his most popular melodies. In "Go Where Glory Waits Thee," although the woman seems to represent Ireland, she takes the active part of the poet as the one who sings to her lover. "Tho' the Last Glimpse of Erin with Sorrow I See" is also written from the perspective of a woman to her love, her "Coulin," but her lover is feminized, as she says she will "gaze on thy gold hair as graceful it wreathes" and "hang o'er thy soft harp."[66] In this poem, Ireland is represented as a man in exile: "wherever thou art shall seem Erin to me"[67] is the statement of the woman to her lover.

"Oh! Blame Not the Bard" depicts the relationship between feminization and colonization in Ireland. The poem expresses the dilemma of a poet who neglects the cause of his country to write pleasantries and to "ceaselessly smil[e] at Fame."[68] The speaker claims that

He was born for much more, and in happier hours
His soul might have burn'd with a holier flame,
The string, that now languishes loose o'er the lyre,
Might have bent a proud bow to the warriors dart;
And the lip, which now breathes but the song of desire,
Might have pour'd the full tide of the patriot's heart.[69]

In the final stanza, he contents himself with the thought that even "tho' glory be gone, and tho' hope fade away," he can remember Erin in his poetry, and his songs will be so plaintive that Ireland's masters "Shall pause at the song of their captive, and weep!"[70] The poem indicates how the process of colonization works to feminize the colonized, as Moore represents the bard retreating to the "bowers." However, the footnotes to this work complicate this representation, as they suggest that this figure is itself a stereotypical creation of the colonizer's gaze: "We may suppose this apology to have been uttered by one of those wandering bards, whom Spenser so severely, and, perhaps, truly, describes in his State of Ireland."[71] It is Spenser, then, whom Moore presents as offering a feminized image of the Irish bards, as he praises their poetry for being "sprinkled with some pretty flowers of their natural device, which have good grace and comeliness unto them."[72]

Moore's strategy of ambiguity was designed to appeal to different audiences at the same time. In their original form, the songs and music play with the gendered representation of Ireland, twisting it and translating it. With the publication of the lyrics on their own, however, the *Irish Melodies* lost a great deal of their political impact.[73] The first legitimate edition of the lyrics without the music appeared in 1820, published by Longman's. This was corrected and reprinted with the "Prefatory Letter on Music" in 1821. In 1840–1841, Longman published the *Melodies* in the ten-volume *Poetical Works of Thomas Moore,* again without music. Moore himself resisted the separation of the lyrics from the music. In the notes to the *Melodies* published in the 1840–1841 edition, he writes, "Though an edition of the Poetry of the Irish Melodies, separate from the Music, has long been called for, yet, having, for many reasons, a strong objection to this sort of divorce, I should with difficulty have consented to a disunion of the words from the airs, had it depended solely upon me to keep them quietly together."[74] He contends that he was eventually persuaded to accede to this because the works were being pirated in America, on the Continent, and in "a volume full of typographical errors"[75] in Dublin. He indicates, nevertheless, that he is well aware that his verses "must lose even more than the '*animae dimidium*' in being detached from the beautiful airs to which it was their good fortune to be associated."[76] What happened, however, with the publication of the poems on their own, was what we might call a dehybridization. All of the elements that constituted the dynamic Irishness in the *Melodies* were omitted. The original Irish titles disappeared and with them the traces of the original tunes. All that remained were the titles that Moore himself had supplied. In *The Work of Writing,* Clifford Siskin notes that the literary mass market after 1830 was "configured hierarchically into different levels of 'culture' through procedures of reprinting, anthologizing, and illustration."[77] This cultural hierarchy also played a large part in depoliticizing Moore's work, each subsequent reprinting rendering it more harmless and nostalgic rather than potentially disruptive.

The provocative illustrations that had appeared on the covers of the various editions of the *Melodies* were replaced by illustrations that were much less ambiguous. The frontispiece done by Daniel Maclise for volume 3 of the 1840–1841 Longman edition of *The Poetical Works of Thomas Moore* (the volume that featured the *Irish Melodies*) features a domestic scene with a man and woman sitting by a hearth with their two faithful dogs (figure 6.4). An old harper is playing for them, but he is depicted as an itinerant musician who has just put down his shabby hat and walking stick long enough to play a tune and collect a meal. The angle of his head and his downward glance associates him with the woman, rendering him even more harmless. The only indication of anything disturbing in the illustration is the collection of military paraphernalia in the shadowy background, but these weapons are safely stored as if in a museum collection. Underneath the illustration is a stanza from "The Legacy" that confirms a nostalgic rather than dynamic construction of Irishness:

> Then if some bard who roams forsaken,
> Revive its soft note in passing along,
> Oh! one thought of its master waken
> Your warmest smile for the child of song.

The title page of this edition features an image of two lovers in a boat (see figure 6.5). The woman dominates the man, bending over him as she sits in the prow. Although the woman has a harp in her hand, she seems to be using it more for balance than for any musical purpose. The illustrations in the original volumes of the *Melodies* employed symbols of Irish identity, juxtaposing them and infusing new meaning into them. The illustrations in the editions of poems from the *Melodies*, however, present these symbols as static icons.

The 1846 edition of *Moore's Irish Melodies* published by Longman contains even more elaborate illustrations by Maclise for every poem. In the preface to this edition, Moore writes of his sense that Maclise is furthering the national cause. Although he qualifies his statements by suggesting that "the whole source and soul of the Irish Melodies lies in their matchless music," he speaks of his delight that "to complete [the *Melodies*'] national character, an Irish pen-

Figure 6.4. Frontispiece by Daniel Maclise from Thomas Moore, *The Poetical Works of Thomas Moore*, vol. 3 (London: Longman, Orme, Brown, Green, and Longmans, 1840–1841). Courtesy of the Special Collections Department, University of Edinburgh Library.

cil has lent its aid to an Irish pen in rendering due honour and homage to our country's harp."[78] But in fact, Maclise's elaborate medievalizations de-emphasize the Irish context of the poems and replace ambiguity with senti-mental nostalgia (see figure 6.6). Maclise's illustrations are interwoven with the text of the poems, simultaneously containing and overwhelming them. Maclise's own relationship to Ireland has been debated by recent critics.[79] In the case of this edition of Moore's poems, however, his contributions situate the *Melodies* in a market for buyers concerned more with the appearance of books than with their content. With its gilt-edged pages, this edition adver-tises itself as a product of consumption.

As products of consumption, the *Melodies*, as they appeared both with music and without, were caught up in the gendered politics of the market-place. What we see emerging within critical commentary on Moore is a tra-jectory in which the *Melodies* are associated with female consumers and judged as inferior because they are so popular. And as the body of his work was sub-ject to the assessments of an increasingly gendered politics of taste, so, too, was Moore's own body. Whereas early commentary on Moore appearing

Figure 6.5. Title page by Daniel Maclise from Thomas Moore, *The Poetical Works of Thomas Moore*, vol. 3 (London: Longman, Orme, Brown, Green, and Longmans, 1840–1841). Courtesy of the Special Collections Department, University of Edinburgh Library.

soon after his translations of Anacreon viewed him as too licentious, later commentary portrayed him as effeminate and an object of feminine consumption himself.[80]

Reviews of Moore's early poetry stress his threat to female readers. The *Monthly Review* of September 1806, for example, complains that Moore has "substituted mere sensuality for refinement"[81] in his *Epistles, Odes, and Other Poems*. Sydney Owenson articulates this view of Moore in her *Memoirs*, as she describes the song Moore sang for her and her sister when she first met him: "'Will you come to the bower,'" she notes, was "a very improper song, by-the-bye, for young ladies to hear."[82] Francis Jeffrey echoes this concern in his infamous *Edinburgh Review* article of July 1806, writing that Moore is "the most licentious of modern versifiers"[83] and suggesting that women's warm sensibilities render them "peculiarly liable to be captivated by the appearance of

Go where glory waits thee,
But while fame elates thee,
Oh! still remember me.
When the praise thou meetest
To thine ear is sweetest,
Oh! then remember me.

Figure 6.6. Illustration by Daniel Maclise to "Go Where Glory Waits Thee," from *Moore's Irish Melodies* (London: Longman, Brown, Green, and Longmans, 1846), p. 1. Courtesy of the W. A. C. Bennett Library, Simon Fraser University.

violent emotions, and to be misled by the affectation of tenderness or gener-osity."[84] For Jeffrey, Moore's assault on female sensibility is a threat not just to individual reputations but to the nation: "The character and the morality of women exercises already a mighty influence upon the happiness and re-spectability of the nation; and it is destined, we believe to exercise a still higher one," but, he adds, Moore has jeopardized "domestic happiness and private honour" and "public spirit and national industry" with his poems.[85] Jeffrey positions his concerns in terms of what he sees as a "kind of crisis,"[86] cautioning that the regulation of what is available to read is most important at this point in history because "women are now beginning to receive a more extended education, to venture more freely and largely into fields of literature, and to become more of intellectual and independent creatures, than they have yet been in these islands."[87]

According to the reviewer in the June 1812 issue of the *Quarterly Review*, Moore mended his ways with the *Melodies*, no longer sacrificing "decorum at the altar of love."[88] What we see in this review, too, however, is a sense of how much Moore's work coincides with a shift in the participation of women in cultural activity. According to this reviewer, "The abolition of those preju-dices which so long condemned the female part of the community to intellec-tual idleness, has admitted a new and very numerous class to the enjoyments of poetry."[89] The reviewer echoes Jeffrey's belief in women's "extreme sensi-bility" and suggests that they are particularly susceptible to "the charms of music."[90] He also indicates that the "the most important portion" of the po-etry that women read will be found in "the verses that accompany their music."[91] Reviews of Moore's *Melodies* reveal anxiety about female consump-tion, particularly when that consumption occurs outside strictly literary boundaries.[92] Although the review published in the *Quarterly Review* of Octo-ber 1822 suggests that the *Melodies* contain "very little which could be offensive to the most feminine delicacy,"[93] it mentions critics who have objected that "Mr. Moore, considering the thousands of young ladies who would lose half their valuable time in warbling his melodies, should have taken especial care that they came by no other loss."[94] The publication of the ten volumes of the *Irish Melodies* in their original form, then, posed a national threat not just be-cause of their appeal to an Irish population that was potentially disruptive to the foundations of the British constitution but because of their appeal to a fe-male population that was potentially disruptive to the British republic of letters. The *New Monthly Magazine* for January 1, 1820, concludes with "two pic-tures" of Moore that unite concern about his effect on women with concern about his association with Irish nationalism:

I have seen him . . . seated at the piano, surrounded by simpering ma-
trons, some unconscious, some but *too conscious* of the meaning of his war-
blings; . . . rank after rank of beautiful unmarried females trembling on
the verge of impurity, as they crowded and *blushed* around their favorite
minstrel. I have seen him at his *state dinner* in Ireland, surrounded by the
shouting O'Donnells and O'Connells, and all the endless Os of Irish
genealogy, pledging his soul to them in rosy libations of wine for his
patriotism.[95]

Reviews of Moore demonstrate an increasing concern to regulate the impact
of his work by reinforcing the gendered standards both of the national imaginary and of the literary sphere. Moore's popularity among female consumers
and his activity as a singer made him an object of female consumption himself. This association was used to establish the feminine nature of his work,
and, correspondingly, the judgment of his work as feminine was used to
weaken its politically radical potential.

Although it discusses Moore's susceptibility to the "charms" of "any
given numbers of young ladies," the October 1822 *Quarterly Review* blames
characteristics that are essentially feminine for what it describes as the superficial nature of Moore's poetry: "Our very greatest wits have not been men of
a gay or vivacious disposition. . . . Mr. Moore's wit is here such as we should
have looked for from his general turn of mind, pleasant and harmless, neither
powerful nor severe." [96] The *Monthly Repository* (September 1827) observed:
"Like a lovely woman, fond of ornament, the muse of Moore is covered with
too great a profusion of glittering diamonds and jewels, all most elegant indeed of their kind, and disposed with the greatest taste, but destroying in
some degree that graceful simplicity which is not more becoming to female
than to poetical beauty."[97] Not only is Moore's muse feminized here as the
object of the male gaze, but he is also represented as a feminine consumer who
is too caught up with the activity of consumption to exhibit proper taste.

Criticisms of Moore appearing in the mid-Victorian era were exacerbated by a general downturn in the status of poetry as well as a solidification
of gender roles. The review of Lord Russell's *Memoirs, Journal and Correspondence
of Thomas Moore* (1853–56) in the *National Review* for July 1856 (Russell's work appeared after Moore's death) stresses his "boyish, careless, and unapprehensive
spirit" and suggests that "[h]e was always an amateur rake rather than a real
one."[98] The reviewer also suggests that Moore is a second-rate poet whose
work is essentially superficial: "Its surface is highly attractive; but it yields all
its charms to the first glance."[99] This poetic inadequacy is connected in the

reviewer's mind with bodily inadequacy: "He was a delightful companion, a devoted son, a tender husband; he had a genial temper and a kindly nature; but he was small."[100] The slippage between poetic ability and bodily size is seen in the reviewer's definition of "manhood." Moore, he says, was "manly in the sense of being high-spirited, but he wanted something of the breadth of manhood."[101] The characteristics of a great poet and a true man appear identical here. Both involve a "power of motion."[102] Moore is described time and time again in this review as effeminate, as passive rather than active. Moreover, his effeminacy is particularly linked with his performance of his songs, an activity that, as we have seen, was part of his contract with the Powers. He is described as a "singing-bird," a "carpet poet" with a "boudoir education," who instead of going out into the natural world is more "fitted for the dining and drawing-room."[103]

The gendered politics of taste that influenced judgments about both Moore's work and his body cannot be separated from the gendered colonial relationship between Ireland and England. As Mary Jean Corbett points out, "[I]n the English-Irish context, gender provides perhaps the most fundamental and enduring discursive means for signifying Irish political incapacity."[104] It was an Englishman, William Hazlitt, who, in *The Spirit of the Age*, recognized the potential denial of the Irish nation as a political unit that the *Melodies* as they were marketed could serve. Also critical of Moore's patrician friendships, Hazlitt berates him for converting "the wild harp of Erin into a musical snuff-box."[105] He warns: "If these national airs do indeed express the soul of impassioned feeling in his countrymen, the case of Ireland is hopeless. If these prettinesses pass for patriotism, if a country can heave from its hearts' core only these vapid, varnished sentiments lip-deep, and let its tears of blood evaporate in an empty conceit, let it be governed as it has been."[106] Hazlitt's comments here are useful because they articulate an opposition between "prettiness" and "patriotism" that implies the fundamental gendering of both the nation and the marketplace and illustrates the connection between the two. "Prettiness" is an indication of both lack of literary taste and lack of the qualities necessary for national self-governance. Hazlitt's comments point out the double bind in which Moore found himself. Moore's work was judged as an object of mass consumption rather than of art, and, correspondingly, dismissed as feminine. At the same time, Moore's own body became the subject of this gendered discourse of commodification, as reviews of his work equated his lack of "great" poetic ability with his lack of virility. His feminization on the literary market affected his perceived ability to write a national identity for Ireland, and his position as an Irish writer confirmed his feminization on the marketplace. With Moore, whom Charles Gavan Duffy dubbed the "pet of the petticoats,"[107] as its representative, the Irish nation was viewed not just as feminine but as emasculated and therefore as incapable of the kind of judgment necessary for national self-determination. Moore's hybridized "truly National" project brought Irish patriotism from the podium to the parlor, as Daniel O'Connell suggested, but it also provided a means by which the English could disregard that patriotism as too "pretty."

7

In Moore's Wake

Irish Music in Ireland after the *Irish Melodies*

The feminization of Moore and his work in British cultural venues was echoed in Ireland, where it was associated with a gendered perspective on how the nation should be represented. The editor of *The Citizen: A Monthly Journal of Politics Literature and the Arts* for December 1839, for example, laments:

> Moore has devoted so much of his time to [the service of the young English gentlepeople]; instead of working for his own country, which admitted of, and greatly needed a nobler and more strenuous devotion of life to literary toil. Had he spent the last forty years of his life in Ireland, and worked but half as hard, to supply a few of her many wants, as he has been compelled to do for the booksellers in England, his position, in Ireland and in Europe, had been far different now. Instead of being, as it were, the ambassador of the national genius in England, he might have been, for a time, its honoured chieftain at home.[1]

Instead of devoting his life to "literary toil," Moore is harnessed to market interests. He is "compelled" to work for "booksellers." Rather than presenting Moore as his nation's "chieftain," or even its "ambassador," the writer emphasizes Moore's feminine qualities. But instead of representing the feminized colonial here, Moore in the hands of his fellow Irishmen becomes an image of an unnatural Mother Ireland. The metaphor of a maternal Moore dominates the passage: "How many myriads are there of the present generation, with whose dearest recollections he is inseparably mingled,—whose young hearts he cradled in a new delight, and rocked them with those sweet songs, into Elysian dreams, such as otherwise they had never known?"[2] Moore's maternity, however, is presented as a failure due to his abandonment of his native land. The projects that, had he remained in Ireland, "must have suggested themselves to his fertile, all-embracing spirit, are now among the still-born children of time," while those that he did produce "have yet an untimely paleness, as reared in a strange clime, and wear not that hue of strength and gladness which they would, had they been born beneath our skies, nursed 'mid the bloom of our mountain heather, and dipped in the lively current of our own unshackled streams."[3] They are beautiful, the editor suggests, but "there is a weakness in their beauty,"[4] as opposed to the vigor necessary for national formation. These "children" are the products of cultural hybridity rather than purity. The comments on Moore in *The Citizen* indicate not only the prevalence of gendered images in the discourse on Irish music but also how those comments are configured in racialized and biological terms in Ireland itself.

The Citizen was not the only work to register anxiety about the *Melodies'* long-term effect on Irish music and national identity and to reject the hybrid nature of his work in a search for greater cultural purity. This chapter will examine the discourse on Irish music in the wake of Moore, considering first the strategies of James Hardiman and Thomas Davis to counteract what they see as the problems with Moore's representation of Ireland. For Hardiman, the emphasis on hybridity in Moore's work denied Gaelic culture's unique claim to Irish identity. For Davis, Moore was too elitist and failed to provide the basis for a vigorous Irish "spirit of the nation," or "raciness," in Davis's terms, that would include Catholic and non-Catholic people from the lower and middle classes. The implications of the gendering of Moore were picked up by Davis in particular, who responded to the feminizing of Moore and of Irish music by asserting the masculine nature of Irish culture. Finally, I consider the configuration of music and identity that George Petrie asserted in his *Ancient Music of Ireland,* a configuration that served to associate Irish music with loss, exile, and, again, the feminine.

In 1831, two years after the Catholic Emancipation, James Hardiman's two-volume *Irish Minstrelsy, or Bardic Remains of Ireland with English Poetical Translations* appeared. The title of Hardiman's work capitalizes on the popularity of Walter Scott's *Minstrelsy of the Scottish Border* (republished the previous year), and Hardiman himself concedes that "[t]he borrowed term 'Minstrelsy' is used in the title of this collection, only because it is familiar to the public ear, for others more appropriate might be found in our language."[5] But Hardiman also yokes the word *minstrel,* a term whose meaning was the subject of much dispute, to the concept of the Irish bards.[6] In addition, Hardiman's *Minstrelsy* is ambiguously located between the literary and the oral legacies of the Gaelic culture, between the "book" and the "songs." The title page of both volumes features a quotation by John Philpot Curran that indicates this hybrid quality: "I will give thee a book—it containeth the Songs of the bards of ERIN, of the bards of the days that are gone."

Hardiman starts his *Irish Minstrelsy* on an optimistic note, suggesting that the current intellectual climate is favorable to a revival of interest in "the ancient literature of Ireland": "Those memorials which have hitherto lain so long unexplored, now appear to awaken the attention of the learned and the curiosity of the public; and thus, the literary remains of a people once so distinguished in the annals of learning, may be rescued from the oblivion to which they have been so undeservedly consigned."[7] He suggests that part of his concern is to claim for the Irish cause some of the popularity that was accorded James Macpherson: "It has long been a subject of regret, with the writer, that the remains of our national bards . . . should be consigned to obscurity at home, while a neighbouring nation derived so much literary fame from a few of those remains, boldly claimed and published as its own."[8] But it is equally clear that Hardiman has also been influenced by the "literary fame" that a fellow Irishman won, as, in many ways, he sets out to correct the impact of Thomas Moore's *Melodies* on the representation of Ireland at home and abroad. Hardiman's remark that "[t]he music of Ireland is better known to the world, at the present day, than its poetry"[9] is an indirect comment on the influence of Moore. Hardiman explains the popularity of Irish music by suggesting that music is more easily appreciated because it is more accessible than Irish poetry: "In the sweetest strains of natural feeling, the former found its ready way to every heart, and became endenizened in every clime, while the latter, wrapped in an ancient and expressive but proscribed and insulated language, has been generally neglected."[10] Hardiman's metaphor prepares the way for the translation of the Irish poetry featured in his work, as he implies that the Irish language is like a garment that covers the true essence of the poetry.[11] In many cases, Hardiman argues, the original Irish lyrics have been replaced by "vulgar ballads, composed in English, during the last 150 years."[12] Hardiman presents the result as a kind of sexual violence, invoking the marriage allegory applied so commonly to the relationship between England and Ireland: the English words are "a disgrace to our sweet and simple melodies, to which they have been so cruelly and unnaturally united."[13] He rails against "this trash, which modern *collectors* have dignified with the title of 'National Irish Song'!!!"[14] Although he is careful here to make an exception for Moore's *Melodies,* he is intent on restoring a sense of purity and authenticity to the songs by returning to the original sources and remasculinizing the nation by concentrating on war songs and elegies for warriors.[15]

Despite Hardiman's attempt to draw the reader's attention to the original Gaelic songs, however, the project of the *Irish Minstrelsy* is made highly problematic by the process of translation. David Lloyd comments on the "team of translators who versified the Gaelic in a mode that uneasily combines the conventions of late Augustan descriptive verse with those of Romantic meditative and ballad poetry."[16] The translations of the Irish poetry in the *Irish Minstrelsy,* like Moore's *Melodies,* oscillate between promoting Gaelic Irish identity and equating that identity with loss. The last section in the collection is devoted to "Odes, Elegies, Etc.," and includes poems that both praise and mourn fallen heroes. "Ode to the Milesians" encourages the "champions of the Gaël"[17] in language that sounds very much like Moore's:

> Forth warriors, forth, with heaven to speed,
> Proud in your country's cause to bleed;
> They best may hope the victor's wreath,
> Whose watch word's "liberty or death."[18]

"Elegy on the Death of Denis Mac Carthy," on the other hand, laments the "prime leader of the Gaël," whose followers now are "defeated, in disgrace": "Mac Carthy More is lost, and long we're doom'd to *sigh and wail.*"[19]

Despite the similarities between Moore's and Hardiman's texts, however, the *Irish Minstrelsy* actually tries to revise the impact not only of Moore's melodies but of Moore himself on the Irish public. Whereas the popularity of Moore centered on the celebration of the individual genius, Hardiman shifts the focus from genius to genealogy, depicting Moore as the successor of a rich legacy of poets of the Irish language. He portrays the community of Irish music and poetry as developing over time, as he moves from praising the ancient bards for their "patriotism, genius, and learning" to presenting the poets of the more recent centuries as "their successors."[20] The first volume of the *Minstrelsy* includes a two-page list of the poets of "the last two centuries," a list that, although ostensibly given "in the margin," overwhelms the two lines of the narrative text at the top, drawing the reader's attention to the large number of names.[21] Similarly, although the last section, "Odes, Elegies, Etc.," begins with a quotation from the "Dissertation concerning the Poems of Ossian,"[22] Hardiman argues that Ireland's claim to a "high poetic character" does not depend on Ossianic poetry alone, nor "on any single class of poetical composition."[23]

Hardiman's emphasis on the poetic community as opposed to individual poets such as Moore becomes more apparent in the section entitled "Memoir of Thomas Furlong," one of the translators of the *Irish Minstrelsy,* in which Hardiman includes a speech given at a Dublin dinner by Furlong. The speech begins by expressing admiration for Moore—"the mere introduction of his name is calculated to excite a warmer, a livelier feeling"[24]—and for Moore's patriotism: "[W]e esteem him not merely as the eager and impassioned advocate of general liberty—but we love him as the lover of his country. We hail him as the denouncer of her wrongs, and the fearless vindicator of her rights."[25] Furlong contrasts Moore's conscious decision to write about Ireland with the "spiritless, slavish" behavior of poets like Parnell, Roscommon, and Goldsmith who did not draw attention to their national origin. As the speech continues, however, Furlong redraws the metaphorical map so that Moore becomes not so much the initiator of a new patriotic spirit as a contemporary manifestation of "the fine mind of the nation" that is "unfolding itself."[26] Furlong continues: "Justly has Ireland been called 'The Land of Song,' the very atmosphere is poetical—the breezes that play around us seem the very breathings of melody. The spirits of our ancient bards are looking down, inviting the youth of the soil to participate in their glory. How could Moore, when speaking of Ireland, be otherwise than poetical? how could he touch on such a subject without catching an added spirit of inspiration?"[27] It is now not Moore as an individual genius who inspired "a warmer, a livelier feeling" but rather, a feeling, or national spirit, that inspired Moore.

Hardiman further emphasizes the subsuming of individual genius within a national "spirit of inspiration" by concluding this section with a poem of Furlong's entitled "The Spirit of Irish Song." The speaker of the poem contrasts poetic artfulness with "Nature," urging the reader to "fling the forms of art aside" and take up "the simple songs of our sires."[28] The true "minstrelsy," he suggests, is based on an oral tradition: "What to the spirit more cheering can be / Than the lay whose ling'ring notes recal [sic] / The thoughts of the holy—the fair—the free."[29] In contrast, the "forms of art" cut the reader off from this oral tradition. They "dull" and "enthral" the ear. "The Spirit of Irish Song" reads ironically in the context of Hardiman's project in the *Irish Minstrelsy* to concentrate on poets "such as wrote solely in their native language,"[30] as Furlong employs a highly artful style of written English in order to praise Irish song. But the poem nevertheless sums up Hardiman's corrective ideal, as it suggests the existence of a "spirit" of Irish song that is passed down from generation to generation and that can be identified by the effect it produces:

> Give me the full responsive sigh,
> The glowing cheek and the moisten'd eye;
> Let these the minstrel's might attest,
> And the vain and the idle—may share the rest.[31]

That this "spirit of Irish song" is meant to transcend the individual "min-strel" is further suggested by Hardiman's comment that the poem was "the last which issued from the pen of Mr. Furlong, written a few days before his death."[32] The individual may die, but the spirit of the nation lives on.

Hardiman's most radical response to Moore in the *Irish Minstrelsy*, however, was to foreground the political context of Irish music, a foregrounding that attempted to make Irish music and the Gaelic Catholic cause synonymous. Moore, as seen in chapter six, provided hints about radical readings of his poems in the *Melodies*, but for the most part, they read ambiguously. In this strategic ambiguity lies their ability to appeal to different audiences in different contexts. Hardiman makes a point, however, of recontextualizing the songs to claim them for the Gaelic Catholic cause. In the "Memoir of Carolan," for example, the harper is presented as suffering from the persecutions against Catholics. His family is identified as belonging to the clan Mac-Brady, whose lands were gradually taken away from them for offences such as not teaching English to the children of their estate, being on the wrong side of the Civil War, and supporting James II.[33] While he admits that Carolan wrote songs for both English and Irish individuals, Hardiman emphasizes Carolan's particular sympathy for the "Milesian" nobility: "it was in his favorite county of ROSCOMMON, that Carolan always found and felt himself most at home, and for the natives there, particularly the old Irish, and, above all, the ancient and princely stocks of O'Conor, and M'Dermott, he poured forth some of his sweetest strains."[34] In the notes to the "Remains of Carolan," Hardiman details the history of Irish oppression that lies behind Carolan's songs. The notes for "Planxty Stafford" explain that the Stafford family was "'transplanted' by Cromwell from Wexford to Roscommon, where they had a grant of lands, trifling in comparison to those which they lost in their native county."[35] "Edward O'Corcoran" is revealed as a hero of the siege of Limerick, and Hardiman notes, "its capitulation, the articles of surrender, and their flagrant violation, are already known throughout the civilized world."[36] It is also telling that Hardiman decided to use an illustration of the actual eighteenth-century portrait of Carolan in the *Minstrelsy* rather than any stylized Ossianic rendering such as had more recently been offered in the *Irish Magazine* of 1809 (see figures 1.3 and 1.4). Hardiman's concern is historical context.

Hardiman continues this practice of politicizing the songs throughout the two volumes. He supplies the reader with the political details of "Uile Can Dubh O," or "The Song of Sorrow," which was translated by Mary Balfour as an apolitical parlor piece for Bunting's 1809 volume: "The words were composed by one of the unfortunate sufferers expelled from Ulster, in the reign of James I. when almost the entire of that province was confiscated, and planted with English and Scotch adventurers."[37] Where the politics of a song have been identified previously, Hardiman goes further. Charlotte Brooke, for example, had indicated that Edmond Ryan, otherwise known as "Emon a Knock," or "Ned of the Hill," "commanded a company of those unhappy free booters called Rapparees, who, after the defeat of the Boyne, were obliged to abandon their dwellings and possessions."[38] Hardiman rewrites this in a harsher tone. Ned is "said to have been one of those numerous adherents of James the Second, who, on the defeat of that monarch, were outlawed, and had their estates confiscated."[39] Hardiman also draws attention to the textual history of the song, commenting that "Miss Brooke has translated this as an 'Elegiac Song.'"[40] The *Irish Minstrelsy* is not only a recontextualization of the songs themselves but a recontextualization and correction of previous collections that contained those works.

Hardiman represents Gaelic culture as a fount of oral information. Its continuance depends on remembering the contexts in which the songs evolved and the metaphors they relied on. Brooke interpreted "Emon a Knock" as pertaining to Ned's "desertion" by his "mistress," adding, "I have not been able to discover the name of this fair inconstant."[41] Although Brooke was probably aware of the use of the song as a Jacobite allegory, she failed to include this information with her notes. As well as providing historical information that glosses the songs, Hardiman wants to draw the reader's attention to the covert Jacobite politics of some of the songs. He asserts that "Emon a Knock" is "purely allegorical, Ireland being designated by the beautiful female addressed; but the allegory being now forgotten, the composition is known only as a love effusion, and has been therefore included in the present part of this work."[42] He indicates a similar history behind "Roisin Dubh," or "Little Black Rose," which is "an allegorical ballad, in which strong political feelings are conveyed, as a personal address from a lover to his fair one. . . . By *Roisin Dubh*, supposed to be a beloved female, is meant Ireland."[43] Hardiman suggests that the song is now "safe" to include in such an anthology because its political meaning has now disappeared: "The allegorical meaning has been long since forgotten, and the verses are now remembered, and sung as a plaintive love ditty."[44] Hardiman expands on the nature of allegory in Irish song in the second volume of the *Irish Minstrelsy*, which features a section on "Jacobite Relics": "It may be necessary here to observe, that a custom prevailed among our modern bards, to supply stanzas, particularly of a political nature, for the finest national tunes."[45] However, in his elaboration on the subject, Hardiman reverses his account of the nature of the allegory, commenting that the lyrics "of a political nature" have survived the original words: "[T]hese [political] compositions, in general, supplanted the older words, which fell into disuse and were soon forgotten."[46]

The idea of an oral Gaelic culture that creates its own community is suggested by Hardiman's allusions to the tunes to the poems. Some tunes are indicated with reference to Moore's *Melodies* and to Bunting's *Ancient Music*.[47] But in other cases, Hardiman merely mentions the name of a tune. For those unfamiliar with common tunes, attempting to map out which tune goes with which set of lyrics is impossible. In the case of "In This Calm Sheltered Villa," for example, the description leads back on itself. Hardiman begins by observing that "[t]his is one of the many pleasing ballads to the favorite air of *Coolin*; and the words, like most others to the same charming melody, are inexpressibly sweet and tender."[48] However, in the next sentence, he moves from another ballad that is sung to "Coolin" to still another air: "The 'Lov'd Maid of Broka' in Bunting's Collection of the Ancient Music of Ireland, versified by Hector Mac Neill, from a literal translation of the Irish, is one of those ballads, though there coupled with a different air."[49] The original tunes are unknown to the English reader, however, even though he or she may be given a translation of the song. In fact, Hardiman's translators make a point of changing the usual combination of lyrics and airs.[50] The case of Carolan offers such an example: "His lively style, so different from the slow plaintive strains of our ancient music; the rapidity of his turns; his abrupt changes and terminations, so unexpected yet so pleasing, could be followed only in the language in which he thought, composed, and sung."[51] The accompanying air has been changed accordingly so that "Whiskey Is the Potion" is "here translated to the characteristic air of 'Carolan's Receipt,'"[52] while the "air of the old song, called the 'Farmer,' which was written by a Catholic priest," is "found to answer" the translation of "Edward O'Corcoran."[53]

By such means, Hardiman builds up a picture of a Gaelic song culture as "counteractivity" to official regulation. The song culture is as compelling and as exclusive as a religion: "Clothed in the language of the Country, which was always regarded and still is cherished with national enthusiasm, and addressed to the religious and political feelings of the multitude, these [Jacobite] songs helped, in no small degree, to counteract the effects even of the penal laws. They were transmitted from sire to son, and imprinted on the memory with nearly the same degree of reverence as the doctrines of Christianity."[54] Hardiman suggests that the songs exercised an unofficial power over the Gaelic population that defied official government power: "For a long period . . . after

the revolution, the last of the race of our bards, indignant at the national op-
pressions, and disregarding the terrors of death or exile, which inevitably followed detection, poured forth their feelings of political hope, enmity, revenge, or despair, in strains, which roused and strengthened those passions in
the breasts of their desponding countrymen."[55] The songs, he indicates, were
remembered by the people, and, "as it was treason to sing them openly, they
were chaunted [sic] at private meetings, or by the cottage fire-sides throughout
the land, with feelings little short of religious enthusiasm."[56] It is this song
culture, then, which is still kept partially secret from the English reader, hidden within the notes or only hinted at. And Hardiman suggests that secrecy
is a dangerous thing, as he notes that it was the "spell of secrecy" surrounding the songs that gave them such power and that was directly responsible for
the violence of 1798: "By these means, the embers of discontent were fanned
and kept alive, until they burst forth in those terrible conflagrations which afterwards entailed so much misery on the country."[57] If the government had
been able to "give publicity to those proscribed stanzas," Hardiman suggests,
"the charm from which they derived their principal influence" might have
been dissolved.[58]

But such a reliance on an oral culture creates an opposition between Gaelic oral culture and English publication, between secret Gaelic songs "transmitted from sire to son, and imprinted on the memory" and print culture.
Such a split would further reinforce stereotypes of Irish primitivism that
were already in circulation.[59] To avoid such a dichotomy, Hardiman creates a
Gaelic underground textual culture in addition to the underground oral culture. The structure of the *Irish Minstrelsy* promises a parallel English translation of Gaelic poems. But this parallel breaks down in the notes, which
contain numerous stanzas and entire poems not translated into English. Hardiman notes in several places that he adds these for the benefit of the "Irish
reader." The result is extreme in the notes to the last section, where the non-
Irish reader is confronted by twelve pages of "Irish Proverbs" in Irish type.
(Hardiman used a type known as the Figgins type, used in only one other
book.)[60] As in Brooke's *Reliques*, the untranslated text serves to draw attention
to the existence of Gaelic culture. But whereas in Brooke the Gaelic text was
chiefly confined to a section appearing after the English translations, in Hardiman's *Irish Minstrelsy* Irish text continually disrupts the narrative of the English notes. While the translations of particular poems in Hardiman's work
repeat the ambiguity found in Moore's *Melodies*, the structure of the text works
to overcome this ambiguity. The instability of the allegory, the elusiveness of

the tunes, and the labyrinthine notes in the *Irish Minstrelsy* serve to conceal Irish culture from the English reader, creating a vague apprehension that the embers of Irish discontent may not be completely cold.

The section on Jacobite relics combines a conciliatory perspective with what can only be considered veiled threats of violence. This latter element was particularly unsettling to Samuel Ferguson, who reviewed the *Irish Minstrelsy* for the *Dublin University Magazine* in 1834.[61] Throughout this section, Hardiman emphasizes the oppression that the Irish have experienced at the hands of the English, drawing an analogy between the Irish and another disenfranchised population: "The political situation of the Irish with respect to England, has been frequently compared with that of the Greeks in their relation to Turkey."[62] He suggests, however, that the English have "excelled the most furious followers of Mahomet in Greece"[63] in their tyranny. Hardiman adds to this apprehension with his various warnings to the English administration: "Ireland has been rendered a paralyzed limb on the empire, but sufficient nerve remains, by which, in some frenzied or convulsive moment, it may inflict a sudden and deadly wound on the body which it ought to protect, support, and adorn. May this awful truth sink deep in the minds of those who have it yet in their power to avert so dreadful a retribution."[64] He concludes the section on Jacobite relics by reflecting on the changes that have now occurred and notes his pleasure "that the children of the tyrant and slave, the oppressor and the oppressed, now mingle, without distinction, in the great mass of society; and that the angry passions which formerly raged with violence, are generally and rapidly declining." However he also adds: "[M]ay no untoward circumstance occur to interrupt this happy procedure."[65]

While Hardiman's project, by pointing to the inaccessible but persistent (and threatening) presence of a past pure Gaelic oral and textual culture, suggests an inevitable gap between the Gaelic- and the English-speaking populations of Ireland, Thomas Davis is concerned to forge a national identity that will ostensibly accommodate both populations.[66] According to Davis, Irish nationality must "contain and represent the races of Ireland. It must not be Celtic, it must not be Saxon—it must be Irish."[67] In the process of trying to achieve this goal, Davis, like Hardiman, both capitalizes on the popularity of Moore, and attempts to redirect that popularity. In his essay "On Irish Music and Poetry," Davis expresses his concern to preserve what he considers an essential Irishness in Irish music. He is particularly worried that English speakers in Ireland are losing touch with Irish music: "Varied and noble as our music is, the English speaking people in Ireland have been gradually losing their knowledge of it, and a number of foreign tunes—paltry scented things from Italy, lively trifles from Scotland, and German opera cries—are heard in our concerts, and, what is worse, from our Temperance bands."[68] Essentially, there has been no Irish music written by Irish composers "since Carolan's death," suggests Davis: "Not that we were without composers, but those we have do not compose Irish-like music, nor for Ireland. Their rewards are from a foreign public—their fame, we fear, will suffer from alienage."[69] While Davis expresses a desire to create what is in effect a hybrid national identity, consisting of Gaelic and English elements, he also wants to claim a purity for that national identity that derives from its connection to the Irish soil, its essential "raciness."

Like Hardiman, Davis pays formal tribute to Thomas Moore for his patriotism, for his ability to produce "Irish-like music . . . for Ireland": "Fortunately there was one among us . . . who can smite upon our harp like a master, and make it sigh with Irish memories, and speak sternly with Irish resolve."[70] But in his essay on "Irish Songs," Davis also suggests the limitations of Moore. For one thing, he is too highbrow: "It may be said that Moore is lyrist enough for Ireland. He is immeasurably our greatest poet, and the greatest lyrist, except Burns and Beranger, that ever lived; but he has not given songs to the middle and poor classes of Irish."[71] Davis expresses class differences in gendered terms, equating Moore's appeal to an elite class with effeminacy: "We might show that though he is perfect in his expression of the softer feelings, and unrivalled even by Burns in many of his gay songs, yet, that he is often deficient in vehemence, does not speak the sterner passions, spoils some of his finest songs by pretty images, is too refined and subtle in his dialect, and too negligent of narrative."[72] Moore's work, then, resembles the "foreign tunes"—the "paltry scented things" and "trifles"—that lack the racial roots and masculinity Davis envisages as necessary for imagining the Irish nation.

For Davis, the project of creating an Irish nationality in opposition to British imperialism involves revising the representation of the nation's gender. Davis rejects Ireland's feminized colonial status and attempts to depict native Irish music as masculine, as his description of the ancient Irish music suggests: "Its antique war-tunes . . . stream and crash upon the ear like the warriors of a hundred glens meeting; and you are borne with them to battle, and they and you charge and struggle amid cries and battle-axes and stinging arrows. Did ever a wail make man's marrow quiver, and fill his nostrils with the breath of the grave like the *ululu* of the north or the *wirrastrue* of Munster?"[73] Even non—war tunes are portrayed as martial in spirit: "The Irish jigs and planxties are not only the best dancing tunes, but the finest quick marches in the world."[74] This masculinization is embodied in the cover of *The Spirit of the Nation*, which Davis suggests is "a monument to bardic power, to patriotism, to our music and our history."[75] The bard on the cover is a picture of the youthful virility that Davis wants to emphasize:

> On one side of the picture is a young bard, harp-bearing. The hills of Ireland are behind him, he has come down full of strength, and wisdom, and faith. He played with the fair hair of the cataract till his ears grew filled with its warnings—he has toiled up the mountain till his sinews stiffened and his breath deserted him, for he was full of passion and resolve. . . . [N]o he has another, or rather his one great mission, the dream of his childhood before him, and he moves along through the land. . . . [H]e is full of his great thought, abstracted from all else, even from his own echoes.[76]

This youth is contrasted with the other bard on the cover, who is modeled on the Ossianic tradition. The young man serves to reanimate the representative of this other tradition: "An old bard, vast, patriarchal, rigid with years for he might have harped at the landing of Owen Roe) [*sic*] sat tranced and clutching his harp of broken chord. The singing of the ministrel [*sic*] of the Nation has broken the old harper's spell, and his hand is rising, and there is life coming into his huge rocky face."[77] The nation is joined in a form of homosocial bonding, as the song of the young bard also invigorates two other young men: "Two young brothers in arms (friends and patriots) are looking wilding [*sic*] at the passing bard, and as his song swells louder, there is fierce daring in their eyes and limbs."[78] The feminine is literally marginalized in this depiction of the nation, as the figures of four women, representative of the regions of Leinster, Munster, Ulster, and Connaught, are confined to the corners: "Disconnected from this immediate group (and sunk in the corners of the structure, beneath whose antique arch the minstrel has past [sic]) are figures of the four provinces."[79] Where the men constitute the spirit of the nation, the women represent its body, its geographical surfaces.

Given this gendered image of Ireland's national music, it is not surprising that in his essay "Irish Music and Poetry" Davis's solution to the elitism of Moore also includes remasculinizing the music, rendering it in a lower voice: "A reprint of Moore's *Melodies* on lower keys, and at *much* lower prices, would probably restore the sentimental music of Ireland to its natural supremacy."[80] But Davis wants not just to re-present Moore's work but to find new ways of making music represent a more masculine nation. This involves the creation of a new canon of national music. The music of the past has been inadequate, he suggests. He dismisses even the native songs of the Irish-speaking people as "very defective": "Most of those hitherto in use were composed during the last century, and, therefore, their structure is irregular, their grief slavish and despairing, their joy reckless and bombastic, their religion bitter and sectarian, their politics Jacobite, and concealed by extravagant and tiresome allegory."[81] To counteract songs like Moore's that dwell on the nation's weakness, Davis suggests a deliberate project of selecting music to represent the strength of the nation. He proposes two collections: "'Songs of the Irish Nation,' *to be published with music, either in parts or in single songs,* and 'Songs for the Fields and Streets.'"[82] Only songs appropriate for a nation building a masculine image would be chosen. These collections, he suggests, would not just take existing songs as they are but select and edit them.[83] A popular editor of the songs, Davis suggests, "could condense them into three or four verses each—cut them so as exactly to suit the airs, preserve the local and broad historical allusions, but remove the clumsy ornaments and exaggerations."[84] The ideal national song should be regular, direct, and unadorned. It should remain essentially masculine and not be subject to feminine ornamentation.

But in addition to forging a new canon of representative songs, Davis envisages a new genre that would represent the Irish nation: a "Ballad History of the Nation," as he calls it in an essay with that title. According to Davis, prose history is important for giving dates of events, but something more is needed to properly convey the nation's history:

> To hallow or accurse the scenes of glory and honor, or of shame and sorrow; to give to the imagination the arms, and homes, and senates, and battles of other days; to rouse, and soften, and strengthen, and enlarge us with the passions of great periods; to lead us into love of self-denial, of justice, of beauty, of valour, of generous life and proud death; and to set up in our souls the memory of great men, who shall then be as models and judges of our actions—these are the highest duties of history, and these are best taught by a Ballad History.[85]

Davis's ballad history serves the citizens of the nation in both a maternal and a paternal capacity, nurturing them through the various stages of life. But it is the paternal aspect that is more important for Davis. A ballad history is "welcome to childhood" due to "its rhymes, its high colouring, and its aptness to memory."[86] The "violent passions," "vague hopes," and "romantic sorrow" that it contains are suitable for the "fitful and luxuriant feelings" of boyhood.[87] However, he suggests, "in manhood we prize the condensed narrative, the grave firmness, the critical art, and the political sway of ballads."[88] Finally, "in old age [the ballads] are doubly dear; the companions and reminders of our life, the toys and teachers of our children and grand-children."[89] In contrast to "Mother" Moore's songs, which, according to *The Citizen,* have "cradled" the children of Ireland into "Elysian dreams," Davis's ballad history would ensure the correct channeling of "fitful and luxuriant feelings" into patriotic and masculine "firmness."

The narrative of the nation becomes the representative model for each individual's history from the nursery to the grave. As Davis suggests, "Every generation finds its account in [the patriotic ballads]" that constitute the ballad history.[90] This idea of narrative is very important to Davis, both as a way of suggesting the parallel chronological development of the nation and its individual citizens from childhood to maturity and as a way of encouraging an equivalence between the practice of reading and economic behavior. A narrative encourages the individual in the labor of reading, a labor that ultimately leads to a goal, rather than catching him up in refinement and ornament and spending his resources without progress. Where Moore's songs are "too negligent of narrative," allowing the reader to luxuriate in feeling, the ballad history would provide a narrative path for the reader to follow.

It is the labor involved in reading that Davis wants to encourage. He pays lip-service to the oral nature of the proposed ballad history, suggesting that patriot ballads that will go into creating that history will "pass from mouth to mouth like salutations."[91] But what he also describes is a desire for the elimination of oral transmission. Davis suggests that in ancient times all "ballads were made to music, and the minstrel sang them to his harp or screamed them in recitative"[92] to ensure their dissemination. But mechanical reproduction is now able to take over this role: "Printing so multiplies copies of ballads, and intercourse is so general, that there is less need of this adaptation to music now."[93] Printing, the materialization and commodification of the ballads, is yet another means of ensuring conformity and of eliminating "excess" and ornament. It is also a way of eliminating the history of allusions and the hybridity that, as we have seen, is an integral aspect of the ballads and tunes and that Hardiman suggested as a kind of "counteractivity." Davis wants to eliminate the ambivalent traces of meaning belonging to the ballads and to concentrate the reader's attention on the present meaning and the present moment: "Moreover, it may be disputed whether the dramatic effect in the more solemn ballads is not injured by lyrical forms. . . . Were we free to do so, we could point out instances in the *Spirit of the Nation* in which the rejection of song-forms seems to have been essential to the awfulness of the occasion."[94] Whereas in Moore's case the elimination of the music in the later editions turned the powerful ambivalence of the text into sentimentality, Davis wants the elimination of the music to result in the creation of a nation simultaneously forged from and purged of the traces of the past.

Where Hardiman's project involved placing Moore within a historical genealogy of Gaelic Catholic poets, Davis wants to use Moore as a starting point for a new program based on—but free from—historical partisanship. He suggests that the success of *The Spirit of the Nation* was partially attributable to the popularity of Moore: "To him, to his patriotism, to his genius, and, we may selfishly add, to his friendship, we owe our ability now to give to Ireland music fit for 'The Memory of the Dead' and 'The Hymn of Freedom.'"[95] Moore becomes a tenuous link here, merely a conduit for the music that he passed on. Davis suggests that the poetry of *The Spirit of the Nation* will supplant Moore's own poetry, just as the music that Moore passed on will ideally be supplanted by words.

Both Hardiman's and Davis's attempts to forge the Irish nation through reconfiguring its oral tradition were ultimately disrupted by the devastation that became known as "The Great Hunger."[96] In the aftermath of the Famine, the editor and antiquarian George Petrie attempted to compile a complete collection of Irish tunes with all the local variants.[97] The result was *The Ancient Music of Ireland*, published in 1855, which, with its musical scores, commentary on the tunes, and historical accounts of Ireland's music, attempts to imagine a national identity for contemporary Ireland based on the relics of the past. In *The Ancient Music of Ireland*, Petrie ponders the devastating effects of the Famine on Irish music: "'The land of song' was no longer tuneful; or, if a human sound met the traveller's ear, it was only that of the feeble and despairing wail for the dead."[98] According to Petrie, while hunger and emigration worked to depopulate "the green pastoral plains, the fruitful valleys, as well as the wild hill sides and the dreary bogs," it was this lack of Irish song that brought home the dreadful national loss. Hunger might kill bodies, but lack of music killed the soul: "This awful, unwonted silence, which, during the famine and subsequent years, almost everywhere prevailed, struck more fearfully upon their imaginations, as many Irish gentlemen informed me, and gave them a deeper feeling of the desolation with which the country had been visited, than any other circumstance which had forced itself upon their attention."[99] And it is to fill "that awful unwonted silence"[100] that Petrie states he accepted the proposal to publish his collection of songs, setting himself the task "to fix, as far as practicable, by evidences, the true forms of our melodies, where already published or not; and to throw all available light upon their past history."[101] Petrie's interest in the authenticity of Irish music is connected not with ethnic or racial purity but with the "true forms" of the melodies.

A large part of this concern with purity in the *Ancient Music*, however, is setting right the genealogy of Irish music collecting, in particular elevating Bunting over Moore. But while Petrie is quick to praise Bunting as a pioneer in the history of music collection in Ireland, one who, more than Moore, has been responsible for the preservation of Irish music, he also devotes a great deal of space in his introduction to distinguishing himself from Bunting. Bunting commented that the popularity of a tune fixes it in the people's ears, thus establishing "a tribunal of the utmost accuracy and of unequalled impartiality (for it is unconscious of the exercise of its own authority) governing the musical traditions of the people."[102] Petrie comments that the songs are not, "like so many modern melodies, mere *ad libitum* arrangements of a pleasing succession of tones, unshackled by a rigid obedience to metrical laws; they are arrangements of tones, in a general way expressive of the sentiments of the songs for which they were composed, but always strictly coincident with, and subservient to, the laws of rhythm and metre which govern the construction of those songs, and to which they consequently owe their peculiarities of structure."[103] Where Bunting's authority comes from popular consensus, Petrie's comes from a notion of basic laws. Petrie's appeal to these basic laws allows the music to be rigidly categorized: "And hence it obviously follows that the entire body of our vocal melodies may be easily divided into, and arranged under, as many classes as there are metrical forms of construction in our native lyrics—but no further; and that any melody that will not naturally fall into some one or other of those classes must be either corrupt or altogether fictitious."[104] Petrie makes Irishness equate with a specific structure.[105]

Bunting expressed his belief in the oral tradition of music: "A strain of music, once impressed on the popular ear, never varies."[106] Petrie qualifies the efficacy of the oral tradition, limiting it to singing. Petrie's preference for the human voice over instrumental music as the more authentic way of conveying tunes can be seen as far back as his review essay on Bunting and Moore for the *Dublin Examiner* in August 1816. In that piece, he praises the contemporary interest in national music as "an omen of a purer and more natural taste, being likely to take the place of the tawdry and artificial one that has so long governed the musical world."[107] Petrie takes aim at the compositions of the last century, which are, he suggests, too "refined" to be considered authentic.

The complexity of the eighteenth-century tunes means that they lose their continuity with the past, he suggests, as they are played differently by different players: "The compositions of this period have an instrumental character—the older ones a vocal—and in consequence of this difference, we rarely hear any of the modern airs in a perfect form, or two performers play them alike; for their intricacies, and length, and want of striking character, make them difficult to commit to, or retain in the memory, while the ancient airs are sung in all parts of the kingdom with but little variation."[108] Petrie's concern is to establish new criteria for authenticity.

In the *Ancient Music*, he elaborates on his earlier comparison of the accuracy of vocal versus instrumental transmission, complaining that Bunting's most "common authorities" are "harpers and other instrumentalists."[109] For Petrie, a tune must come from the singing of a native singer to be authentic: "[I]t was only from the chanting of vocalists, who combined words with the airs, that setting could be made which would have any stamp of purity and authenticity."[110] According to Petrie, Irish melodies,

> even when in the hands of those players whose instruments will permit a true rendering of their peculiar tonalities and features of expression, assume a new and unfixed character, varying with the caprices of each unskilled performer, who, unshackled by any of the restraints imposed upon the singer by the rhythm and metre of the words connected with those airs, thinks only of exhibiting, and gaining applause for, his own powers of invention and execution, by the absurd indulgence of barbarous licenses and conventionalities, destructive not only of their simpler and finer song qualities, but often rendering their essential features undeterminable with any degree of certainty.[111]

While Petrie suggests that a tune needs to be situated in the body of a native singer, he assumes that that body will act as a pure conduit for the music. Whereas the body of an instrumentalist will act upon a tune, modifying it into something "new and unfixed," the body of a singer, according to Petrie, lacks the agency to effect changes.

Like Davis, Petrie connects Irishness with a connection to "the soil." The most authentic Irish airs, Petrie suggests, are derived not just from any native singer but from those who live in the most "purely" Irish locations. He notes, "I have availed myself of every opportunity in my power to obtain the purest settings of the airs, by noting them from the native singers, and more particularly from such of them as resided, or had been reared, in the most purely Irish districts."[112] For Bunting, an Irish tune can be preserved from generation to generation as long as there are people to play it. For Petrie, the tune must be collected from a "native singer" in the most "Irish" geographical location possible. For Bunting, a tune can travel essentially unchanged in time and space: "It may be made the vehicle of many different sets of words, but they are adapted to *it*, not it to *them*, and it will no more alter its character on their account than a ship will change the number of its masts on account of an alteration in the nature of its lading."[113] Petrie condemns "the irrationality and untruthfulness" of this idea.[114] For Petrie, Irish tunes exist in a bewildering number of forms: "I rarely, if ever, obtained two settings of an *unpublished* air that were strictly the same; though, in some instances, I have gotten as many as fifty notations of the one melody."[115] The task for Petrie is to establish and fix the most Irish tune in order to find the national standard: "I have sedulously endeavored to test their accuracy, and free them from the corruptions incidental to local and individual recollections, by seeking for other settings from various localities and persons."[116] Through comparing variants and establishing "the superior accuracy, and perhaps beauty, of one over others,"[117] he attempts to purge the tune of local "corruptions" and therefore derive the national *Ur*-tune.[118] In the body of his text he is constantly noting how he has selected "the truest from a variety of versions."[119] Bunting optimistically conveys the sense that a tune is carried forward unchanging on a sea of performances. Petrie endows the oral tradition with a great deal of anxiety. Tunes, for him, are constantly beset by corrupting influences. Each transfer from the original body from which the tune is uttered threatens the purity of the tune.

The purity of the tune is also related to considerations of gender and class. Petrie alluded to a feminine representation of Ireland in his *Irish Penny Journal* (December 19, 1840) when describing John Hogan's monument to James Doyle: "[I]n the figure of the prostrate female we recognize at a glance the attributes of our country," a "country . . . personified by a beautiful female figure."[120] In Hogan's statue, Ireland is a majestic crowned image bearing a harp. The *Ancient Music*, however, suggests a connection between Irish identity and laboring-class women. Many of the tunes derive from the performances of women of this class. "The Cunning Young Man," for example, was taken down "from the singing of a fisherman's wife," who in turn learned it "from the singing of her mother."[121] The version of "The Silken Article" that Petrie includes was derived "from the singing of a woman named Biddy Monahan," who was, "from her love for music, a rare depository [*sic*] of the melodies which had been current in her youth in the romantic peninsula of *Cuil Iorra*."[122] "Molly Hewson" was "one of many tunes noted down about forty years since, from the singing of a now aged lady—a near connexion of my own—those airs having been learned in her child-days from the singing of an old woman, who was frequently brought in to assist in washing in her father's house."[123] Alternatively, tunes that are noted from the singing of men are generally remembered "as heard in [their] youth."[124] The original songs, then, are associated with femininity or immaturity, not with adult masculinity. As such, Petrie anxiously suggests, they are subject to change and must be regulated. The "true forms" of the melodies must be "fixed."

Petrie suggests that the only way to "fix" the tunes so that they are protected from corruption is to publish them. This was the basic tenet of the Society for the Preservation and Publication of the Melodies of Ireland, which sponsored Petrie's endeavor. The preface in the *Ancient Music* expresses the society's concern with "the Preservation and Publication of the immense quantity of National Music still existing in Ireland . . . of which much is yet unwritten."[125] The society's goals are to be facilitated by "the collection and classification of all such as has been already noted down on paper, and by the formation of a central depôt in Dublin, to which persons having opportunities of noting down what is still unwritten may be invited to send copies of any airs which they can obtain, either in Ireland or among our countrymen in other lands"[126] and by the publication of collections such as Petrie's, which is envisioned as the first of many. The society's elevation of print above oral culture is also evident in the text of the *Ancient Music*, as Petrie hints at his own predisposition toward print in his comments regarding Bunting's lack of interest in print sources. He indicates that he knows Bunting had at his disposal "all the oldest printed, as well as many MS., settings of a large number of our airs, together with an extensive collection of the Irish songs sung to them, and other materials now difficult, if not impossible, to procure,"[127] but that he hardly made any use of them. Indeed, Petrie comments that Bunting "appears to have had a rooted aversion" to "the use of all printed authorities" and that "in all cases, he preferred the statement of facts on his own unsupported authority to every one."[128] Petrie rises to the podium in his denunciation of Bunting's reliance on oral transmission as his source:

[W]hat reliance can we place on the statements to one who, in reference to that strange musical farrago . . . called "the Irish cry as sung in Ulster" . . . tells us that it was procured in 1799 "from O'Neill, harper, and from the hired mourners or keeners at Armagh; and from a MS. above 100 years old"?—or who gravely acquaints us that he obtained the well-known tune called "Patrick's Day," in 1792, from "Patrick Quin, harper;"

as if he could not have gotten as accurate a set of it from any human being in Ireland that could either play, sing, or whistle a tune; and though he knew that the air had been printed—and more correctly too—in Playford's "Dancing Master," more than a century previous. Thus, in like manner, he refers us to dead harpers as his authorities for all those tunes of Carolan, and many others, which he printed; nearly all of which had been already given in Neal's, and other publications of the early part of the last century.[129]

Petrie suggests that a London publication of Irish tunes, Playford's, is more "correct" than the playing of contemporary Irish musicians. His questioning the authority of "dead harpers" in comparison to the published *Collection of the most Celebrated Irish Tunes* suggests his ultimate preference for print.

Ironically, although Petrie is very concerned to "fix" tunes correctly using the singing of informants, he does not often provide words for the tunes. In almost every case in which he notes a tune from a native singer, he comments that he "neglected to make a record"[130] of the words sung to the tune and has forgotten the name in Irish by which "the melody was known in [the singer's] native county."[131] He is eager to point out the value of lyrics in conveying information about peasant life. Even the political ballads are interesting "as expressive of the popular mind during periods of its excitement to disaffection."[132] But the words are arbitrary to Petrie, and he makes many editorial decisions about them. The tune for "The Blackthorn Cane with a Thong" was "noted down" from the singing of Biddy Monahan, but Petrie supplies it with a song that "was written by Owen Roe O'Sullivan . . . a scholar and Irish poet of some eminence."[133] He joins the fragments of one ancient song to another that is "modern" to illustrate what he considers "one of the better and abiding traits of the Irish peasant nature, in strong contrast to those partially acquired and temporary ones which had been superinduced by untoward circumstances."[134] And he decides which words might be "unfit for publication" due to their questionable moral content. The words that do appear in the *Ancient Music* serve as general indicators of peasant life, highly mediated by editorial intervention. They are fragments of a vanished peasant culture that are pieced together.

In contrast, the tunes are presented as intact and correct in every way possible. However, unlike Bunting's collections—or those of Owenson, Moore, or even Hardiman or Davis—the *Ancient Music* is not designed for utility. The tunes are certainly designed to be playable. Harmonies suitable for the keyboard and indications of tempo are provided with each tune. For "persons not provided with a Metronome,"[135] Petrie includes an indication of how long a pendulum should be for one beat to correspond to a particular note in each tune. But each tune is separated by commentary that sometimes occupies several pages. The *Ancient Music* is not a collection of tunes to be kept on the piano for performance. It is a reference work whose chief concern is the preservation of tunes. Moore's collections of songs invited the active participation of their consumers, at least those with a certain amount of musical training, in such a way as to turn the object of consumption into a site of production. Petrie's collection does not encourage such participation. The readers of the *Ancient Music* consume the tunes as artifacts, "accidentally discovered vestiges of an ancient and peculiar race of people."[136] Derived originally from singing, the songs have lost their specific meaning and serve only as general signs of orality.[137]

The association of music with the loss of oral culture is further complicated, as the bodies of the peasants who preserved the songs have now been subject to the ravages of the Famine. Petrie notes the effect of the Famine and the concomitant emigration on the different generations of Irish citizens. The old, "who had still preserved as household gods the language, the songs, and traditions of their race and their localities," have perished, while the middle-aged who survived have fled from the "plague and panic stricken land."[138] As a result, the young are now displaced from the nurturing of traditional society, a nurturing whose musical aspect is particularly associated with the feminine: they are raised "where no mother's eyes could make them feel the mysteries of human affections—no mother's voice could soothe their youthful sorrows, and implant within the memories of their hearers her songs of tenderness and love."[139] While they have also lost the "traditions and characteristic peculiarities of feeling" that are associated with the "father's instructions," it is the maternal "voice" that is linked with "song."

But Petrie's depiction of the loss of peasant traditional life is more complex than this. In his introduction, Petrie suggests that he was motivated to collect Irish melodies by, among other things, a "desire to aid in the preservation of remains so honourable to the national character of my country."[140] He indicates that he was ultimately persuaded to publish his findings by the catastrophe of the Famine, which had killed so many Irish people and threatened the rest with the loss of their culture: "I could not but feel that what must have been, at no distant time, the inevitable result of the changes in the character of the Irish race which had been long in operation, and which had already almost entirely denationalized its higher classes, had been suddenly effected, as by a lightning flash, by the calamities which, in the year 1846–7, had struck down and well nigh annihilated the Irish remnant of the great Celtic family."[141] Here the Famine appears not as the cause of the loss of Irish oral culture but merely as a catalyst that accelerated an ongoing process of general erosion of the "racy feeling of nationality" in Ireland.[142]

Although Petrie suggests that the Irish upper classes have been "denationalized," it is the lower classes who manifest a specific symptom of the lack of "national character": an inability to distinguish authentic from inauthentic Irish melodies. He comments that "[t]he thoughtless, impulsive Irishman, of a lower social grade, will prefer the airs of 'Patrick's day,' or 'Garryowen,' to all the lively melodies of his country."[143] Although he hints that the Irish people have grown "accustomed . . . to the use of food of a coarser and more exciting nature" because of "adversities," those adversities are never specified. Instead, Petrie is left to lament the lack of taste of his countrypeople: "I could not but fear that I might be vainly labouring to cultivate mental fruit which, however indigenous to the soil, was yet of too refined and delicate a flavour to be relished, or appreciated."[144] In particular, he identifies this lack of taste as responsible for the current vogue of Thomas Moore: "[T]he finest of our Irish melodies have obtained their just appreciation far less from any immediate estimate of their merits, than from their accidental union with the lyrics of Moore and others, which had taken a hold on the popular mind."[145] Music becomes not only the distinguishing characteristic of Ireland—"the only skill for which our English neighbours ever deigned to allow us any credit," as Moore suggested—but also a way of identifying a particular kind of Irishness: general and tasteful, but not "popular." Petrie wants to change the "musical sensations of the Irish people." In particular, using authentic melodies, he wants to develop a new sense of Irish identity, based on the melodies of peasant singing but refined by having been for the most part divorced from its original lyrics and surrounded by explanatory notes.

In the *Ancient Music,* Petrie promotes the authenticity of the oral tradition in the form of the voice, which is variously linked to the feminine and to immaturity, but he also suggests that that authenticity can be preserved only through the technology of print, which erases the voice, masculinizing it by fixing it in a correct form. And as the authenticity of the music can be preserved only through a disavowal of the (female) human body that was its original site, that disavowal becomes necessary to ensure its authenticity. The body of the printed text serves not as a replacement of the human body but as a sign of its loss. Print becomes a marker of a vanished orality. The *Ancient Music,* then, associates Irish music inherently with loss and suggests the representation of Ireland as a feminine symbol of the past and of exile.

8

Irish Music, British Culture, and the Transatlantic Experience

Fintan O'Toole identifies two Irelands, one located at home and one abroad: "Considered geographically," he suggests, "Ireland is a pre-given space, standing sharply out from the ocean that surrounds it. But considered demographically, Ireland is an unbounded sprawl, an incoherent network of memories and resentments, dreams and desperations, moving between the island itself and its diaspora in Britain, the United States, Australia, Canada and elsewhere."[1] The first can be read, "albeit problematically, as the result of a given past."[2] But the second "demographic Ireland" is "a nation that cannot be read but must be written."[3] O'Toole's formulation of the Irish diaspora suggests the kind of ambivalence that has been the focus of much of this book, as he remarks that because this second nation must be written, "it could be written otherwise."[4] This chapter will examine a number of ways this diasporic identity has been written—and written "otherwise"—by looking at representations of Irish music in England and North America in the mid–nineteenth century.

A number of critics have investigated negative stereotypes of the Irish current in England in the nineteenth century.[5] English representations of Irish flaws took on particular significance during and just after the Famine years, when the condemnation of the essentially flawed Irish character was paramount in justifying England's role in failing to adequately address the problem. The burden of Carlyle's *Reminiscences of My Irish Journey in 1849*, for example, is to exonerate England by vilifying Ireland. Carlyle sees nothing worthwhile in Ireland. Faced with scene after scene of poverty, Carlyle's compassion turns to abhorrence: "Poor wretches, after all; but human *pity* dies away into stony misery and disgust in the excess of such scenes."[6] His observation that newly established workhouses are not being used as fully as they could be leads him to the conclusion that the English government has in fact done too much: "[E]verywhere in Ireland one finds that the 'Government,' far from stinginess in public money towards Ireland, has erred rather on the other side; making, in all seasons, extensive *hives* for which the *bees* are not yet found."[7] At the end of his trip, Carlyle's solution for Irish difficulties is to lay the blame on Irish people: "Remedy for Ireland? To cease generally from following the devil: no other remedy that I know of."[8]

Although Carlyle was certainly one of Ireland's more colorful detractors, other less flamboyant writers share his views. Nassau Senior manages to convey the same disparagement of Irish society in the wake of the Famine as Carlyle. Senior, an economist and government policy advisor, had earlier risked the wrath of the Church of England by advocating using the lands of the Catholic Church to support Catholic priests.[9] In his numerous accounts of the Irish situation, however, Senior, like Carlyle, blames insecurity, ignorance, and indolence in Ireland for the lack of capital being sent to help the Irish people. He connects these qualities with Irish character flaws, as he notes that "[t]he INSECURITY of person and of property in Ireland arises from the tendency to violence and resistance to law which is the most prominent, as well as the most mischievous, part of the Irish character. It is the quality which most distinguishes Ireland from Great Britain."[10] In "Relief of Irish Distress in 1847 and 1848," he compares the impact of the potato famine in Ireland and in England, concluding that the relatively light impact of the famine in England was due to that nation's being more "civilised":

> The consequence in England was distress; but as the English, like every civilised nation, use many different kinds of food, and employ a large portion of their incomes for purposes other than the purchase of food, the difficulty was met by an increased consumption of other articles, which would otherwise have been given to domestic animals . . . and by a diminished expenditure in clothes and other commodities not absolutely indispensable. In Ireland the consequence was Famine—a calamity which cannot befall a civilized nation.[11]

Both Carlyle and Senior conclude that the British Empire is the only thing that has the potential to save Ireland from itself. Carlyle writes, "Society is at an end here, with the land uncultivated, and every second soul a pauper.— 'Society' here would have to eat itself, and end by cannibalism in a week, if it were not held up by the rest of our empire still standing afoot!"[12] And Senior, asserting that "the people of England and of Ireland . . . are among the most dissimilar nations in Europe,"[13] suggests that it is precisely the difference between the nations that gives England the right to rule Ireland: "[I]n legislating for Ireland, we must legislate for her, not as if she were a distinct State, but as a member of the Empire."[14]

Both Carlyle's and Senior's accounts betray their fear of Irish contamination. In Senior's work, poverty is portrayed as a disease and a poison that threatens both the Irish and the English social body: "[W]e may be sure that, if we allow the cancer of pauperism to complete the destruction of Ireland, and then to throw fresh venom into the already pre-disposed body of England, the ruin of all that makes England worth living is a question only of time."[15] What is significant here, however, is that England is already "pre-disposed" to the "cancer of pauperism." At the same time that he wants to emphasize Ireland's difference, Senior registers anxiety about just how related the two nations are and therefore how susceptible England is to Irish influence. In *Reminiscences of My Irish Journey in 1849*, it is Carlyle's own body that represents English suffering caused by Irish contamination, as he recounts for the reader the multiple ailments he experiences during his time abroad. He notes that he experiences insomnia during his entire trip, lamenting that "[o]ne's 'powers of observation' act under sad conditions, if the nerves are to be continually in a shatter with want of sleep and what it brings! Under that sad condition, as of a gloomy pressure of waking nightmare, were all my Irish operations, of observation or other, transacted."[16] Senior also employs the nightmare image in "Ireland in 1843" to describe the Irish situation, as he suggests that "[f]or many years past, Ireland has been the most painful subject on which a liberal writer could employ himself. . . . When Irish questions, or rather the *Irish Question* . . . has been forced on our attention, we have felt, like a dreamer in a nightmare, oppressed by the consciousness that some great evil was rapidly advancing—that mere exertion on our part would avert it, but that we had not the power to will that exertion."[17] Carlyle's "waking nightmare" and Senior's "dreamer in a nightmare" collapse their professedly rational accounts of the "Irish Question" into images of Gothic obscurity.

The accounts of Carlyle and Senior indicate the prejudice and fear that characterized British attitudes to Ireland during the mid–nineteenth century. But Carlyle's work also gives an indication of British interest in a particular aspect of Irish culture, for among the subjects upon which Carlyle comments in his "waking nightmare" is Irish music. During one of his forays, he observes a keening ritual: "Funeral overtaken by us; the 'Irish howl;'—totally disappointing, there was no sorrow whatever in the tone of it. A pack of idle women, mounted on the hearse as many as could, and the rest walking; were hoh-hoh-ing with a grief quite evidently hired and not worth hiring."[18] And in Limerick, he notes, "[Charles Gavan] Duffy reads *choice* Irish ballads to me,—unmusical enough."[19] Although Carlyle is as disparaging about Irish music as he is about everything else in Ireland, his comments make clear that he had high expectations of Irish music before he embarked on his journey. He was familiar enough with the ideal of the "Irish howl" to find the actual performance that he witnessed unsatisfying. Similarly, the "choice" ballads strike him as unmusical, despite what he has heard about them. Carlyle's awareness of and anticipation of Irish musical performance suggest the currency of Irish music across the Irish Sea.

Indeed, around the same time that Carlyle, Senior, and others were writing their negative impressions of the Irish national character and the English government was debating what course to take regarding the Famine in Ireland, Irish music was enjoying a renewed vogue in England. Samuel Lover was performing evenings of Irish song in London and achieving great popularity with a play and a novel based on one of his songs, "Rory O'More." Frederick Horncastle, too, was presenting his "Entertainment on the National Music of Ireland." And the symbolic conflation of Ireland and music was embodied at the Great Exhibition of 1851 with Arthur Jones's "Temple of Music," carved out of Irish bogwood. Lover, Horncastle, and Jones offer positive representations of Irishness at a time when the Irish were being treated with suspicion. Although all three represent Irish music as an object of cultural consumption in England, aligning Irishness with tradition and sentiment while asserting English modernity, their representations also constitute a positive resistance to the British imperial vision.

Samuel Lover began his career as an artist of miniatures, then became a writer, contributing songs, stories, and sketches to leading Dublin magazines. His biographer, William Bayle Bernard, notes that many of these, "when published collectively [as *Legends and Stories of Ireland* (1831)], obtain[ed] him a second fame in England."[20] He moved to London in 1834, where, like Thomas Moore, he was an extremely popular guest at drawing-room receptions because of his performing abilities. After his eyesight began to fail in 1844, he gave up painting and became an entertainer on the London stage, performing his own songs and stories in what became known as "Lover's Irish Evenings."[21] His début was in March 1844 at the Princess Theatre, London. For the next seven years, he presented his "Evenings," accompanied by two young ladies who sang. Lover followed in the footsteps of Moore, benefiting from Moore's popularity in England, but at the same time he attempted to carve out a different niche than his predecessor.

In the fourth edition of Lover's collection of *Songs and Ballads,* in which, as he notes, the songs are "divorced from the music to which they have been wedded," Lover attempts to address the kind of criticism Moore received for his songs' lack of masculine vigor, for their being "pleasant and harmless, neither powerful nor severe," as the October 1822 *Quarterly Review* put it. [22] Lover writes, "I would beg to remind the critic that a song . . . must not be measured by ordinary rules of criticism" because "the song-writer is limited within many bounds to which other writers are not restricted." [23] He continues, "A critic may consider a song to want grandeur or vigour of expression, —a want which the writer himself has lamented, very probably, but he has been compelled to use good *singing* words, rather than *reading* ones; and this should be kept in mind when we read songs that have been made for singing." [24] Lover gives examples from Milton's *Comus* and Byron's "Stanzas for Music" that, though they qualify as grand poetry, "are not suited to singing" [25] because of their complicated nature. Lover counters the kind of criticism Moore received by asserting that songs must be judged according to different rules. To consider merely the language of the song, Lover suggests, is to consider only part of the song's "vigour," for the music also supplies its own "vigour": "[I]t absolutely *increases* the power of the lines." [26]

Lover also manages to avoid the gendered criticisms leveled at Moore by shifting his focus away from genteel lovers pining for their lost nation and their beloved to less "feminized" subjects: the working-class Irish. Bernard, writing in 1874, describes the difference between Moore and Lover: "It was the greatest triumph of Moore that his enchanting melodies had the effect of attracting sympathy to Ireland when England, still engaged in an exhausting foreign struggle, was most indifferent to her cries; and I think it may be said of Lover, that he sought to direct this awakened feeling to the quarter of all others which required its influence the most—that of the derided Irish peasant." [27] Lover's "Rory O'More; Or, Good Omens," one of the most popular songs from the "Irish Evenings," in fact makes fun of such genteel declarations of love as are found in Moore's songs when Kathleen teases Rory by claiming that Mike loves her better: "The ground that I walk on he loves, I'll be bound." [28] Rory replies by appealing to practicalities: "Faith . . . I'd rather love *you* than the ground." [29] Bernard describes the negative stereotypes that Lover was attempting to change: "National prejudice had so long encrusted [the lower-class Irishman] with vulgarity and coarseness . . . that English society had only been able to enjoy his humour under restraint, and could not avoid being repelled from him even when it was most diverted." [30] He contends that Lover, like Moore, attempted to use Irish music to further a political cause, and he describes Lover's idea: "[I]f this truer picture of the man could be shown in a series of songs adapted to popular national airs, or other music as appropriate, and addressed to the taste and sympathy of good society, Irish and English, it would not only supply its hearers with a new and welcome entertainment, but possibly awaken in English circles a kindlier feeling towards a class which they had so little understood, and so imperfectly been pleased with."[31] In his account, Bernard engages in anti-English stereotyping that counterbalances the stereotyping of the Irish as "vulgar" and "coarse." He accuses the English of "torpor" and "dullness": "Our [English] national reserve and sombreness still cling to us like a bad cold that defies all effect of stimulants. Wit, music, singing, dancing seem to serve but as so much limelight to make our pensiveness more visible. . . . To resuscitate a group from its good old Anglo-Saxon torpor, to lift from its soul a weight of dullness which so many think a due propriety, is mostly a labour that needs a Hercules quite as much as it does a Momus."[32] Far from being associated with feminine weakness, in Bernard's account, Lover's work provides a powerful "stimulant" to rouse the English from their "torpor."

But Lover's project to promote a more positive view of the Irish peasantry in his "Irish Evenings" and other work remains problematic. For one thing, his portrayals of Irish peasants reinforce an association between the Irish nation and the rural past that presents Ireland as the antithesis of a modern England. Bernard notes that Lover gathered his materials from his own past, drawing his anecdotes from meetings with peasants in Wicklow: "In later and longer rambles he may have gathered the rich material with which he illustrated their character, the manifold traits and jests and incidents which he has embalmed in song and legend; but the spirit in which he painted them was ever that of boyhood."[33] In addition to connecting the songs and stories to his own "boyhood," Lover represents Irish superstitiousness in a number of his songs. Each of the three stanzas of "Rory O'More" illustrates a superstition—wearing a cloak inside out, dreaming in "conthrairies," and performing activities an odd number of times. Rory proceeds to turn these superstitions to his advantage in wooing Kathleen. When Kathleen complains that Rory teases her until she puts her coat on backwards and avows that she dreams every night that she hates him, Rory replies, "'[T]is all for good luck." When she tells him to leave her alone, as he has kissed her eight times that day, he uses the information to steal another kiss as "there's luck in odd numbers." Other songs like "The Falling Star" and "The Four-Leaved Shamrock" also foreground Irish superstitions. By drawing a connection between Irish songs, childhood, and primitive society, Lover's songs associate Ireland with irrationality. His anecdotes of Irish rural peasant life were especially appealing during and after the Famine, when the rural areas of Ireland were being depopulated, as the songs represented Ireland as chronologically retarded during a time in which England was gaining in global influence. The songs "embalm" an Irish identity rooted in the past, preserving it for eternity for the consumption of a modern English audience.

At the same time, Lover's songs constitute a resistance to British power. The name of the main character in his most popular song, play, and novel, "Rory O'More," is indicative of that resistance, as it harks back to the O'More who was the main instigator of the 1641 Ulster Rebellion against English rule. Bernard notes that the song "Rory O'More" "attained, in a brief period, to an imperial reputation. United to one of the most hilarious and inspiring of national airs, *I'll follow you over the Mountain, my dear* . . . it flew with the wings of a swallow over Ireland and England, and at length crossing the ocean, became a favorite in every city and almost every village of the West."[34] Bernard continues,

> Their graceful and piquant mirthfulness, underlain by a delicate fervour which stole into the feelings unawares amidst the laughter, were to many English listeners as much a surprise as an enjoyment. Its music also, descending from the drawing-room to the streets, was ground into public favour on every barrel-organ in the kingdom, and with the military bands succeeded to all the honours of the *British Grenadiers*. The tune indeed, like the tricolour, made the circuit of the world. The course of the sun, it has been said, is followed by the roll of the British drum, and for many years the imperial strain brightened its summons, morning and evening, with the buoyant lilt of the Irish peasant.[35]

In Bernard's account, Lover's songs offer a challenge to British hegemony, working to put the Irish peasant on the "imperial" circuit. In fact, Bernard credits "Rory O'More" with having the same cultural power as the militaristic "British Grenadiers." The original Rory O'More may have lost the rebellion (and eventually his life), but Lover's efforts ensured that his name survived to fight on the cultural front.

Lover rendered his presentations on Irish music into more permanent form, publishing a collection entitled *Mr. Lover's Irish Evenings* in 1844. The publication features only the lyrics from the "Irish Evenings," not Lover's commentary. All of the songs, with the exception of Moore's "Go Where Glory Waits Thee," were written by Lover. The majority are love songs, several of which dwell on the parting of lovers. In "Mary Ma Chree," for example, Mary mourns the departure of her young soldier:

Her lover was gone to a far distant land,
And Mary, in sadness, would pace the lone strand,
And tearfully gaze o'er the dark rolling sea,
That parted her soldier from Mary *ma chree*.[36]

None of the songs are overtly political, not even to the extent of equating the beloved with the figure of Ireland, as is common in Moore's *Melodies*. But *Mr. Lover's Irish Evenings* also offers some idea of the political fashion in which Lover framed his audience's perception of these songs. The subtitle of the work refers to "The Irish Brigade," and the program included in the publications indicates how Lover used the history of the brigade to assert an Irish military identity. The Irish Brigade were originally "Wild Geese" who had fled to fight for France. The program indicates their "expatriation," then launches into descriptions of Irish martial prowess, including the "Brilliant achievements of the Brigade in Flanders, Spain and Italy," the "Distinction in Foreign service" that the "Youth of Ireland" enjoyed, and the "Military Talents" of Patrick Sarsfield (a hero of the siege of Limerick during the Williamite wars). The narrative of the program alludes to the threat to England that an Ireland united with either France or Scotland would constitute, as it notes how the brigade was well received by Louis XIV and how the "Irish and Scots engaged in a common cause" during the Jacobite Rebellion. These threats are ultimately downplayed, however, as the performance apparently ends by indicating how the Irish Brigade was finally dissolved and how the Irish were "incorporated with the English and Scotch, in the British Army." Yet despite this military amalgamation, the Irish (and the "Scotch") maintain their cultural distinctiveness in their "Love . . . for their National Music." While Lover's commentary diffuses the military threat that the Irish constituted historically, both by discussing the combined British military and by interspersing the military narrative with love songs (which are interpreted as concerning members of the brigade and their sweethearts), the burden of the program is to present the "Rollicking Spirit of the Irish" as a force to be reckoned with. While the songs themselves suggest a feminized version of Irish music, especially as they were performed by female singers, the context in which Lover presents them, the history of the Irish Brigade, reasserts a masculine identity for Irish music.

Lover was not the only one offering performances of Irish music in London at the time. In January 1843, Frederick W. Horncastle, a former organist at St. Patrick's Cathedral, Armagh, presented his "Entertainment on the National Music of Ireland with Vocal and Instrumental Illustrations" at the

Music Hall in Bedford Square. Accompanying him were the Misses Williams, who sang, a Miss LeRoy, who played harp, and a Mr. Thomas O'Hannigan, who played the union pipes. Horncastle's "Entertainment" strung together performances of Irish songs (many of which were Moore's versions) with lectures on the structure and history of Irish music and Irish legends and anecdotes. The event was very well received, obtaining eight encores, according to contemporary newspapers. One of these encores was for the "Caoine, or Funeral Cry," which, despite (or perhaps because of) the artificial context in which it was performed, was considerably more moving than the actual keening that Carlyle witnessed. Like "Lover's Irish Evenings," Horncastle's "Entertainment" seems to have worked in several ways. On the one hand, it represented Irish music in a positive way, suggesting its historical interest. On the other hand, the "Entertainment" reinforced an opposition between Irish music as a primitive tradition and English taste as indication of modernity. The *Morning Post* attested that "the whole entertainment afforded great delight to a numerous audience," while the *Britannia* suggested that the event's popularity was proof "that the people are becoming alive to the eloquent beauty of national music, illustrating, as it does, every phase of national character."[37] Like Lover's songs, Horncastle's "Entertainment" associates Irish music with what would have been considered "primitive"—legends and superstitions. Horncastle himself, by explaining and historicizing the music, serves to make his audience metropolitan experts on the subject of Irish music. The audience at Horncastle's "Entertainment" could indulge their taste for the "primitive" while inside the theatrical venue and re-emerge into the modern city once the evening was over.

It is in its print form as *The Music of Ireland as Performed in Mr. Horncastle's Irish Entertainments* (1844) that Horncastle's work is most politically subversive, however. Although Horncastle's *Music of Ireland* is not so direct in illustrating Irish resistance to British hegemony as Lover's publication, it, too, encourages an association of Ireland and military power by including a number of "Marches" along with "[t]he Bardic and Connaught Caoines, Songs, Fairy Chants & Songs, Rural Ballads" and "Songs of Occupation." "Burn's March," for example, presents an image of masculine military vigor:

> See the bold Chieftain marching o'er the mountain
> While in the cold breeze his banners are streaming
> And the soft rays of moonlight are gleaming
> See the bold Chieftain marching o'er the mountain

Soon will the fire of War be glowing
And the red blood in streams be flowing.[38]

"Brian Boroimhe's March," while unaccompanied by lyrics, contains a note indicating that "[t]his March was played at the battle of Clontarf, where Brian Boroimhe, Monarch of all Ireland was killed A.D. 1014. It is the martial music, or gathering sound by which the Irish Troops were said to have been formed into Battalions, and Marched to the plains of Clontarf."[39] While the *Music of Ireland* encourages the association between Ireland and conceptions of the primitive and of fairies, it also highlights the actual history of Irish resistance to English rule.

Both Lover and Horncastle published their work in London. But Horncastle at least seems to have had some interest in testing the waters in Ireland. While the audience was numerous in London, however, this was not the case when he took his "Entertainment" to Dublin in February 1843. The *Dublin Magazine* that came out that same month notes with regret that the "Entertainment" attracted a much smaller audience in Dublin. Clearly it was the metropolitan citizens who were the most interested in the display of musical culture from the periphery, a display they judged to be a worthy demonstration of Irish "national character."[40]

Edward Said discusses the relationship between display, the expanding British empire in the nineteenth century, and discourses of judgment, suggesting that "[t]here is a convergence between the great geographical scope of the empires, especially the British one, and universalizing cultural discourses. Power makes this convergence possible, of course; with it goes the ability to be in far-flung places, to learn about other people, to codify and disseminate knowledge, to characterize, transport, install, and display instances of other cultures (through exhibits, expeditions, photographs, paintings, surveys, schools), and above all to rule them."[41] This convergence was nowhere more evident than at the Great Exhibition of the Works of Industry of All Nations held in London in 1851, which displayed Ireland along with dozens of other nations. Jeffrey Auerbach suggests that Ireland's representation at the exhibition was even worse than that of Wales: "Only Belfast, Dublin, and Cork contributed more than a few items, and out of 13,000 exhibitors from the British Isles, fewer than 300 were Irish. On the whole, the exhibition seems to have passed Ireland by," even though Henry Cole had visited Dublin "as part of his first tour of the manufacturing regions in 1849."[42] One of the three hundred Irish items, however, was so notable as to warrant a lengthy description and engraving in the *Official Descriptive and Illustrated Catalogue of the Great Exhibition*, Tallis's *History and Description of the Crystal Palace, and the Exhibition of the World's Industry in 1851*, and *The Illustrated Exhibitor, a Tribute to the World's Industrial Jubilee*. This object was a "music temple," carved in bog-yew, by Arthur Jones, a furniture maker in Dublin (figure 8.1). Tallis's introductory comments on the piece draw a familiar connection between music and Irish identity: "We will now make mention of a contribution from 'the Emerald Isle.' . . . As in all periods of their history, the Irish have been passionately fond of music, the decorative piece of furniture embodying this characteristic, was certain to acquire importance and prominence."[43] The description in Tallis's *History* (an abbreviated version of that found in the *Official Catalogue*) suggests how Irish music serves as a focal point for displaying the Irish national character in the metropolitan center, but it also reveals a resistance to Ireland's being subsumed into that center. Once again, the concept of hybridity is useful to keep in mind. The act of encounter—this time, the encounter between an object (which serves to represent the Irish nation) and the metropolitan citizen—simultaneously produces and contests the identities of both groups. The description reads:

> A statuette of Ollamh Fouhdla, the founder of the Irish monarchy, and also of the Palace of Tara, naturally surmounted the temple. He was represented in his capacity of monarch and lawgiver, delivering the laws to the Irish nation, holding forth the beechen boards, on which were inscribed passages from the Brehon laws, engraved in the ancient Irish character:—

> "Seven things bear witness to a king's improper conduct:
> "An unlawful opposition in the senate.
> "An overthrow of the law.
> "An overthrow in battle.
> "A dearth.
> "Barrenness in cows.
> "Blight of fruit.
> "Blight of seed in the ground.
> "These are the seven candles lighted to expose the misgovernment
>   of a king."

> He was seated on the Lia Fail, or enchanted stone, said to be deposited in Westminster Abbey; he sat in the centre of a platform, representing all

Figure 8.1. Irish "Music Temple" carved in bog-yew for London's Great Exhibition, from *The Illustrated Exhibitor, a Tribute to the World's Industrial Jubilee* (London: J. Cassell, 1851). Reproduced from the original held by the Department of Special Collections of the University Libraries of Notre Dame.

Ireland mapped out under him. The panel in front represented, in relief, the opening of the triennial convention at Tara, in the reign of Cormac "Ufalda," or "Long Beard," in the early part of the third century, anterior to the introduction of Christianity into the island. Cormac sat in the centre of the hall, surrounded by ten principal officers of state, who always accompanied the monarch on state occasions. The opposite panel represented the harpers in Tara Hall performing before the monarch and his queen; a canopy formed by the fossil antlers and skull of the giant deer, supported the drapery, an opening in which discovered the undulating hills of Tara.[44]

The association of Irish identity with the medieval past, as suggested in the description, implies a contrast with the exhibition's representation of Britain as at the forefront of a rapidly industrializing Europe. Viewers of the "Temple of Music," like audiences at "Lover's Irish Evenings" and Horncastle's "Entertainment," were encouraged to associate Ireland with the past rather than the future. The piece was assessed and scrutinized as an Irish contribution to the skills and wealth of the empire. But wood carving was not considered as technologically progressive as other skills. Tallis's comments on the place of wood carving among the decorative arts are applicable to the exhibition's work in reinforcing the imperial project at home and abroad. He suggests that "[a]mongst the decorative arts, wood carving has a distinct and legitimate position, and confined within due limits is always effective. Still its province is restricted, or ought to be, to the ornamentation of material when applied to a useful purpose; it can never assume the dignity of art *per se*."[45] In an analogous fashion, the exhibition confirmed that the "province" of Ireland was "confined within due limits" by being displayed in London. The "Temple" also features an embodiment, carved into its very material, of its own ambivalent status of asserting yet subordinating Irish identity. The *Official Catalogue* points out that "[t]he lower stretcher is ornamented in the centre by a bunch of shamrocks, embosomed in the heart of which are the letters V and A [for Queen Victoria and Prince Albert], tied by a true lover's knot, and the date 1851 inserted. The four curious antique letters E.R.I.N. are copied from the ornamental capital letters in the Book of Kells—one of the most ancient Irish manuscripts."[46] Such a convoluted image suggests an intimate connection between the assertion of Irish musical identity and the appeal to imperial taste.[47]

Further complicating the image of Irish identity that the "Temple of Music" conveys is the fact that the piece features references to both Irish independence and the loss of that independence. It is dominated by the image of Ollamh Fodhla, the poet-king reputed to have introduced a triennial gathering at Tara that served in some sense as a parliament.[48] His image recalls seated images of Queen Victoria but also contrasts with them as it connotes patriarchal authority. He is presenting panels on which are inscribed the Brehon Laws, the detailed ancient Gaelic laws. Both Gaelic civility and literacy are suggested with this image. Jones actually draws on the same repertoire of symbols that groups such as the Repeal Association and Young Ireland did. The membership card of the Repeal Association, for example, also featured an image of Ollamh Fodhla along with other representatives of Irish independence and the inscription: "There Is But One Hope In Ireland—The Restoration of Her Domestic Parliament." And one of the subjects Thomas Davis had suggested in his essay on "National Art" was *Ollamh Fodhla Presenting his Laws to his People*.[49] The temple's reference to Tara suggests the same kind of contestation of British rule that O'Connell and Davis advocated. Tara was one of the two principal centers of Gaelic Ireland. John O'Beirne Ranelagh observes that it retained a powerful hold on the Irish popular imagination even up to the eighteenth and nineteenth centuries: "In 1798 Irish rebels gathered at Tara spontaneously, as if possessed of some ancestral memory. In 1843, Daniel O'Connell organized one of the largest assemblies in Irish history at Tara, clearly calculating that the folk knowledge of the site was an important additional weapon in his campaign for Irish home rule."[50] Even the material out of which the temple was constructed connotes resistance to English domination. In his essay "Of the Bogs and Loughs of Ireland," published in the *Philosophical Transactions* (1685), William King laments the presence of bogs as a sign of Irish "want of industry" but notes that the bog had served to preserve the Irish "from the conquest of the English."[51] The image of the bog also suggests the failure of land reclamation projects of the eighteenth century, as Katie Trumpener suggests: "Bog drainage synecdochically represents the project of Enlightenment land reform."[52]

Jones's piece also hints at the disastrous consequences of British conquest of Ireland. Tallis's account notes that the "enchanted stone," presumably the coronation seat for the High King of Ireland, is now "deposited in Westminster Abbey." And informed spectators would know that the Brehon Laws were abolished in the sixteenth century as part of the renewed attempt to "civilize" Ireland. Jones's piece presents a *tableau vivant* of the historical erosion of Irish independence due to conquest, as Tallis inadvertently notes: "The whole subject formed a sort of chronological series, commencing 700 years B.C., the date of the foundation of the Irish monarchy—touching the flourishing state of the kingdom under Cormac—passing through the chivalrous age of the Crusaders—and ending with the present agricultural age of Ireland."[53] The "flourishing" state of the ancient kingdom contrasts with the "present agricultural age," when Ireland has just been devastated by a famine that was blamed by many on English agricultural policy and governmental indifference. The temple both celebrates an Irish national past and laments its passing. Although the long sides of the piece feature images of the Triennial Convention at Tara and harpers playing before the monarch, suggesting how "in all periods of their history, the Irish have been passionately fond of music," the short sides tell a different story, mapping the beginning and end of the harping tradition with portraits of Onaoi, the first musician who accompanied the sons of Milesius to Ireland, and Carolan, often considered the last of the bardic line. Jones's "Temple" serves as a corrective to the imperial project at the heart of the exhibition, a reminder of the adverse effects of British colonialism.

As the ambiguities inherent in the musical representations of Lover, Horncastle, and Jones imply, the display of Irish music in England constituted a threat to English power—and to English culture. The widespread popularity of Irish music at the time highlighted the relationship between national identity and music. As a writer for the *North British Review* suggested in a review of Bunting's 1840 edition of the *Ancient Music of Ireland,* "Music, like all the other arts, is intimately allied in its development with the life of nations, and supplies one of the modes of expressing their individual existence; we can therefore trace in the music of a people the outlines of their peculiar character and history."[54] The popularity of Irish music put the English in the uncomfortable position of trying to define a musical identity of their own. An article entitled "National Music and Musicians" in the Irish journal *The Citizen* (January 1840) makes Irish music's challenge to English musical identity explicit. The article depicts Ireland as a Cinderella whose singing is much sweeter than that of her stepsisters (suggesting England and perhaps Scotland), despite the advantages of wealth and education that they enjoy. "Poor Ireland is our Cinderella," the article asserts, and, correspondingly, "Our melodies are the native songs of our Cinderella."[55] The article contends that England is incapable of producing native musicians of its own. Michael Balfe, it suggests, was the first native composer of opera in the British Isles, and he was Irish. Although Balfe did not write specifically native Irish music, the article ties his success to the musical tradition of Ireland, as it reiterates the organic connection between music and the inhabitants of the nation: "It is evident,—it lies upon the surface of the history of music,—that the more composers have consulted national music—the music of the people—the more have the beauties and attractions of their style been enhanced."[56] The article ends with a denunciation of England, suggesting that because it has no native music of its own, it is unable to produce composers of any merit.

Entertainments like Lover's and Horncastle's traced the "peculiar character and history" of the Irish people in their music, as did the work of Bunting and Petrie. But what "peculiar character and history" could be traced in English music? If, as the author of the *North British Review* article suggested, "The stronger the national feeling, the more distinctly marked will be the music of the people,"[57] it was imperative for the English to find some way of identifying the distinct markings of their music—and asserting its superiority over its Irish counterpart. The concern in England about the lack of native music and musicians is indicated by a number of attempts to rectify the situation. The Society of British Musicians was founded in 1834 to promote "the advancement of native talent in composition and performance."[58] Collections of English song and music found eager publishers. The oboist W. T. Parke, for example, attempted to fill in the recent history of English music in his two-volume *Musical Memoirs; Comprising an Account of the General State of Music in England from the First Commemoration of Handel in 1784, to the Year 1830* (1830).[59] William Chappell sought for evidence of English music further back in history with his two two-volume editions, *Collection of National English Airs, Consisting of Ancient Song, Ballad and Dance Tunes* (1838–40) and *Popular Music of the Olden Time* (1855–59).[60]

The periodical press also took up the cause of asserting the merits of English music and containing Irish music. In a piece entitled "The Origin of Music," published originally in 1848 in the *Quarterly Review*, then reprinted in separate form in 1852, Elizabeth Rigby paradoxically both identifies what might pass as English national music and disavows the need to do so. Rigby holds forth on the nature of national music, asserting in a vein similar to that of the author of the *North British Review* article that music is connected to the "inward national character."[61] She seizes on the glee-book as an example of English national music, as she traces the movement of music from Italy to Britain:

[Music] agreed with the domestic habits which have ever characterized old England. It suited that best of all clubs—a large family party; it was welcome to that best of all earthly abodes—a good old country-house. Father and mother, brothers and sisters, could all take a part in this domestic chorus; and on joyous occasions, when sons returned to the paternal mansion, and married daughters met again beneath the roof . . . the old glee-book was pulled out.[62]

The glee-book serves to perform Englishness within the individual family and, by implication, within the national family, for, as Anne McClintock asserts, "The family offered an indispensable metaphoric figure by which national difference could be shaped into a single historical genesis narrative."[63] According to Rigby, the glee-book also provides the means through which to save England from foreign cultural intrusions: "Who has not experienced the beautiful moral of this class of music, when, by the request of some revered elder in the family, the modern Italian trio or quartet . . . has been forsaken for some old English glee."[64] Glees are credited with reflecting national sentiments and policies:

> It is pleasant to turn over the leaves of such an old collection, and muse on their words of deep national significance. There is a regular declaration of English rights and principles in them, with their sound piety, broad fun, perfect liberty of speech, and capital eating and drinking. One may look upon them as a stronghold of moral as well as musical principles during that gloomy interregnum [of Puritanism].[65]

Rigby acknowledges that England lacks any composers of its own: "In the nationalities of modern music, . . . we are aware that our own land does not take a distinguished part."[66] However, she asserts, England does "adopt" musicians from other nations:

> But if, since the early death of Purcell, England has produced but few native composers of eminence, we may be satisfied in remembering that she has adopted more than any other country. It may be said without presumption that in no other respect is the national pride and prejudice so utterly forgotten as in our taste for music: nowhere does the public ear embrace a wider range of musical enjoyment and knowledge; nowhere do the various professors of musical art find fairer hearing or better pay.[67]

Rigby's England is both a connoisseur whose "taste for music" is cosmopolitan and an employer who is able to take numerous international employees, including Ireland, under its wing.

What is also interesting in Rigby's piece is the way she elevates musical taste, the possession of which in some ways becomes more important than playing music—at least at an amateur level. She laments that "the class of individuals who contentedly perform that species of self-serenade which goes by the ominous title of 'playing a little'" actually have little love for music.[68] Moreover, such amateurs are subject to vanity: "[T]he draught of excitement is pernicious to all alike, and one which we instinctly [*sic*] shrink from seeing at the lips of those we love."[69] The amateur players to which Rigby refers in particular are women, and her comments also reveal the gender politics at stake in the commodification of the musical field:

> Upon the whole we are inclined to think that the most really enviable partaker of musical felicity, the one for whom the pleasure is most pure for himself and least selfish for others, is he who has no stake of vanity or anxiety in the matter—but who sits at an overture, symphony, or chorus with closed eyes and swimming senses—brightens at major keys, saddens at minors—smiles at modulations, he knows not why,—and then goes forth to his work next morning with steady hand and placid brow, while ever and anon the irrepressible echoes of past sounds break forth over desk or counter into jocund or plaintive hummings, as if the memory were rejoicing too much in her sweet thefts to be able to conceal them.[70]

What Rigby describes is the activity of a bourgeois subject in a market economy that ostensibly provides a seamless connection between production and consumption. The subject, who is gendered male, acts the part of the good consumer during his time off, consuming music played by a professional musician, then "goes forth" the next day to perform his labors of production "over desk or counter."[71] As "sweet thefts," the "hummings" appear to operate outside the market economy, but in fact they serve to link women to this regime: "Happy hummings these for wife or sister, to whose voice or piano he is for ever a petitioner for pleasures it is a pleasure to give, and who leads him with 'that exquisite bit of Beethoven' as with a silken string."[72] Women are prevented from indulging in the "vanity or anxiety" of amateur playing by being directed in their performance. Although Rigby suggests that wives and sisters "lead" their husbands or brothers, it is in fact the man who regulates what is played, making it match what he has heard the previous day. Like the singing of glees, the performance of Beethoven in the right context serves to consolidate the power of the "paternal mansion" and, by analogy, the nation. Rigby's male bourgeois subject provides the center that holds it all together. Rigby's commentary elevates cultural consumption above production but also serves to masculinize and regulate that consumption.

The male subject she describes is able to experience emotions—he "brightens at major keys, saddens at minors"—but he is not overwhelmed by them. The activity of masculine judgment and the cultivation of taste prevail over all feelings. Rigby's subject is an imperial citizen, trained to perceive himself as superior to the female members of his own household within the nation and also to the citizens of the nation's outposts.

A review article entitled "Celtic Music" that also appeared in the *Quarterly Review* (March 1869) exploits this contrast between masculine judgment and feminine feeling in order to assert the national superiority of English over Irish music.[73] The reviewer notes that "[t]he principal characteristics of Celtic music are originality, pathos, and simplicity. Its genius is unfavorable to elaborate development."[74] The review distinguishes the feminine sentimentality of the Celtic music from the more masculine and organized character of English and German national music, a character that derives, suggests the reviewer, from the "Saxon or Teutonic element" in these nations. This reviewer agrees with Rigby's assessment that glees are the most characteristic English national music: "In all ages the English have been partial to duets, glees, catches, madrigals, and rounds: they make first-rate choristers."[75] But in addition, this review makes an implicit connection between social organization and music. The Celtic nations' "unsusceptibility to musical concord or harmony" suggests their inability to work together.[76] The characteristics of Celtic music are carried over by the reviewer into a discussion of Celtic taste: "Such things as fugues, symphonies, sonatas and the like, do not suit the impulsive Celt."[77] The Celts "care little for part-singing; but the English and the Germans are passionately fond of it."[78]

An article written a decade earlier in the *North British Review* makes similar gendered comparisons. The reviewer acknowledges the strong identification between Celts and their music: "Music seems in truth to be interwoven with the whole existence of the Celtic people."[79] According to this account, Celtic music, though once a very powerful means of articulating the national spirit, is now merely useful as a reflection of the past glory of the Celts. While music once served to "civilize" and "humanize" the Celtic race, it now "mourns over its grave."[80] According to the reviewer, the distinguishing characteristics of Celtic music are the "long drawn wailing Trochee"[81] and the "emphatic sixth major,"[82] which, combined, produce a bittersweet effect: "Their fond memory of bygone happier days is characteristically expressed with more or less force in the music of all Celtic races."[83] And the reviewer notes that the music of the Irish bards is "the purest of Celtic musical compositions": "[I]n their music we hear most distinctly the mingling of half laughing and half sobbing sounds which seem to be the voice of the race."[84] The reviewer confuses the cause of the characteristics of Celtic music, however. The "laughing and sobbing" is presented both as a quality inherent in the music and as an effect of historical losses. Most importantly, Celtic music presents an articulation of loss that is universally understood: "What an interesting fact, that a race which has run its course in its old home should leave behind it, in its music, a language of grief so affecting, that other people, although strangers to its fate, listen with deep emotion to the heart-rending sounds that this fallen race sends forth like a dying swan."[85]

Like the *Quarterly Review* article, the *North British Review* article contends that Celtic music is essentially characterized by emotion, specifically by an Ossianic commingling of joy and grief. "Teutonic music," the precursor of English music, on the other hand, conveys a philosophical idea: "the idea of individuality."[86] The iambic rhythms that characterize Teutonic music reflect "a bold energy indicating the enterprising spirit of the Teutonic race," while the "full tonic accord at the concluding cadence" imparts to the music "a fulness [*sic*] of expression and harmony, corresponding with the comprehensive and idealistic nature of the people, making their music adequate to their highest expectations."[87] This gendered configuration is echoed in Matthew Arnold's *On the Study of Celtic Literature* (1867), in which Arnold discusses the subordination of the "Celtic spirit" to the Saxon "genius." Arnold notes that the Celts have "a peculiarly near and intimate feeling of nature and the life of nature"[88] that he associates with the feminine: "The sensibility of the Celtic nature, its nervous exaltations, have something of the feminine in them."[89] According to Arnold, the Celt is "peculiarly disposed to feel the spell of the feminine idiosyncrasy. . . . [H]e is not far from its secret."[90] Arnold uses his characterization of Celt and Saxon as both explanation and justification of their political situations. The Celt is passionate and impractical, always reacting against *"the despotism of fact,"* unable to accomplish anything of practical worth.[91] The Saxon, on the other hand, is "disciplinable and steadily obedient within certain limits, but retaining an inalienable part of freedom and self-dependence."[92] In Arnold's book, as in Rigby's article and the articles of the *Quarterly Review* and *North British Review,* the Saxon or Teutonic ancestors of the English are associated with the ability to regulate emotion and become effective political subjects. In contrast, Celticism, particularly Irishness, is associated with lack of control and with lack of political capacity.

The 1853 *North British Review* article represents the Celtic spirit not as vanishing but as being absorbed, for "national elements are as imperishable in the economy of nature as physical atoms; they only change their form."[93] The author describes the "monuments" that the Celts will leave behind in Europe: certain inheritable physical characteristics, words, customs and superstitions, and, most importantly, music. "It is even more extraordinary," he or she asserts, "that from among these tones of grief the ear is sometimes pierced by a cry of merriment, sounding like mockery amidst the usual strain of sorrow; it is like the sun breaking through the rain clouds. Such is the music which we inherit from the Celtic race."[94] The article only obliquely mentions the fate of the actual bodies of the Celts, as it hints at the process of emigration that was removing so many Irish to North America at the time: "The last representatives of the Celtic race are hastening to bid farewell to the hemisphere which harboured them so long, and are seeking a new home and brighter destinies across the Atlantic."[95] According to the article, this emigration effectively constitutes the end of the Celts as an "individual race": "The part which they had to play as an individual race on the old continent has ceased, and the elements of their national existence are to be mixed up with those of other races on another soil, in order to become a constituent particle in the formation of a new and herculean people."[96] The article presents a salve to English anxieties about both Irish culture and the Irish people: Irish music will be "inherited" by the "old continent," while the Irish themselves will be diffused through intermingling with other "races" in the New World.

Neither of these projections happened exactly as imagined by the author of the *North British Review.* The Irish did not all leave Europe, and in fact some of those that remained made their presence clear by establishing the Fenian Brotherhood in the 1860s to challenge British policy. Moreover, instead of "mixing up" the "elements of their national existence" with other races in North America, the Irish remained ethnically distinct, perhaps partially as a result of so many of them emigrating at once. As Dale Knobel points out, "With only two exceptional years, the Irish . . . constituted the largest single ethnic component of European immigration to America between 1820 and 1854."[97] And Irish music did not just become absorbed in the Old World but remained a popular cultural form in both Britain and North America. For at the same time that it was being presented in the British metropolitan center, Irish music was being performed across the Atlantic in individual homes through song sheets and on the stage in variety shows and theater. While Irish music in Britain both affirmed and challenged Britain's alleged superiority over a nation incapable of governing itself, Irish music as it was presented in the United States mapped Irishness onto discourses of authenticity and individuation. The imagining of Ireland became a useful component in America's attempt to distinguish itself from England.

Much has been written about negative stereotypes of Irish immigrants in the United States. Mick Moloney notes, for example, that the caricature of the "stage Irishman" "found a ready home in nineteenth[-]century America where the establishment was British and Protestant and the immigrant Irish were the first major urban underclass of unskilled, uneducated wage earners."[98] Such negative stereotypes fed back into the culture so that, as Knobel writes, "from the [18]20s to the [18]60s, the verbal image of the Irish evolved into a rigid form" which suggested that it "was more difficult for the immigrant Irish to shake off their background and become acceptable republicans."[99] But as in England, there were also positive representations of Irishness available to Americans. In particular, the association of Irish music with nostalgia seems to have found an appreciative audience both among Irish Americans and non–Irish Americans.[100]

Moloney suggests that Irish song in general is notable for its "celebration of place" but that "the tradition of immigrant songs is even more oriented towards place, with song titles and themes in the Irish-American song tradition abounding in published and recorded song material between 1800 and 1940. The genre idealizes the homeland or a particular area of the homeland and expresses nostalgic longing for the country or locality left behind."[101] The song tradition of nineteenth-century Irish American sheet music exploited just this relationship between Irishness and nostalgia. Williams notes that "[i]n 1800, sheet music was a new cultural artifact in the United States," although the sheet music industry would grow immensely by the end of the nineteenth century.[102] Thus, according to Williams, "the Irish stereotype in America developed within an area of popular culture that was itself evolving at the same time."[103] Moloney confirms this observation, suggesting that "[s]heet music was a huge influence in the popularizing of Irish-American nostalgic song particularly in the years before sound recordings became widely available."[104] Many of these nostalgic songs were influenced by the work of Thomas Moore, who enjoyed a huge popularity in North America. Charles Hamm comments, "It would be simplistic to suggest that this theme [nostalgia] was transmitted to the United States only by Moore's *Irish Melodies*; however, these had much greater currency in the United States than any other works treating the same theme. And certainly, the post-Moore American songwriters, who dealt with this theme for a good half-century, took Moore as their model."[105] He adds, "The *Irish Melodies* were the most popular songs in America in the second and third decades of the nineteenth century. They were instrumental in shaping indigenous popular music in America; every American songwriter in the half-century after 1810 was strongly affected by both melodies and texts of the *Irish Melodies*; and their commercial success was a factor in the developing music publishing business."[106]

The nostalgic songs served a number of purposes. In *Communities across Borders: New Immigrant and Transnational Cultures*, Paul Kennedy and Victor Roudometof, examining the current era of globalization, suggest that "migrant, ethnic/diasporic, transnational communities" experience their "locality" of origin "symbolically."[107] For such communities, they suggest, "locality" "consists of an imagined homeland or place understood through nostalgia, memory, history, or constructed cultural sites."[108] The nostalgic songs in Irish American sheet music create a positive "imagined homeland" that Irish emigrants can celebrate. But they also produce a gendered cartography of diaspora in which the homeland is symbolized as the cherished but lost female and the New World is figured as the individuated male.

As Hamm suggests, many Irish songs published in nineteenth-century America capitalize on the theme of loss that Moore explored. But whereas the majority of Moore's nostalgic songs concern the loss of a past era of Ireland's glory, the songs in popular American song sheets figure that loss as more personal. In addition, they elide the temporal with the geographical, as the nostalgia for the past becomes a nostalgia for a place. In an 1843 song sheet entitled *The Lament of the Irish Emigrant. A Ballad*, for example, Ireland is associated with a past era of happiness for the emigrant. A note to the song reads: "Portraying the feelings of an Irish peasant previous to his leaving home, calling up the scenes of his youth under the painful reflection of having buried his wife and child, and what his feelings will be in America."[109] Another song, *Lament of the Irish Exile, A Ballad*, also associates Ireland with a youth that the emigrant leaves behind:

> Soon did the light winds bear,
> Erin Aroon,
> Me from thy shores so fair,
> Erin Aroon,
> Lovely as youth's fond dream,
> Was thy last distant gleam,
> Smiling in evening's beam,
> Erin Aroon.[110]

As in Moore's songs, Ireland is typically associated with the beloved. In *Dear Little Colleen*, the speaker, who is "Leaving old Erin to see it no more," asks his beloved to bring him "One sweet bit of shamrock from over the sea" in order to "Whisper dear Colleen of home unto me."[111]

While numerous song sheets imagine a return to Ireland and the beloved, others suggest a cutting off from the past that is often represented through the end of the relationship or the death of the beloved.[112] The speaker in *Mary! Avourneen: An Irish Ballad* laments his beloved's indifference to him when he does return from working in the United States: "Mary! dear Mary! I've come back to thee, / But cold is the welcome you now give to me!"[113] *Mavourneen Machree* concerns a man who has left his "Mary" behind to work in the United States in order to save her from "poverty's stings." He amasses a fortune and returns to Ireland only to find that Mary is in her grave:

> I return'd to the spot where I left thee, in sadness,
> With a heart every pulse of which beat but for thee
> Now I bend o'er thy cold grave lamenting in madness,
> The dark hour we parted, Mavourneen Machree.[114]

Such songs, like the work of Lover, Horncastle, and Jones in London, offer positive representations of Irish identity that contrast with images of the Irish as pugilistic or stupid. The song sheets associate the Irish with loyalty, domestic attachment, hard work, and forbearance in times of difficulty.

However, the Irish American song sheets simultaneously foreclose on the possibilities of Irishness. Specifically, the song sheets promote an association of Ireland with immaturity and with the feminine. This association is reinforced iconographically by the covers on a number of song sheets. Many of these portray a demure young woman with an Irish name. *Kate Kearney,* for example, features a young woman clasping a bunch of shamrocks on its cover (see figure 8.2). On the cover of *Beautiful Songs of Erin,* the name "Erin" indicates both the Irish nation and a particular woman (figure 8.3). The cover of *Coolun: A Favorite Irish Air* depicts the same feminized image of Carolan featured in the 1809 *Irish Magazine* article on the harper.

While such songs iconically represent the Irish nation as feminine, they also suggest a rejection of the feminine. Just as Petrie's *Ancient Irish Music* indicated the need to translate songs collected from women into a more masculine environment, so the authors of Irish American song sheets also suggest the need to transcend the feminine associations of their songs. Songs that relate the severing of the relationship with Ireland and the beloved, for example, suggest a translation of the physical relationship to a higher state. In *The Lament of the Irish Emigrant,* the speaker emphasizes:

Figure 8.2. Cover of *Kate Kearney* (song sheet). Courtesy Lilly Library, Indiana University, Bloomington, Indiana.

I'm bidding you a long farewell,
My Mary, kind and true,
But I'll not forget you darling,
In the land I'm going to,
They say there's bread and work for all,
And the sun shines always there;
But I'll not forget old Ireland,
Were it fifty times as fair.[115]

The physical relationship is translated into a metaphysical one made possible through memory. *The Answer to the Lament of the Irish Emigrant* suggests this kind of translation even more strongly, as the wife describes her and her child's continuing presence as spirits:

Though Erin's shores you leave, Willie,
An angel follows thee;
Thy baby's spirit linked with mine,
Shall watch thee o'er the sea;
And when beneath the stranger's sod
Thy wearied form shall lie,
Our triune shade will peaceful seek
Its home beyond the sky.[116]

Although Ireland is associated with a state of youth and with the feminine, the nostalgic songs of exile also attempt to cancel out that association by carrying it "beyond" physical boundaries, placing it within the speaker's mind and memory. The process of emigration as it is depicted in nostalgic songs becomes a process of reaching a more mature masculine and progressive state of modernity. The cover of *Lament of the Irish Exile* makes this gendering explicit (figure 8.4). The bottom half of the cover recalls the image found in volume 4 of *The Irish Melodies* (see figure 6.3), a female Ireland with spear, shield, helmet, and harp. She stands on an island, surrounded by numerous ships in full sail. The "Irish exile," on the other hand, depicted on the upper half of the cover, is male. He has picked up the harp of Ireland, while the spear and the shield lie on a pile at the beach. The image of tradition—in this case, a feminine Ireland—must be preserved because the articulation of the state of modernity depends upon the existence of a premodern state from which it has emerged. But for modernity to be considered authentic, the distinction between the two must be seen to be clear.

Figure 8.3. Cover of *Beautiful Songs of Erin* (song sheet). Courtesy Lilly Library, Indiana University, Bloomington, Indiana.

Many of the songs from the song sheets were further popularized by their use in theatrical productions. The early to mid–nineteenth century saw a profusion of Irish performers singing Irish songs for minstrel and variety shows in the United States. Irish music also featured prominently in more middlebrow theater. As Mick Moloney points out, "[T]hroughout the whole nineteenth century there was a plethora of related popular theatrical performance contexts where Irish music was played, Irish songs sung and Irish dramatic sketches and routines enacted. [Many] of these elements were present in the melodramatic creations that dominated the popular stage in the latter decades of the nineteenth century."[117] In song sheets and on the stage, Ireland was depicted as a traditional, feminine nation situated in the past, an image that could be contrasted with the modern nation of the United States.

But as O'Toole suggests, for each writing of diasporic culture, there is a writing "otherwise." It was an Irish-born playwright, Dion Boucicault, an immigrant to England and then America, who troubled existing representations of Irish national identity in the mid-nineteenth-century American imagination. Boucicault's three major Irish plays, *Colleen Bawn, Arrah-na-Pogue,* and the *Shaughraun,* while drawing on images of a feminized Ireland found in contemporary song sheets and theatrical performances, also recontextualized those images, altering their significance for both the Irish and the American nations.

The man whom Elizabeth Butler Cullingford identifies as "the most popular playwright in the English-speaking world between 1840 and 1900"[118] was born Dionysius Lardner Boursiquot in Dublin, most probably an illegitimate child of a Protestant middle-class mother and her lover, Dionysius Lardner, a lecturer at Trinity College Dublin. Mother and children moved to London in 1828, where the future playwright was educated. Boucicault was already well established as a theatrical performer and playwright by the time he turned his writerly attention to Irish matters.[119] Cullingford argues that Boucicault used the popular form of melodrama to raise awareness of the Irish situation: "In Boucicault's Irish plays, character, setting, and plot are constructed to produce not rational assent, but warm feelings. Mass culture, he understood, operates not through intellectual analysis, but through the politics of empathy."[120] According to Cullingford, Boucicault employed a number of strategies to develop that empathy. He "exploited his popularity as an actor in favour of the Irish underdog; his most sympathetic characters, Myles-na-Coppaleen, Shaun the Post, and Conn the Shaughraun, were all Irish Catholic peasants. He also manipulated his 'sensation scenes' so that technical triumphs of staging were invested with non-verbal political affect."[121] With the

Figure 8.4. Cover of *Lament of the Irish Exile, A Ballad* (New York: William Vanderbeck, n.d.). Courtesy Lilly Library, Indiana University, Bloomington, Indiana.

exception of "The Wearing of the Green" from *Arragh-Na-Pogue*, Cullingford does not discuss the music of the plays in her analysis, but the music was a crucial element in conveying the plays' "political affect."

The origin of Boucicault's first Irish play, the *Colleen Bawn, or the Bride of Glengarry*, connects it with the genre of "Irish plays" popular at the time in American theatres. Boucicault began the play in response to a request from an Irish American actor-manager, Barney Williams. According to Richard Fawkes, Williams and his wife "had been touring the States for many years playing in Irish comedies. In 1855 they had gone to London, and when they returned to New York, they wanted a new play to add to their repertoire. Who better to ask than the leading Irish dramatist of the age?"[122] In fact, Boucicault brought the play out at Laura Keene's Theatre in New York on March, 29, 1860, when he needed to provide Keene with a new play. The story of the *Colleen Bawn* is derived from an actual event that took place in the vicinity of Limerick in 1819. A wealthy young gentleman, Lieutenant John Scanlan, married a beautiful working-class girl, Ellen Hanley, then arranged for her to be murdered when he tired of her. Gerald Griffin had attended the trials of Scanlan and his servant, and used the story as the basis of his novel, *The Collegians* (1829), which became the source for Boucicault's play. In his reworking, Boucicault altered the story to produce a comic version of events, a happy ending, and a memorable character, Myles-na-Coppaleen. Boucicault himself played the character of Myles-na-Coppaleen, and, as Fawkes notes, "It was to see Myles (and Boucicault playing him) as much as to see the play that audiences flocked to Laura Keene's Theatre."[123] After its tremendous success in New York, the *Colleen Bawn* moved to London, where it opened at the Adelphi on September 10, 1860. Again, it was immensely popular, becoming, as Fawkes suggests, "the biggest success seen in London for decades."[124] It played for 278 performances at the Adelphi Theatre and was also turned into an opera entitled *The Lilly of Killarney*, written by John Oxenford and composer Julius Benedict with help from Boucicault.[125] The opera, too, was in high demand. Boucicault then decided to return to Dublin after an absence of nearly twenty years to produce his play. The *Colleen Bawn* opened at the Theatre Royal, Hawkins Street, in Dublin, on April 1, 1861, where it played for twenty-four nights.[126]

Boucicault took the title *Colleen Bawn*, or "fair maid," from a popular song circulating in sheet form at the time, "Willy Reilly and His Colleen Bawn." Four complete songs are written into the play, one and a half sung by the character of Eily and two and a half sung by Myles. In addition, Myles is constantly singing snippets from other songs. It is he who sings the title song,

"The Colleen Bawn," also known after its first line as "Limerick Is Beautiful." The songs comment on the relationship between Ireland and England and also Ireland and America. Several of the songs in the play present images of Irish insubordination to English hegemony.[127] The lyrics of the "Colleen Bawn," for example, draw an equation between the power and wealth of the "Emperor of Russia," "Julius Caesar," and the "Lord Lieutenant" of Ireland. The song envisions each of these powerful personages giving up "all my wealth, my manes . . . my army" for the privilege of marrying the Irish "Colleen Bawn."[128] "Cruiskeen Lawn" and "Pretty Girl Milking Her Cow" also convey criticism of England in the traces of previous forms in which they have appeared. The tune of "Cruiskeen Lawn," sung by Eily in the play, was used by Moore for his song "Song of the Battle Eve." Moore's "Song of the Battle Eve" translates the drinking-song theme of "Cruiskeen Lawn" into a military situation, envisioning Irish troops "quaffing" wine for encouragement as they boost their morale. The song ends with a condemnation of "Saxon" and "Dane" and a promotion of the Irish cause:

> Let those, who brook the chain
> Of Saxon or of Dane,
> Ignobly by their fire-sides stay;
> One sigh to home be given,
> One heartfelt prayer to heaven,
> Then, for Erin and her cause, boy, hurra! hurra! hurra!
> Then, for Erin and her cause, hurra!

The tune of "Pretty Girl Milking Her Cow," which appeared in Bunting's 1796 collection as "Calin deas scruidadh na mbo,"[129] was used by Moore for his song entitled "Song of O'Ruark, Prince of Breffni." Moore's song concerns the story of Bearbhorgil, whose betrayal of her husband gave England its "first opportunity of profiting by our divisions and subduing us," according to Moore. Like "Song of the Battle Eve," "Song of O'Ruark" ends by pitting Saxon tyranny against Irish honor:

> They come to divide, to dishonour,
> And tyrants they long will remain.
> But onward!—the green banner rearing,
> Go, flesh every sword to the hilt;
> On our side is Virtue and Erin,
> On theirs is the Saxon and Guilt.

A song sheet of "The Pretty Girl Milking Her Cow" as sung in "Bouci-cault's *Colleen Bawn*," published in New York in 1860, appends Moore's ver-sion of the song to Boucicault's lyrics, making the political traces of the song explicit.[130]

At the end of the *Colleen Bawn*, Boucicault represents the core of a demo-cratic state for Ireland that is achieved after the elimination of all elements that threaten the democracy: the Irish Catholic sycophant, Danny, and the corrupt Anglo-Irish magistrate, Corrigan, with his Redcoat sidekicks. More-over, in its depiction of the marriage of Eily and Hardress, the play recalls "national tales" such as the *Wild Irish Girl* that depict a cross-cultural marriage between an Irish woman and an English man.[131] Although the plot of the play channels pro-Irish sentiment in a nonmilitant direction, the music retains its traces of insurgence. While the plot reiterates the gendered stereotypes of Irishness as female and Englishness as male, reaffirming a colonial relation-ship between the two nations, the music in the *Colleen Bawn* suggests a mascu-line Irish nation that resists British rule.

The combination of music and plot has different implications for the re-lationship between Ireland and America. Two of the songs, "Cruiskeen Lawn" and "Brian O'Linn," confirm the association between the Irish and drinking and comic songs that Mick Moloney identifies in the American variety shows of the midcentury.[132] The love songs "The Colleen Bawn" and "Pretty Girl Milking Her Cow," however, offer a more genteel image of Irish music, em-ploying conventions similar to those of the emigrant songs considered above. In "The Colleen Bawn," a lover laments that his beloved is "proud and cold" toward him. "Pretty Girl Milking Her Cow" tells the story of an upper-class lover and his working-class beloved. Like the emigrant songs, "Pretty Girl Milking Her Cow" establishes a connection between the beloved and the "true" Ireland, in this case, represented by a rural working girl. This connec-tion is also suggested elsewhere in the play, as Eily's upper-class husband, Hardress, tries to get her to alter her accent and to stop singing the Irish songs, which he considers "vulgar." The priest urges Eily to resist both of these pressures: "May the brogue of Ireland niver forsake your tongue—may her music niver lave yer voice—and may a true Irishwoman's virtue niver die in your heart."[133] Like the Irish American song sheets, the *Colleen Bawn* presents American audiences with a familiar image of Ireland as a musical nation as-sociated with feminine virtue, a positive image of Irish roots.

But the plot of the *Colleen Bawn* revises the gendered images of Ireland popular in song sheets at the time by refusing to subordinate a femi-nized Irish nation to a more mature masculine America. America is briefly mentioned in the play by the scheming Danny, but only as a possible location to which Eily might be exiled: "Sure she might be packed off across the wather to Ameriky, or them parts beyant."[134] Moreover, "Ameriky" is a place where people lose their identities, their roots: "Who'd ever ax a word afther her?"[135] Ireland, rather than America, is presented as the "mature" nation, for at the end of the play, Ireland is transformed into a democratic land of opportunity, where working-class Eily and her upper-class lover can be united and Eily can find "friends" among the upper-class and acceptance of the way she "spakes." The ending of the play reinforces American democratic ideals. But it also challenges America's self-proclaimed role as the land of the free, for it depicts those ideals as indigenous to Ireland.

Capitalizing on the success of the *Colleen Bawn*, Boucicault's two subsequent Irish plays also feature Irish music and song.[136] *Arrah-na-Pogue* opened November 7, 1864, at the Old Theatre Royal, Dublin, at the height of Fenian organization in Ireland; an abortive Fenian rebellion took place in 1867. *Arrah-na-Pogue* is set several years after the 1798 Rebellion and is explicit about the politically resistant role that music can play. At the wedding scene, Shaun the Post, who, like Myles in the *Colleen Bawn*, is a constant vehicle of Irish song, is asked to sing "The Wearing of the Green." In response, he comments: "Whisht, boys, are ye mad? is it sing that song and the soldiers widin gunshot? Sure there's sudden death in every note of it."[137] "The Wearing of the Green" had been popular in the 1798 Rebellion. It also appeared in the 1845 version *Spirit of the Nation* to the words "Up for the Green," and was quoted by Samuel Lover in *Rory O'More*.[138] As Cullingford notes, Boucicault retained only the lines about Napper Tandy in his version of the song: "[T]he opening lines of the first stanza and the whole of the second and third were his own."[139] Like its predecessors, Boucicault's rendition of the song expresses indignation against the English suppression of the Irish: "[T]here's a bloody law again the wearing of the green. . . . They are hanging men and women for the wearing of the green."[140] It also advocates Irish resistance, suggesting that the Irish will continue to fight against injustice: "You may take the shamrock from your hat and cast it on the sod, / But 'twill take root and flourish there, though under foot 'tis trod."[141]

Boucicault's version of "The Wearing of the Green" relies on the same formulation of a feminine Ireland as did the Irish American emigrant song sheets, but this time "Erin" is figured not as the beloved, but as the mother:

But if at last our colour should be torn from Ireland's heart,
Her sons with shame and sorrow from the dear old isle will part;

I've heard a whisper of a country that lies beyond the sea
Where rich and poor stand equal in the light of freedom's day.
O Erin, must we leave you, driven by a tyrant's hand?
Must we ask a mother's blessing from a strange and distant land?[142]

However, in Boucicault's hands, the burden of the song is not just to criticize English policy toward England but to flatter American audiences into believing that America can be more tolerant toward the Irish than Britain. America, after all, had its own anti-Irish sentiments to contend with as a result of the draft riots of 1863.[143] In Boucicault's song, America is figured as a place "Where the cruel cross of England shall nevermore be seen, / And where, please God, we'll live and die still wearing of the green."[144] The figuration of Erin as the mother who conveys her "blessing" to her children "beyond the sea" suggests a continuing link between the two nations of Ireland and America and implies the obligation that the sons still retain to look after their "mother" nation. Unlike the *Colleen Bawn*, then, *Arrah-na-Pogue* envisions America as a positive destination for the oppressed Irish. In fact, the triangulated relationship between Ireland, Britain, and America that "The Wearing of the Green" suggests is played out in the history of the song itself, which had very different fates in England and America. Cullingford notes that "The Wearing of the Green" was banned at performances of *Arrah-na-Pogue* throughout the British Empire after Fenians "blew up the wall of Clerkenwell prison, killing twelve people and injuring a hundred more" in December 1867.[145] In America, however, "The Wearing of the Green" became a popular sheet music song.[146] "The Wearing of the Green" continued to represent the connection between the sons "beyond the sea" and their mother-nation when a version of the song published in Philadelphia in 1865 was "Dedicated to the Fenian Brotherhood."[147]

The *Shaughraun*, which opened on November 14, 1874, at Wallack's Theatre in New York, registers an awareness of the multiple meanings that music can have in different contexts. After Robert, the Fenian rebel, has been recaptured, Father Dolan berates Conn for singing in the midst of the tragedy and asks him where he has been all night. Conn replies that he has been under Robert's prison window, "keeping up his heart wid the songs and the divarshin." As it turns out, his songs have provided "divarshin" in more than one sense, as they have diverted the attention of the English soldiers and offered a way for Robert to communicate with Conn right under his captors' noses. Conn tells Father Dolan how, with his dog, Tatthers, he had taken up a position entertaining the English soldiers where Robert could hear him.

The names of the tunes he plays served as a code that only Robert could understand and respond to:

> Sure I had all the soldiers dancing to my fiddle, and I put Tatthers through all his thricks. I had 'em all in fits of laffin' when I made him dance to my tunes. That's the way the masther knew I was waiting on him. He guessed what I was at, for when I struck up "Where's the slave?" he answered inside with "My lodging is on the cowld ground"; then when I made Tatthers dance to "Tell me the sorrow in my heart"—till I thought they'd have died wid the fun—he sung back "The girl I left behind me" . . . an' I purtended that the tears runnin' down my nose was with the laffin'.[148]

The two audiences, the soldiers and Conn and Robert, have different prior experiences of Irish music. For the English soldiers, the tunes are empty of meaning. They hear only lively music that makes them want to dance. For the two Irishmen, the tunes are inseparable from their words, words that the characters then relate to their own situation. The soldiers are enjoying the music so much that Conn says, "I thought they'd have died wid the fun," yet all the while the music is being used to subvert their attempt to discipline the Irish rebel. Adding further to the double valence of the music is the fact that Conn is masking his own tears. Although on the surface he appears to be laughing along with the soldiers, in fact he is weeping for his friend. In this scene, Boucicault illustrates the hybrid quality of Irish music and the different effects of that hybridity on different audiences. It is a lesson learned, no doubt, as a result of the transnational location of his own work on the stages of England, Ireland, and America.

The songs that Boucicault presented, songs that, employed in particular ways in his plays, offered multiple, sometimes contradictory images of the nation, were subsequently published as sheet music and reintroduced into American parlors. The covers of the songs advertise their performance context by referring to the fact that they were sung "in the drama[s]" of Boucicault. These songs contest the static feminine images of the Irish nation found in many songs of exile published in sheet form. Moreover, Boucicault's three Irish plays, the *Colleen Bawn, Arrah-na-Pogue,* and the *Shaughraun,* offer another crucial intervention into the gendering of the Irish nation abroad. In the characters of Eily, Arrah, and Fanny, the plays allude to the identification of Ireland with the feminine. But they also present a competing masculine symbol of Ireland in the characters of Myles, Shaun, and Conn. In his role as these three characters, Boucicault followed in the footsteps of Irish tenors like Moore and Lover. But whereas Moore was criticized and, ultimately, feminized for his refined parlor performances, and whereas Lover attempted to avoid such criticisms by singing of lower-class heroes who stole kisses from their lower-class girlfriends, Boucicault's singing male characters refuse categorization according to class and heterosexual gender roles. Myles, Shaun, and Conn the Shaughraun all live on the perimeter of society. Myles is an awkward outcast. Although he is in love with the Colleen Bawn and indeed rescues her from death, at the end of the play, he notes that he is content to have his love remain platonic. Conn is a poacher and a drunk who, like Shaun, is referred to as a "vagabone" and "thief o' the world."[149] The latter two men are more successful than Myles in securing a heterosexual attachment. But their sentimentalism prevents them from conforming to the roles of conventional masculine heroes of nineteenth-century melodrama. They are closer to eighteenth-century "men of feeling," although they are far from "civilized." What Boucicault presents in his plays is a hybrid vision of Ireland: the rooted homeland embodied by the female beloved or mother and the ever-changing "thief o' the world," the rootless sentimental wanderer, who, though in the cases of Shaun and Conn, is engaged to be married to a woman, nevertheless retains elements of his wandering life. Boucicault's ambiguous representation of Ireland—as both feminine and masculine, static and fluid—offers an important way of writing the Irish diasporic image "otherwise" and of avoiding the pitfalls of gendering the nation into which earlier cultural figures had fallen.

Boucicault's plays have been largely forgotten. The opportunities that they offered for hybridizing gendered representations of the nation were overlooked in the next century as figures such as William Scanlan and Chauncey Olcott took the spotlight in promoting Irish identity in America. As Mari Kathleen Fiedler points out, although Olcott himself didn't set foot in Ireland until he was an adult, the songs that he "popularized at the turn of the century were (and still are) included in countless anthologies of Irish music and were tagged as 'Irish' everywhere in America."[150] With songs like "Mother Machree" and "The Old Fashioned Mother," Olcott, and those who followed in his wake, encouraged an image of a Mother Ireland smiling over her diasporic children. It was an image that appealed not just to those of Irish heritage but to many in America. As William H. A. Williams suggests, "[T]he more America changed, the more Ireland and Irishness became repositories for the qualities that might be lost."[151] And it was an image that would remain current, further popularized by Hollywood musicals with singers like Bing Crosby, until supplemented by music from the folk revival of the 1960s.

Afterword

As the preceding chapters have suggested, the history of Irish music is a history of the desire for cultural purity. Both nationalist and colonial discourses have been heavily invested in establishing the authenticity of Irish music. In the nationalist account of Joseph Cooper Walker, for example, authenticity meant a direct connection to a glorious bardic past. For Edward Bunting, establishing the authenticity of Irish tunes over words became a way of eliminating any debate over Irish history, for the tunes could be relied on with "certainty and precision." For Thomas Davis, the authenticity of Irish music came to rest on the quality of "raciness," which could foster a collective identity shared by Catholics and Protestants. All of these projects connected musical authenticity to national legitimacy for Ireland. Ironically, in colonial discourse, the authenticity of Irish music was seen to be tied to a lack of national legitimacy. The articles in the *Quarterly Review* and the *North British Review* examined in chapter 8, for example, allow Irish music an ancient and pure Celtic pedigree in order to assert the superiority of English culture. For these authors, Irish music's "unsusceptibility to musical concord or harmony" was direct proof of Ireland's need to be ruled by Britain. Each chapter, whether concerning nationalist or colonial formations, has explored the gendered implications of the search for musical purity, for as Nira Yuval-Davis reminds us, "[A] proper understanding of either [gender or nation] cannot afford to ignore the ways they are informed and constructed by each other."[1]

In considering these varied representations of Irish music, this book has argued that each claim for Irish music's cultural purity has had its uncanny double that has served to trouble the narrative of authenticity. Brooke's bardic poetry was hybridized through translation. Davis's account of the power of Irish music was seen to be dependent on the erasure of its orality, its musicality. In Petrie's account, the medium of print worked to complicate the issue of musical authenticity. As such cases suggest, the history of Irish music can be reconsidered in such a way as to emphasize the music's fundamental hybridity rather than its purity. It is precisely this hybridity that has allowed Irish music to mean different things in different contexts—to transgress boundaries, in Said's formulation, and to provide multiple means of "divarshin," in Boucicault's terms. Moore's work serves as a paradigmatic example of music that means different things to different groups and also as an anomaly in its author's use of hybridity as a deliberate strategy. The quest for musical authenticity explored here continues to resonate in our present-day experiences of Irish music in such phenomena as the popularity of recordings of Irish traditional music and the success of the Irish music and dance spectacle *Riverdance*. These current examples of the musical construction of Irish identity, like the ones considered earlier, reflect and are reflected in gendered terms. In the present cases, however, the operative other against which the Irish self is defined is not British colonial authority dominating a British market but the global market for culture.

The popularity of Irish traditional music in the international arena dates back to the folk revival of the 1960s and 1970s, when groups like the Clancy Brothers, the Bothy Band, the Chieftains, Planxty, and Clannad established reputations in Ireland and beyond. Since the 1990s, however, Irish music has enjoyed a vogue under the category of "world music," a title invented in 1986 to accommodate the growing interest in African and non-Western musics.[2] Sally K. Sommers Smith discusses the process by which Irish music has expanded beyond Ireland and Irish diasporic communities: "Ethnomusicologists may once have been able to localize the practice of Irish traditional dance music to Ireland, and to immigrant communities in North America or Australia. It is no longer possible to do so. Irish music has become a 'world music.'"[3] But the issue of authenticity continues to haunt the discourse on traditional Irish music—live and recorded—in both local and world arenas. In its more recent guise, the concern with authenticity appears as an assertion of tradition as opposed to innovation. Martin Stokes and Philip Bohlman comment on the current quest for musical purity: "[T]he search for a hitherto misapprehended 'real' coupled with a (less explicit) demand for its institutional habilitation remain unshaken ideological components in thinking and writing about music on the Celtic fringe."[4] Irish musicians based in Ireland and abroad, individuals who claim a diasporic connection with the Irish community, and consumers who have no such claim are all variously invested in establishing a "real" Irish traditional music.

Scott Reiss discusses the debate among players of Irish music regarding tradition versus innovation, a debate that he suggests is embodied in the dialogue between Tony MacMahon and Micheál Ó Súilleabháin at *Crosbhealach an Cheoil*, the Crossroads Conference in 1996. MacMahon, an accordion player, television producer, and self-professed purist, accused Ó Súilleabháin, a pianist, composer, and director of the Irish World Music Center at the University of Limerick, of wreaking havoc with tradition. MacMahon described a piece on the CD *A River of Sound* that Ó Súilleabháin created with Donal Lunny as "Hiberno jazz scrubbed clean of its roots, ritual and balls."[5] What is striking in the current debate by musicians, however, is how naturalized the idea of tradition has become—and how vital a sign of national legitimacy, just as in the nationalist accounts of Irish music examined previously in this book. Even those musicians who describe themselves as innovators still unquestioningly accept the notion of a tradition and want to see themselves working within its parameters. Reiss quotes Martin Hayes, an Irish-born fiddler now living in Portland: "I am trying to walk that very narrow line between pushing the boundaries innovatively and staying completely within the tradition."[6] Reiss himself seems to promote the virtues of tradition over innovation in his discussion. Although he acknowledges that the playing of traditional music reflects an imagined set of beliefs, he still invokes a standard of purity in his description of local Irish music: "[P]laying traditional music in Ireland . . . enacts a culture of orality, an awareness of heritage and lineage, and an aesthetic of spontaneous creativity."[7]

What is at stake in the current claims for the purity of tradition is, as in earlier centuries, an insistence on national integrity in the face of denationalizing influences. In the current case, however, the denationalizing influences are a consequence not of British but of global consumption—the influence of other world musics or the alleged "rootlessness" of jazz, for example. For musicians in Ireland, determining what is traditional in traditional music is a way of establishing not only musical but also national boundaries in the midst of global cultural flows. What is important to bear in mind, however, is the complexity of the concept of tradition. Fintan Vallely provides a useful intervention in his discussion of traditional music's association, dating from the late nineteenth century, with "a Republican political consciousness," with "traveling people and their myth of dispossessed grandeur," with "the gentry (*uilleann* pipers in particular, who contributed artistic focus and many tunes)," and with "the suppressed indigenous classical music of the onetime court harpers who had become redundant due to Gaelic dispossession prior to the eighteenth century."[8] As Vallely indicates, what has become known today as Irish traditional music is a hybrid mix of histories.

It is not just musicians in Ireland who engage in the debate regarding the authenticity of Irish traditional music. There are many musicians outside Ireland who are interested in Irish music.[9] The determination of what is "real" Irish music has different implications for musicians beyond the national borders of Ireland than for those within the nation, however, offering them a connection to a rooted community. But ironically, at the same time as they seek authenticity in the music that they play, musicians who play traditional Irish music outside Ireland are necessarily altering its practice. Like eighteenth-century Anglo-Irish players of Gaelic music, non-Irish players of Irish traditional music have different contexts for playing and experiencing Irish traditional music. Even as they attempt to protect traditional Irish music, they exert a further hybridizing influence on it. They also extend the concept of the community of Irish traditional playing from the local to the global arena. As Timothy Taylor remarks, "It would perhaps be more accurate to say that the 'community' of Irish music is less place-based than ever, though it still has ties to place, and has cultural power to invoke place."[10]

This "cultural power to invoke place" is of particular interest to people outside Ireland who claim Irish heritage.[11] As the product of a "white" folk culture, Irish music represents an ethnic connection for those who have not previously considered themselves ethnic per se. Cyberspace forums of the Irish diaspora assert a strong association between music and Irish identity. "Irish Music" is the only cultural form indicated on the Web site of the "Virtual Irish Community," for example, squeezed between other links that include "Irish Accommodation," "Irish Chat," "Irish Gifts," and "Irish Roots."[12] The IrishNet Web site, which bills itself as concerned with building "the global Irish community," is hosted by and includes a link to Ceolas, "the home of celtic music on the internet."[13] Like Aran knit sweaters and Claddagh rings, Irish music can be seen as an advertisement of one's Irish roots. For members of the "global Irish community," as for those musicians who choose to play Irish music, the appeal of Irish music is its offer of a rooted identity in a rootless world.

The popularity of recorded Irish traditional music as a sign of rooted identity is not limited to those who claim Irish ancestry. Irish music also serves as an artifact that can connect anyone in the global arena to rootedness and tradition.[14] Sommers Smith points out how members of listservs such as the IRTRAD, "the premier discussion group for Irish traditional music on the Internet," debate what Irish music is most "traditional." Like musicians in Ireland, members of IRTRAD and other virtual groups value the music's connection with "a culture of orality, an awareness of heritage and lineage, and an aesthetic of spontaneous creativity," in Reiss's words; their connection with these qualities, however, comes not through a diasporic connection with Ireland but through their consumption of its music. Like the audiences of Lover's *Irish Evenings*, contemporary consumers of traditional music identify

Irish traditional music as a symbol of an authentic, premodern culture. In the current context, that premodern culture is validated as an Edenic alternative to postmodern malaise. As Sommers Smith suggests, however, the global consumption of Irish traditional music also affects the kind of music identified as traditional: "The increasing professionalism [resulting from the popularity of the music] means that who and what gets recorded may be decided at least as much by market factors as by the musical tastes of the performers or by a desire to provide an accurate representation of the tradition."[15] More and more, Irish traditional music is being altered in the process of being consumed internationally. Not only are only certain kinds of music being selected for recording, but those selected are often commingled with other types of music in a constant attempt to tap into new markets.[16]

This representation of Irish music in the global market has had notable gendered implications. During the 1960s folk revival, traditional Irish music was largely represented by male artists: the Clancy Brothers and Tommy Makem, with their tweed caps and energetic renditions of rebel ballads and working songs, and the Chieftains, with their multiple male instrumentalists. The Irish nation of the folk revival, like the bardic nations of Walker and Bunting, was a musical creation of men. In the aftermath of the revival, both male and female artists have been involved in the production of Irish traditional music and the blending of Irish music with other genres of world music. But it was a female singer, Enya, who took Irish music to a wider audience at the end of the last century. Significantly, her musical representations imagine Ireland not as a contemporary nation but as a precursor to modernity. Born Eithne Ní Bhraonáin, Enya is younger sister to a number of the musicians of Clannad, with whom she played for three years. Clannad began what Fintan Vallely describes as a "'Celtic-hush' style of popular music that made great use of electronic enhancement,"[17] and Enya capitalized on this technique to produce her own highly technical brand of New Age music. But in so doing, she also produced Irish music with mainstream appeal, in a form that the UK *Times* labeled "Ethereal pop."[18] Her 1988 album *Watermark* with its hit single "Orinoco Flow (Sail Away)" has sold over eight million copies worldwide.[19] Enya herself stakes her compositions' claim to the traditional world, as she asserts: "My melodies have the feel of traditional Irish music. They're the real strength of my music—the real backbone. It almost doesn't matter what the lyrics sound like."[20] But the pieces draw less on actual traditional tunes and more on the New Age interest in Ireland as a site of mysticism and Celtic mythology. "The Celts," for example (with lyrics by Roma Ryan), represents the Celts as an omnipresent spiritual force:

Saol na saol,
Tús go deireadh.
Tá muid beo
Go deo.

[Life of lives,
Beginning to the end.
We are alive
Forever.][21]

The fact that the lyrics are written in Gaelic reinforces the connection between Ireland and this spiritual force, while the music, with its electronic lay-
ering and reverb, creates a sense of disembodiment that further adds to the
ethereality. [22] The Web site "Enya: Magic and Melody" features an eclectic
section on "Celtic Mythology" that reflects the connections Enya's music encourages consumers of her music to make and includes links not only to "Cú
Chulainn, Champion of Ireland" and "The Druids" but also to "Arthurian
Legend" and "Boadicia and the Iceni." With the two songs she produced
for *The Fellowship of the Rings* in 2001, Enya offered consumers the opportunity
to draw connections between Irish mythology and the fictional world of
J. R. R. Tolkien. Ironically, these connections encourage the idea that Enya's
music is more deeply traditional than other forms of Irish folk music because
it reflects an ancient Celtic as opposed to an Irish world. In Charlotte Brooke's
and Sydney Owenson's work the voice of a woman offered important assertions of contemporary national identity. In Enya's work a woman's voice associates Ireland with Celtic mythology, reconfiguring Irishness as a premodern
symbol in a postmodern marketplace.

Similar gendered associations of Ireland with the past, this time both
mythical and historical, occur in another late-twentieth-century expression
of Irish popular culture: *Riverdance*. Evolving from a seven-minute interval
showpiece in the 1994 Eurovision Song Contest, *Riverdance: The Show* has been
an extraordinary success, selling out at box offices in Dublin, London, and
New York and eventually splitting into two touring companies. It has inspired numerous spinoffs like Michael Flatley's *Lord of the Dance* and *Feet of
Flames* and Alan Harding's *Spirit of the Dance* and has given rise to a worldwide interest in Irish dancing. As Frank Hall observes, "One would be hard
pressed to think of another dance show of any kind that has reached such a
level of popularity."[23] Like a contemporary version of "Rory O'More," *Riverdance* has "made the circuit of the world," attaining, not an "imperial," but

a global reputation.[24] In *Riverdance: The Story*, Sam Smyth's coffee-table book outlining the history of the show, *Riverdance* is described as "a metaphor for a new Ireland dancing into the twenty-first century."[25] According to its creators and producers, part of the show's success lies in its successful union of tradition and innovation, featuring music by former Planxty member Bill Whelan, which, according to Smyth, "was crafted so skillfully that audiences were convinced all the tunes and songs were traditional classics."[26] Smyth describes *Riverdance* as "a contemporary affirmation of an ancient Irish tradition,"[27] suggesting that it links past and present in a powerful representation of contemporary Irish identity.

What is interesting, however, is that the show's reputed integration of tradition and innovation depends on exactly the kind of gender stereotyping that we saw operating in earlier representations of Irish identity in Britain and the United States: a gendering of tradition as female and modernity as male.[28] In the 1995 video of *Riverdance: The Show*, the bulk of the traditional dancing is done by women, while the male dancers do the majority of the innovations and crossing over of traditions.[29] The first piece, "Reel around the Sun," for example, presents a chorus of women dancers. There are six men as well, but the overwhelming impression is made by the female dancers. They all dance in a "traditional" style, arms down and expressing little emotion.[30] The principal male dancer, Michael Flatley, however, bursts onto the stage in running leaps with open arms. Throughout the performance, his dancing is characterized by novelty. In "Distant Thunder," he and the male dancers integrate steps with clapping. In "Firedance," he joins in the flamenco dance with Maria Pagés. In "Riverdance International," he trades taps with the drummers. When he dances with the chorus, his presence introduces novelty. In contrast, the principal female dancer, Jean Butler, dances fairly traditionally throughout, indulging in only the occasional arm stretching (in "The Countess Cathleen") or hair flipping (in "Riverdance"). When she dances with the male dancers in the "Countess Cathleen" episode, she performs traditional steps to each one in turn, while they answer with nontraditional leaps. Furthermore, in the "Lift the Wings" episode, it is Jean Butler who gazes backward (presumably to Ireland) before heading for the New World. *Riverdance*, at least in the form in which it is packaged for a global video-watching audience, appeals to the same gendering of "home" and "away" that was depicted so forcefully in American song sheets like the *Lament of the Irish Exile*.[31]

Critics have credited the core of the success of *Riverdance* to its being supported so well by "the Irish diaspora around the world,"[32] and it is useful to examine further how that diaspora is invoked. *Riverdance* moves between portraying the rooted quality of Irish identity and its lack of a center. The performance begins with a focus on an imagined Ireland that is connected, like Enya's image of Ireland, to the "elemental forces" of Celtic mythology. Bill Whelan explains the concept behind the first act: "In Act One, the show deals with the themes that are at the heart of a lot of the early music and dance, songs in praise of the earth, sun, fire, the moon and other elemental forces that are common to all cultures. Act One is more purely Celtic in form and content."[33] Sam Smyth suggests that the "accumulation of these experiences culminat[es] in [the Irish people's] bond with home."[34] Robert Ballagh's sets, which include projected images of the passage tombs at Newgrange, Knowth, and Dowth for "Heart's Cry" and of a dolmen for "Distant Thunder," encourage this identification of Irish identity with the primitive. In contrast, Act Two focuses on the Irish diaspora. In Whelan's words: "Act Two tells how the native culture has been forced to emigrate and, by so doing, is exposed to the forms of expression of other cultures, both in dance and music."[35] Whelan promotes the show as both an affirmation of Irish identity and a celebration of transnationality: "People recognise themselves in the show. How else would African Americans, Australians, people from the north of England identify with the show? Sure, the Irish feel proud to be Irish, but it is international too—and it's not just because of the Spanish or Russian dancers. In Belfast, both Protestants and Catholics identified with it; it transcends nationalism."[36] *Riverdance* appeals to both nationalist and transnationalist impulses.

In "Traditionalism and Homelessness in Contemporary Irish Music," Kieran Keohane contends that Irish emigrant culture is constituted by "a profound and irreconcilable ambivalence": "On the one hand, the culture of emigration is animated by a desire to be anchored, temporally and spatially, by the particularity of tradition. . . . On the other hand, what we fear about the processes of globalisation—loss of coherence of place and time, homelessness—we simultaneously desire."[37] He asserts that "[t]here is a desire for post-national, cosmopolitan identification, to escape from the bonds of tradition to a free, but fearfully lonely, existential condition of rootlessness and, at the same time, a desire to return to, to re-collect and re-live in the tradition(s) of 'real' (that is to say imagined) Ireland(s)."[38] What Keohane describes, the simultaneous desire to belong and not to belong to a national culture or home, is not unique to Irish emigrant culture. It is a common experience of contemporary Western society. And this explains the appeal of *Riverdance* to non–Irish diaspora audiences.[39] Ireland provides an effective national focus for this paradoxical postmodern desire because it is historically associated with both music and emigration; both are seen as intrinsic to the Irish character. As we have seen in previous chapters, in the eighteenth and nineteenth centuries, music became organically associated with Irishness. Music became the "first faculty of the Irish," in the words of Thomas Davis. And beginning in the nineteenth century, according to Jim MacLaughlin, emigration also became specifically associated with Irishness, defined as both *"natural* and *traditional"* in the Irish case.[40] *Riverdance* draws on the rootedness associated with Irish music and dance while at the same time suggesting a "natural" process whereby Irish music and dance have crossed over to influence (and be influenced by) music and dance forms in both the Old and New Worlds. *Riverdance: The Story* articulates the appeal to musical rootedness in its opening words: "Throughout history Irish men and women have kicked out in time to express an inner joy and stepped in rhythm to consolidate their social circle."[41] Meanwhile, the show itself naturalizes the narrative of the Irish diaspora night after night with its performances around the globe. Precisely because of the ways in which it has been figured in popular culture up to the present, then, Ireland offers a model of how to be rooted and rootless at the same time.

The "Homecoming" episode that ends the show is billed as an integration of "the influences picked up abroad,"[42] and as such, it represents a utopian integration of national and transnational identity. Smyth describes it as "the merging of diverse cultures in a shared adventure that is then transported back home, completing the circle as Ireland celebrates taking its place in the world."[43] What I have been suggesting, however, in this Afterword and in my earlier discussion of the discourse on Irish music, is how much Ireland's "place in the world" has been and still is determined not in isolation but in uneven negotiation with other places in the world. That negotiation has historically produced a rich source of ambiguities and ambivalences, as I have attempted to indicate. Viewed in this light, the popularity of Irish traditional music and of *Riverdance* offers contemporary examples of negotiation similar to those found in eighteenth-century printed collections of music and in the work of writers from Walker to Petrie.

We cannot forget, however, that the current "shared adventure," the "merging of diverse cultures" that Sam Smyth celebrates, is to a great degree determined by who holds the power over music and that increasingly that power is held not by individuals, governments, or nations at all but by corporate and commercial interests. As Steven Feld writes in the context of world music: "[N]o matter how inspiring the musical creation, no matter how affirming its participatory dimension, the existence and success of world music returns to one of globalization's basic economic cliches: the drive for more and more markets and market niches."[44] In this situation, the question that remains is to what extent contemporary music—specifically Irish music, but for that matter any music—can work within and resist the structures of globalization. How can Irish music continue to defy the social systems, historical visions, and theoretical totalizations to which Edward Said refers?[45] Given the homogenizing pressures of a global market, the stakes are high for Irish music to articulate a nation whose citizens, like those of other nations, are engaged in a struggle to articulate multiple identities, identities based not on essential purity but on hybridity. It is my hope that this reconsideration of the history of Irish music, of the figures who have helped shape that history, and of their works will prove valuable in articulating a new relationship between music and identity for Ireland in the twenty-first century.

Notes

INTRODUCTION

1. Giraldus served as royal clerk to Henry II and as tutor to his son, John. Bartlett notes that "[d]uring his service as a royal clerk [to Henry II], Gerald was actively involved in the containment of the native Welsh." Robert Bartlett, *Gerald of Wales, 1146–1223* (Oxford: Clarendon Press, 1982), 15. Giraldus was sent by Henry to Ireland in 1185 on John's mission of conquest. According to A. B. Scott and F. X. Martin, Giraldus was also sent by Richard I to "keep the Welsh borders peaceful during the dangerous transition period" after the death of Henry II. Giraldus Cambrensis, *Expugnatio Hibernica: The Conquest of Ireland*, ed. and trans. A. B. Scott and F. X. Martin (Dublin: Royal Irish Academy, 1978), xiv–xv.

2. Giraldus Cambrensis, *The Historical Works of Giraldus Cambrensis. Containing the Topography of Ireland, and the History of the Conquest of Ireland*, trans. Thomas Forester (1863; reprint, New York: AMS Press, 1968), 10.

3. Ibid.

4. Ibid., 122.

5. Ibid., 124.

6. Ibid., 125.

7. David Cairns and Shaun Richards, *Writing Ireland: Colonialism, Nationalism, and Culture* (New York: St. Martin's Press, 1988), 3.

8. Giraldus Cambrensis, *Topography*, 126.

9. Ibid., 8.

10. Ibid., 126.

11. Ibid.

12. Christopher Highley notes similar ambiguities in Giraldus's *Conquest of Ireland* when Giraldus both presents a cultural chauvinism but also "calls into question the entire 'colonial' enterprise in Ireland and levels national differences." *Shakespeare, Spenser, and the Crisis in Ireland* (Cambridge: Cambridge University Press, 1997), 11.

13. Giraldus Cambrensis, *Topography*, 127.

14. Ibid.

15. Ibid., 128.

16. Ibid.

17. Ibid.

18. The sentence in Latin as quoted by Joseph Cooper Walker reads: "Mirum, quod in tanta tam praecipiti digitorum rapacitate, musica servatur proportio, et arte per omnia indemni, inter crispatos modulos, organaque multipliciter intricata,

tam suavi velocitate, tan dispari paritate, tam discordi concordia, consona redditur et completur melodia, seu Diatesseron, seu Diapente chordae concrepent, semper tamen ab molli incipiunt, et in idem redeunt, ut cucncta sub jucundae sonoritatis dulcedine compleantur." *Historical Memoirs of the Irish Bards* (1786; reprint, New York: Garland, 1971), 102.

19. Edward Said, *Musical Elaborations* (London: Vintage, 1991), xii.

20. Ibid., x. Moreover, Said suggests that music "is also an art whose existence is premised undeniably on individual performance, reception, or production" (x). See also Richard Leppert and Susan McClary, *Music and Society: The Politics of Composition, Performance and Reception* (Cambridge: Cambridge University Press, 1987), and John Shepherd, *Music as Social Text* (Cambridge: Polity Press, 1991).

21. Richard Leppert, *Music and Image* (Cambridge: Cambridge University Press, 1988), 159.

22. Michael Chanan, *Musica Practica: The Social Practice of Western Music from Gregorian Chant to Postmodernism* (London: Verso, 1994), 6.

23. Ibid.

24. For examples of works dating from the early twentieth century that explore the connection between Irish music and society, see W. H. Grattan Flood, *A History of Irish Music* (Dublin: Browne and Nolan, 1905); Aloys Fleischmann, ed., *Music in Ireland: A Symposium* (Cork: Cork University Press, 1952); Ita Margaret Hogan, *Anglo-Irish Music, 1780–1930* (Cork: Cork University Press, 1966).

25. David Lloyd, *Ireland after History* (Notre Dame, IN: University of Notre Dame Press, 1999), 37. In his chapter "Adulteration and the Nation" in *Anomalous States: Irish Writing and the Post-colonial Moment* (Durham, NC: Duke University Press, 1993), Lloyd considers how the "hybrid quality" of ballads in nineteenth-century Ireland works to "exceed the monologic desire of cultural nationalism" (89).

26. For examples of recent work examining how literature works to create and contest Irish identity, see Cairns and Richards, *Writing Ireland*; Mary Jean Corbett, *Allegories of Union in Irish and English Writing, 1790–1870: Politics, History and the Family from Edgeworth to Arnold* (Cambridge: Cambridge University Press, 2000); Seamus Deane, *Celtic Revivals: Essays in Modern Irish Literature, 1880–1980* (London: Faber, 1985) and *Strange Country: Modernity and Nationhood in Irish Writing since 1790* (Oxford: Clarendon Press, 1997); Terry Eagleton, *Crazy John and the Bishop* (Cork: Cork University Press, 1998) and *Heathcliff and the Great Hunger: Studies in Irish Culture* (New York: Verso, 1995); Terry Eagleton, Frederic Jameson, and Edward Said, eds., *Nationalism, Colonialism, and Literature* (Minneapolis: University of Minnesota Press, 1990); Luke Gibbons, *Transformations in Irish Culture* (Notre Dame, IN: University of Notre Dame Press, 1996); Declan Kiberd, *Inventing Ireland: The Literature of the Modern Nation* (Cambridge, MA: Harvard University Press, 1995); Joep Leerssen, *Mere Irish and Fíor-Ghael: Studies in the Idea of Irish Nationality, Its Development and Literary Expression Prior to the Nineteenth Century* (Notre Dame, IN: University of Notre Dame Press, 1997) and *Remembrance and Imagination: Patterns in the Historical and Literary Representation of Ireland in the Nineteenth Century* (Notre Dame, IN: University of Notre Dame Press, 1997); Lloyd, *Anomalous States, Ireland after History*, and *Nationalism and Minor Literature: James Clarence Mangan and the Emergence of Irish Cultural Nationalism* (Berkeley: University of California Press, 1987);

Thomas McLoughlin, *Contesting Ireland: Irish Voices against England in the Eighteenth Century* (Dublin: Four Courts Press, 1999).

27. Harry White's *The Keeper's Recital: Music and Cultural History in Ireland, 1770–1970* (Notre Dame, IN: University of Notre Dame Press, 1998) is the most notable of works attempting to put music back on center stage in the debate about Irish culture. Referring to Seamus Deane's assertion that the "enforced intimacy between literature and politics was unique and tragic in Ireland," White suggests that "the intimacy between music and politics was closer still" (ix). Marie McCarthy's *Passing It On: The Transmission of Music in Irish Culture* (Cork: Cork University Press, 1999) also presents a critical perspective on the use of music in Irish society. Chapter 3 of Helen Burke's *Riotous Performances: The Struggle for Hegemony in the Irish Theater, 1712–1784* (Notre Dame, IN: Notre Dame University Press, 2003) addresses the complex ideologies at play in the creation, performance, and consumption of Irish music in late-eighteenth-century Ireland. Ciaran Carson's *Last Night's Fun: A Book about Music, Food and Time* (London: Pimlico, 1996), while not an academic work, also explores the connection between Irish music and national identity. Fintan Vallely has recently edited an important reference work, *The Companion to Irish Traditional Music* (Cork: Cork University Press, 1999), that should contribute to the critical discussion of Irish music.

28. Pierre Bourdieu, *The Field of Cultural Production: Essays on Art and Literature* (New York: Columbia University Press, 1993), 110.

29. Said, *Musical Elaborations*, 55.

30. James Usher, *Clio: Or, A Discourse on Taste* (1769; reprint, New York: Garland, 1970), 151.

31. The discourse of music, then, reflects the ambivalence that, according to Homi Bhabha, "haunts the idea of the nation, the language of those who write it and the lives of those who live it." *Nation and Narration* (New York: Routledge, 1990), 1.

32. For further discussion of the importance of postcolonial theory to Irish studies, see Corbett, *Allegories of Union*, 7–11; Gibbons, *Transformations in Irish Culture*, chap. 14; Lloyd, *Anomalous States*, 5ff.; and Gerry Smyth, "The Past, the Post and the Utterly Changed: Intellectual Responsibility and Irish Cultural Criticism," *Irish Studies Review* 10 (1995): 25–29. On the related topic of revisionism in Irish studies, see Ciaran Brady, *Interpreting Irish History: The Debate on Historical Revisionism* (Blackrock: Irish Academic Press, 1994); D. George Boyce and Alan O'Day, eds., *Modern Irish History: Revisionism and the Revisionist Controversy* (London: Routledge, 1996); and Eagleton, *Crazy John*, 308–27.

33. Stephen Slemon argues that the term *postcolonialism* is most useful when it "locates a specifically anti- or *post*-colonial discursive purchase in culture, one which begins in the moment that colonial power inscribes itself onto the body and space of its Others and which continues as an often occulted tradition into the modern theatre of neo-colonialist international relations." "Modernism's Last Post," in *Past the Last Post*, ed. Ian Adam and Helen Tiffin (London: Harvester Wheatsheaf, 1991), 3.

34. I see *postcolonial* as a hybrid term, invoking both local specificities too often left out and universal considerations.

35. Colin Graham and Willy Maley, "Irish Studies and Postcolonial Theory," *Irish Studies Review* 7, no. 2 (1999): 150.

36. Sara Suleri, *The Rhetoric of English India* (Chicago: University of Chicago Press, 1992), 1.

37. Graham and Maley, "Irish Studies," 151.

38. Gyan Prakash, *After Colonialism: Imperial Histories and Postcolonial Displacements* (Princeton, NJ: Princeton University Press, 1995), 3.

39. Giraldus Cambrensis, *Topography*, 126–27.

40. The term *double inscription* is cited by Stuart Hall as an alternative to "the clearly demarcated inside/outside of the colonial system on which the histories of imperialism have thrived for so long." "When Was 'the Post-colonial'? Thinking at the Limit," in *The Post-colonial Question: Common Skies, Divided Horizons*, ed. Iain Chambers and Lidia Curti (New York: Routledge, 1996), 247.

41. Patrick Williams and Laura Chrisman, *Colonial Discourse and Post-colonial Theory: A Reader* (New York: Harvester Wheatsheaf, 1993), 16. See Bill Ashcroft, *Post-colonial Transformations* (New York: Routledge, 2001), for a fuller analysis of the kinds of transformations that occur in a situation of colonization.

42. Stuart Hall, "Cultural Identity and Diaspora," in Williams and Chrisman, *Colonial Discourse*, 247.

43. Lloyd, *Anomalous States*, 111–12.

44. See Homi Bhabha, *The Location of Culture* (New York: Routledge, 1993). In his essay for the Web site "Re-inventing Britain," Bhabha envisions a hybridization that emphasizes "culture as a form of historic and political movement that intervenes and intercedes in a kind of 'subaltern' strategy within the interstices, those in between times and spaces that are blocked in the largely spatial binary division of High/Low, Major/Minor." He continues: "It is the ability of hybridisation to take seriously those moments of transition or survival, its specific creativities and transgressions, that makes it a particularly productive perspective for narrating the 'here and now,' the present moment of our history as it is forming in our lives, shaping in our hands, slipping beyond reach." "Minority Culture and Creative Anxiety," 2000, retrieved January 20, 2001, from the "Re-inventing Britain" Web site: www.britcoun. org/studies/reinventingbritain/bhabha_2.htm. See also Robert Young, *Colonial Desire: Hybridity in Theory, Culture and Race* (New York: Routledge, 1995), for a genealogy of the term *hybridity* that critiques Bhabha's celebration of the concept.

45. Srinivas Aravamudan, *Tropicopolitans: Colonialism and Agency, 1688–1804* (Durham, NC: Duke University Press, 1999), 14.

46. I believe that this understanding of hybridity can also be brought to bear on the uses of postcolonial theory that I offer here. Like other hybrid forms, postcolonialism is context dependent. At times, as A. Dirlik argues, postcolonialism can be seen to be complicit in strategies of globalization. "The Postcolonial Aura: Third World Criticism in the Age of Global Capitalism," *Critical Inquiry* 20 (Winter 1992): 328–56. However, I also believe it can offer a way of describing and grappling with that globalization. What remains crucial to the uses made of postcolonial theory is consideration of the specific circumstances surrounding its reference to and embedding in the material world.

47. A recent multidisciplinary field influenced by cultural materialist, sociological, and postmodernist theories as well as traditional book history, print culture focuses, among other things, on the ways the meaning of a text is bound up with its

material presence and history and its creators' as well as its consumers' presuppositions about its relation to other texts. For the related field of book history criticism, see David Finkelstein and Alistair McCleery, *The Book History Reader* (New York: Routledge, 2002).

48. Bartlett notes that "the number of manuscripts [of Giraldus's works] surviving from the medieval period indicates their popularity. Medieval translations and abridgements were made, and printed editions appeared in the sixteenth and early seventeenth centuries" (*Gerald of Wales*, 178).

49. Matthew Pilkington, "The Progress of Music in *Ireland*. To Mira," in *The Field Day Anthology of Irish Writing*, ed. Seamus Deane (New York: Norton, 1991), 1:410. The theme of *concordia discors* was common among eighteenth-century British poets.

50. Charles O'Conor, *Dissertations on the History of Ireland*, 2nd ed. (Dublin, 1755), 55. O'Conor was also the author of *The Case of the Roman-Catholics of Ireland. Wherein the Principles and Conduct of that Party are fully Explained and Vindicated* (Dublin, 1753).

51. William Powers excerpted this statement from a 1807 letter of Moore's to Sir John Stevenson.

52. Sydney Owenson, *The Wild Irish Girl* (1806; reprint, New York: Garland, 1979), 1:222–23.

53. Thomas Davis, *Spirit of the Nation* (Dublin, 1843), vi. Marie McCarthy suggests: "In the various phases of nationalism from the late eighteenth to the mid-twentieth century, Ireland's musical heritage was drawn upon consistently as a means of revitalizing and legitimising an authentic Gaelic culture. In the process, myths and images about the origins and development of music were reinvented, and they became part of the cultural canon that was transmitted to succeeding generations" (*Passing It On*, 29). David Lloyd eloquently unravels the political complications in the Young Irelanders' cultural project of developing a nonsectarian national character in *Nationalism and Minor Literature*.

54. In his 1882 essay "What Is a Nation?" Ernst Renan remarks that "[f]orgetting, I would even go so far as to say historical error, is a crucial factor in the creation of a nation." In Bhabha, *Nation and Narration*, 11. In this book, I suggest that the "historical errors" of the colonizing nation also play a part in the self-definition of the colonized nation.

55. Anthony Bradley and Maryann Gialanella Valiulis, introduction to *Gender and Sexuality in Modern Ireland*, ed. Anthony Bradley and Maryann Gialanella Valiulis (Amherst: University of Massachusetts Press, 1997), 2.

56. Éibhear Walshe, *Sex, Nation and Dissent in Irish Writing* (Cork: Cork University Press, 1997), 3.

57. See Adele Dalsimer and Vera Kreilkamp, "Re/Dressing Mother Ireland: Feminist Imagery in Art and Literature," in *Re/Dressing Cathleen: Contemporary Works from Irish Women Artists*, ed. Jennifer Grinell and Alston Conley (Chestnut Hill, MA: Charles S. and Isabella V. McMullen Museum of Art, Boston College, 1997), 37–42; and Belinda Loftus, *Mirrors: William III and Mother Ireland* (Dundrum Down: Picture Press, 1990). Fintan Cullen also refers to the use made of female representations of Ireland in art. See *Visual Politics: The Representation of Ireland, 1750–1930* (Cork: Cork University Press, 1997), 152–59.

58. Dalsimer and Kreilkamp, "Re/Dressing Mother Ireland," 37.

59. Gibbons, *Transformations in Irish Culture*, 20.

60. Ibid., 21–22.

61. Ibid., 21.

62. Ibid.

63. Mary Louise Pratt comments on the anomaly between how women are used on metaphorical level and the prescribed roles of living women: "As mothers of the nation [women] are precariously other to the nation." "Women, Literature and National Brotherhood," *Nineteenth-Century Contexts* 18, no. 1 (1994): 30. Carol Coulter suggests that the opportunities for women to become politically involved in the nationalist struggles in the "colonised world" were greater than those in imperialist nations due to the existence of mass movements, "the widespread rejection of existing political institutions and culture, and the different family relationships which existed in colonial countries." *The Hidden Tradition: Feminism, Women and Nationalism in Ireland* (Cork: Cork University Press, 1990), 3. But she adds that they were later excluded by the new state they helped to create.

64. Nira Yuval-Davis and Floya Anthias, eds., *Woman-Nation-State* (New York: St. Martin's Press, 1989), 7.

65. Joseph Valente, "The Myth of Sovereignty: Gender in the Literature of Irish Nationalism," *ELH* 61 (1994): 193.

66. Ibid.

67. Ibid.

68. Nira Yuval-Davis, *Gender and Nation* (Thousand Oaks, CA: Sage Publications, 1997), 4.

69. In *Ireland's Others: Gender and Ethnicity in Irish Literature and Popular Culture* (Notre Dame, IN: University of Notre Dame Press, 2001), Elizabeth Butler Cullingford discusses "works that vary the analogy between femininity and Irish nationality" (7). She traces, for example, "an alternative narrative of homosocial or homoerotic bonding between English and Irish males, which constitutes an imaginative attempt to overcome the antipathy between the two countries" (7).

70. Anne McClintock, *Imperial Leather: Race, Gender and Sexuality in the Colonial Conquest* (New York: Routledge, 1995), 5.

71. G. J. Barker-Benfield, *The Culture of Sensibility: Sex and Society in Eighteenth-Century Britain* (Chicago: University of Chicago Press, 1992), xxiv.

72. Ibid., xxv.

73. Ibid., xxvii–xxviii.

74. Ibid., 1.

75. Pratt, "Women, Literature," 30.

76. Ibid.

77. Ibid.

78. Lawrence Klein, "Gender and the Public/Private Distinction in the Eighteenth Century: Some Questions about Evidence and Analytic Procedure," *Eighteenth-Century Studies* 29, no. 1 (1993): 99.

79. Ibid., 102.

80. Harriet Guest, *Small Change: Women, Learning, Patriotism, 1750–1810* (Chicago: University of Chicago Press, 2000), 13–14. See also Elizabeth Eger, Charlotte Grant,

Clíona Ó Gallchoir, et al., eds., *Women, Writing and the Public Sphere, 1700–1830* (Cambridge: Cambridge University Press, 2001).

81. Klein, "Gender," 101.

82. Guest, *Small Change*, 12.

83. Margaret Kelleher and James H. Murphy, eds., *Gender Perspectives in Nineteenth-Century Ireland: Public and Private Spheres* (Dublin: Irish Academic Press, 1997), 16.

84. Klein, "Gender," 104.

85. In "An Underground Gentry? Catholic Middlemen in Eighteenth-Century Ireland" (in *The Tree of Liberty: Radicalism, Catholicism and the Construction of Irish Identity, 1760–1830* [Cork: Cork University Press, 1996]). The cases that Whelan examines, which turn on the difference between public perception and private knowledge, offer more proof for the argument about the permeability of public and private.

86. Pratt, "Women, Literature," 30.

87. Walker, *Historical Memoirs*, 21.

88. Pratt, "Women, Literature," 31.

89. Charlotte Brooke, *Reliques of Irish Poetry* (1789; reprint, Gainesville, FL: Scholar's Facsimiles and Reprints, 1970), iii.

90. Sydney Owenson, *Twelve Original Hibernian Melodies, with English Words, Imitated and Translated from the Works of the Ancient Irish Bards* (London, 1805), 1.

91. See Nancy Curtin, "Matilda Tone and Virtuous Republican Femininity," John Gray, "Mary Ann McCracken: Belfast Revolutionary and Pioneer of Feminism," and Kevin O'Neill, "Mary Shackleton Leadbeater: Peaceful Rebel," all in *The Women of 1798*, ed. Dáire Keogh and Nicholas Furlong (Dublin: Four Courts Press, 1998), 26–46, 47–63, and 137–63 respectively.

92. Pratt, "Women, Literature," 30.

93. George Petrie, *The Ancient Music of Ireland* (Dublin: M. H. Gill, 1855), xii.

94. For purposes of this argument, I focus on Irish emigration to the United States, recognizing that the specifics of Irish emigration to Canada were quite different. See Cecil J. Houston and William Smyth, *Irish Emigration and Canadian Settlement: Patterns, Links, and Letters* (Toronto: University of Toronto Press, 1990); and David Wilson, *The Irish in Canada* (Ottawa: Canadian Historical Association, 1989).

95. Richard Kirkland, "Questioning the Frame: Hybridity, Ireland and the Institution," in *Ireland and Cultural Theory: The Mechanics of Authenticity*, ed. Colin Graham and Richard Kirkland (Houndmills: Macmillan, 1999), 211.

96. Ibid.

CHAPTER 1. NATION AND NOTATION: IRISH MUSIC AND
PRINT CULTURE IN THE EIGHTEENTH CENTURY

1. McCarthy, *Passing It On*, 7.

2. See Ann Buckley, "'And his voice swelled like a terrible thunderstorm . . .': Music as Symbolic Sound in Medieval Irish Society," and Ríonach Uí Ógáin, "Traditional Music and Irish Cultural History," both in *Irish Musical Studies*,

vol. 3, *Music and Irish Cultural History*, ed. Gerard Gillen and Harry White (Blackrock: Irish Academic Press, 1995), 13–76 and 77–100 respectively. Ó Ciosáin's comments on the difficulties of documenting the "local and popular cultures of eighteenth- and nineteenth-century Ireland" also apply to the musical sphere: "The words and beliefs of the majority are rarely, if ever, available in forms which are not heavily mediated." Niall Ó Ciosáin, *Print and Popular Culture in Ireland, 1750–1850* (New York: St. Martin's Press, 1997), 1.

3. Hogan, *Anglo-Irish Music*, xiv.

4. Brian Boydell, *Four Centuries of Music in Ireland* (London: British Broadcasting Corporation, 1979), 11.

5. White, *The Keeper's Recital*, 7.

6. For general commentary on the employment of the model of two separate nations in Irish historiography, see Brady, *Interpreting Irish History*. See also Boyce and O'Day, *Modern Irish History*.

7. Boydell, for example, comments that Gaelic music is the "result of an amalgam of many streams of native and European influence." "Music before 1700," in *A New History of Ireland*, vol. 4, *Eighteenth-Century Ireland, 1691–1800*, ed. T. W. Moody and W. E. Vaughan (Oxford: Clarendon Press, 1986), 546.

8. Tom Dunne argues that "the nature of the Anglo-Irish tradition . . . has been too narrowly conceived by both historians and literary scholars." He lists three main, interconnected strands of that tradition: "[t]he Old English emphasis on their cultural distinctiveness and political autonomy, and their role as interpreters and civilisers of the barbaric native Irish world"; "the 'New English' . . . radicalisation of existing colonist perspectives, including a greater hostility to the Gaelic world, and the infusion of the political and religious dimensions of Protestantism"; and the "assimilation by writers from the Gaelic, colonised population of colonist techniques of argument and persuasion, in order to make the case for equality of treatment." "Haunted by History: Irish Romantic Writing, 1800–1850," in *Romanticism in National Context*, ed. R. Porter and M. Teich (Cambridge: Cambridge University Press, 1988), 70–71. In her study of Irish historiography, Jacqueline Hill makes a similar point regarding Catholic perspectives: "References to 'the Catholic viewpoint,' for instance, do not take us very far, because there was more than one Catholic viewpoint, as well as more than one Protestant position." "Popery and Protestantism, Civil and Religious Liberty: The Disputed Lessons of Irish History, 1690–1812," *Past and Present* 118 (February 1988): 98. Whelan (*Tree of Liberty*) has also helped question the idea of an unbridgeable gap between the two cultures.

9. Patrick O'Donoghue, for example, speculates that "[t]he employment of secular song style—largely the achievement of Guilliaume de Machaut in the first half of the fourteenth century—may have paved the way for the use of popular folk tunes as the musical bases for polyphonic Mass settings." "Music and Religion in Ireland," in Gillen and White, *Irish Musical Studies*, 3:122. Buckley also comments on the interaction between the two cultures: "Following the formal establishment of English administration in Ireland under Henry II, rather than Ireland becoming anglicized in any uniform or totalising way, the new French- and English-speaking settlers engaged in patronage of Gaelic harpers and poets just like the longer-established chieftains. However, they also introduced other types of artistic expression,

particularly in the form of English rites, to the new ecclesiastical centres which they established. . . . And so alongside the Use of Sarum, the cathedral choir schools, and Corpus Christi processions in urban centres, the culture of the old Gaelic courts continued to flourish" ("'And his voice . . . ,'" 3:57).

10. Hall, "When Was 'the Post-colonial'?" 251.

11. This tune corresponds to the song known today as "The Croppy Boy." Tomás Ó Canainn, *Traditional Music in Ireland* (London: Routledge and Kegan Paul, 1978), 10.

12. Andrew Carpenter, *Verse in English from Eighteenth-Century Ireland* (Cork: Cork University Press, 1998), 3.

13. Neil McKendrick, John Brewer, and J. H. Plumb, *The Birth of a Consumer Society: The Commercialization of Eighteenth-Century England* (London: Europa Publications, 1982), 9. For a critical evaluation of the methodology of this work, see Grant Mc-Cracken, *Culture and Consumption: New Approaches to the Symbolic Character of Consumer Goods and Activities* (Bloomington: Indiana University Press, 1988), 4–7.

14. Neil McKendrick, "The Consumer Revolution," in McKendrick, Brewer, and Plumb, *Birth of a Consumer Society*, 11.

15. This boom, he suggests, can be "discerned in the 1690's, and by 1750 and 1760 leisure was becoming an industry with great potentiality for growth." J. H. Plumb, "The Commercialization of Leisure in Eighteenth-Century England," in McKendrick, Brewer, and Plumb, *Birth of a Consumer Society*, 265.

16. Ann Bermingham and John Brewer, eds., *The Consumption of Culture 1600–1800: Image, Object, Text* (New York: Routledge, 1995), 6.

17. Ibid., 9.

18. "Mr Johnston's Great Room" in Crow Street was, according to Brian Boydell, "built at the request of members of the Musical Academy for the practice of Italian music in 1731." "Music, 1700–1850," in *New History of Ireland*, 4:576. Mercer's Hospital invited Handel to Dublin in 1741 (4:579). The *Messiah* was first performed in Dublin in 1742 with Matthew Dubourg on violin.

19. Pilkington, "Progress of Music," 1:410.

20. According to Brian Boydell, "Between the acts there was singing, dancing, and instrumental music; and often further diversion in the form of tumbling, rope dancing, and conjuring tricks" ("Music, 1700–1850," 4:586).

21. Boydell notes among these venues Dublin Castle, cathedrals for special celebrations, the New Music Hall in Fishamble Street, the Philharmonic Room in Fishamble Street, and the Rotunda Room, built in 1767 "in association with Dr Mosse's Lying-in Hospital." Ibid., 581.

22. The latter of these was, along with the *Beggar's Opera*, the most popular ballad opera in the eighteenth century. Murray Pittock refers to an Irish song in his interpretation of John Gay's *Beggar's Opera* as a "jacobitical" reading of English society: "Macheath may sing 'Lillibulero,' but the set expressed to the air is one which deprecates the money-based society of Whig England." *Inventing and Resisting Britain: Cultural Identities in Britain and Ireland, 1685–1789* (New York: St. Martin's Press, 1997), 93.

23. See chapter 3 of Burke's *Riotous Performances* and Frank Llewelyn Harrison, "Music, Poetry and Polity in the Age of Swift," *Eighteenth-Century Ireland* 1 (1986):

37–63, for further discussion of the political use of Irish song in eighteenth-century theater.

24. Petrie, *Ancient Music of Ireland*, 33. In his discussion regarding an unnamed tune, Petrie also comments on the mixing of popular with elite traditions that such encounters produce: "The second part of the air was sung in chorus, accompanied by the beating of the singers' feet,—a mode of giving effect to such movements, which some, at least of my readers may remember to have been common amongst 'the gods,' at the Dublin Theatre, during the singing by Jack Johnstone of many of his exciting songs" (Ibid., 66).

25. Andrew Carpenter suggests that "[t]he increasing popularity of traditional Irish music in the Anglo-Irish drawing room in the 1720s and 1730s was a sign of a changing and mellowing society." "Changing Views of Irish Musical and Literary Culture in Eighteenth-Century Anglo-Irish Literature," in *Irish Literature and Culture*, ed. Michael Kenneally (Gerrards Cross: Colin Smythe, 1992), 11.

26. David Johnson, *Scottish Fiddle Music in the Eighteenth Century* (1994; reprint, Edinburgh: Mercat, 1997), 34. According to Johnson, "Every single professional violinist in eighteenth-century Scotland . . . had to earn his living part of the time by playing folk-fiddle music." *Music and Society in Lowland Scotland in the Eighteenth Century* (London: Oxford University Press, 1972), 18–19.

27. J. C. Beckett, "Introduction: Eighteenth-Century Ireland," in Moody and Vaughan, *New History of Ireland*, 4:xxxix. This is best exemplified in William Molyneux's *Case of Ireland's Being Bound by Acts of Parliament in England, Stated* (Dublin, 1698). Molyneux also argued that if England was allowed to legislate for Ireland, there should be Irish members of Parliament in Westminster. See J. G. Simms, "The Establishment of a Protestant Ascendancy, 1691–1714," in Moody and Vaughan, *New History of Ireland*, 4:6. The Union of Scotland and England in 1707 further exacerbated the resentment of the Irish.

28. Simms, "Establishment."

29. For the consumption of Irish goods as a statement of national affiliation, see Sarah Foster, "Buying Irish: Consumer Nationalism in Eighteenth-Century Dublin," *History Today* 47 (June 1997): 44–51. Barra Boydell, however, argues against reading the increasing use of Irish tunes as a feature of "local nationalism": "The use of traditional airs in concertos and solo keyboard pieces became increasingly popular toward the end of the [eighteenth] century. This tendency has sometimes been interpreted as a reflection of the increase in nationalist feelings that were apparent in the two decades before 1798, but an examination of London programmes during the same period reveals a similar fashion for the use of Scottish, Welsh and Irish melodies in instrumental works, particularly concertos." "The Iconography of the Irish Harp as a National Symbol," in *Irish Musical Studies*, vol. 5, *The Maynooth International Musicological Conference, 1995: Selected Proceedings*, ed. Patrick F. Devine and Harry White (Blackrock: Irish Academic Press, 1996), 105. Boydell attributes the national tunes' popularity to their musical function, commenting on "the suitable role which such melodies could play in the post-baroque form so frequently used for the final movement of concertos, or as a theme for variations in the slow movement." Boydell's depoliticization of the use of national tunes ignores the complex ideological role that

they played, but his comments are useful in pointing out the relationship between the production of Irish tunes in Ireland and in Britain.

30. Ferdinando Warner, *History of Ireland from the Earliest Authentic Accounts to the Year 1171* (Dublin, 1770), 1:vi–vii.

31. Quoted in Thomas McLoughlin, *Contesting Ireland: Irish Voices against England in the Eighteenth Century* (Dublin: Four Courts Press, 1999), 19.

32. Nicholas Carolan, *The Most Celebrated Irish Tunes: The Publishing of Irish Music in the Eighteenth Century* (Cork: Irish Traditional Music Society of University College Cork, 1990), 10.

33. Plumb suggests that the boom for music publishing was in the 1690s ("Commercialization of Leisure," 271). Brian Boydell comments that "there is only one definite mention before the eighteenth century of the publication of printed music in Ireland," an advertisement in the two issues of the *Dublin News Letter* of 1686 for "All the choicest new songs, with musical notes" ("Music before 1700," 557).

34. Deane, *Strange Country*, 55.

35. Max Weber identifies the system of Western music with the same rational drive that accompanied the development of capitalism. *Rational and Social Foundations of Music*, trans. Don Martindale, Johannes Riedel, and Gertrude Neuwirth (Carbondale: Southern Illinois University Press, 1958). John Shepherd extends Chanan's observation to consider the introduction of a system of scales that accompanies notation: "[P]reviously autonomous melodic shapes eventually became subservient to a unified harmonic scheme. It was not sonic events themselves which were henceforth important, but the various functions that could be visited on them." "Music and Male Hegemony," in *Music and Society: The Politics of Composition, Performance and Reception*, ed. Richard Leppert and Susan McClary (Cambridge: Cambridge University Press, 1987), 161.

36. Anne Willis, "The Neals' Celebrated Irish Tunes," unpublished master's thesis, 8. Photocopy in author's possession.

37. Chanan, *Musica Practica*, 77. He continues: "Notation erected a block in the Western ear against the inner complexities of non-Western musics. A strange kind of deafness appeared in the most sophisticated ears. . . . Under the hegemony of notation, the Western psyche came to fear the embrace of what it repressed, and responded to any music which manifested this repressed material as if it were a threat to civilization" (76–77).

38. Shepherd, "Music and Male Hegemony," 158.

39. Chanan, *Musica Practica*, 112.

40. Carolan, *Most Celebrated Irish Tunes*, 4.

41. Lawrence Whyte, "A Dissertation on *Italian* and *Irish* Music, With Some Panegyrick on *Carralan* Our Late *Irish Orpheus*" in *Field Day Anthology*, 1:414.

42. Mary Hamer, "Putting Ireland on the Map," *Textual Practice* 3, no. 2 (1989): 184.

43. Gibbons, *Transformations in Irish Culture*, 358–59. David Lloyd makes a similar claim with reference to Walter Benjamin's "Theses on the Philosophy of History," which argues for "forms of popular memory" that erupt, "interrupting the forward movement of 'progress and development.'" Lloyd, *Ireland after History*, 41.

44. Chanan, *Musica Practica*, 38.

45. Nicholas Carolan suggests c. 1724 for the date of the *Collection*, whereas Anne Willis gives 1726 as the most likely date. According to Carolan, "The earliest piece of Irish music published in the eighteenth century in England" is found in John Abell's *Collection of Songs in Several Languages* (London, 1701) (*Most Celebrated Irish Tunes*, 8–9). In addition, several Irish tunes had appeared in editions of John Playford's *The English Dancing Master*, dating from 1651 onwards, and in Thomas Durfey's *Pills to Purge Melancholy*, 6 vols. (London, 1698–1720). But the Neals's was the first collection of tunes to call attention to its contents' peculiarly Irish character (Carolan, *Most Celebrated Irish Tunes*, 8–9). See Willis, "Neals' Celebrated Irish Tunes," 2–3, for information on the dating of the publication of the *Colection*. Willis observes that "there is no evidence of any Irish tunes having been printed in Dublin by printers other than the Neals, though there were other printers of music in Dublin at the time" (6). The first collection of Scottish tunes printed in Scotland came out around the same time: Adam Craig's *Scots Tunes* (c. 1725). Allan Ramsay's *Tea-table Miscellany* (1723) had included words, but no music, to a number of popular folksongs.

46. According to Willis, John Neal and his son, William, were "impresarios, instrument makers, printers and publishers of engraved music" who "managed most of the entertainments in Dublin in the first half of the eighteenth century" ("Neals' Celebrated Irish Tunes," 1). John Neal, under the auspices of "The Charitable and Musical Society," organized subscription concerts for the relief of debtors. 1.

47. Ibid., 6.

48. Ibid., 13.

49. See ibid., 4. Willis notes, however, that "of the forty-nine tunes in the Neal collection, eighteen are not playable on the flute, and eleven of these are not playable on the oboe." She speculates that this is because the Neals were not familiar with the range of this new variety of flute, which had only been introduced in London around 1705.

50. Ibid., 3.

51. Boydell, "Music, 1700–1850," 4:591.

52. Donal O'Sullivan, *Carolan: The Life, Times and Music of an Irish Harper* (1968; reprint, London: Ossian, 1991), 294. The fact that the tune appears as "PleaRar keh na Rough" on the title page but as "Plea Rarkeh na Rourkough" on page 6 emphasizes the fluidity of the process of translating speech into print.

53. Willis, "Neals' Celebrated Irish Tunes," 6.

54. Ibid.

55. In fact there are sixteen other tunes by Carolan in the *Celebrated Irish Tunes* for which the composer's name is not given.

56. Mary Helen Thuente, *The Harp Re-strung: The United Irishmen and the Rise of Irish Literary Nationalism* (Syracuse, NY: Syracuse University Press, 1994), 50.

57. Joseph Cooper Walker, *Historical Memoirs*, Appendix 81.

58. Willis, "Neals' Celebrated Irish Tunes," n.p.

59. Ibid.

60. This incident is immortalized by Swift in his "Drapier's Letters." Murray Pittock points out that this episode was particularly galling to Irish citizens because

of the recent Williamite devaluation of the "Gunmoney" minted during the Jacobite adminstration (Pittock, *Inventing and Resisting Britain,* 82).

61. Willis, "Neals' Celebrated Irish Tunes," 12.

62. This is the same Dermod O'Connor who published a translation of Geoffrey Keating's *Foras feasa ar Éirinn (A General History of Ireland)* in Dublin in 1723.

63. Burke Thumoth also published *Twelve English and Twelve Irish Airs* around the same date (London, c. 1750).

64. Brian Boydell dates the change in the presentation of Irish music to the 1780s and attributes it to "the growing sense of national consciousness that marked the closing decades of the century" ("Music, 1700–1850," 4:603). The connection between Irish music and "national consciousness" begs further exploration, however.

65. O'Conor, *Dissertations,* 57–58.

66. Ibid., 53. O'Conor was an influence on many Anglo-Irish writers, a number of whom were personal friends of his. In his *Dissertations,* O'Conor suggests that the uncivilized state of Ireland frequently noted by later historians is a consequence of the Irish people's suffering under oppression: "In truth, our people were in no time savages. . . . Their barbarism, in later ages, was owing to a civil state, the worst that can possibly exist" (x).

67. Thomas Campbell, *A Philosophical Survey of the South of Ireland, in a series of letters to John Watkinson, M.D.* (Dublin: W. Whitestone, 1778), 451.

68. Ibid., 453. Gibbons points out how Campbell's generous attitude toward the Irish past changed as a result of the political situation in the 1780s. "From Ossian to O'Carolan: The Bard as Separatist Symbol," in *From Gaelic to Romantic: Ossian Translations,* ed. Fionna Stafford and Howard Gaskill (Amsterdam: Rodopi, 1995), 226–51.

69. Walker, *Historical Memoirs,* 62.

70. Charles Vallancey, *A Vindication of the Ancient History of Ireland wherein is shewn, 1. The Descent of its Old Inhabitants from the Phaeno-Scythians of the East 2. The early Skill of the Phaeno-Scythians, in Navigation, Arts and Letters 3. Several Accounts of the Ancient Irish Bards, authenticated from parallel History, Sacred and Profane* (Dublin, 1786), 88.

71. Samuel Thompson, Ann Thompson, and Peter Thompson, *The Hibernian Muse: A Collection of Irish Airs* (London, 1787), 3.

72. Campbell, *Philosophical Survey,* 453.

73. Leerssen discusses a "shift in historical consciousness between 1760 and 1890: a shift in which Ireland's social elite, originally English in ethnic background, cultural outlook and political allegiance, redefined its self-image and began to place itself under Gaelic auspices" (*Remembrance and Imagination,* 11). He relates this to a breakdown in relations "between the Anglo-Irish elite and the British government" (12). David Cairns and Shaun Richards read the Anglo-Irish projects at the time as an attempt "to produce forms of sentimental connection which would make it possible for the Ascendancy to assume the leadership of the people—nation—with their material and cultural dominance preserved"(*Writing Ireland,* 21).

74. See Lawrence Lipking, *The Ordering of the Arts in Eighteenth-Century England* (Princeton, NJ: Princeton University Press, 1970), 218.

75. Jean-Jacques Rousseau, "Essay On the Origin of Languages," in *On the Origin of Language,* ed. John H. Moran and Alexander Gode (Chicago: University of

Chicago Press, 1966), 59. Rousseau also put forward the idea that people of different nations relate to different songs: "[E]ach needs tunes with familiar melodies and understandable lyrics. Italian tunes are needed for Italians; for Turks, Turkish tunes. Each is affected only by accents familiar to him. His nerves yield only to what his spirit predisposes them. One must speak to him in a language he understands, if he is to be moved by what he is told" (60).

76. O'Conor, *Dissertations*, 53–54.

77. Ibid., 54.

78. Pilkington, "Progress of Music," 1:409.

79. Giraldus Cambrensis, *Historical Works*, 128.

80. Roger North, *Roger North on Music*, ed. John Wilson (London: Novello, 1959), v.

81. James Harris, "A Discourse on Music, Painting and Poetry," in *Three Treatises* (1765; reprint, New York: Garland, 1970), 80.

82. Ibid. In contrast, in his *Essays: On Poetry and Music*, James Beattie denies that music can be considered to any great extent imitative: "Music . . . is pleasing, not because it is imitative, but because certain melodies and harmonies have an *aptitude* to raise certain passions, affections, and sentiments in the soul." *Essays: On Poetry and Music* (London: Routledge, 1996), 136.

83. John Brown, *A Dissertation on the Rise, Union, and Power, the Progressions, Separations, and Corruptions, of Poetry and Music* (1763; reprint, New York: Garland, 1971), 223.

84. Charles Avison, *An Essay on Musical Expression* (London, 1752), 70. More recently, Caryl Flinn notes the way that music became marginalized in relation to sight: "Sound has thus come to function as sight's lesser counterpart, performing the role of an irrational, emotional 'other' to the rational and epistemologically treasured visual term." *Strains of Utopia: Gender, Nostalgia, and Hollywood Film Music* (Princeton, NJ: Princeton University Press, 1992), 6.

85. Kevin Barry, "James Usher and the Irish Enlightenment," *Eighteenth-Century Ireland* 3 (1988): 120.

86. Usher, *Clio*, 151.

87. Whyte, "Dissertation," 1:412.

88. Ibid.

89. O'Sullivan discusses the various theories explaining how Swift came to be acquainted with the song (*Carolan*, 294), and notes that in their *History of the City of Dublin* (1818), John Warburton, James Whitelaw, and Robert Walsh suggest that Carolan helped Swift in his translation of the poem (*Carolan*, 56). In *Riotous Performances*, Burke argues that Swift and Anthony Raymond, the "Protestant clergyman and fellow of Trinity College who was Swift's collaborator in this translation" were participating "however unwittingly" in a form of "nationalist transmission" (98–99).

90. Jonathan Swift, "The Description of an *Irish-Feast*, Translated almost literally out of the Original *Irish*," in Deane, *Field Day Anthology*, 1:399. I am indebted to Andrew Carpenter's notes both on this poem and on "The Parson's Revels" in his *Verse in English*, 20 and 207–14.

91. William Dunkin, "The Parson's Revels," in Deane, *Field Day Anthology*, 1:447.

92. Ibid., 1:446.

93. O'Conor, *Dissertations*, 54.

94. Ibid., 54–55.

95. Ibid., 55.

96. Barker-Benfield, *Culture of Sensibility*, xxv.

97. Ibid.

98. John Brewer, *The Pleasures of the Imagination: English Culture in the Eighteenth Century* (Chicago: University of Chicago Press, 2000), 82.

99. Ibid.

100. Ibid.

101. In *Intimate Enemy: Loss and Recovery of Self under Colonialism* (Delhi: Oxford University Press, 1983), Ashis Nandy explores the connection between "political and socio-economic dominance" (4) and masculinity.

102. Pilkington, "Progress of Music," 1:409.

103. Ibid., 1:409.

104. Ibid.

105. Ibid., 1:411.

106. Whyte, "Dissertation," 1:413.

107. Ibid., 1:413–14.

108. Ibid., 1:415.

109. See Burke for a discussion of Whyte's own ambiguous social and political position (*Riotous Performances*, 94–98).

110. Pilkington, "Progress of Music," 1:410.

111. Sandra Joyce suggests that the inclusion of Carolan's compositions in eighteenth-century opera was a "significant contributing factor to the spread of [his] fame." "An Introduction to O'Carolan's Music in Eighteenth-Century Printed Collections," in *Irish Musical Studies*, vol. 4, *The Maynooth International Musicological Conference, 1995: Selected Proceedings*, ed. Patrick F. Devine and Harry White (Dublin: Irish Academic Press, 1996), 305.

112. See O'Sullivan, *Carolan*, 78.

113. This collection was sponsored by the Reverend Patrick Delany and published by Dermot Connor (Carolan, *Most Celebrated Irish Tunes*, 13).

114. Michel Foucault, "What Is an Author?" in *Language, Counter-Memory, Practice*, ed. Donald F. Bouchard (New York: Cornell University Press, 1977), 127.

115. Chanan, *Musica Practica*, 67.

116. Campbell, *Philosophical Survey*, 452.

117. Oliver Goldsmith, "The History of Carolan, the Last Irish Bard," in Deane, *Field Day Anthology*, 1:667.

118. Ibid.

119. Ibid., emphasis mine.

120. Ibid.

121. Ibid., 1:668.

122. Campbell, *Philosophical Survey*, 451.

123. Ibid., 453.

124. Ibid., 452–53.

125. For a thorough treatment of this issue, see O'Sullivan, *Carolan*.

126. White, *Keeper's Recital*, 15.

127. Katie Trumpener, *Bardic Nationalism: The Romantic Novel and the British Empire* (Princeton, NJ: Princeton University Press, 1997), xii.

128. Ibid.

129. Cheryl Herr, "The Erotics of Irishness," in *Identities*, ed. Kwame Anthony Appiah and Henry Louis Gates (Chicago: University of Chicago Press, 1995), 276–77.

130. Goldsmith, "History of Carolan," 1:668.

131. Campbell, *Philosophical Survey*, 453.

132. Walker, *Historical Memoirs*, Appendix, 85.

133. Ibid., Appendix, 84.

134. Ibid.

135. Ibid., Appendix, 83.

136. Ibid., Appendix, 84–85.

137. Ibid., Appendix, 84.

138. Rev. Charles O'Conor, D.D., *Memoirs of the Life and Writings of the Late Charles O'Conor of Belanagare ESQ, M.R.I.A* (Dublin, 1796), 162.

139. Ibid.

140. The *Memoirs* was suppressed by the author after the first volume because of his fear that its pro-Catholic sympathies would compromise his family. Writing in 1831, James Hardiman also links Carolan's body and national music with the Catholic cause by calling attention to the use of his skull as a "relic": "On opening the grave in 1750 to receive the remains of a Catholic clergyman, whose dying request was to be interred with the Bard, the skull of the latter was taken up. The Hon. Thos. Dillon, brother to the Earl of Roscommon, caused it to be perforated a little in the forehead, and a small piece of ribbon to be inserted in order to distinguish it from similar disinterred remnants of mortality. It was placed in a niche over the grave, where it long remained an object of veneration, several persons having visited the church for the sole purpose of seeing the relic of a man so universally admired for his musical talents." *Irish Minstrelsy, or Bardic Remains of Ireland* (1831; reprint, New York: Barnes and Noble, 1971), 1:lxv. Moreover, in Hardiman's account, the skull becomes metonymic for the Catholic population in general: a "person on horseback, and in the garb of a gentleman—but supposed to have been a Northern Orangeman" arrived at the church desiring to see the skull. When it was brought to him, he "discharged a loaded pistol at it, by which it was shattered to pieces. Then, damning all Irish Papists, he rode away. . . . The brutal act could be perpetuated only through the demoniac spirit of party rage, which then disgraced the unhappy Country" (1:lxv). The existence and location of Carolan's skull were debated throughout the nineteenth and early twentieth centuries.

141. Gibbons, "From Ossian to O'Carolan," 226–28.

142. Ibid., 228.

143. Ibid., 250.

144. Ibid., 249

145. "Life of Carolin," *Irish Magazine*, October 1809, 434.

146. Ibid., 435.

147. *A Favorite Collection of Irish Melodies, The Original and Genuine Compositions of Carolan, The Celebrated Bard* (Dublin, n.d.).

CHAPTER 2. HARPING ON THE PAST: JOSEPH COOPER WALKER'S
HISTORICAL MEMOIRS OF THE IRISH BARDS AND THE
"HORIZONTAL BROTHERHOOD" OF THE IRISH NATION

1. According to Lipking, "Hawkins tries to write a peculiarly English history, using materials gathered at home; Burney tries to bring England into the continental mainstream, using the collections he gathered as the most famous musical traveller of his time" (*Ordering of the Arts*, 230).

2. John Hawkins, *A General History of the Science and Practice of Music*, 2 vols. (1776; reprint, New York: Dover, 1963), 1:xix.

3. Ibid.

4. Charles Burney, *A General History of Music, from the earliest Ages to the present Period*, 4 vols. (London, 1776–89), 1:xi.

5. Ibid., 1:x.

6. Ibid., 1:xvii.

7. Hawkins, *General History*, 265.

8. Ibid., 561.

9. Ibid., 564.

10. Ibid.

11. Burney, *General History*, 351–52.

12. Ibid., n. 109.

13. Keating's *Foras feasa ar Éirinn* was translated into English by Dermod O'Connor and published as *The General History of Ireland* in 1723. In that work, Keating notes the "great Encomium" that Giraldus bestowed upon Irish music and comments that this praise comes from "a Writer who renounc'd all Partiality in Favour of the *Irish*" (xi–xii).

14. Highley, *Shakespeare, Spenser*, 70. Highley suggests that in the sixteenth century "Ireland was discursively mapped in the context of a larger set of discourses about England's Celtic borderlands, discourses that made particular use of the fraught connections between Ireland and Wales" (67).

15. Hardiman, *Irish Minstrelsy*, 1:353.

16. Janet Harbison, "The Legacy of the Belfast Harpers' Festival, 1792," *Ulster Folklife* 35 (1989): 113.

17. But for a discussion of British government policy to reestablish control over Ireland in response to Ireland's new independence, see James Kelly, *Prelude to Union: Anglo-Irish Politics in the 1780s* (Cork: Cork University Press, 1992).

18. R. Foster comments: "O'Conor and his friends epitomize not only the preoccupations of the Catholic gentry and intellectuals, but also the obsession with Gaelic antiquity that would spread to Protestant society also by the 1780's. . . . In the upper classes of both traditions, an intellectual fascination with the Irish past

had taken hold, which would have diverse and far-reaching results." *Modern Ireland, 1600–1972* (Harmondsworth: Penguin, 1989), 210. See also Thuente, *Harp Re-strung,* chap. 2.

19. Ó Ciosáin, *Print and Popular Culture,* 172.

20. Leerssen, *Mere Irish and Fíor-Ghael,* 376. As I suggested in chap. 1, the work of Whelan (*Tree of Liberty*) has served to complicate such a perceived binary opposition between Anglo-Irish elite and a disenfranchised Gaelic culture by pointing to the pervasiveness of an influential Catholic element in eighteenth-century Irish society.

21. Benedict Anderson, *Imagined Communities: Reflections on the Origins and Spread of Nationalism,* rev. ed. (London: Verso, 1991), 11.

22. Joep Leerssen, "Anglo-Irish Patriotism and Its European Context: Notes towards a Reassessment," *Eighteenth-Century Ireland* 3 (1988): 20.

23. The other appendices are "Inquiries Concerning the Ancient Irish Harp" and "A Letter to Joseph C. Walker, Member of the Royal Irish Academy; on the Style of the Ancient Irish Music," both by Edward Ledwich; "An Essay on the Poetical Accents of the Irish," by William Beauford; an essay in Italian by Signor Canonico Orazio Maccari di Cortona about a statue of a bagpipe player; "Memoirs of Cormac Common," a famous singer and storyteller, by Ralph Ousley; "The Life of Turlough Carolan," by Walker himself; "An Account of Three Brass Trumpets Found Near Cork," containing descriptions of the trumpets that appeared in the Antiquarian Society of London's *Vetusta Monumenta*; "Essay on the Construction and Capability of the Irish Harp," by William Beauford; and "Select Irish Melodies." The appendices are paginated separately from the main text (but continuously with each other). All further page citations to the appendices will be preceded by "A."

24. Jean-Jacques Rousseau, "Essay," 50.

25. Walker, *Historical Memoirs,* 66. See also his opening remarks: "An attempt . . . to trace the arts of Poetry and Music to their source, in this, or in any country, must be unsuccessful: they are coeval with its original inhabitants; for man is both a poet and a musician by nature" (1–2).

26. Ibid., 65.

27. Ibid. Rousseau writes: "[E]ach [citizen] needs tunes with familiar melodies and understandable lyrics. . . . Each is affected only by accents familiar to him" ("Essay," 60).

28. Walker, *Historical Memoirs,* 65.

29. Ibid.

30. Ibid., 66 n.

31. Ibid., 6.

32. Quoted in ibid., 135.

33. Ibid., 6.

34. Ibid., 9–10.

35. Leerssen reads Walker's enterprise as representative of an attempt to invest the Gaelic past with the "lofty ideals of a Patriot hue" (*Remembrance and Imagination,* 29). See also Norman Vance, "Celts, Carthaginians and Constitutions: Anglo-Irish Literary Relations 1780-1820," *Irish Historical Studies* 22 (March 1981): 216–38.

36. Linda Colley, *Britons: Forging the Nation, 1707–1837* (New Haven, CT: Yale University Press, 1992), 238.

37. Pratt, "Women, Literature," 30.

38. Penny Fielding, *Writing and Orality: Nationality, Culture, and Nineteenth-Century Scottish Fiction* (Oxford: Oxford University Press, 1996), 10–12.

39. The relative value of oral texts was one of the most hotly debated issues in the Ossianic controversy. Trumpener reads Johnson's *Journey to the Western Islands of Scotland*, for example, as an attempt to establish "the primacy of a cosmopolitan and imperial vision of Enlightenment activity over what it sees as Scotland's nationalist Enlightenment, of the forces of linguistic normalization over those of vernacular revival, and of a London-centered, print-based model of literary history over a nationalist, bardic model based on oral tradition" (*Bardic Nationalism*, 70).

40. Walker, *Historical Memoirs*, 66.

41. Ibid., 65–66.

42. Quoted in ibid., 7.

43. Ibid., 3.

44. Ibid., 5.

45. Ibid., 12.

46. Ibid.

47. Ibid., 51.

48. Ibid., 154.

49. Ibid., 155.

50. Ibid., 19–20.

51. Ibid., 19.

52. Clare O'Halloran, "Irish Recreations of the Gaelic Past: The Challenge of Macpherson's *Ossian*," *Past and Present* 124 (1989): 85.

53. Ibid.

54. Walker, *Historical Memoirs*, 37 n.

55. Ibid.

56. Ibid., n.

57. Ibid., 110 n.

58. Ibid., 74.

59. Ibid., 137.

60. Ibid., A92.

61. Ibid., 111.

62. Ibid., 106.

63. Ibid.

64. Ibid., 138.

65. Ibid., 137.

66. Quoted in ibid., 139–40.

67. Ibid., 141.

68. Ibid., 155.

69. Ibid., 155–56.

70. Ibid., 156.

71. Ibid., 158.

72. Ibid., 160.

73. Ibid., 158.

74. Ibid., 159.

75. Ibid., 161.
76. Ibid.
77. Ibid., 4.
78. Ibid., 101, my emphasis.
79. Ibid., 53.
80. Ibid.
81. Ibid., 57.
82. Ibid.
83. Ibid., 67.
84. Ibid.
85. Ibid., 125.
86. Ibid.
87. Ibid.
88. Ibid., 125–26.
89. Ibid., 126.
90. Ibid., 127–28.
91. Ibid., 128.
92. Ibid.
93. Leerssen notes both of Walker's explanations for the melancholy nature of Irish music but fails to comment on the implications of this ambivalent view (*Mere Irish and Fíor-Ghael*, 373).
94. Quoted in Walker, *Historical Memoirs*, 61 n.
95. Ibid.
96. Walker, *Historical Memoirs*, A11.
97. Ibid.
98. Ibid.
99. As Barra Boydell points out, the harp on Tudor coinage introduced by Henry VIII had "a decorative curled foot, a feature which has no parallel on Irish harps. Thus, the first widespread use of the harp as the symbol of Ireland depicted the instrument not as it was known in Ireland, but according to the perception of outsiders." "Iconography," 133.
100. Walker, *Historical Memoirs*, A126.
101. Ibid.
102. Ibid., 134.
103. Ibid., A126.
104. Ibid., 19.
105. Quoted in ibid., 19 n.
106. Ibid., 19.
107. Ibid., 20–21.
108. Ibid., 21.
109. Walker notes in particular that a "great revolution" was inspired in "Anno Mundi 3649 . . . by the united powers of female poesy and music" (33). The incident, the story of Maon, would be taken up by Charlotte Brooke in her own revolutionary project to include women in the imagining of the Irish nation, as we will see in chap. 3.
110. Valente, "Myth of Sovereignty," 189.

111. Walker, *Historical Memoirs*, A81.

112. Ibid., A82.

113. Ibid.

114. Valente, "Myth of Sovereignty," 191.

115. Bhabha, *Location of Culture*, 70.

116. Walker, *Historical Memoirs*, A81.

117. Walker notes that "[t]he immortal Dean Swift" asked for a literal translation of the song and "was so charmed with its beauties, that he honoured it with an excellent version" (*Historical Memoirs*, A82). In addition, he writes, "A faithful poetical translation of PLERACA NA RUARCACH has been since published by Charles Wilson, a neglected genius, now struggling with adversity in London" (A81). The tune to "O'Rourke's Feast" was included in the second edition of the *Memoirs* (*Historical Memoirs of the Irish Bards; An Historical Essay on the Dress of the Ancient and Modern Irish; and a Memoir on the Armour and Weapons of the Irish*, 2 vols. [Dublin: James Christie, 1818], 1: A16). (Below, all citations are to first edition.)

118. Walker, *Historical Memoirs*, 62, my emphasis.

119. Burney, review of *Historical Memoirs of the Irish Bards, Monthly Review*, December 1787, 426.

120. Ibid., 427.

121. Ibid., 425−26.

122. Ibid., 425.

123. Ibid., 429.

124. Ibid., 438−39.

125. Trumpener, *Bardic Nationalism*, 57.

126. Burney, review, 425.

127. Ibid., 431.

128. Ibid., 433.

129. Ibid., 430.

130. Ibid., 426−27.

131. Ibid., 427.

132. Harry White, "Carolan and the Dislocation of Music in Ireland," *Eighteenth-Century Ireland* 4 (1989): 55.

133. Ibid.

134. Ibid.

135. Bhabha, *Location of Culture*, 152.

136. Ibid.

137. James W. Phillips, *Printing and Bookselling in Dublin, 1670-1800* (Dublin: Irish Academic Press, 1998), 93 and 77.

CHAPTER 3. "THE UNITED POWERS OF FEMALE POESY AND MUSIC":
CHARLOTTE BROOKE'S *RELIQUES OF IRISH POETRY*

1. Leerssen, *Mere Irish and Fíor-Ghael*, 363. Charles Henry Wilson's *Poems Translated from the Irish Language into the English* appeared in 1782, but it does not seem to have had the same force upon the public as Brooke's translations.

2. Deane, *Strange Country*, 101.

3. Brooke, *Reliques of Irish Poetry*, iii.

4. There is some evidence that nationalism in dependent, or "colonial," nations actually could create a space for women writers. In her study of women's prefaces in nineteenth-century anthologies, for example, Carole Gerson notes female writers' "awareness of their participation in the founding of a new national literature. A Canadian readership might be more forgiving than a British one when presented with literature that was at least . . . essentially Canadian." "The Presenting Face: Prefaces to English-Language Poetry and Fiction Written by Women in Canada, 1850–1940," in *Prefaces and Literary Manifestoes*, ed. E. D. Blodgett and A. G. Purdy (Edmonton: Research Institute for Comparative Literature, 1990), 62. In her discussion of Mary Davys, an earlier Irish woman writer, Siobhán Kilfether argues that prefaces by women in eighteenth-century works can be seen as either aggressive or defensive. She favours reading them as an "assault on the language of fiction and an attempt to inscribe gender on every story." "Beyond the Pale: Sexual Identity and National Identity in Early Irish Fiction," *Critical Matrix* 2, no. 4 (1986): 17.

5. Brooke, *Reliques of Irish Poetry*, vii–viii.

6. Ibid., viii.

7. Ibid.

8. Ibid.

9. Charles Henry Wilson, ed., *Brookiana* (London, 1804), 86–87. Wilson recounts that when a young man at Sheridan's school "addressed some verses to him in the Irish language," Henry Brooke was "so highly pleased with this little nosegay of flowers, that he resolved to learn the Irish language, a resolve, with many others, which he never put into execution" (86–87). J. C. Beckett notes that Brooke was "mainly responsible for his daughter's more persevering and more fruitful interest in Gaelic literature," although it was Joseph Cooper Walker who first encouraged her to collect and translate Gaelic poems. "Literature in English, 1691–1800," in *A New History of Ireland*, vol. 4, *Eighteenth-Century Ireland, 1691–1800,*. ed. T. W. Moody and W. E. Vaughan (Oxford: Clarendon Press, 1986), 469.

10. Walker, *Historical Memoirs*, A92. As in previous citations, "A" refers to the book's appendices, which are paginated separately from the main text.

11. Brooke, *Reliques of Irish Poetry*, ix.

12. Sylvester O'Halloran was the author of *A General History of Ireland, from the Earliest Accounts to the Close of the Twelfth Century*, 2 vols. (London: J. Murray, 1772), and *An Introduction to the Study of the Histories and Antiquities of Ireland* (London: J. Murray, 1772), among other works.

13. Ibid., v.

14. Ibid., viii.

15. Ibid., 246 n.

16. Clare O'Halloran discusses Brooke's lack of reference to Macpherson: "Brooke's absolute silence on the Ossian controversy is all the more remarkable since she was the first to provide Gaelic originals in tandem with her translations, the lack of which had constituted one of the main criticisms of Macpherson's work" ("Irish Recreations," 87). It is interesting to compare Brooke's presentation of Ossianic poetry with that of James Macpherson. The "joy of grief" as recounted by the poet Os-

sian had been a continuous theme of Macpherson's poetry, suggesting his ambiguous relationship to Scottish Highland culture. Brooke does include two "Heroic" pieces featuring dialogues between St. Patrick and Oisin. The first of these, "Magnus," begins with Oisin (her equivalent of Ossian) lamenting the loss of the heroic culture and ends similarly, with Oisin regretting:

> Among thy clerks, my last sad hour
> Its weary scene prolongs;
> And psalms must now supply the pow'r
> Of victory's lofty songs.
> (*Reliques of Irish Poetry*, 65)

But the second of Brooke's "Heroic" poems, "The Chase," ends more triumphantly:

> Now, Patrick of the scanty store,
> And meagre-making face!
> Say, did'st thou ever hear before
>   This memorable Chase?

Indeed, this poem takes as its theme the restoration of Finn to his former strength after he had been prematurely aged by an enchantress. Unlike Macpherson's poems of Ossian, Brooke's *Reliques of Irish Poetry* suggests the continuing vitality of Gaelic culture.

17. Brooke, *Reliques of Irish Poetry*, 55.

18. Ibid., 251 n.

19. Ibid.

20. Ibid., 247 n.

21. Walker, *Historical Memoirs*, A77.

22. Brooke, *Reliques of Irish Poetry*, 246.

23. Ibid., 245.

24. Walker, *Historical Memoirs*, 9–10.

25. Sylvester O'Halloran, *An Introduction to the Study of the Histories and Antiquities of Ireland* (London: J. Murray, 1772); Brooke, *Reliques of Irish Poetry*, 5.

26. Brooke, *Reliques of Irish Poetry*, 5.

27. Walker, *Historical Memoirs*, 233.

28. Ibid., 128.

29. Brooke, *Reliques of Irish Poetry*, 236.

30. Ibid., 237.

31. According to Seymour, Brooke was "compelled to beg for [financial] assistance from Percy" (Brooke, *Reliques of Irish Poetry*, vi) after her father's death left her alone and destitute. Percy's connection with Irish harping is also indicated by his being asked to become the first president of the new Belfast Harp Society in 1808. He declined the offer (Flood, *History of Irish Music*, 319).

32. Thomas Percy, *Reliques of Ancient English Poetry*, 3 vols., ed. Henry B. Wheatley (London: George Allen and Unwin, 1885), 1:1–2.

33. Ibid., 1:346; my emphasis.

34. Ibid., 1:348.

35. Brooke, *Reliques of Irish Poetry*, 229–30.

36. Ibid., 238.

37. Ibid. Her specific targets are Young, Rowe, Thomson, and Gray. Thomson was, of course, a Scot.

38. Ibid., 47 n.

39. Quoted in Aaron Crossley Hobart Seymour, "Memoir of Miss Brooke," in Brooke, *Reliques of Irish Poetry*, xlii.

40. Brooke, *Reliques of Irish Poetry*, 21 n.

41. Ibid., 245. The other two songs included in this section situate themselves in relation to the heroic age; "Song," by Patrick Linden, praises his love as a descendant of Colla the Great of the fourth century, while "The Maid of the Valley" alludes to the story of Deirdre.

42. Ibid., 253.

43. Ibid., 238.

44. Ibid., 237.

45. Ibid., 5.

46. Adam Potkay, "Virtue and Manners in Macpherson's *Poems of Ossian*," *PMLA* 107 (1992): 121.

47. Brooke, *Reliques of Irish Poetry*, vii.

48. Ibid., 74. Leerssen comments that Brooke views her introduction of the Gaelic heritage to an Anglo-Irish readership, not as "an opportunity to capitalize on its exotic value, but rather . . . as a Patriot endeavour in the service of her country: hoping to instill some appreciation for native Gaelic culture among the lettered Irish, and, hence, to raise Ireland and its culture in the British estimate" (*Mere Irish and Fíor-Ghael*, 363).

49. Beth Kowaleski-Wallace, "Milton's Daughters: The Education of Eighteenth-Century Women Writers," *Feminist Studies* 12 (1986): 276–77.

50. Henry Brooke, *A Collection of the Pieces Formerly Published by Henry Brooke, esq. To which are added Several Plays and Poems, now first printed*, 4 vols. (London, 1778), 2:206.

51. Ibid., 2:214.

52. Ibid., 2:152.

53. Brooke, *Reliques of Irish Poetry*, 325.

54. Ibid., 327.

55. Walker, *Historical Memoirs*, 19.

56. Ibid., 33.

57. Brooke, *Reliques of Irish Poetry*, 338.

58. Ibid., 346.

59. Ibid., 347.

60. Ibid., 348.

61. Ibid., 347–48.

62. Ibid., 368.

63. Ibid., 368–69.

64. Ibid., iv.

65. Quoted in Seymour, "Memoir of Miss Brooke," xlii–xliii.

66. Brooke, *Reliques of Irish Poetry*, v.

67. Ibid., vi.

68. Ibid.

69. Robert Welch, *A History of Verse Translation from the Irish, 1789–1897* (Totowa, NJ: Barnes and Noble, 1988), 5–6. Welch's assumption of the male identity of the translator fits my argument about the necessity of considering gender in the articulation of nationalism. He does not seem to accord Brooke the same credit of "signalling the difference" of Gaelic culture that he does this hypothetical male translator.

70. Ibid., 4.

71. E. W. Lynam, *The Irish Character in Print, 1571–1923* (1924; reprint, New York: Barnes and Noble, 1969), 20.

72. Carpenter, "Changing Views," 21.

73. Pat Muldowney and Brendan Clifford, eds., *Bolg an tSoláir* (Belfast: Athol Books, 1999), 138.

74. Ibid., 139.

75. Ibid.

76. Ibid., 64.

77. Pat Muldowney and Brendan Clifford, introduction to ibid., 8.

78. Seymour was the son of the vicar of Cahirelly, diocese of Cashel. He wrote *Vital Christianity Exhibited in a Series of Letters on the Most Important Subjects of Religion, Addressed to Young Persons* (London, 1819) and the *Life and Times of Selina, Countess of Huntingdon*, 2 vols. (London: W. E. Painter, 1839).

79. Seymour, "Memoir of Miss Brooke," cxxv–cxxvi

80. Ibid., xxiii

81. Ibid., xli.

82. Ibid., xlvii.

83. Ibid., iii.

84. Ibid., xxxi.

85. *Dublin Penny Journal*, September 1, 1832, 74.

CHAPTER 4. SEQUELS OF COLONIALISM: EDWARD BUNTING, THE *ANCIENT IRISH MUSIC*, AND THE CULTURAL POLITICS OF PERFORMANCE

1. McDonnell was "founder of the Linen Hall Library, the Belfast Academical institution, and the Ulster Gaelic Society." Brian Ó Cuív, "Irish Language and Literature, 1691–1845," in *A New History of Ireland*, vol. 4, *Eighteenth-Century Ireland, 1691–1800*, ed. T. W. Moody and W. E. Vaughan (Oxford: Clarendon Press, 1986), 414.

2. Edward Bunting, *The Ancient Music of Ireland* (Dublin: Hodges and Smith, 1840), 63.

3. In the 1840 volume, Bunting lists the participants: Daniel Black, Charles Byrne, William Carr, James Duncan, Charles Fanning, Denis Hempson, Hugh Higgins, Rose Mooney, Arthur O'Neill, and Patrick Quinn. First prize went to Fanning.

4. Charlotte Milligan Fox, *Annals of the Irish Harpers* (London: Smith, Elder, 1911), 4–5.

5. Wolfe Tone's famous journal entry for July 13, 1792, "Harpers again. Strum. Strum and be hanged" (quoted in Thuente, *Harp Re-strung*, 5), is often cited as evidence of the separation between the two events. Boydell notes that "Wolfe Tone, though he had no interest in harp music, looked in twice at the festival, and the Society of United Irishmen encouraged the venture" ("Music, 1700–1850," 4:603). Thuente puts the quotation from Tone's journal into perspective, suggesting that Tone had a "strong interest in traditional music" (*Harp Re-strung*, 6).

6. Thuente, *Harp Re-strung*, 125.

7. O'Neill notes that Bunting's mother was "the daughter of an Irish piper named Quinn, whose ancestor, Patrick Grauna O'Quinn, lost his life in the rising of 1641. His father was an English mining engineer from Derbyshire, who came to Ireland to open a coal mine in county Tyrone." Captain Francis O'Neill, *Irish Minstrels and Musicians* (Darby, PA: Norwood Editions, 1973), 137.

8. Harbison, in "Legacy," discusses the changes which occurred from Bunting's manuscripts to the publication of the tunes.

9. See Edward Bunting, *A General Collection of the Ancient Irish Music* (Dublin, 1796), and *A General Collection of the Ancient Music of Ireland* (London: Clementi, 1809). The 1796 volume contains sixty-six tunes. There are seventy-seven tunes in the 1809 volume, thirteen of which are repeated from the 1796 publication. The 1840 volume (simply *Ancient Music of Ireland*) contains one hundred and fifty-one tunes, thirty-one of which had appeared previously.

10. Boydell, "Music, 1700–1850," 4:603.

11. Ibid.

12. Bunting, *General Collection of the Ancient Irish Music* [1796], i.

13. Ibid., ii.

14. Ibid., iv.

15. Colin Graham, "'. . . Maybe That's Just Blarney': Irish Culture and the Persistence of Authenticity," in Graham and Kirkland, *Ireland and Cultural Theory*, 8.

16. Bunting, *General Collection of the Ancient Irish Music* [1796], i.

17. Ibid., ii.

18. Ibid.

19. Harbison suggests that "the harmonisations used by Bunting were hardly appropriate for the harp. They were arranged for ears that were better accustomed to the harmonies of Haydn, Handel and Mozart" ("Legacy," 116).

20. Bunting, *General Collection of the Ancient Irish Music* [1796], iii.

21. Ibid., ii.

22. Ibid., iii.

23. According to Thuente, Bunting taught Russell how to play the harp and went to see him when he was in hiding outside Belfast in 1803 (*Harp Re-strung*, 9).

24. See ibid., chap. 2.

25. Bunting, *General Collection of the Ancient Irish Music* [1796], iii.

26. Trumpener argues for the "important differences of emphasis between [the United Irish] conception of nationalism and that of the nationalist song collectors" (*Bardic Nationalism*, 11).

27. Bunting, *General Collection of the Ancient Irish Music* [1796], iv.

28. Ibid.

29. Kevin Whelan, *Fellowship of Freedom: The United Irishmen and 1798* (Cork: Cork University Press, 1998), 36.

30. Ibid.

31. Ibid., 37. See cover illustration

32. Pratt, "Women, Literature," 31.

33. Curtin, "Matilda Tone," 32. See her article "'A Nation of Abortive Men': Gendered Citizenship and Early Irish Republicanism," in *Reclaiming Gender: Transgressive Identities in Modern Ireland*, ed. Marilyn Cohen and Nancy J. Curtin (New York: St. Martin's Press, 1999), 33–52.

34. Mary Helen Thuente, "Liberty, Hibernia, and Mary Le More: United Irish Images of Women," in Keogh and Furlong, *Women of 1798*, 9–25.

35. Bunting, *General Collection of the Ancient Irish Music* [1796], i.

36. Ibid., iii.

37. Ibid., ii.

38. Ibid.

39. Foster, *Modern Ireland, 1600–1972*, 290.

40. According to Petrie, Bunting was attempting to compete with Moore "by an expensive splendour of typography, not to be found in the musical publications of that poet." "Our Portrait Gallery, No. 41. Edward Bunting," *Dublin University Magazine*, January 1847, 70.

41. Fox suggests, however, that the volume was "too repulsively learned . . . to give it a chance of suiting the tastes or purses of the class of society which had bought the earlier work; and among the higher classes there was then too little of Irish taste to incline them to receive it" (*Annals*, 47). It was pirated the moment it appeared, and it earned Bunting no money. What it did earn him, however, was cultural capital, as it gained him access to two London families who had an interest in Irish music: the Longmans and the Broadwoods.

42. "Historical and Critical Dissertation," in Bunting, *Ancient Music of Ireland*, 1 n.

43. Quoted in ibid., 1.

44. Ibid.

45. Ibid.

46. Ibid., 19.

47. Ibid., 1.

48. Ibid., 15.

49. Bunting, *General Collection of the Ancient Music of Ireland* [1809], 9.

50. Ibid., 27.

51. Ibid., iii.

52. "Historical and Critical Dissertation," 3.

53. Ibid.

54. Ibid.

55. Bunting, *General Collection of the Ancient Music of Ireland* [1809], i.

56. Ibid., ii.

57. Macpherson's *Fingal*, despite the controversy it generated, went a long way towards defusing anti-Scottish prejudice in the years following the 1745 Rebellion.

58. Fox, *Annals*, 224.

59. Bunting, *General Collection of the Ancient Music of Ireland* [1809], i.

60. Ibid.

61. Ibid.

62. See Fox (*Annals*, 41) and White (*Keeper's Recital*, 42) for details of Bunting's relationship with Lynch.

63. Petrie, "Bunting," 36.

64. Bunting, *General Collection of the Ancient Music of Ireland* [1809], 51.

65. Leslie Stephen and Sidney Lee, eds., *Dictionary of National Biography*, 22 vols. (1917; reprint, London: Oxford University Press, 1963), 3:846.

66. Bunting, *General Collection of the Ancient Music of Ireland* [1809], 65.

67. Ibid.

68. Ibid.

69. Ibid.

70. Ibid.

71. Ibid.

72. Petrie, "Bunting," 36.

73. Deane, *Field Day Anthology*, 2:10.

74. Bunting, *General Collection of the Ancient Music of Ireland* [1809], 15.

75. Ibid., 35.

76. Ibid., 4.

77. Ibid., 58.

78. Ibid.

79. Ibid.

80. Ibid., 43.

81. Deane, *Field Day Anthology*, 2:10.

82. Fox, *Annals*, 45.

83. Drennan was tried for seditious libel. Trumpener points out that he thereafter "turned to poetry as his principal mode of political expression" (*Bardic Nationalism*, 11).

84. Bunting, *General Collection of the Ancient Music of Ireland* [1809], ii.

85. "Historical and Critical Dissertation," 24.

86. Ibid., 26. For information on contemporary work on this harp, see Bill Taylor, "The Cloyne Harp," retrieved March 25, 2005, from www.clarsach.net/Bill_Taylor/cloyne.htm.

87. O'Neill, *Irish Minstrels and Musicians*, 140. The source of the "bitterness" to which O'Neill refers was the financial failure of the earlier editions.

88. See Lloyd (*Nationalism and Minor Literature*, chap. 2) for a discussion of the various political and cultural ideologies of the early nineteenth century.

89. Bunting, *Ancient Music of Ireland* [1840], 1.

90. Ibid.

91. Ibid., 2.

92. Ibid.

93. Ibid.

94. Ibid., 5.

95. Ibid., 6.

96. Ibid.

97. Ibid., 10.

98. Ibid., 64. Bunting also indicates that she had won third prize at the second Granard Festival in 1782 (62). It is worth noting as well that eight out of fifteen of those on the adjudication committee were female (Fox, *Annals*, 99).

99. Bunting, *Ancient Music of Ireland* [1840], 81.

100. *Chambers's Edinburgh Journal*, September 19, 1840, 279.

101. Bunting, *Ancient Music of Ireland* [1840], 6–7.

102. Ibid., 7.

103. Ibid., 8.

104. Ibid.

105. Ibid.

106. Ibid.

107. Ibid., 8–9.

108. It also becomes clear, however, that the bards or nobility no longer serve as a source for true Irish melodies; this has now fallen to the "old native people of the country" (10).

109. Lloyd, *Nationalism and Minor Literature*, x.

110. Bunting, *Ancient Music of Ireland* [1840], 11.

111. Fox, *Annals*, 304.

112. Ibid., 299.

113. Bhabha, *Nation and Narration*, 1.

114. Fox notes that the Lord Chamberlain, Lord Belfast, "encouraged and assisted Bunting in his final enterprise, and brought his work before the notice of Queen Victoria and the Prince Consort" (*Annals*, xii).

115. Bunting, *Ancient Music of Ireland* [1840], 4–5.

116. Ibid., iii.

117. Leppert, *Music and Image*, 146.

118. Jeffrey Kallberg, *Chopin at the Boundaries: Sex, History and Musical Genre* (Cambridge, MA: Harvard University Press, 1996), 35.

119. Ibid., 35–36. William Weber concurs, suggesting that for middle-class girls of that period, "learning the piano was virtually a puberty rite, since it was conceived not as a hobby but rather as a social obligation integral to their upbringing." *Music and the Middle Class: The Social Structure of Concert Life in London, Paris and Vienna* (New York: Holmes and Meier, 1975), 30.

120. Leppert, *Music and Image*, 146. He expands on this notion: "The implications of the privatization of women's performances are very great for the music history of England, for among the leisured elite theirs was the gender that had the time and the cultural 'permission' to study music seriously, yet by and large the talents they developed could not be heard beyond their own drawing rooms" (149).

CHAPTER 5. PATRIOTISM AND "WOMAN'S SENTIMENT" IN SYDNEY OWENSON'S *HIBERNIAN MELODIES* AND *THE WILD IRISH GIRL*

1. Barker-Benfield, *Culture of Sensibility*, xxviii.

2. Colley, *Britons*, 253.

3. Ibid., 254.

4. Guest, *Small Change*, 17.

5. Eger et al., *Women, Writing*, 7.

6. In *The Romantic National Tale and the Question of Ireland* (Cambridge: Cambridge University Press, 2002), Ina Ferris discusses Owenson's assertion of "female authorship as a properly public activity answering to a 'general public' outside the controls instituted by the literary field" and of herself as a "national author" (68).

7. Sydney Owenson, *Lady Morgan's Memoirs*, ed. W. Hepworth Dixon and Geraldine Jewsbury (London: W. H. Allen, 1862), 1:229–30.

8. Ibid., 1:230.

9. Ibid. This ability to change the terms of the divisions between the spheres is evident throughout her career. In *Lady Morgan's Memoirs*, for example, she situates political concerns and even science within the female domain, as she describes the Christmas when she was born as "the festival of humanity, of peace and good will to man, of love and liberty and *high distinction to woman*, of glory to the motherhood of nations" (1:7, my emphasis). The terms used to describe the benefits to women here—*liberty* and *high distinction*—are borrowed from the masculine political domain. Owenson turns from the story of Christ to the story of a woman, Eve, rewriting the fortunate fall. The season represents for Owenson "the accomplishment of the first desire of *her*, who was created, not born; the desire 'to be as gods, knowing good from evil'—the head and front of human science" (1:7). The origin of science is credited to woman, and, indeed, national identity is reconfigured as a function of feminine reproduction: "the motherhood of nations."

10. Leppert, *Music and Image*, 22.

11. Owenson, *Lady Morgan's Memoirs*, 1:230.

12. Timothy P. Foley, "Public Sphere and Domestic Circle: Gender and Political Economy in Nineteenth-Century Ireland," in Kelleher and Murphy, *Gender Perspectives*, 21.

13. Owenson, *Lady Morgan's Memoirs*, 1:213.

14. McClintock explores the way that both female and male upper-class identity is shaped through relations with the laboring class. She suggests: "[G]ender is not a separate dimension of identity to which one adds, accumulatively, the dimension of class. Rather, gender is an articulated category, constructed *through and by class*" (*Imperial Leather*, 94).

15. Owenson, *Lady Morgan's Memoirs*, 1:269.

16. Leppert, *Music and Image*, 162.

17. Ibid.

18. Ibid.

19. Ibid.

20. Ibid., 171.

21. Sydney Owenson, *Patriotic Sketches of Ireland, Written in Connaught*, 2 vols. (Baltimore: Dobbin and Murphy, 1809), xii.

22. Walker, *Historical Memoirs*, 65.

23. Owenson, *Twelve Original Hibernian Melodies*, 1.

24. Ibid., 2.

25. Ibid., 1.

26. Walker, *Historical Memoirs*, 65.

27. Owenson, *Twelve Original Hibernian Melodies*, 1.

28. Ibid.

29. Ibid.

30. Brooke, *Reliques of Irish Poetry*, iii.

31. Owenson, *Twelve Original Hibernian Melodies*, 1.

32. Ibid., 2.

33. Ibid.

34. Ibid.

35. Ibid.

36. Ibid.

37. Owenson, *Lady Morgan's Memoirs*, 1:230.

38. Owenson, *Twelve Original Hibernian Melodies*, 1.

39. Ibid.

40. Owenson, *Patriotic Sketches*, i. Tom Dunne notes that Robert Owenson's "notable repertoire of Gaelic songs" "formed the basis" of the *Twelve Original Hibernian Melodies*. Tom Dunne, "Fiction as the 'Best History of Nations': Lady Morgan's Irish Novels," in *The Writer as Witness*, ed. Tom Dunne (Cork: Cork University Press, 1987), 140.

41. Owenson, *Twelve Original Hibernian Melodies*, 2.

42. Ibid., 5.

43. Ibid., 11.

44. Ibid.

45. Ibid., 12.

46. Dunne, "Fiction," 140.

47. Ibid. Moreover, Dunne argues that Sydney Owenson's ambiguous relationship with Gaelic Ireland only "reflected that of her father, who was a fascinating combination of the authentic and theatrical" ("Fiction," 140). See, for comparison, Myers's criticism of Dunne's readings of Maria Edgeworth's narratives as "ventriloquism" of her father's ideas. Mitzi Myers, "'Like the Pictures in a Magic Lantern': Gender, History, and Edgeworth's Rebellion Narratives," *Nineteenth-Century Contexts* 19, no. 4 (1996): 385.

48. Leerssen, *Remembrance and Imagination*, 35.

49. Owenson, *Twelve Original Hibernian Melodies*, 1.

50. Ibid., 9.

51. Ibid.

52. Ibid., 13.

53. Ibid., 18.

54. Ibid.

55. Ibid., 7.

56. Ibid., 8.

57. Ibid., 9.

58. Ibid., 11.

59. In her discussion of *The Wild Irish Girl*, Ina Ferris provides an astute reading of the way sound operates as indicative of a Humean notion of sympathy that disturbs an individual's thoughts (*Romantic National Tale*, 61–63).

60. Owenson, *Patriotic Sketches*, ix.

61. Leerssen, *Remembrance and Imagination*, 61.

62. Ibid., 60.

63. Owenson, *Wild Irish Girl*, 2:73.

64. Ibid., 1:178.

65. Ibid., 1:250.

66. Ibid., 1:106.

67. Ibid., 1:162.

68. Ibid., 1:166.

69. Ibid.

70. Ibid., 2:2.

71. Ibid., 2:38–39.

72. Ibid.

73. Ibid., 2:39–40.

74. Ibid., 1:226.

75. Ibid., 1:221–22.

76. Ibid., 1:111.

77. Ibid., 1:117.

78. Leerssen, *Remembrance and Imagination*, 60–63.

79. Owenson, *Wild Irish Girl*, 1:39 n.

80. Ibid., 1:58–59 n.

81. Ibid., 1:70 n.

82. Ibid., 1:233.

83. Ibid., 2:16 n.

84. Ibid., 1:218–19 n.

85. Ibid., 1:219 n.

86. Ibid., 1: 219.

87. Leerssen, *Remembrance and Imagination*, 61.

88. Ibid.

89. Owenson, *Wild Irish Girl*, 1:80.

90. Ibid., 1:80f.

91. Ibid., 1:85–86.

92. See Walker, *Historical Memoirs*, 134.

93. Owenson, *Wild Irish Girl*, 1:86 n.

94. Ibid., 1:222–23.

95. Ibid., 1:223–24.

96. Walker, *Historical Memoirs*, 66 n.

97. Owenson, *Wild Irish Girl*, 1:227–28.

98. Ibid., 1:228.

99. Ibid., 1:161.

100. Ibid., 2:94.

101. Ibid., 2:119.

102. For a variety of interpretations of the political implications of this marriage, see Corbett, *Allegories of Union*; Ian Dennis, *Nationalism and Desire in Early Historical Fiction* (Houndmills, Basingstoke: Macmillan, 1997); Dunne, "Fiction"; Joseph Lew, "Sydney Owenson and the Fate of Empire," *Keats-Shelley Journal* 39 (1990): 39–65; and Robert Tracy, "Maria Edgeworth and Lady Morgan: Legality versus Legitimacy," *Nineteenth-Century Literature* 40 (June 1985): 1–22.

103. Owenson, *Wild Irish Girl*, 1:93.

104. Ibid., 3:258–59.

105. In *Romantic National Tale*, Ferris notes the way that Glorvina resists Horatio's attempts to "incorporate her into his fantasy" (55), suggesting that "throughout the narrative she tends to keep him off-balance" (56). Nevertheless, it is still Horatio's perceptions of being "off-balance" that the reader sees.

106. Owenson, *Wild Irish Girl*, 1:156.

107. Ibid., 1:162.

108. Ibid., 1:209.

109. Ibid., 1:168.

110. Ibid., 2:46.

111. Ibid., 1:109.

112. Ibid., 1:44.

113. Ibid., 1:232.

114. Ibid., 1:233 n.

115. Leerssen, *Remembrance and Imagination*, 57.

116. Owenson, *Wild Irish Girl*, 1:142.

117. Ibid., 1:209.

118. Anne Fogarty suggests that Owenson, like Edgeworth, produces political fictions that are "at once enlightened, conciliatory and riddled with ambiguity" but that, "in the final reckoning, the belief of these writers in a future which will be uncontaminated by the conflicts of the past is persistently undermined by the spectres of history which haunt their texts." "Imperfect Concord: Spectres of History in the Irish Novels of Maria Edgeworth and Lady Morgan," in Kelleher and Murphy, *Gender Perspectives*, 126. For Fogarty, the Gorgon episode is an example of such a "spectre."

119. Owenson, *Wild Irish Girl*, 1:185.

120. Ibid., 1:186.

121. Ibid., 1:213.

122. Ibid.

123. Ibid., 3:224.

124. Ibid., 3:331.

125. Ibid., 3:334; 3:236.

126. Ibid., 3:224, 3:332, 3:335, and 3:342.

127. Ferris observes: "For all her picturesque posturing, sound is [Glorvina's] primary medium, and her voice unsettles the English hero as her visuals rarely do" (*Romantic National Tale*, 63).

128. Gayatri Spivak, "Can the Subaltern Speak?" in Williams and Chrisman, *Colonial Discourse*, 83.

129. Owenson, *Wild Irish Girl*, 3:241.

130. Owenson, *Lady Morgan's Memoirs*, 1:252.

131. Ibid., 1:260.

132. For the detrimental effects of such racial perspectives, see L. Perry Curtis, *Apes and Angels: The Irishman in Victorian Caricature* (Washington, DC: Smithsonian Institution Press, 1997).

133. Dennis, *Nationalism and Desire*, 49.

134. Fox, *Annals*, 54.

135. Boydell, "Iconography," 140.

136. Ibid.

137. Owenson, *Lady Morgan's Memoirs*, 1:408.

138. Mary Campbell, *Lady Morgan: The Life and Times of Sydney Owenson* (London: Pandora, 1988), 71–72.

CHAPTER 6. A "TRULY NATIONAL" PROJECT: THOMAS MOORE'S *IRISH MELODIES* AND THE GENDERING OF THE BRITISH CULTURAL MARKETPLACE

1. Thomas Moore, *The Poetical Works of Thomas Moore*, 10 vols. (London: Longman, Orme, Brown, Green, and Longmans, 1840–1841), 4:113. The first and second volumes (referred to as "Numbers") of the *Irish Melodies* appeared in 1808. Subsequent volumes appeared in 1810, 1811, 1813, 1815, 1818, 1821, 1824, and 1834.

2. Howard Mumford Jones, *The Harp That Once—: A Chronicle of the Life of Thomas Moore* (1937; reprint, New York: Russell and Russell, 1970), 292.

3. Terence Brown, "Thomas Moore: A Reputation," in *Ireland's Literature: Selected Essays* (Dublin: Lilliput Press, 1988), 18. Brown contrasts this with the one thousand pounds Wordsworth made in his lifetime.

4. White suggests a chronological rise and fall of Moore's political reputation: "The transformation of Moore . . . from romantic agent of Irish emancipation (and specifically Catholic emancipation) to hated darling of the Victorian parlour, is one that belongs to the sectarian projection of Gaelic culture, which in part characterised the Celtic revival of the late 1870's. Between 1807 and the advent of the Famine, however, Moore's voice was the conduit of a romanticised political sentiment which had its origins in the United Irishmen, the failure of the Rebellion and the new symbolic force of the music itself" (*Keeper's Recital*, 44–45). While illuminating, this also seems to downplay criticism of Moore that occurred in the time up to the Famine.

5. Critical discourse on Moore reiterates this split perspective. In *Harp Restrung*, Thuente argues that Moore was carrying on the tradition of United Irish political verse. Harry White concurs with this view, contending that Moore "politicized the ethnic repertory" (*Keeper's Recital*, 52). Leerssen concludes that "the true political importance of the *Melodies* lies in their cultivation of remembering" (*Remembrance and Imagination*, 81). And Eagleton observes that "it would be hard to underestimate the political impact of Thomas Moore's *Irish Melodies*" (*Heathcliff*, 227). At the same time, other critics read Moore's work as more politically ineffectual. Malcolm Brown ar-

gues that "the *Melodies* treat of Irish history as if its true significance was to provide a drawing-room audience with metaphors of its own indulgent sense of personal mutability." *The Politics of Irish Literature: From Thomas Davis to W. B. Yeats* (Seattle: University of Washington Press, 1972), 19–20. McCormack asserts that Moore's songs "signalled the convergence of a defeated Gaelic past and a metropolitan audience that was intellectually curious but not intellectually demanding. *Drawing room* might be emphasized to indicate the abandonment of political rhetoric with the extinction of the Irish parliament, and the elevation in its stead of the family as a collective image of Irish ambition." W. J. McCormack, "Language, Class and Genre," in Deane, *Field Day Anthology*, 1:1079.

    6. White suggests that "[t]he United Irishmen were a formative influence in Moore's education as a (Catholic) student in Trinity College, Dublin, from 1794 until 1800" (*Keeper's Recital*, 45).

    7. Hoover Harding Jordan, *Bolt Upright: The Life of Thomas Moore* (Salzburg: Institut für Englische Sprache und Literatur, Universität Salzburg, 1975), 26.

    8. Ibid., 25–26.

    9. White, *Keeper's Recital*, 45.

    10. Thomas Moore, *Letters*, 2 vols., ed. Wilfred S. Dowden (Oxford: Clarendon Press, 1964), 1:430.

    11. Veronica ní Chinnéide, "The Sources of Moore's Melodies," *Journal of the Royal Society of Antiquaries of Ireland*. 89, no. 2 (1959): 110.

    12. Moore, *Letters*, 1:41–42.

    13. Jordan, *Bolt Upright*, 206.

    14. The *New Monthly Review* (January 1, 1820) picked up on Moore's residence in England, mocking him for being an "absentee" (4).

    15. Moore, *Works*, 3:286.

    16. Ibid.

    17. Miriam De Ford, *Thomas Moore* (New York: Twayne, 1967), 35.

    18. Jones, *The Harp That Once*, 153.

    19. Ibid., 159.

    20. Moore, *Letters*, 1:220.

    21. Ibid.

    22. De Ford, *Thomas Moore*, 35.

    23. Lloyd, *Nationalism and Minor Literature*, x.

    24. Eagleton, *Crazy John*, 141.

    25. Ibid., 140.

    26. In addition, twenty-nine tunes came from Smollet Holden's 1806 *Collection of Irish Slow and Quick Tunes*. Three tunes came from the ballad opera *The Poor Soldier*, by William Shield (with librettos by John O'Keefe). Moore also took two tunes from two other of Shield's works and one tune from Owenson's *Hibernian Melodies* (ní Chinnéide, "Sources of Moore's Melodies," 113–14).

    27. The efforts to recover the original tunes began with Charles Villiers Stanford's *Irish Melodies of Thomas Moore: The Original Airs Restored* (New York, 1895).

    28. Moore comments in a footnote to the Advertisement to the first two volumes of the *Melodies*: "The Writer forgot . . . that the Public are indebted to Mr. BUNTING for a very valuable Collection of Irish Music; and that the patriotic

Genius of Miss OWENSON has been employed upon some of our finest airs" (4:112).

29. Moore, *Works*, 4:120.

30. Ibid., 4:121.

31. Anne Janowitz, *England's Ruins: Poetic Purpose and the National Landscape* (Cambridge, MA: Basil Blackwell, 1990), 3.

32. Thomas Crofton Croker, *Notes from the Letters of Thomas Moore to His Music Publisher, James Power . . . with an Introductory Letter from Thomas Crofton Croker, Esq.* (New York: Redfield, 1854), 48.

33. ní Chinnéide, "Sources of Moore's Melodies," 110.

34. Ibid., 114.

35. Moore, *Works*, 3:234.

36. Dunne, "Haunted by History," 86. Dunne argues that Moore, along with James Hardiman, Gerald Griffin, and James Clarence Mangan, exemplifies "Catholic exploitation of and nostalgia for the past as well as the survival of older Gaelic perspectives" (72).

37. Augustine Martin, "Anglo-Irish Poetry: Moore to Ferguson," *Canadian Journal of Irish Studies* 12, no. 2 (1986): 88.

38. Moore, *Works*, 4:129.

39. Ibid., 4:129–30.

40. Ibid., 4:134.

41. This letter is, in fact, more radical than Moore's original preface, which Harry White suggests Moore repressed because it "would not sit well with the apparently innocent solicitations of a drawing-room *ballade*" (*Keeper's Recital*, 46). Published as an appendix to Moore's satire *Intolerance* (1808), the repressed preface suggests that the poet looking to Irish history for subject matter will find a distinct lack of either heroes or national pride. Instead, he must look to the theme of sorrow, which, he suggests, is "best suited to our Music" (*Works*, 3:57). Moore moves on to describe how this music can be employed in a political act, giving the example of the repression of the Antiochians under the reign of Theodosius, which he directly relates to the situation of the Catholic Irish by describing it as the first "example of a disqualifying penal code enacted by Christians against Christians" (*Works*, 3:58). When their entreaties are rejected, their bishop resorts to teaching the "songs of sorrow which he had heard from the lips of his unfortunate countrymen to the minstrels who performed for the Emperor at table" (*Works*, 3:59). Theodosius relents. Much as Moore suggests the active powers of music to effect political change, what he emphasizes in the anecdote is the Antiochians' desire for forgiveness for the "crimes into which their impatience had hurried them" (*Works*, 3:58). Moore ends his comments by relating the anecdote directly to the Irish situation: "Surely, if music ever spoke the misfortunes of a people, or could ever conciliate forgiveness for their errors, the music of Ireland ought to possess these powers" (*Works*, 3:59). The emphasis is on forgiving crimes, not promoting resistance.

42. Moore, *Works*, 3:225.

43. Ibid., 3:260.

44. Ibid., 3:301.

45. Ibid., 3:257.

46. Ibid., 3:258.
47. Ibid.
48. Ibid., 3:252.
49. Ibid.
50. Deane says that the past in the *Melodies* was "so deeply buried that it was not recoverable except as sentiment" (Deane, *Celtic Revivals*, 14). But for Leerssen this is exactly the political importance of the *Melodies*. Leerssen notes that "the fact that some *Melodies* are sentimental and others are nationalistic has seduced later critics, who viewed them as a whole, into thinking that they were 'sentimentally nationalistic'" (*Remembrance and Imagination*, 248 n. 32). Leerssen concludes that "the true political importance of the *Melodies* lies in their cultivation of remembering" (81).
51. Moore, *Works*, 3:244.
52. Ibid., 3:264.
53. Loftus, *Mirrors*, 60.
54. Moore, *Works*, 3:222–23.
55. Ibid., 3:260.
56. The relationship between the two nations is also expressed in class terms here: it is the *Lord* of the Valley, who has "crost over the moor" and has shamed and disregarded Ireland.
57. Moore, *Works*, 3:250.
58. See Murray Pittock, *Poetry and Jacobite Politics in Eighteenth-Century Britain and Ireland* (Cambridge: Cambridge University Press, 1994), 188 ff.
59. Petrie, *Ancient Music of Ireland*, 37.
60. McClintock, *Imperial Leather*, 5.
61. Moore, *Works*, 3:290.
62. Ibid., 3:248.
63. Ibid.
64. Ibid., 4:18.
65. Ibid., 3:224.
66. Ibid., 3:234.
67. Ibid.
68. Ibid., 3:264.
69. Ibid.
70. Ibid., 3:365–66.
71. Ibid., 3:265 n.
72. Ibid., 3:264 n.
73. Deane comments on the impact of the different representations of the *Melodies*: "In Moore's case, we constantly find ourselves reading the *Melodies* without the music; the music is supplied by memory. So he . . . appears in two forms—with or without the music—and the arguments are conducted on the lines of deformation: the words deform the music, the musical notation is inappropriate to the native forms. . . . [T]he whole territory of Irish music, and by extension of Irish authenticity, is betrayed into print; and yet it is only through such betrayal that it can be preserved at all, for it is only through the medium of print that an audience can be found and established" (*Strange Country*, 66–67). Augener and Company produced a one-volume edition, *A People's Edition of Moore's Irish Melodies* (London, 1859). For the

publication of Moore's melodies in America, see Charles Hamm, *Yesterdays: Popular Song in America* (New York: Norton, 1979), 46ff.

74. Moore, *Works*, 3:219.

75. Ibid.

76. Ibid., 3:220.

77. Clifford Siskin, *The Work of Writing: Literature and Social Change in Britain, 1700–1830* (Baltimore: Johns Hopkins University Press, 1998), 12.

78. Thomas Moore, *Moore's Irish Melodies* (London: Longman, Brown, Green, and Longmans, 1846), iv.

79. Cullen argues that Maclise's paintings make Ireland "acceptable and unproblematic" (*Visual Politics*, 47). Jeanne Sheehy reads Maclise as asserting Gaelic culture, *The Rediscovery of Ireland's Past: The Celtic Revival, 1830–1930* (London: Thames and Hudson, 1980), 45–46.

80. Interestingly, contemporary critics echo this feminization of Moore. White suggests that Moore's favourite theme was "art impoverished, even emasculated, by Irish history" (White, *Keeper's Recital*, 49). Eagleton writes of his work that "[s]adness evokes the reader's pity, but since part of Moore's pathos is a sense of impotence, it also provides a certain relief" (*Crazy John*, 143).

81. *Monthly Review*, September 1806, 61.

82. Owenson, *Memoirs*, 1:183.

83. Francis Jeffrey, *Edinburgh Review*, July 1806, 456.

84. Ibid., 458.

85. Ibid., 459–60.

86. Ibid., 459.

87. Ibid.

88. *Quarterly Review*, June 1812, 378.

89. Ibid., 377.

90. Ibid.

91. Ibid.

92. George Petrie also suggested such an association, at least with regard to the music of the *Melodies*, when he commented in an untitled review published in the August 1816 issue of the *Dublin Examiner* that the symphonic additions to the *Melodies* "are too much in the common style of the second-rate composers of the day, whose works obtain a popularity by being adapted to the taste, as well as the fingers of the young ladies to whom more finished productions would be unintelligible" (250).

93. *Quarterly Review*, October 1822, 143.

94. Ibid., 142–43.

95. *New Monthly Magazine*, January 1, 1820, 4.

96. *Quarterly Review*, October 1822, 139–40.

97. *Monthly Repository*, September 1827, 649.

98. *National Review*, July 1856, 11.

99. Ibid., 41.

100. Ibid. In *Mansex Fine: Religion, Manliness and Imperialism in Nineteenth-Century British Culture* (Manchester: Manchester University Press, 1998), David Alderson discusses Robert Knox's similar emphasis on Celtic physical inferiority to the Saxon in his *The Races of Men: A Fragment* (1850), 115.

101. *National Review*, July 1856, 41.

102. Ibid., 45.

103. Ibid., 42.

104. Corbett, *Allegories of Union*, 16.

105. William Hazlitt, "Mr. T. Moore.—Mr. Leigh Hunt," in *The Spirit of the Age, or Contemporary Portraits*, ed. W. Carew Hazlitt (New York: George Bell and Sons, 1906), 326.

106. Ibid.

107. Quoted in Charles Gavan Duffy, "Thomas Moore," in Deane, *Field Day Anthology*, 1:1251.

CHAPTER 7.   IN MOORE'S WAKE: IRISH MUSIC IN IRELAND
AFTER THE *IRISH MELODIES*

1. *The Citizen: A Monthly Journal of Politics Literature and the Arts*, December 1, 1839, 88.

2. Ibid.

3. Ibid., 88–89.

4. Ibid., 89.

5. Hardiman, *Irish Minstrelsy*, 1:xxxvi–xxxvii.

6. Thomas Percy and Joseph Ritson's dispute over the term is perhaps the most famous example of this controversy. See Dianne Dugaw, ed., *The Anglo-American Ballad: A Folklore Casebook* (New York: Garland, 1995).

7. Hardiman, *Irish Minstrelsy*, 1:i.

8. Ibid., 1:xxxviii.

9. Ibid., 1:lxxix.

10. Ibid.

11. For a discussion of the uses of translation "as an unrefractive medium" in both the nationalist and unionist causes, see Lloyd, *Nationalism and Minor Literature*, 94.

12. Hardiman, *Irish Minstrelsy*, 1:lxxvii.

13. Ibid.

14. Ibid.

15. He notes: "It is considered scarcely necessary here to state, what every reader is already aware of, that Mr. Moore's words to our 'Irish Melodies,' form a splendid exception to the foregoing *general* censure" (lxxvii).

16. Lloyd, *Nationalism and Minor Literature*, 84. Lloyd also observes the tensions that exist between the "tenor of Hardiman's commentaries and the 'refined,' Englished style of the versifications" (89).

17. Hardiman, *Irish Minstrelsy*, 2:281.

18. Ibid., 2:285.

19. Ibid., 2:279.

20. Ibid., 1:xxi.

21. Ibid., 1:xxii–xxiii.

22. Ibid., 2:172.

23. Ibid., 2:175.

24. Ibid., 1:lxxviii.

25. Ibid.

26. Ibid.

27. Ibid., 1:lxxviii–lxxix.

28. Ibid., lxxx.

29. Ibid.

30. Ibid., 1:xxi.

31. Ibid., 1:lxxx.

32. Ibid.

33. Ibid., 1:xli–xlii.

34. Ibid., 1:lix. He also politicizes English literature: "The admirers of [Spenser] may be gratified by a few particulars concerning him and his family (extracted from original documents) which may serve to correct some errors of his biographers, or supply information which they do not appear to have possessed" (1:319). He notes, "Here on the banks of the Awbeg, the poet's 'gentle Mulla,' was written the Faery Queen. But Spenser was not so devoted to the muses, as to neglect his newly acquired possessions; on the contrary he stands charged with having unjustly attempted to add to them" (1:320). This is followed by an account of Spenser's attempt to encroach on the MacCarthys' and others' estates.

35. Ibid., 1:109–10.

36. Ibid., 1:111.

37. Ibid., 1:351–52.

38. Brooke, *Reliques of Irish Poetry*, 205.

39. Hardiman, *Irish Minstrelsy*, 1:358.

40. Ibid.

41. Brooke, *Reliques of Irish Poetry*, 206.

42. Hardiman, *Irish Minstrelsy*, 1:358.

43. Ibid., 1:351.

44. Ibid.

45. Ibid., 2:143.

46. Ibid.

47. See, for example, ibid., 1:120.

48. Ibid., 1:359.

49. Ibid.

50. One of Hardiman's translators was the poet William Hamilton Drummond. Drummond published his own collection, *Ancient Irish Minstrelsy*, in 1852.

51. Hardiman, *Irish Minstrelsy*, 1:106.

52. Ibid., 1:109.

53. Ibid., 1:110.

54. Ibid., 2:149. Hardiman emphasizes the political effectiveness of song by supplying an example to which the English reader can relate: "Lord Wharton boasted, that he rhymed King James out of Ireland by the old Williamite ballad Lillibulero: and Bishop Percy noticing that song in his Reliques of ancient English poetry . . . quotes his brother prelate, Bishop King, to shew that it 'contributed not a little to the great revolution of 1688!'" (2: 148).

55. Ibid., 2:7.

56. Ibid.

57. Ibid.

58. Ibid. Hardiman indicates that the songs are now sung "more for the sake of the charming airs with which they are associated, than for any political sentiments which they may contain" (2:8).

59. For examples, see Curtis, *Apes and Angels*.

60. Lynam, *Irish Character*, 27.

61. Ferguson's review appeared in four parts in April, August, October, and November.

62. Hardiman, *Irish Minstrelsy*, 2:3–4.

63. Ibid., 2:5.

64. Ibid., 2:160.

65. Ibid., 2:168–69.

66. Lloyd examines the inherent contradictions in Davis's and the Young Irelanders' nationalism: "[T]he nationalism of a colonized people requires that its history be seen as a series of unnatural ruptures and discontinuities imposed by an alien power while its reconstruction must necessarily pass by way of deliberate artifice. Almost by definition, this anti-colonial nationalism lacks the basis for its representative claims and is forced to invent them" (*Anomalous States*, 89).

67. Thomas Davis, *Selections from His Prose and Poetry* (London: Gresham, 1914), 367–68.

68. Ibid., 160–61.

69. Ibid., 162.

70. Ibid.

71. Ibid., 269.

72. Ibid.

73. Ibid., 160.

74. Ibid.

75. Ibid., 163.

76. Ibid., 164–65.

77. Ibid., 165.

78. Ibid.

79. Ibid.

80. Ibid., 161.

81. Ibid., 271.

82. Ibid., 264.

83. Lloyd considers Davis's concern to edit the mass of street ballads and to create new ballads as a struggle to bring the "hybrid quality of popular forms" into conformity with "the monologic desire of cultural nationalism, a desire which centres on the lack of an Irish epic" (Lloyd, *Anomalous States*, 89).

84. Davis, *Prose and Poetry*, 271.

85. Ibid., 240.

86. Ibid.

87. Ibid., 240–41.

88. Ibid., 241.

89. Ibid.

90. Ibid.

91. Ibid.

92. Ibid.

93. Ibid.

94. Ibid.

95. Ibid., 162.

96. For just a sampling of the variety of work on the Famine, see Christine Kinealy, *This Great Calamity: The Irish Famine, 1845–52* (Dublin: Gill and Macmillan, 1994); Joel Mokyr, *Why Ireland Starved: A Quantitative and Analytical History of the Irish Economy, 1800–1850* (Boston: Allen and Unwin, 1983); and the classic study by Cecil Woodham Smith, *The Great Hunger* (New York: Harper and Row, 1962).

97. Leerssen calls Petrie "a cardinal figure in the re-emergence of Irish anti-quarianism" (*Remembrance and Imagination*, 89). In the 1830s, he was joint editor with John O'Donovan of the *Dublin Penny Journal*, which was designed to disseminate knowledge of Irish antiquities. He was put in charge of the topographical section of the Ordnance survey project from 1838 to 1841.

98. Petrie, *The Ancient Music of Ireland*, xii.

99. Ibid.

100. Ibid.

101. Ibid., xiii.

102. Bunting, *Ancient Music of Ireland* [1840], 2.

103. Petrie, *Ancient Music of Ireland*, xvi.

104. Ibid., xvi–xvii.

105. Petrie disagrees with Bunting about the presence of the submediant in-dicating an authentically Irish tune. Petrie comments: "I cannot concur with Mr. Bunting that it is an essential, or even the most characteristic feature of a true Irish melody" (*Ancient Music of Ireland*, 48).

106. Bunting, *Ancient Music of Ireland* [1809], 1.

107. George Petrie, untitled review essay on Thomas Moore's *Irish Melodies*, *Dublin Examiner*, August 1816, 243.

108. Ibid., 248.

109. Petrie, *Ancient Music of Ireland*, xvi.

110. Ibid.

111. Ibid.

112. Ibid., xviii. Petrie notes he himself does not have a "perfect" collection, as he, too, has been forced to obtain songs "sometimes from pipers, fiddlers, and such other corrupting and uncertain mediums; sometimes from old MS., or printed music books; and often, at second-hand, from voluntary contributors, who had themselves acquired them in a similar manner. And though the airs thus acquired have but rarely borne the stamp of unsullied purity, they have often retained such an approach to beauty as seemed to entitle them to regard, and as would not permit me, willingly, to reject them as worthless" (xvii–xviii).

113. Bunting, *Ancient Music of Ireland* (1840), 1.

114. Petrie, *Ancient Music of Ireland*, xv.

115. Ibid. Petrie suggests that this kind of inaccuracy has been responsible for a number of mistakes in the work of Moore, for example, as Petrie claims that he listed the same tune as two different airs in several cases.

116. Ibid., xviii.

117. Ibid.

118. Petrie notes that when he cannot decide on the more accurate tune, he preserves several variations (*Ancient Music of Ireland*, xviii).

119. Ibid., 49.

120. Quoted in Sheehy, *Rediscovery of Ireland's Past*, 55. Pittock comments that this quotation looks "back to the *aisling* as well as to the sacrificial nationalism of twentieth-century Ireland." Murray Pittock, *Celtic Identity and the British Image* (Manchester: Manchester University Press, 1999), 64.

121. Petrie, *Ancient Music of Ireland*, 6.

122. Ibid., 7.

123. Ibid., 40.

124. Ibid., 54.

125. Ibid., v.

126. Ibid., vi.

127. Ibid., xiv.

128. Ibid.

129. Ibid.

130. Ibid., 61.

131. Ibid.

132. Ibid., 54.

133. Ibid., 36.

134. Ibid., 56.

135. Ibid., xxv.

136. Ibid., 65.

137. The introductory note in Petrie's *Ancient Music of Ireland* regarding the Society for the Preservation and Publication of the Melodies of Ireland states that "the volumes eventually completed by this Society will contain a complete, satisfactory, and popular explanation of the structure, character, and peculiarities of Irish National Music, an accurate account of its history as far as known (and it reaches back for many centuries), and a Collection which in extent, rarity, and beauty, will surpass anything of the kind ever attempted. The genius and expression of our Music will thus be fixed, and its noblest stores preserved for the admiration of future ages, and the perpetual pride of the Irish race" (vi). But his collection, although designed for "the perpetual pride of the Irish race," was not "published generally"; rather it was "distributed to *the members of the Society only*" (vi). Paradoxically, access to and participation in Petrie's Irish nation depends upon the "payment of One Pound, annual subscription" (vi).

138. Ibid., xii.

139. Ibid.

140. Ibid., x.

141. Ibid., xii.

142. Eagleton comments on some of these demographic and economic changes (*Heathcliff*, 274).

143. Petrie, *Ancient Music of Ireland*, xx.

144. Ibid., xi.

145. Ibid., xx.

CHAPTER 8.   IRISH MUSIC, BRITISH CULTURE, AND
THE TRANSATLANTIC EXPERIENCE

1. Fintan O'Toole, "The Ex-Isle of Erin: Emigration and Irish Culture," in *Location and Dislocation in Contemporary Irish Society: Emigration and Irish Identities*, ed. Jim MacLaughlin (Cork: Cork University Press, 1997), 161.

2. Ibid.

3. Ibid.

4. Ibid.

5. For historical approaches, see also John Archer Jackson, *The Irish in Britain* (London: Routledge and Kegan Paul, 1963); Lynn Hollen Lees, *Exiles of Erin: Irish Migrants in Victorian London* (Ithaca, NY: Cornell University Press, 1979); and Roger Swift and Sheridan Gilley, *The Irish in Britain, 1815–1939* (Savage, MD: Barnes and Noble, 1989). Focusing on the writing of Elizabeth Gaskell, Thomas Carlyle, Friedrich Engels, and James Kay, Mary Jean Corbett points out how Irish immigrants to mid-nineteenth-century England were figured as "the primitive, the diseased, or the essentially inferior" (*Allegories of Union*, 83). Corbett argues, however, that "English colonial discourse [regarding Ireland] is by no means . . . monotonously monolithic and insensitive to historical change" (15).

6. Thomas Carlyle, *Reminiscences of My Irish Journey in 1849* (London: S. Low, Marston, Searle and Rivington, 1882), 137.

7. Ibid., 178–79.

8. Ibid., 258–59.

9. See Nassau Senior, *On National Property* (London: B. Fellowes, 1835).

10. Nassau Senior, *Journals, Conversations and Essays Relating to Ireland*, 2 vols. (London: Longmans, Green, 1868), 1:31.

11. Ibid., 1:208.

12. Carlyle, *Reminiscences*, 206.

13. Senior, *Journals*, 1:198.

14. Ibid., 1:201.

15. Ibid., 1:264.

16. Carlyle, *Reminiscences*, 39.

17. Senior, *Journals*, 1:18.

18. Carlyle, *Reminiscences*, 130.

19. Ibid., 167.

20. William Bayle Bernard, *The Life of Samuel Lover, R.H.A., Artistic, Literary and Musical, with Selections from his Unpublished Papers and Correspondence* (London: H. S. King, 1874), 65.

21. Samuel Lover also published *Lover's Irish Evenings* (London, 1844).

22. *Quarterly Review*, October 1822, 140.

23. Samuel Lover, *Songs and Ballads* (London: Houlston and Wright, 1858), vi. This collection was originally published in 1839 by Chapman and Hall.

24. Ibid.

25. Ibid., vii.

26. Ibid., ix–x.

27. Bernard, *Life of Samuel Lover*, 91.

28. Lover, *Songs and Ballads*, 3; l.15.

29. Ibid.

30. Bernard, *Life of Samuel Lover*, 91–92.

31. Ibid., 92.

32. Ibid., 73.

33. Ibid., 14.

34. Ibid., 107. "Rory O'More" is the first poem in Lover's *Songs and Ballads*. The song's popularity led Lover to attempt his first novel, based on the narrative. *Rory O'More* was published in 1837 and was later dramatized by Lover.

35. Bernard, *Life of Samuel Lover*, 108.

36. Samuel Lover, *Mr. Lover's Irish Evenings* (London: W. S. Johnson, 1844), 4.

37. Quoted in *Dublin Monthly Magazine*, February, 1843, 11 and 10 respectively.

38. Frederick W. Horncastle, *The Music of Ireland as Performed in Mr. Horncastle's Irish Entertainments* (London, 1844), 59–61.

39. Ibid., 67.

40. Horncastle also published *Music of Ireland* in London the following year.

41. Edward Said, *Culture and Imperialism* (New York: Knopf, 1993), 108.

42. Jeffrey Auerbach, *The Great Exhibition of 1851: A Nation on Display* (New Haven, CT: Yale University Press, 1999), 85. Auerbach notes that "[t]he Great Exhibition revealed markedly different levels of integration between Scotland, Wales, Ireland, and England. Not the least of these differences were varying levels of industrialization: The proportion of employed males engaged in non-agricultural occupations as of 1851 was between 50 and 60 percent in England, Scotland, and Wales, but less than one-third in Ireland" (85–86).

43. John Tallis, *Tallis's History and Description of the Crystal Palace, and the Exhibition of the World's Industry in 1851*, 3 vols. (London: John Tallis, 1852), 1:73. Other commodities suggesting the connection between Ireland and music were also popular at the time. Sheehy observes that Waterhouse and Company, Dublin jewelers, commercialized the Tara Brooch and "also produced brooches of a different kind, adapted from the shape of the ancient Irish harp, notably the one known as Brian Boru's harp in Trinity College, Dublin" (Sheehy, *Rediscovery of Ireland's Past*, 87).

44. Tallis, *Tallis's History*, 1:73–74.

45. Ibid., 1:70.

46. *Official Descriptive and Illustrated Catalogue of the Great Exhibition 1851*, 3 vols. (London: Spicer Brothers, 1851), 1:738.

47. Sheehy suggests the involvement of the bog oak carving industry in this interconnection. Pieces of bog oak furniture, replete with iconographic images of Ireland like harps and wolfhounds, were bought by Irish citizens (Daniel O'Connell

even purchased several pieces). At the same time, souvenirs of bog oak were very popular in England, beginning with the presentation of a walking stick of bog oak to George IV upon his visit to Dublin in 1821 (Sheehy, *Rediscovery of the Irish Past*, 84). Sheehy indicates that bog oak was so much in demand that it was "even faked" in England (85).

48. In the preface to the second edition of his *Dissertations on the History of Ireland*, Charles O'Conor comments on the "OLLAMH FODHLA, who reigned long, and who, to the authority of a great monarch, joined the influence of a great philosopher, in forming the minds of the national youth. It was he, who planned, regulated, and endowed the college of the learned in Treamor; laid down a new system of education; and made this model of the several provincial schools, for cultivating the arts intellectual and military" (O'Conor, *Dissertations*, vi).

49. Sheehy, *Rediscovery of the Irish Past*, 31.

50. John O'Beirne Ranelagh, *A Short History of Ireland* (1983; reprint, Cambridge: Cambridge University Press, 1994), 13.

51. William King, "Of the Bogs and Loughs of Ireland," in Deane, *Field Day Anthology*, 1:969; 1:967.

52. Trumpener, *Bardic Nationalism*, 42.

53. Tallis, *Tallis's History*, 1:74.

54. *North British Review* 20 (1853): 341–60.

55. "National Music and Musicians," *Citizen*, January 1840, 192.

56. Ibid., 196.

57. *North British Review* 20 (1853): 186.

58. Joel Sachs, "London: The Professionalization of Music," in *The Early Romantic Era: Between Revolutions, 1789 and 1848*, ed. Alexander Ringer (Englewood Cliffs, NJ: Prentice Hall, 1991), 218.

59. W. T. Parke, *Musical Memoirs; Comprising an Account of the General State of Music in England from the First Commemoration of Handel in 1784, to the Year 1830*, 2 vols. (London: Henry Colburn and Richard Bentley, 1830).

60. William Chappell, *Collection of National English Airs, Consisting of Ancient Song, Ballad and Dance Tunes*, 2 vols. (London, 1838–40), and *Popular Music of the Olden Time; A Collection of Ancient Songs, Ballads and Dance Tunes*, 2 vols. (London, 1855–59).

61. Elizabeth Rigby, Lady Eastlake, *Music and the Art of Dress* (London: John Murray, 1852), 5. Rigby's main claim to fame is her review of *Vanity Fair* and *Jane Eyre* published in the *Quarterly Review* of December 1848.

62. Ibid., 32.

63. McClintock, *Imperial Leather*, 357.

64. Rigby, *Origin of Music*, 32.

65. Ibid., 33.

66. Ibid., 41.

67. Ibid., 41–42.

68. Ibid., 16.

69. Ibid., 17.

70. Ibid., 17–18.

71. Rigby's commentary can be seen in the context of William Weber's observations regarding the "modernization" of musical life in London between 1830 and 1848: "By 1848 performing roles had taken on a high degree of rationalization: public concerts were now the undisputed province of professionals" (Weber, *Music and the Middle Class*, 115). According to Weber, "the economic gain of the professional" now dominated public concerts, rather than "the personal self-improvement of the amateur" (115).

72. Rigby, *Origin of Music*, 17–18.

73. Bronwen Walters discusses the gendered aspect of perceptions of the Irish in the nineteenth century. While "[m]asculine images were of uncontrolled subhumans incapable of self-government," she suggests, "[f]eminine images were of weakness requiring protection." Bronwen Walters, "Gendered Irishness in Britain: Changing Constructions," in Graham and Kirkland, *Ireland and Cultural Theory*, 80.

74. *Quarterly Review*, March 1869, 348.

75. Ibid., 349.

76. Ibid.

77. Ibid., 348.

78. Ibid., 349.

79. *North British Review* 20 (1853): 188.

80. Ibid.

81. Ibid.

82. Ibid., 188.

83. Ibid.

84. Ibid.

85. Ibid.

86. Ibid., 190.

87. Ibid.

88. Matthew Arnold, *The Complete Prose Works of Matthew Arnold*, 10 vols., ed. R. H. Super (Ann Arbor: University of Michigan Press, 1962), 3:347.

89. Ibid. See also Pittock, *Celtic Identity* (chap. 2), for the evolution of the association of Celtic identity with emotion.

90. Arnold, *Complete Prose Works*, 3:347.

91. Ibid., 3:344.

92. Ibid., 3:347.

93. *North British Review* 20 (1853): 188.

94. Ibid.

95. Ibid.

96. Ibid.

97. Dale T. Knobel, *Paddy and the Republic: Ethnicity and Nationality in Antebellum America* (Middletown, CT: Wesleyan University Press, 1986), 13. In *Ireland after History*, Lloyd discusses Ireland's systematic underdevelopment and the phenomenon of emigration: "Unlike most other colonial and postcolonial locations, emigration has been for Ireland a *programmatic* instrument of colonial rule and policing, and remained the enabling condition of postcolonial economic development for both de

Valera's isolationist Free State and the later, modernizing states north and south of the border" (11). For an interesting account of a "world-systems theory" perspective on Irish emigration, see MacLaughlin, *Location and Dislocation.*

98. Mick Moloney, *Irish Music on the American Stage* (Cork: Irish Traditional Music Society, 1993), 11.

99. Knobel, *Paddy and the Republic,* 12.

100. Kerby Miller notes that the connection between Irishness and nostalgia is derived from the notion of exile, which he traces to Irish Catholicism and loss of the Gaelic culture; see *Emigrants and Exiles: Ireland and the Irish Exodus to North America* (New York: Oxford University Press, 1985). But for criticism of Miller, see Donald Harman Akenson, "The Historiography of the Irish in the United States," in *The Irish in the New Communities,* vol. 2, *The Irish World Wide: History, Heritage, Identity,* ed. Patrick O'Sullivan (Leicester: Leicester University Press, 1992), 99–127.

101. Moloney, *Irish Music,* 32.

102. William H. A. Williams, *'Twas Only an Irishman's Dream: The Image of Ireland and the Irish in American Popular Song Lyrics, 1800–1920* (Urbana: University of Illinois Press, 1996), 4. Williams's book was useful in directing me to the Starr Collection of the Lilly Library at Indiana University at Bloomington, which contains roughly 850 examples of "Irish" songs. Williams suggests that this represents about one-third to one-half of what was commercially available at the time (11).

103. Ibid., 4.

104. Moloney, *Irish Music,* 35.

105. Hamm, *Yesterdays,* 54.

106. Ibid., 57–58.

107. Paul Kennedy and Victor Roudometof, *Communities across Borders: New Immigrant and Transnational Cultures* (New York: Routledge, 2002), 24.

108. Ibid.

109. Hon. Mrs. Price Blackwood (words) and William Dempster (music), *The Lament of the Irish Emigrant. A Ballad* (Boston: George. P. Reed, 1843), 3. This song is included in Deane, *Field Day Anthology,* 2:103. Mrs. Price Blackwood (Lady Dufferin) was born in London, the granddaughter of Richard Brinsley Sheridan. The title of the 1843 song sheet advertises that the song was written "by a Lady, The Daughter of an Eminent Exile."

110. *Lament of the Irish Exile, A Ballad. Poetry by a Lady, The Daughter of an Eminent Exile* (New York: William Vanderbeck., n.d.).

111. George Cooper (words) and C. M. Pyke (music), *Dear Little Colleen* (New York: Spear and Dehnhoff, 1877), 3–4.

112. A number of songs from this period, like "Kathleen O'Moore" and "The Lament of the Irish Lover," are based on men mourning women who have died, although they are not songs of exile.

113. Cooper and Pyke, *Dear Little Colleen,* 4.

114. Madame Anna Ablamowicz (words), and E. W. Mason (music), *Mavourneen Machree. Ballad* (Louisville, KY: Tripp and Cragg, 1852), 4–5.

115. Blackwood, *Lament,* 9.

116. John Murphy (words) and T. Bissell (music), *The Answer to the Lament of the Irish Emigrant* (Boston: Keith's Music Publishing House, 1844), 5.

117. Moloney, *Irish Music*, 17. Moloney points out that Irish-Americans were prominent in popularizing the "black-face" tradition of minstrelsy.

118. Elizabeth Butler Cullingford, "The Stage Englishman of the Irish Drama: Boucicault and the Politics of Empathy," in *Ireland's Others*, 13–36, 17.

119. While it shared certain features with the kinds of "Irish comedies" in which Williams and his wife acted, the *Colleen Bawn* also differed from them in a number of ways. Fawkes remarks that the appearance of Myles, a more well-rounded character than the typical Stage Irishman, "marked a major step forward towards a truly indigenous Irish drama." Richard Fawkes, *Dion Boucicault: A Biography* (London: Quartet Books, 1979), 117.

120. Cullingford, "Stage Englishman," 18.

121. Ibid.

122. Fawkes, *Dion Boucicault*, 114–15.

123. Ibid., 117.

124. Ibid., 121.

125. Boucicault was not happy with opera, however. In his opinion, "All the sentiment, all the tenderness, all the simple poetry was swept away." Ibid., 122.

126. Fawkes points out the innovations in theater practices and payment that Boucicault initiated, noting that Boucicault and his wife made over 23,000 pounds from the *Colleen Bawn*. Ibid., 137.

127. The date in which Boucicault set his play also appears designed to put an English audience on alert. The actual murder of Ellen Hanley took place in 1819. Although there is little indication of the historical era in the events of the play, apart from the presence of Redcoat soldiers who go with Corrigan to arrest Hardress, the notes on the "Costumes" indicate that it is set in the period of "1798," the time of the Irish Rebellion.

128. Ibid., 106.

129. Bunting, *General Collection of the Ancient Irish Music* [1796], 54.

130. *The Pretty Girl Milking Her Cow as Sung by Mrs. Agnes Robertson and Mrs. John Wood in Boucicault's Drama of the "Colleen Bawn"* (New York: John J. Daly, 1860).

131. Cullingford notes that Boucicault's plots were contrived so that "the internal logic of his drama . . . constructed his audiences as Irish sympathizers" ("Stage Englishman," 19).

132. Moloney, *Irish Music*, 12.

133. Dion Boucicault, *The Dolmen Boucicault*, ed. Davis Krause (Dublin: Dolmen Press, 1964), 65.

134. Ibid., 76.

135. Ibid., 76.

136. Several other plays such as *The Rapparees* and *Robert Emmet* also deal with Irish matters, but the three considered here were by far the most popular.

137. Boucicault, *Dolmen Boucicault*, 133.

138. Lover also quotes the ballad in *Rory O'More: A National Romance* (New York: Atheneum Society, 1901), 282.

139. Cullingford, "Stage Englishman," 21.

140. Boucicault, *Dolmen Boucicault*, 134.

141. Ibid.

142. Ibid.

143. Gary A. Richardson, "The Greening of America: The Cultural Business of Dion Boucicault's *The Shaughraun*," *American Drama* 3, no. 2 (1996): 12.

144. Boucicault, *Dolmen Boucicault*, 134.

145. Cullingford, "Stage Englishman," 24.

146. It also became the inspiration for a song called "The Wearing of the Grey," which was concerned to boost Confederate morale after the Civil War:

> The fearful struggle's ended now, And peace smiles on our land,
> And though we've yielded, we have proved ourselves a faithful band;
> We fought them long, We fought them well, We fought them night and day,
> And bravely struggled for our rights, While wearing of the Grey!

The Wearing of the Grey (New Orleans: A. E. Blackmar, 1865). Retrieved from the Web site of the Lester S. Levy Collection of Sheet Music, Milton S. Eisenhower Library of Johns Hopkins University: http://levysheetmusic.mse.jhu.edu/otcgi/llscgi6o.

147. *Wearing of the Green as Sung by J. E. McDonough, in E. H. House & Dion Boucicoult's [sic] Celebrated Irish Drama of Arrah Na Pogue* (Philadelphia: Charles W. A. Trumpler, 1865). Retrieved from the Web site of the University of Pennsylvania's Keffer Collection of Sheet Music, ca. 1790–1895: www.library.upenn.edu/collections/rbm/keffer/b3on79.html.

148. Boucicault, *Dolmen Boucicault*, 202–3.

149. Ibid., 119.

150. Mari Kathleen Fiedler, "Chauncey Olcott: Irish-American Mother-love, Romance, and Nationalism," *Eire-Ireland* 22, no. 2 (1987): 5.

151. William H. A. Williams, "From Lost Land to Emerald Isle: Ireland and the Irish in American Sheet Music, 1800–1920," *Eire-Ireland* 26, no. 1 (1991): 41.

AFTERWORD

1. Yuval-Davis, *Gender and Nation*, 21.

2. See Scott Reiss, "Tradition and Imaginary," in *Celtic Modern: Music at the Global Fringe*, ed. Martin Stokes and Philip Bohlman (Lanham, MD: Scarecrow Press, 2003), 161; and Fintan Vallely, "The Apollos of Shamrockery," in Stokes and Bohlman, *Celtic Modern*, 209.

3. Sally K. Sommers Smith, "Irish Traditional Music in a Modern World," *New Hibernia Review 5/Iris Éireannach Nua: A Quarterly Record of Irish Studies* 5 (Summer 2001): 116.

4. Martin Stokes and Philip Bohlman, introduction to *Celtic Modern*, 5.

5. Reiss, "Tradition and Imaginary," 158.

6. Ibid, 157.

7. Ibid., 148.

8. Vallely, "Apollos of Shamrockery," 204.

9. Reiss draws a distinction between "'Celtic' music, understood as media-driven and existing within a virtual community, and the community-based traditional musics of Ireland" ("Tradition and Imaginary," 146).

10. Timothy Taylor, "Gaelicer Than Thou," in Stokes and Bohlman, *Celtic Modern*, 280.

11. Natasha Casey points out that "almost 14 percent of white Americans consider themselves of Irish ancestry, and that number jumps to 16 percent if one includes the confounding category of Scotch-Irish." "*Riverdance*: The Importance of Being Irish American," *New Hibernia Review 5/Iris Éireannach Nua: A Quarterly Record of Irish Studies* 6 (Winter 2002): 24.

12. "Irish Music," retrieved March 18, 2004, from "Virtual Irish Community" Web site: www.vic.ie/.

13. "IrishNet," retrieved March 18, 2004, from www.ceolas.org/IrishNet.

14. In "Gaelicer Than Thou," Taylor discusses how Americans "tend to create identities through what they buy" and how "[r]ace and ethnicity have become something that Americans can now consume" (278).

15. Sommers Smith also points out, however, the ways mediation may also "ensure, in the long run, the overall survival of the genre": "[D]istrust of the commercial must be balanced with the realization that commercial recordings are now by far the most significant means by which the music is transmitted" ("Irish Traditional Music," 118).

16. Fintan Vallely expresses concern about the commodification of Irish music in the guise of world music, suggesting that "[u]ltimately, this is an economic struggle; the borrowing of traditional music's language of self-description is not just a battle of words for minds, but for credibility, power, audiences, and performance space" ("Apollos of Shamrockery," 214). Other critics acknowledge the ambivalence of Irish music's popularity, however. Timothy Taylor, for example, concludes that commodification is only part of the story: "[M]usic, especially 'Celtic' or Irish or Scottish or Welsh or Breton or what have you that spans different music industry categories . . . and has many local practitioners, is caught up in a myriad commodifying, noncommodifying, and uncommodifying practices at any one time and in any particular place" ("Gaelicer Than Thou," 282). Martin Stokes and Philip Bohlman sidestep the issue of whether commodification is good or bad as they suggest that "[t]o note the commoditized aspect of Celtic musical identities is . . . to ask questions about how . . . the commodity form and commoditized attitudes toward music making produce such diverse sociomusical realities on the Celtic fringe" (introduction to *Celtic Modern*, 17).

17. Vallely, *Companion*, 73.

18. David Toop, "Surprising Rise of Ethereal Pop," *Times* (London), January 7, 1989, retrieved March 18, 2004, from the Web site "Enya: Magic and Melody": http://enya.org/p_trans4/b003.htm.

19. David Gritten, "Enya and the Cult of the Celt," *Daily Telegraph*, January 4, 1996, retrieved March 18, 2004, from the Web site "Enya: Magic and Melody": http://enya.org/p_trans3/t045.htm4.

20. Dennis Hunt, "Digging up the Irish Roots of Enya's Melodies," *Los Angeles Times*, February 15, 1992, retrieved March 18, 2004, from the Web site "Enya: Magic and Melody": http://enya.org/p_trans3/t047.htm.

21. "The Celts," lyrics retrieved March 18, 2004, from "Enya: The Official Website": http://discography.enya.com/index_01.asp. "The Celts" appeared originally on the album *Enya* (1987), which was re-released as *The Celts* in 1993.

22. "Orinoco Flow" makes a direct connection between Ireland and mythical spaces: "From Bissau to Palau—in the shade of Avalon, / From Fiji to Tiree and the Isles of Ebony." Lyrics retrieved March 18, 2004, from "Enya: The Official Website": http://discography.enya.com/index_01.asp.

23. Frank Hall, "Your Mr. Joyce Is a Fine Man but Have You Seen *Riverdance?*" *New Hibernia Review 5/Iris Éireannach Nua: A Quarterly Record of Irish Studies* 1 (Autumn 1999): 134.

24. Bernard, *Life of Samuel Lover*, 108.

25. Sam Smyth, *Riverdance: The Story* (London: Andre Deutsch, 1996), 15.

26. Ibid., 56.

27. Ibid., 15.

28. McClintock points out that: "the temporal anomaly within nationalism . . . is temporarily resolved by figuring the contradiction in the representation of *time* as a natural division of *gender*. Women are represented as the atavistic and authentic body of national tradition (inert, backward-looking and natural), embodying nationalism's conservative principle of continuity. Men, by contrast, represent the progressive agent of national modernity (forward-thrusting, potent and historic) embodying nationalism's progressive, or revolutionary principle of discontinuity" (*Imperial Leather*, 358–59).

29. There have been a number of different variations on the original performance of *Riverdance: The Show* in different venues and at different times. My remarks are based on the Tyrone/RTE 1995 video, which was filmed live at the Point Theatre, Dublin. In her fascinating piece on Riverdance, Hazel Carby points out that only Flatley is "allowed to break and transcend the traditional conventions of form, moving his arms freely in stark contrast to the chorus of female and subordinate male dancers," but she does not pursue the implications of this gendering process. "What Is This 'Black' in Irish Popular Culture?" *European Journal of Cultural Studies* 4, no. 3 (2001): 333.

30. I should note as well that what is known today as "traditional" Irish dancing here is itself an invention of the twentieth century. Although based on styles dating back to medieval times, "Solo and group step dancing have been refined in the twentieth century into the costumed and choreographed kinds we see at competitions today" (Vallely, *Companion*, 101).

31. When Colin Dunne took over the lead role from Flatley, he dropped the "flamenco-style" arms in preference for arms "loosely held but never rigid." See Jann Parry, "The Irish Dance Phenomenon: Celtic Crossover," *Dance Magazine*, October 1997, 72.

32. See Parry, "Irish Dance Phenomenon," and Casey, "*Riverdance.*"

33. Smyth, *Riverdance*, 87.

34. Ibid., 82.

35. Ibid., 87.

36. Ibid., 90.

37. Kieran Keohane, "Traditionalism and Homelessness in Contemporary Irish Music," in Jim MacLaughlin, *Location and Dislocation*, 274.

38. Ibid., 302.

39. As Murray Pittock suggests in *Celtic Identity and the British Image*, "Simplistic and populist as many contemporary manifestations of the 'Celtic' may be, . . . they are not merely designer flotsam, but the latest descendants of questions deeply lodged in history" (*Celtic Identity*, 7).

40. MacLaughlin, introduction to *Location and Dislocation*, 5.

41. Smyth, *Riverdance*, 10.

42. Ibid., 87.

43. Ibid., 82.

44. Ibid., 167.

45. Said, *Musical Elaborations*, 55.

References

Abell, John. *A Collection of Songs in Several Languages*. London, 1701.

Ablamowicz, Madame Anna (words), and E. W. Mason (music). *Mavourneen Machree. Ballad*. Louisville, KY: Tripp and Cragg, 1852.

Akenson, Donald Harman. "The Historiography of the Irish in the United States." In *The Irish in the New Communities*, vol. 2, *The Irish World Wide: History, Heritage, Identity*, ed. Patrick O'Sullivan, 99–127. Leicester: Leicester University Press, 1992.

Alderson, David. *Mansex Fine: Religion, Manliness and Imperialism in Nineteenth-Century British Culture*. Manchester: Manchester University Press, 1998.

Anderson, Benedict. *Imagined Communities: Reflections on the Origins and Spread of Nationalism*. Rev. ed. London: Verso, 1991.

Aravamudan, Srinivas. *Tropicopolitans: Colonialism and Agency, 1688–1804*. Durham, NC: Duke University Press, 1999.

Arnold, Matthew. *The Complete Prose Works of Matthew Arnold*. 11 vols. Ed. R. H. Super. Ann Arbor: University of Michigan Press, 1962.

Ashcroft, Bill. *Post-colonial Transformations*. New York: Routledge, 2001.

Auerbach, Jeffrey. *The Great Exhibition of 1851: A Nation on Display*. New Haven, CT: Yale University Press, 1999.

Avison, Charles. *An Essay on Musical Expression*. London, 1752.

Barker-Benfield, G. J. *The Culture of Sensibility: Sex and Society in Eighteenth-Century Britain*. Chicago: University of Chicago Press, 1992.

Barry, Kevin. "James Usher and the Irish Enlightenment." *Eighteenth-Century Ireland* 3 (1988): 115–22.

Bartlett, Robert. *Gerald of Wales, 1146–1223*. Oxford: Clarendon Press, 1982.

Beattie, James. *Essays: On Poetry and Music*. London: Routledge, 1996.

Beckett, J. C. "Introduction: Eighteenth-Century Ireland." In *A New History of Ireland*, vol. 4, *Eighteenth-Century Ireland, 1691–1800*, ed. T. W. Moody and W. E. Vaughan, xxxix–lxiv. Oxford: Clarendon Press, 1986.

———. "Literature in English, 1691–1800." In *A New History of Ireland*, vol. 4, *Eighteenth-Century Ireland, 1691–1800*, ed. T. W. Moody and W. E. Vaughan, 424–69. Oxford: Clarendon Press, 1986.

Bermingham, Ann, and John Brewer, eds. *The Consumption of Culture, 1600–1800: Image, Object, Text*. New York: Routledge, 1995.

Bernard, William Bayle. *The Life of Samuel Lover, R.H.A., Artistic, Literary and Musical, with Selections from His Unpublished Papers and Correspondence*. London: H. S. King, 1874.

Bhabha, Homi K. *The Location of Culture*. New York: Routledge, 1993.

————. "Minority Culture and Creative Anxiety." 2000. Retrieved January 20, 2001, from "Re-inventing Britain" Web site: www.britcoun.org/studies/reinventingbritain/bhabha_2.htm.

————, ed. *Nation and Narration.* New York: Routledge, 1990.

Boucicault, Dion. *The Dolmen Boucicault.* Ed. David Krause. Dublin: Dolmen Press, 1964. Bourdieu, Pierre. *The Field of Cultural Production: Essays on Art and Literature.* New York: Columbia University Press, 1993.0

Boyce, D. George, and Alan O'Day, eds. *Modern Irish History: Revisionism and the Revisionist Controversy.* London: Routledge, 1996.

Boydell, Barra. "The Iconography of the Irish Harp as a National Symbol." In *Irish Musical Studies,* vol. 5, *The Maynooth International Musicological Conference, 1995: Selected Proceedings,* ed. Patrick F. Devine and Harry White, 131–45. Blackrock: Irish Academic Press, 1996.

Boydell, Brian. *Four Centuries of Music in Ireland.* London: British Broadcasting Corporation, 1979.

————. "Music before 1700." In *A New History of Ireland,* vol. 4, *Eighteenth-Century Ireland, 1691–1800,* ed. T. W. Moody and W. E. Vaughan, 542–67. Oxford: Clarendon Press, 1986.

————. "Music, 1700–1850." In *A New History of Ireland,* vol. 4, *Eighteenth-Century Ireland 1691–1800,* ed. T. W. Moody and W. E. Vaughan, 568–628. Oxford: Clarendon Press, 1986.

Bradley, Anthony, and Maryann Gialanella Valiulis, eds. *Gender and Sexuality in Modern Ireland.* Amherst: University of Massachusetts Press, 1997.

Brady, Ciaran. *Interpreting Irish History: The Debate on Historical Revisionism.* Blackrock: Irish Academic Press, 1994.

Brewer, John. *The Pleasures of the Imagination: English Culture in the Eighteenth Century.* Chicago: University of Chicago Press, 2000.

Brooke, Charlotte. *Reliques of Irish Poetry.* 1789. Reprint, Gainesville, FL: Scholar's Facsimiles and Reprints, 1970.

Brooke, Henry. *A Collection of the Pieces Formerly Published by Henry Brooke, esq. To which are added Several Plays and Poems, now first printed.* 4 vols. London, 1778.

Brown, John. *A Dissertation on the Rise, Union, and Power, the Progressions, Separations, and Corruptions, of Poetry and Music.* 1763. Reprint, New York: Garland, 1971.

Brown, Malcolm. *The Politics of Irish Literature: From Thomas Davis to W. B. Yeats.* Seattle: University of Washington Press, 1972.

Brown, Terence. "Thomas Moore: A Reputation." In *Ireland's Literature: Selected Essays.* Dublin: Lilliput Press, 1988. 14-28.

Buckley, Ann. "'And his voice swelled like a terrible thunderstorm . . .': Music as Symbolic Sound in Medieval Irish Society." In *Irish Musical Studies,* vol. 3, *Music and Irish Cultural History,* ed. Gerard Gillen and Harry White, 13–76. Blackrock: Irish Academic Press, 1995.

Bunting, Edward. *The Ancient Music of Ireland.* Dublin: Hodges and Smith, 1840.

————. *A General Collection of the Ancient Irish Music.* Dublin, 1796.

————. *A General Collection of the Ancient Music of Ireland.* London: Clementi, 1809.

Burke, Helen. *Riotous Performances: The Struggle for Hegemony in the Irish Theater, 1712–1784.* Notre Dame, IN: Notre Dame University Press, 2003.

Burney, Charles. *A General History of Music, from the earliest Ages to the present Period.* 4 vols. London, 1776–89.

———. Review of *Historical Memoirs of the Irish Bards.* *Monthly Review,* December 1787, 425–39.

Cairns, David, and Shaun Richards. *Writing Ireland: Colonialism, Nationalism, and Culture.* New York: St. Martin's Press, 1988.

Campbell, Mary. *Lady Morgan: The Life and Times of Sydney Owenson.* London: Pandora, 1988.

Campbell, Thomas. *A Philosophical Survey of the South of Ireland, in a series of letters to John Watkinson, M.D.* Dublin: W. Whitestone, 1778.

Carby, Hazel. "What Is This 'Black' in Irish Popular Culture?" *European Journal of Cultural Studies* 4, no. 3 (2001): 325–49.

Carlyle, Thomas. *Reminiscences of My Irish Journey in 1849.* London: S. Low, Marston, Searle and Rivington, 1882.

Carolan, Nicholas. *The Most Celebrated Irish Tunes: The Publishing of Irish Music in the Eighteenth Century.* Cork: Irish Traditional Music Society of University College Cork, 1990.

Carpenter, Andrew. "Changing Views of Irish Musical and Literary Culture in Eighteenth-Century Anglo-Irish Literature." In *Irish Literature and Culture,* ed. Michael Kenneally. Gerrards Cross: Colin Smythe, 1992.

———. *Verse in English from Eighteenth-Century Ireland.* Cork: Cork University Press, 1998.

Carson, Ciaran. *Last Night's Fun: A Book about Music, Food and Time.* London: Pimlico, 1996.

Casey, Natasha. "*Riverdance*: The Importance of Being Irish American." *New Hibernia Review 5/Iris Éireannach Nua: A Quarterly Record of Irish Studies* 6 (Winter 2002): 9–25.

Chanan, Michael. *Musica Practica: The Social Practice of Western Music from Gregorian Chant to Postmodernism.* London: Verso, 1994.

Chappell, William. *Collection of National English Airs, Consisting of Ancient Song, Ballad and Dance Tunes.* 2 vols. London, 1838–40.

———. *Popular Music of the Olden Time; A Collection of Ancient Songs, Ballads and Dance Tunes.* 2 vols. London, 1855–59.

Colley, Linda. *Britons: Forging the Nation, 1707–1837.* New Haven, CT: Yale University Press, 1992.

Cooper, George (words), and C. M. Pyke (music). *Dear Little Colleen.* New York: Spear and Dehnhoff, 1877.

Corbett, Mary Jean. *Allegories of Union in Irish and English Writing, 1790–1870: Politics, History and the Family from Edgeworth to Arnold.* Cambridge: Cambridge University Press, 2000.

Coulter, Carol. *The Hidden Tradition: Feminism, Women and Nationalism in Ireland.* Cork: Cork University Press, 1990.

Craig, Adam. *Scots Tunes.* Edinburgh, 1725.

Croker, Thomas Crofton. *Notes from the Letters of Thomas Moore to His Music Publisher, James Power [. . .] with an Introductory Letter from Thomas Crofton Croker, Esq.* New York: Redfield, 1854.

Cullen, Fintan. *Visual Politics: The Representation of Ireland, 1750–1930*. Cork: Cork University Press, 1997.

Cullingford, Elizabeth Butler. *Ireland's Others: Gender and Ethnicity in Irish Literature and Popular Culture*. Notre Dame, IN: University of Notre Dame Press, 2001.

Curtin, Nancy. "Matilda Tone and Virtuous Republican Femininity." In *The Women of 1798*, ed. Dáire Keogh and Nicholas Furlong, 26–46. Dublin: Four Courts Press, 1998.

———. "'A Nation of Abortive Men': Gendered Citizenship and Early Irish Republicanism." In *Reclaiming Gender: Transgressive Identities in Modern Ireland*, ed. Marilyn Cohen and Nancy J. Curtin, 33–52. New York: St. Martin's Press, 1999.

Curtis, L. Perry. *Apes and Angels: The Irishman in Victorian Caricature*. Washington, DC: Smithsonian Institution Press, 1997.

Dalsimer, Adele, and Vera Kreilkamp. "Re/Dressing Mother Ireland: Feminist Imagery in Art and Literature." In *Re/Dressing Cathleen: Contemporary Works from Irish Women Artists*, ed. Jennifer Grinell and Alston Conley, 37–42. Chestnut Hill, MA: Charles S. and Isabella V. McMullen Museum of Art, Boston College, 1997.

Davis, Thomas. *Selections from His Prose and Poetry*. London: Gresham, 1914.

———. *Spirit of the Nation*. Dublin, 1843.

De Ford, Miriam. *Thomas Moore*. New York: Twayne, 1967.

Deane, Seamus. *Celtic Revivals: Essays in Modern Irish Literature, 1880–1980*. London: Faber, 1985.

———. *Strange Country: Modernity and Nationhood in Irish Writing since 1790*. Oxford: Clarendon Press, 1997.

———, ed. *The Field Day Anthology of Irish Writing*. 3 vols. New York: Norton, 1991.

Dennis, Ian. *Nationalism and Desire in Early Historical Fiction*. Houndmills, Basingstoke: Macmillan, 1997.

Dirlik, Arif. "The Postcolonial Aura: Third World Criticism in the Age of Global Capitalism," *Critical Inquiry* 20 (Winter 1992): 328–56.

Duffy, Charles Gavan. "Thomas Moore." In *The Field Day Anthology of Irish Writing*, ed. Seamus Deane, 1:1250–54. New York: Norton, 1991.

Dugaw, Dianne, ed. *The Anglo-American Ballad: A Folklore Casebook*. New York: Garland, 1995.

Dunkin, William. "The Parson's Revels." In *The Field Day Anthology of Irish Writing*, ed. Seamus Deane, 1:444–47. New York: Norton, 1991.

Dunne, Tom. "Fiction as the 'Best History of Nations': Lady Morgan's Irish Novels." In *The Writer as Witness*, ed. Tom Dunne, 133–59. Cork: Cork University Press, 1987.

———. "Haunted by History: Irish Romantic Writing, 1800–1850." In *Romanticism in National Context*, ed. R. Porter and M. Teich, 68–91. Cambridge: Cambridge University Press, 1988.

Durfey, Thomas. *Pills to Purge Melancholy*. 6 vols. London, 1698–1720.

Eagleton, Terry. *Crazy John and the Bishop*. Cork: Cork University Press, 1998.

———. *Heathcliff and the Great Hunger: Studies in Irish Culture*. New York: Verso, 1995.

Eagleton, Terry, Frederic Jameson, and Edward Said, eds. *Nationalism, Colonialism, and Literature*. Minneapolis: University of Minnesota Press, 1990.

Eger, Elizabeth, Charlotte Grant, Clíona Ó Gallchoir, and Penny Warburton, eds. *Women, Writing and the Public Sphere, 1700–1830*. Cambridge: Cambridge University Press, 2001.

A Favorite Collection of Irish Melodies, The Original and Genuine Compositions of Carolan, The Celebrated Bard. Dublin, n.d.

Fawkes, Richard. *Dion Boucicault: A Biography*. London: Quartet Books, 1979.

Ferris, Ina. *The Achievement of Literary Authority: Gender, History and the Waverley Novels*. Ithaca, NY: Cornell University Press, 1991.

———. *The Romantic National Tale and the Question of Ireland*. Cambridge: Cambridge University Press, 2002.

Fiedler, Mari Kathleen. "Chauncey Olcott: Irish-American Mother-Love, Romance, and Nationalism." *Eire-Ireland* 22, no. 2 (1987): 4–26.

Fielding, Penny. *Writing and Orality: Nationality, Culture, and Nineteenth-Century Scottish Fiction*. Oxford: Oxford University Press, 1996.

Finkelstein, David, and Alistair McCleery. *The Book History Reader*. New York: Routledge, 2002.

Fleischmann, Aloys. *Music in Ireland: A Symposium*. Cork: Cork University Press, 1952.

Flinn, Caryl. *Strains of Utopia: Gender, Nostalgia, and Hollywood Film Music*. Princeton, NJ: Princeton University Press, 1992.

Flood, W. H. Grattan. *A History of Irish Music*. Dublin: Browne and Nolan, 1905.

Fogarty, Anne. "Imperfect Concord: Spectres of History in the Irish Novels of Maria Edgeworth and Lady Morgan." In *Gender Perspectives in Nineteenth-Century Ireland: Public and Private Spheres*, ed. Margaret Kelleher and James H. Murphy, 116–26. Dublin: Irish Academic Press, 1997.

Foley, Timothy P. "Public Sphere and Domestic Circle: Gender and Political Economy in Nineteenth-Century Ireland." In *Gender Perspectives in Nineteenth-Century Ireland: Public and Private Spheres*, ed. Margaret Kelleher and James H. Murphy, 21–35. Dublin: Irish Academic Press, 1997.

Foster, R. F. *Modern Ireland, 1600–1972*. Harmondsworth: Penguin, 1989.

Foster, Sarah. "Buying Irish: Consumer Nationalism in Eighteenth-Century Dublin." *History Today* 47 (June 1997): 44–51.

Foucault, Michel. "What Is an Author?" In *Language, Counter-Memory, Practice*, ed. Donald F. Bouchard, 113–38. Ithaca, NY: Cornell University Press, 1977.

Fox, Charlotte Milligan. *Annals of the Irish Harpers*. London: Smith, Elder, 1911.

Gerson, Carole. "The Presenting Face: Prefaces to English-Language Poetry and Fiction Written by Women in Canada, 1850–1940." In *Prefaces and Literary Manifestoes*, ed. E. D. Blodgett and A. G. Purdy, 56–71. Edmonton: Research Institute for Comparative Literature, 1990.

Gibbons, Luke. "From Ossian to O'Carolan: The Bard as Separatist Symbol." In *From Gaelic to Romantic: Ossianic Translations*, ed. Fionna Stafford and Howard Gaskill, 226–51. Amsterdam: Rodopi, 1995.

———. *Transformations in Irish Culture*. Notre Dame, IN: University of Notre Dame Press, 1996.

Giraldus Cambrensis. *Expugnatio Hibernica: The Conquest of Ireland*. Ed. and trans. A. B. Scott and F. X. Martin. Dublin: Royal Irish Academy, 1978.

————. *The Historical Works of Giraldus Cambrensis. Containing the Topography of Ireland, and the History of the Conquest of Ireland.* Trans. Thomas Forester. London: H. G. Bohn, 1863. Reprint, New York: AMS Press, 1968.

Goldsmith, Samuel. "The History of Carolan, the Last Irish Bard." In *The Field Day Anthology of Irish Writing*, ed. Seamus Deane, 1:667–68. New York: Norton, 1991.

Graham, Colin. ". . . Maybe That's Just Blarney": Irish Culture and the Persistence of Authenticity." In *Ireland and Cultural Theory: The Mechanics of Authenticity*, ed. Colin Graham and Richard Kirkland, 7–28. Houndmills: Macmillan, 1999.

Graham, Colin, and Richard Kirkland, eds. *Ireland and Cultural Theory: The Mechanics of Authenticity.* Houndmills: Macmillan, 1999.

Graham, Colin, and Willy Maley. "Irish Studies and Postcolonial Theory." *Irish Studies Review* 7, no. 2 (1999): 149–52.

Gray, John. "Mary Ann McCracken: Belfast Revolutionary and Pioneer of Feminism." In *The Women of 1798*, ed. Dáire Keogh and Nicholas Furlong, 47–63. Dublin: Four Courts Press, 1998.

Guest, Harriet. *Small Change: Women, Learning, Patriotism, 1750–1810.* Chicago: University of Chicago Press, 2000.

Hall, Frank. "Your Mr. Joyce Is a Fine Man but Have You Seen *Riverdance*?" *New Hibernia Review 5/Iris Éireannach Nua: A Quarterly Record of Irish Studies* 1 (Autumn 1999): 134.

Hall, Stuart. "Cultural Identity and Diaspora." In *Colonial Discourse and Post-colonial Theory: A Reader*, ed. Patrick Williams and Laura Chrisman, 392–403. New York: Harvester Wheatsheaf, 1993.

————. "When Was 'the Post-colonial'? Thinking at the Limit." In *The Post-colonial Question: Common Skies, Divided Horizons*, ed. Iain Chambers and Lidia Curti. New York: Routledge, 1996.

Hamer, Mary. "Putting Ireland on the Map." *Textual Practice* 3, no. 2 (1989): 184–201.

Hamm, Charles. *Yesterdays: Popular Song in America.* New York: Norton, 1979.

Harbison, Janet. "The Legacy of the Belfast Harpers' Festival, 1792." *Ulster Folklife* 35 (1989): 113–28.

Hardiman, James, ed. *Irish Minstrelsy, or Bardic Remains of Ireland.* 2 vols. 1831. Reprint, New York: Barnes and Noble, 1971.

Harris, James. "A Discourse on Music, Painting and Poetry." In *Three Treatises*, 49–103. 1765. Reprint, New York: Garland, 1970.

Harrison, Frank Llewelyn. "Music, Poetry and Polity in the Age of Swift." *Eighteenth-Century Ireland* 1 (1986): 37–63.

Hawkins, John. *A General History of the Science and Practice of Music.* 2 vols. 1776. Reprint, New York: Dover, 1963.

Hazlitt, William. "Mr. T. Moore.—Mr. Leigh Hunt." In *The Spirit of the Age, or Contemporary Portraits*, ed. W. Carew Hazlitt, 317–32. New York: George Bell and Sons, 1906.

Herr, Cheryl. "The Erotics of Irishness." In *Identities*, ed. Kwame Anthony Appiah and Henry Louis Gates, 271–304. Chicago: University of Chicago Press, 1995.

Highley, Christopher. *Shakespeare, Spenser, and the Crisis in Ireland.* Cambridge: Cambridge University Press, 1997.

Hill, Jacqueline. "Popery and Protestantism, Civil and Religious Liberty: The Disputed Lessons of Irish History, 1690–1812." *Past and Present* 118 (February 1988): 96–129.

Hogan, I. M. *Anglo-Irish Music, 1780–1830.* Cork: Cork University Press, 1966.

Horncastle, Frederick. *The Music of Ireland, as Performed in Mr. Horncastle's Irish Entertainments.* London, 1844.

Houston, Cecil J., and William Smyth. *Irish Emigration and Canadian Settlement: Patterns, Links, and Letters.* Toronto: University of Toronto Press, 1990.

The Illustrated Exhibitor, a Tribute to the World's Industrial Jubilee. London, J. Cassell, 1851.

"Irish Music." Retrieved March 18, 2004, from "Virtual Irish Community" Web site: www.vic.ie/.

"IrishNet." Retrieved March 18, 2004, from www.ceolas.org/IrishNet/.

Jackson, John Archer. *The Irish in Britain.* London: Routledge and Kegan Paul, 1963.

Janowitz, Anne. *England's Ruins: Poetic Purpose and the National Landscape.* Cambridge, MA: Basil Blackwell, 1990.

Johnson, David. *Music and Society in Lowland Scotland in the Eighteenth Century.* London: Oxford University Press, 1972.

———. *Scottish Fiddle Music in the Eighteenth Century.* 1984. Reprint, Edinburgh: Mercat, 1997.

Jones, Howard Mumford. *The Harp That Once—: A Chronicle of the Life of Thomas Moore.* 1937. Reprint, New York: Russell and Russell, 1970.

Jordan, Hoover Harding. *Bolt Upright: The Life of Thomas Moore.* Salzburg: Institut für Englische Sprache und Literatur, Universität Salzburg, 1975.

Joyce, Sandra. "An Introduction to O'Carolan's Music in Eighteenth-Century Printed Collections." In *Irish Musical Studies,* vol. 4, *The Maynooth International Musicological Conference, 1995: Selected Proceedings,* ed. Patrick F. Devine and Harry White, 296–309. Dublin: Irish Academic Press, 1996.

Kallberg, Jeffrey. *Chopin at the Boundaries: Sex, History and Musical Genre.* Cambridge, MA: Harvard University Press, 1996.

Keating, Geoffrey. *The General History of Ireland: A full and impartial Account of the Original of that Kingdom With the Lives and Reigns of an Hundred and Seventy-four Succeeding Monarchs of the Milesian Race The Original of the Gadelians, Their Travel into Spain, and from thence into Ireland.* Trans. Dermot O'Connor. London, 1723.

Kelleher, Margaret, and James H. Murphy, eds. *Gender Perspectives in Nineteenth-Century Ireland: Public and Private Spheres.* Dublin: Irish Academic Press, 1997.

Kelly, James. *Prelude to Union: Anglo-Irish Politics in the 1780s.* Cork: Cork University Press, 1992.

Kennedy, Paul, and Victor Roudometof. *Communities across Borders: New Immigrant and Transnational Cultures.* New York: Routledge, 2002.

Keogh, Dáire, and Nicholas Furlong, eds. *The Women of 1798.* Dublin: Four Courts Press, 1998.

Keohane, Kieran. "Traditionalism and Homelessness in Contemporary Irish Music." In *Location and Dislocation in Contemporary Irish Society: Emigration and Irish Identities,* ed. Jim MacLaughlin, 274–304. Cork: Cork University Press, 1997.

Kiberd, Declan. *Inventing Ireland: The Literature of the Modern Nation.* Cambridge, MA: Harvard University Press, 1995.

Kilfether, Siobhán. "Beyond the Pale: Sexual Identity and National Identity in Early Irish Fiction." *Critical Matrix* 2, no. 4 (1986): 1–31.

Kinealy, Christine. *This Great Calamity: The Irish Famine, 1845–52.* Dublin: Gill and Macmillan, 1994.

King, William. "Of the Bogs and Loughs of Ireland." In *The Field Day Anthology of Irish Writing,* ed. Seamus Deane, 1:967–70. New York: Norton, 1991.

Kirkland, Richard. "Questioning the Frame: Hybridity, Ireland and the Institution." In *Ireland and Cultural Theory: The Mechanics of Authenticity,* ed. Colin Graham and Richard Kirkland, 210–28. Houndmills: Macmillan, 1999.

Klein, Lawrence. "Gender and the Public/Private Distinction in the Eighteenth Century: Some Questions about Evidence and Analytic Procedure." *Eighteenth-Century Studies* 29, no. 1 (1993): 97–109.

Knobel, Dale T. *Paddy and the Republic: Ethnicity and Nationality in Antebellum America.* Middletown, CT: Wesleyan University Press, 1986.

Kowaleski-Wallace, Beth. "Milton's Daughters: The Education of Eighteenth-Century Women Writers." *Feminist Studies* 12 (1986): 275–93.

Lament of the Irish Exile, A Ballad. Poetry by a Lady, The Daughter of an Eminent Exile. New York: William Vanderbeck, n.d.

Lee, John. *A Favourite Collection of the So Much Admired Old Irish Tunes.* Dublin, 1780.

Leerssen, Joep. "Anglo-Irish Patriotism and Its European Context: Notes towards a Reassessment." *Eighteenth-Century Ireland* 3 (1988): 7–24.

———. *Mere Irish and Fíor-Ghael: Studies in the Idea of Irish Nationality, Its Development and Literary Expression Prior to the Nineteenth Century.* Notre Dame, IN: University of Notre Dame Press, 1997.

———. *Remembrance and Imagination: Patterns in the Historical and Literary Representation of Ireland in the Nineteenth Century.* Notre Dame, IN: University of Notre Dame Press, 1997.

Lees, Lynn Hollen. *Exiles of Erin: Irish Migrants in Victorian London.* Ithaca, NY: Cornell University Press, 1979.

Leppert, Richard. *Music and Image.* Cambridge: Cambridge University Press, 1988.

Leppert, Richard, and Susan McClary. *Music and Society: The Politics of Composition, Performance and Reception.* Cambridge: Cambridge University Press, 1987.

Lew, Joseph. "Sydney Owenson and the Fate of Empire." *Keats-Shelley Journal* 39 (1990): 39–65.

"Life of Carolin." *Irish Magazine, or Monthly Asylum,* October 1809, 433–36.

Linley, Margaret. "Dying to Be a Poetess: The Conundrum of Christina Rossetti." In *The Culture of Christina Rossetti: Female Poetics and Victorian Contexts,* ed. Mary Arseneau, Antony H. Harrison, and Lorraine Janzen Kooistra, 285–314. Athens: Ohio University Press, 1999.

Lipking, Lawrence. *The Ordering of the Arts in Eighteenth-Century England.* Princeton, NJ: Princeton University Press, 1970.

Lloyd, David. *Anomalous States: Irish Writing and the Post-colonial Moment.* Durham, NC: Duke University Press, 1993.

———. *Ireland after History.* Notre Dame, IN: University of Notre Dame Press, 1999.

————. *Nationalism and Minor Literature: James Clarence Mangan and the Emergence of Irish Cultural Nationalism.* Berkeley: University of California Press, 1987.

Loftus, Belinda. *Mirrors: William III and Mother Ireland.* Dundrum Down: Picture Press, 1990.

Lover, Samuel. *Lover's Irish Evenings.* London, 1844.

————. *Rory O'More: A National Romance.* New York: Athenaeum Society, 1901.

————. *Songs and Ballads.* London: Houlston and Wright, 1858.

Lynam, E. W. *The Irish Character in Print, 1571–1923.* 1924. Reprint, New York: Barnes and Noble, 1969.

MacLaughlin, Jim, ed. *Location and Dislocation in Contemporary Irish Society: Emigration and Irish Identities.* Cork: Cork University Press, 1997.

Martin, Augustine. "Anglo-Irish Poetry: Moore to Ferguson." *Canadian Journal of Irish Studies.* 12, no. 2 (1986): 84–104.

McCarthy, Marie. *Passing It On: The Transmission of Music in Irish Culture.* Cork: Cork University Press, 1999.

McClintock, Anne. *Imperial Leather: Race, Gender and Sexuality in the Colonial Conquest.* New York: Routledge, 1995.

McCormack, W. J. "Language, Class and Genre." In *The Field Day Anthology of Irish Writing,* ed. Seamus Deane, 1:1070–82. New York: Norton, 1991.

McCracken, Grant. *Culture and Consumption: New Approaches to the Symbolic Character of Consumer Goods and Activities.* Bloomington: Indiana University Press, 1988.

McKendrick, Neil, John Brewer, and J. H. Plumb. *The Birth of a Consumer Society: The Commercialization of Eighteenth-Century England.* London: Europa Publications, 1982.

McLoughlin, Thomas. *Contesting Ireland: Irish Voices against England in the Eighteenth Century.* Dublin: Four Courts Press, 1999.

Miller, Kerby. *Emigrants and Exiles: Ireland and the Irish Exodus to North America.* New York: Oxford University Press, 1985.

Mokyr, Joel. *Why Ireland Starved: A Quantitative and Analytical History of the Irish Economy, 1800–1850.* Boston: Allen and Unwin, 1983.

Moloney, Mick. *Irish Music on the American Stage.* Cork: Irish Traditional Music Society, 1993.

Molyneux, William. *The Case of Ireland's Being Bound by Acts of Parliament in England, Stated.* Dublin, 1698.

Moore, Thomas. *Irish Melodies.* 10 vols. London and Dublin, 1808–32.

————. *Letters.* 2 vols. Ed. Wilfred S. Dowden. Oxford: Clarendon Press, 1964.

————. *Moore's Irish Melodies.* London: Longman, Brown, Green and Longmans, 1846.

————. *A People's Edition of Moore's Irish Melodies.* London: Augener, 1859.

————. *The Poetical Works of Thomas Moore.* 10 vols. London: Longman, Orme, Brown, Green, and Longmans, 1840–1841.

Murphy, John (words), and T. Bissell (music). *The Answer to the Lament of the Irish Emigrant.* Boston: Keith's Music Publishing House, 1844.

Myers, Mitzi. "'Like the Pictures in a Magic Lantern': Gender, History, and Edgeworth's Rebellion Narratives." *Nineteenth-Century Contexts* 19, no. 4 (1996): 373–412.

Nandy, Ashis. *Intimate Enemy: Loss and Recovery of Self under Colonialism.* Delhi: Oxford University Press, 1983.

Neal, John, and William Neal. *A Colection [sic] of the most Celebrated Irish Tunes.* Dublin, c. 1724.

ní Chinnéide, Veronica. "The Sources of Moore's Melodies." *Journal of the Royal Society of Antiquaries of Ireland.* 89, no. 2 (1959): 109–34.

North, Roger. *Roger North on Music.* Ed. John Wilson. London: Novello, 1959.

Ó Canainn, Tomás. *Traditional Music in Ireland.* London: Routledge and Kegan Paul, 1978.

Ó Ciosáin, Niall. *Print and Popular Culture in Ireland, 1750–1850.* New York: St. Martin's Press, 1997.

O'Conor, Charles. *The Case of the Roman-Catholics of Ireland. Wherein the Principles and Conduct of that Party are fully Explained and Vindicated.* Dublin, 1753.

———. *Dissertations on the History of Ireland.* Dublin, 1755.

O'Conor, Rev. Charles, D.D. *Memoirs of the Life and Writings of the Late Charles O'Conor of Belanagare ESQ, M.R.I.A.* Dublin, 1796.

Ó Cuív, Brian. "Irish Language and Literature, 1691–1845." In *A New History of Ireland*, vol. 4, *Eighteenth-Century Ireland 1691–1800*, ed. T. W. Moody and W. E. Vaughan. Oxford: Clarendon Press, 1986.

O'Donoghue, Patrick. "Music and Religion in Ireland." In *Irish Musical Studies*, vol. 3, *Music and Irish Cultural History*, ed. Gerard Gillen and Harry White. Blackrock: Irish Academic Press, 1995.

Official Descriptive and Illustrated Catalogue of the Great Exhibition 1851. 3 vols. London: Spicer Brothers, 1851.

O'Halloran, Clare. "Irish Recreations of the Gaelic Past: The Challenge of Macpherson's *Ossian.*" *Past and Present* 124 (1989): 69–95.

O'Halloran, Sylvester. *A General History of Ireland, from the Earliest Accounts to the Close of the Twelfth Century.* 2 vols. London: J. Murray, 1772.

———. *An Introduction to the Study of the Histories and Antiquities of Ireland.* London: J. Murray, 1772.

O'Neill, Captain Francis. *Irish Minstrels and Musicians.* Darby, PA: Norwood Editions, 1973.

O'Neill, Kevin. "Mary Shackleton Leadbeater: Peaceful Rebel." In *The Women of 1798*, ed. Dáire Keogh and Nicholas Furlong, 137–63. Dublin: Four Courts Press, 1998.

O'Sullivan, Donal. *Carolan: The Life, Times and Music of an Irish Harper.* 2 vols. London: Routledge and Paul, 1958.

O'Toole, Fintan. "The Ex-Isle of Erin: Emigration and Irish Culture." In *Location and Dislocation in Contemporary Irish Society: Emigration and Irish Identities*, ed. Jim MacLaughlin, 158–78. Cork: Cork University Press, 1997.

Owenson, Sydney. *Lady Morgan's Memoirs.* 2 vols. Ed. W. Hepworth Dixon and Geraldine Jewsbury. London: W. H. Allen, 1862.

———. *Patriotic Sketches of Ireland, Written in Connaught.* 2 vols. Baltimore: Dobbin and Murphy, 1809.

———. *Twelve Original Hibernian Melodies, with English Words, Imitated and Translated from the Works of the Ancient Irish Bards.* London, 1805.

———. *The Wild Irish Girl.* 3 vols. 1806. Reprint, New York: Garland, 1979.

Parke, W. T. *Musical Memoirs; Comprising an Account of the General State of Music in England from the First Commemoration of Handel in 1784, to the Year 1830.* 2 vols. London: Henry Colburn and Richard Bentley, 1830.

Parry, Jann. "The Irish Dance Phenomenon: Celtic Crossover." *Dance Magazine,* October 1997, 70–73.

Pascoe, Judith. *Romantic Theatricality: Gender, Poetry and Spectatorship.* Ithaca, NY: Cornell University Press, 1997.

Percy, Thomas. *Reliques of Ancient English Poetry.* 3 vols. Ed. Henry B. Wheatley. London: George Allen and Unwin, 1885.

Petrie, George. *The Ancient Music of Ireland.* Dublin: M. H. Gill, 1855.

———. "Our Portrait Gallery, No. 41. Edward Bunting." *Dublin University Magazine,* January 1847, 64–73.

———. Review of Thomas Moore's *Irish Melodies. Dublin Examiner,* August 1816, 241–53.

Phillips, James W. *Printing and Bookselling in Dublin, 1670–1800.* Dublin: Irish Academic Press, 1998.

Pilkington, Matthew. "The Progress of Music in *Ireland.* To Mira." In *The Field Day Anthology of Irish Writing,* ed. Seamus Deane, 1:409–12. New York: Norton, 1991.

Pittock, Murray. *Celtic Identity and the British Image.* Manchester: Manchester University Press, 1999.

———. *Inventing and Resisting Britain: Cultural Identities in Britain and Ireland, 1685–1789.* New York: St. Martin's Press, 1997.

———. *Poetry and Jacobite Politics in Eighteenth-Century Britain and Ireland.* Cambridge: Cambridge University Press, 1994.

Playford, John. *The English Dancing Master.* London, 1651.

Plumb, J. H. "The Commercialization of Leisure in Eighteenth-Century England." In *The Birth of a Consumer Society: The Commercialization of Eighteenth-Century England,* ed. Neil McKendrick, John Brewer, and J. H. Plumb, 265–85. London: Europa Publications, 1982.

Potkay, Adam. "Virtue and Manners in Macpherson's *Poems of Ossian.*" *PMLA* 107 (1992): 120–30.

Prakash, Gyan. *After Colonialism: Imperial Histories and Postcolonial Displacements.* Princeton, NJ: Princeton University Press, 1995.

Pratt, Mary Louise. "Women, Literature and National Brotherhood." *Nineteenth-Century Contexts* 18, no. 1 (1994): 27–47.

The Pretty Girl Milking Her Cow, as Sung by Mrs. Agnes Robertson and Mrs. John Wood in Boucicault's Drama of the "Colleen Bawn." New York: John J. Daly, 1860.

Price Blackwood, the Hon. Mrs. *The Lament of the Irish Emigrant. A Ballad.* Music by William Dempster. Boston: George. P. Reed, 1843.

Ramsay, Allan. *Tea-table Miscellany.* Edinburgh, 1723.

Ranelagh, John O'Beirne. *A Short History of Ireland.* 1983. Reprint, Cambridge: Cambridge University Press, 1994.

Reiss, Scott. "Tradition and Imaginary." In *Celtic Modern: Music at the Global Fringe,* ed. Martin Stokes and Philip Bohlman. Lanham, MD: Scarecrow Press, 2003.

Renan, Ernst. "What Is a Nation?" Trans. Martin Thom. In *Nation and Narration*, ed. Homi Bhabha, 8–22. New York: Routledge, 1990.

Richardson, Gary A. "The Greening of America: The Cultural Business of Dion Boucicault's *The Shaughraun.*" *American Drama* 3, no. 2 (1996): 1–28.

Rigby, Elizabeth. *Music and the Art of Dress*. London: John Murray, 1852.

Rousseau, Jean-Jacques. "Essay on the Origin of Languages." In *On the Origin of Language*, ed. John H. Moran and Alexander Gode, 1–74. Chicago: University of Chicago Press, 1966.

Sachs, Joel. "London: The Professionalization of Music." In *The Early Romantic Era: Between Revolutions, 1789 and 1848*, ed. Alexander Ringer, 201–35. Englewood Cliffs, NJ: Prentice Hall, 1991.

Said, Edward. *Culture and Imperialism*. New York: Knopf, 1993.

———. *Musical Elaborations*. London: Vintage, 1991.

A Selection of Tunes by Carolan. Dublin, 1748.

Senior, Nassau. *Journals, Conversations and Essays Relating to Ireland*. 2 vols. London: Longmans, Green, 1868.

———. *On National Property*. London: B. Fellowes, 1835.

Seymour, Aaron Crossley Hobart. *Life and Times of Selina, Countess of Huntingdon*. 2 vols. London: W. E. Painter, 1839.

———. "A Memoir of Miss Brooke." In *Reliques of Ancient Irish Poetry*, by Charlotte Brooke. Gainesville, FL: Scholar's Facsimiles and Reprints, 1970.

———. *Vital Christianity Exhibited in a Series of Letters on the Most Important Subjects of Religion, Addressed to Young Persons*. London, 1819.

Sheehy, Jeanne. *The Rediscovery of Ireland's Past: The Celtic Revival, 1830–1930*. London: Thames and Hudson, 1980.

Shepherd, John. "Music and Male Hegemony." In *Music and Society: The Politics of Composition, Performance and Reception*, ed. Richard Leppert and Susan McClary. Cambridge: Cambridge University Press, 1987.

———. *Music as Social Text*. Cambridge: Polity Press, 1991.

Simms, J. G. "The Establishment of a Protestant Ascendancy, 1691–1714." In *A New History of Ireland*, vol. 4, *Eighteenth-Century Ireland, 1691–1800*, ed. T. W. Moody and W. E. Vaughan, 1–30. Oxford: Clarendon Press, 1986.

Siskin, Clifford. *The Work of Writing: Literature and Social Change in Britain, 1700–1830*. Baltimore: Johns Hopkins University Press, 1998.

Slemon, Stephen. "Modernism's Last Post." In *Past the Last Post*, ed. Ian Adam and Helen Tiffin. London: Harvester Wheatsheaf, 1991.

Smyth, Gerry. "The Past, the Post and the Utterly Changed: Intellectual Responsibility and Irish Cultural Criticism." *Irish Studies Review* 10 (1995): 25–29.

Smyth, Sam. *Riverdance: The Story*. London: Andre Deutsch, 1996.

Sommers Smith, Sally K. "Irish Traditional Music in a Modern World." *New Hibernia Review/Iris Éireannach Nua: A Quarterly Record of Irish Studies* 5 (Summer 2001): 111–25.

Spenser, Edmund. "A View of the Present State of Ireland." In *The Works of Edmund Spenser*, vol. 10, *Spenser's Prose Works*, ed. Rudolf Gottfried, 39–323. Baltimore: Johns Hopkins University Press, 1949.

Spivak, Gayatri. "Can the Subaltern Speak?" In *Colonial Discourse and Post-colonial Theory: A Reader,* ed. Patrick Williams and Laura Chrisman, 66–111. New York: Columbia University Press, 1994.

Stanford, Charles Villiers. *Irish Melodies of Thomas Moore: The Original Airs Restored.* New York, 1895.

Stokes, Martin, and Philip Bohlman, eds. *Celtic Modern: Music at the Global Fringe.* Lanham, MD: Scarecrow Press, 2003.

Suleri, Sara. *The Rhetoric of English India.* Chicago: University of Chicago Press, 1992.

Swift, Roger, and Sheridan Gilley. *The Irish in Britain, 1815–1939.* Savage, MD: Barnes and Noble, 1989.

Tallis, John. *Tallis's History and Description of the Crystal Palace, and the Exhibition of the World's Industry in 1851.* 3 vols. London: John Tallis, 1852.

Taylor, Timothy. "Gaelicer Than Thou." In *Celtic Modern: Music at the Global Fringe,* ed. Martin Stokes and Philip Bohlman. Lanham, MD: Scarecrow Press, 2003.

Thompson, Samuel, Ann Thompson, and Peter Thompson. *The Hibernian Muse: A Collection of Irish Airs.* London, 1787.

Thuente, Mary Helen. *The Harp Re-strung: The United Irishmen and the Rise of Irish Literary Nationalism.* Syracuse, NY: Syracuse University Press, 1994.

———. "Liberty, Hibernia, and Mary Le More: United Irish Images of Women." In *The Women of 1798,* ed. Dáire Keogh and Nicholas Furlong, 9–25. Dublin: Four Courts Press, 1998.

Thumoth, Burke. *Twelve English and Twelve Irish Airs.* London, c. 1750.

———. *Twelve Scotch and Twelve Irish Airs with Variations.* London, c. 1750.

Tracy, Robert. "Maria Edgeworth and Lady Morgan: Legality versus Legitimacy." *Nineteenth-Century Literature* 40 (June 1985): 1–22.

Trumpener, Katie. *Bardic Nationalism: The Romantic Novel and the British Empire.* Princeton, NJ: Princeton University Press, 1997.

Uí Ógáin, Ríonach. "Traditional Music and Irish Cultural History." In *Irish Musical Studies,* vol. 3, *Music and Irish Cultural History,* ed. Gerard Gillen and Harry White, 77–100. Blackrock: Irish Academic Press, 1995.

Usher, James. *Clio: Or, A Discourse on Taste.* 1769. Reprint, New York: Garland, 1970.

Valente, Joseph. "The Myth of Sovereignty: Gender in the Literature of Irish Nationalism." *ELH* 61 (1994): 189–210.

Vallancey, Charles. *A Vindication of the Ancient History of Ireland wherein is shewn, 1. The Descent of its Old Inhabitants from the Phaeno-Scythians of the East 2. The early Skill of the Phaeno-Scythians, in Navigation, Arts and Letters 3. Several Accounts of the Ancient Irish Bards, authenticated from parallel History, Sacred and Profane.* Dublin, 1786.

Vallely, Fintan. "The Apollos of Shamrockery." In *Celtic Modern: Music at the Global Fringe,* ed. Martin Stokes and Philip Bohlman. Lanham, MD: Scarecrow Press, 2003.

———, ed. *The Companion to Irish Traditional Music.* Cork: Cork University Press, 1999.

Vance, Norman. "Celts, Carthaginians and Constitutions: Anglo-Irish Literary Relations 1780-1820." *Irish Historical Studies.* 22 (March 1981): 216–38.

Walker, Joseph Cooper. *Historical Memoirs of the Irish Bards.* Dublin, 1786.

————. *Historical Memoirs of the Irish Bards; Historical Essay on the Dress of the Ancient and Modern Irish; and A Memoir on the Armour and Weapons of the Irish.* 2nd ed. 2 vols. Dublin: James Christie, 1818.

Walshe, Éibhear. *Sex, Nation and Dissent in Irish Writing.* Cork: Cork University Press, 1997.

Walters, Bronwen. "Gendered Irishness in Britain: Changing Constructions." In *Ireland and Cultural Theory: The Mechanics of Authenticity,* ed. Colin Graham and Richard Kirkland, 77–98. Houndmills: Macmillan, 1999.

Warner, Ferdinando. *History of Ireland from the Earliest Authentic Accounts to the Year 1171.* 2 vols. Dublin, 1770.

Weber, Max. *Rational and Social Foundations of Music.* Trans. Don Martindale, Johannes Riedel, and Gertrude Neuwirth. Carbondale: Southern Illinois University Press, 1958.

Weber, William. *Music and the Middle Class: The Social Structure of Concert Life in London, Paris and Vienna.* New York: Holmes and Meier, 1975.

Welch, Robert. *A History of Verse Translation from the Irish, 1789–1897.* Totowa, NJ: Barnes and Noble, 1988.

Whelan, Kevin. *Fellowship of Freedom: The United Irishmen and 1798.* Cork: Cork University Press, 1998.

————. *The Tree of Liberty: Radicalism, Catholicism and the Construction of Irish Identity, 1760–1830.* Notre Dame, IN: University of Notre Dame Press, 1996.

White, Harry. "Carolan and the Dislocation of Music in Ireland." *Eighteenth-Century Ireland* 4 (1989): 55–64.

————. *The Keeper's Recital: Music and Cultural History in Ireland, 1770–1970.* Notre Dame, IN: University of Notre Dame Press, 1998.

Whyte, Lawrence. "A Dissertation on *Italian* and *Irish* Music, With Some Panegyrick on *Carralan* Our Late *Irish Orpheus.*" In *The Field Day Anthology of Irish Writing,* ed. Seamus Deane, 1:412–14. New York: Norton, 1991.

Williams, Patrick, and Laura Chrisman. *Colonial Discourse and Post-colonial Theory: A Reader.* New York: Columbia University Press, 1994.

Williams, William H. A. "From Lost Land to Emerald Isle: Ireland and the Irish in American Sheet Music, 1800–1920." *Eire-Ireland* 26, no. 1 (1991): 19–45.

————. *'Twas Only an Irishman's Dream: The Image of Ireland and the Irish in American Popular Song Lyrics, 1800–1920.* Urbana: University of Illinois Press, 1996.

Willis, Anne. "The Neals' Celebrated Irish Tunes." Unpublished master's thesis. Photocopy in author's possession.

Wilson, Charles Henry, ed. *Brookiana.* London, 1804.

Wilson, David A. *The Irish in Canada.* Ottawa: Canadian Historical Association, 1989.

Woodham Smith, Cecil. *The Great Hunger.* New York: Harper and Row, 1962.

Worgan, Thomas Danvers. *The Musical Reformer.* London, 1829.

Wright, Daniel. *Aria di Camera.* London, c. 1730.

Young, Robert. *Colonial Desire: Hybridity in Theory, Culture and Race.* New York: Routledge, 1995.

Yuval-Davis, Nira. *Gender and Nation.* Thousand Oaks, CA: Sage Publications, 1997.

Yuval-Davis, Nira, and Floya Anthias, eds. *Woman-Nation-State.* New York: St. Martin's Press, 1989.

Index

LEITH DAVIS is associate professor of English at Simon Fraser University in Burnaby, British Columbia.